George S. Norton, Timothy F. Allen

Ophthalmic Therapeutics

George S. Norton, Timothy F. Allen

Ophthalmic Therapeutics

ISBN/EAN: 9783337815561

Printed in Europe, USA, Canada, Australia, Japan

Cover: Foto ©Andreas Hilbeck / pixelio.de

More available books at **www.hansebooks.com**

THERAPEUTICS.

BY

GEO. S. NORTON, M.D.,

PROFESSOR OF OPHTHALMOLOGY IN THE COLLEGE OF THE NEW YORK OPH-
THALMIC HOSPITAL, SENIOR SURGEON TO THE NEW YORK OPH-
THALMIC HOSPITAL, OPHTHALMIC AND AURAL
SURGEON TO THE HOMŒOPATHIC
HOSPITAL ON WARDS
ISLAND.

WITH AN INTRODUCTION BY PROF. T. F. ALLEN, M.D.

SECOND EDITION,

Re-written and Revised, with Copious Additions.

BOERICKE & TAFEL:

NEW YORK:
145 GRAND STREET.

PHILADELPHIA:
1011 ARCH STREET.

1882.

TO THE

NEW YORK OPHTHALMIC HOSPITAL

THIS LITTLE MANUAL IS

DEDICATED,

IN APPRECIATION OF THE FACILITIES IT AFFORDS FOR THE RELIEF OF SUF-
FERING AND THE ADVANCEMENT OF MEDICAL KNOWLEDGE.

INTRODUCTION.

When the New York Ophthalmic Hospital was placed under the care of surgeons who prescribed drugs in accordance with the homœopathic law of cure, there was but little precedent for them to follow. The whole of our literature was searched for cases of eye complaints cured homœopathically, with meagre results; either the alleged cure was doubtful, or the diagnosis obscure, and the symptoms so vague that no opinion could be formed as to the real nature of the malady. The surgeons were compelled to begin *de novo*, and build up a clinical record; and we may be permitted to say that most satisfactory cures were made. The patient was examined with two distinct objects in view, *first*, to make a thorough diagnosis, *second*, to obtain symptoms, local and general, which should indicate a remedy. We were handicapped with no prejudice in favor of or against any drug, because of a diagnosis, and were perfectly ready to prescribe any drug in the Materia Medica, from A to Z, for any form of disease. The writer, not unfrequently, devoted the larger part of an afternoon to a single case, and, often a part of a night, poring over our imperfect symptomatology; he compiled a large work in manuscript, arranged in sections (of the eye and its appendages) for ready reference; and gradually there grew a system of approved indications which will always endure. This method and its results (the brilliant cure of supposed incurables, and the wonderfully rapid growth of the Hospital as a consequence) became widely known, and for years we were importuned to publish our observations; finally, our manuscript was turned over to Dr. Norton, who had become associated with us in the work, and he put into form for the press, what we had collected; which, with his own additions, was published as *Allen and Norton's Ophthalmic Therapeutics*. Some years have elapsed since the issue of that work, the edition has been sold, and a new one demanded. Our colleague, Dr. Norton, has continued to work in the field with unwearied perseverance and with striking success; the writer has been called to labor more particularly in the broader field of general Materia Medica, and deems it proper that his name should not continue to be associated with Dr. Norton's in this work, simply because to Dr. Norton is wholly due the honor of having revised and enlarged this work.

While there is no doubt that the conditions of the eye, in diseases of that organ, is a most important factor in the selection of the remedy, still we must not forget that eye diseases are often, perhaps generally, the expression of a general cachexia, the remedy for which can only be found by a close examination of the whole individual. A knowledge of remedies for any disease of the eye has been attained *in the beginning*, only by a study of the whole case; and, if it has been found that for certain pathological states but few drugs are appropriate, it must still be kept in view that new remedies are to be found, and that any case may require a drug hitherto unused, for its cure. Among the most brilliant pathological generalizations in ophthalmic therapeutics may be mentioned the use of *Gelsemium* for intra-ocular inflammations characterized by serous exudation; *Rhus tox.* for suppurative intra-ocular and orbital inflammations; Bryonia for plastic exudation, and, we may be permitted to add, the American Aconite (A. uncinatum) for ciliary and peri-orbital neuralgia. No therapeutist will, however, be content to limit his remedial resources, in any one of the above diseases, to the remedy mentioned. Pilocarpine may be required instead of Gelsemium; Silicea in place of Rhus; Phytolacca in place of Bryonia, or Spigelia instead of Aconite; how shall we decide? And the selection must be accurate and prompt, for in the eye, more than anywhere else, delay is dangerous: *the symptoms must always be studied.*

T. F. ALLEN.

PREFACE TO THE SECOND EDITION.

The many additions to ophthalmic therapeutics, within the past six years, have rendered necessary a complete revision of this little manual.

Part First has been wholly rewritten, and several new remedies added. The verified symptomatology, which precedes the clinical application of each drug, has been taken from *Allen's Encyclopedia of Pure Materia Medica,* with such other confirmations as have been made by the author. The clinical indications have, however, received chief attention, as a further experience of six years in a large ophthalmic clinic has naturally developed new remedies, and new indications for old remedies. Much valuable aid has also been received from leading oculists throughout the country, who have kindly sent cases and clinical indications from their own practice; to which their names will be found appended as authority. More space has been given, as will be noticed, to illustrative cases, with a view of showing the actual symptoms of the disease, for which the remedy should be prescribed, and the results of treatment. In order to make this section as practical and reliable as possible, considerable matter found in the first edition has been eliminated. For instance, all material gathered from doubtful sources, from practitioners not personally known to the writer, or, in whom he has not the most implicit confidence as to their ability to correctly diagnosticate and

(7)

truthfully report their cases, also all statements which further experience has failed to verify—are omitted in this edition. Statements and clinical cases in the first edition which were only verified by Dr. Allen are so indicated in the text. In every instance when no authority is given, the author may be considered responsible.

Part Second has been thoroughly revised, and copious additions made. To prevent useless repetition in this portion of the work, only a few characteristic indications for each remedy are usually given. *For a more complete picture, reference should always be made to the description of the drug in Part First.* Believing that all diagnoses should be made in Latin, but recognizing the fact that it is more convenient for general use to employ the English language, it has been deemed advisable to give both the Latin and English diagnoses for all diseases in this part.

A carefully prepared glossary of all the special medical terms used in this book has been compiled by Dr. Malcolm Leal. In addition to which will be found a general index of remedies, diseases, and authors.

154 West Thirty-fourth Street,
    December 15th, 1881.

GEO. S. NORTON.

PREFACE TO THE FIRST EDITION.

MATERIAL for this work has been accumulating for many years, especially since the adoption of the homœopathic method by the New York Ophthalmic Hospital.

When we first took our chairs in that institution, there were few indications for remedies associated with definite lesions of the eye; our cases were diagnosticated, and then carefully examined at all points for indications of the remedy, and from time to time groups of remedies have become associated with definite lesions, and characteristic local indications recognized.

These local indications seem at times to be purely clinical or empirical, but they have always, or nearly always, been discovered while co-existing with positive and pure symptoms of the remedy, but they so often occur independently of the latter that they frequently assume a relatively greater importance.

Our knowledge of the pure effects of drugs upon the eye is unfortunately meagre, often quite indefinite and unsatisfactory; still, we have endeavored to keep to the standard, and have only permitted the introduction of clinical matter when the evidence has seemed to justify.

It is proper to explain that the plan of this work is substantially the same as that projected by Dr. Allen a few years since, and prematurely announced; the material then in hand has been augmented by the observations of Dr. Norton, the whole work written out by him and revised by us jointly.

Incomplete as we know it to be, we feel that its publication should not be longer delayed, and we offer it to the profession for most critical examination. *All the symptomatology given in this work has been verified;* when no authority is referred to, the editors are responsible, except when general reference is made to cases reported. Some observations may be ill-founded; many, we feel sure, will prove reliable and contribute to the preservation and restoration of sight.

T. F. ALLEN.

GEO. S. NORTON.

CONTENTS.

PART FIRST.

PART SECOND.

PART I.

OPHTHALMIC
THERAPEUTICS.

ACETIC ACID.

Clinical.—The benefit obtained from Acet. ac. in croupous inflammation of the air-passages, led to its use in croupous conjunctivitis. Though empirically prescribed at first, it has proved of decided value in certain forms of this inflammation. It is adapted to those cases, in which *the false membrane is dense, yellow-white, tough, and so closely adherent* that removal is almost impossible; thus differing from Kali bichr., in which the membrane is loosely attached, easily rolled up, and separated in shreds or strings. The lids are œdematously swollen and red, especially the upper, which hangs down over the lower. It does not seem to correspond to the diphtheritic form of conjunctivitis, for, though the false membrane is closely adherent, it does not extend deeply into the conjunctival tissue,—no scars remaining after resolution—and at no time is there firm, rigid infiltration of the lids. Little or no benefit can be derived from its use, if the discharge is profuse and purulent, mixed with small portions of the membrane, or if the cornea has become involved.

Compare Arg. nitr., Pulsat. and Hepar.

2

ACONITE.

Objective.—*The lids (especially the upper) are swollen, red and hard*, with a tight feeling; worse mornings. Edges of lids sore, red and inflamed. *The conjunctiva is intensely hyperæmic and œdematous*, mostly towards the inner canthus. Inflammation extremely painful, so that one may wish to die. Lachrymation with local inflammations is usually slight, if any.

Subjective.—In the lids, *dryness, burning, sensitiveness to air*. Pressure in the upper lids, as if the whole ball were pushed into the orbit, causing a bruised pain in the eye; itching, smarting, *burning in the eyes*, especially worse in the evening. Sticking and tearing pains around the eyes, worse at night. The eye is generally sensitive, with *much heat, burning, and aching*, worse on looking down or turning the eyes; feeling as if the eyes were swollen, or as if sand were in them. The ball, especially the upper half, is sensitive if moved; feeling as if it would be forced out of the orbit relieved on stooping; the ball feels enlarged, as if protruding and making the lids tense. Vision as through a veil; it is difficult to distinguish faces; with anxiety and vertigo. Photophobia.

Clinical.—Aconite is the remedy for inflammations of the eye in general, which are very painful, with *heat and burning*, as well as dryness; also for inflammatory conditions *resulting from injuries*, ranging from those of a most severe character, as when all the tissues of the globe have been injured by a perforating wound, to those dependent upon the irritant action of foreign bodies in the cornea or conjunctiva, or the irritation caused by ingrowing lashes. Sometimes it is indicated in acute inflammation of the lids or lachrymal sac, though not as frequently as some other remedies.

The verifications of this drug in the following forms of inflammation of the conjunctiva are every day occurrences: *Catarrhal inflammation* (first stage, prior to exudation), marked by great redness, heat, burning, and pain; chemosis, with pain so terrible that patient wishes to die. Early in purulent inflammation, as illustrated in the case of a child with following conditions:—Lids red and swollen; intense redness of conjunctiva, and chemosis, worse in the right eye; much purulent discharge with heat and sticking pains, aggravated in the morning. Under Aconite[3], with ice externally, a rapid cure resulted.

Acute aggravations of granular lids and pannus, with excessive hyperæmia, heat and dryness, especially if the aggravation be induced by overheating from violent exercise, or by exposure to dry, cold air.

Affections of the cornea seldom require its use, except when of traumatic origin, although one case of superficial ulceration of the left cornea, in a woman fifty years of age, which had been present ten days, with burning heat in the eye and sharp pain on looking at the light, or reading, was quickly relieved under Aconite[3], after Hepar had failed.

Benefit may be derived in the acute stage of scleritis, with contracted pupils, sticking or tearing pains, photophobia, blue circle around the cornea and aching in the ball. (Compare Spigel.)

For *traumatic* iritis Aconite is one of the first remedies to be thought of. It may also be required in simple plastic iritis when caused by exposure to cold, or in recurrent iritis as shown in the following case:—A lady, æt. 42, had, in both eyes, quite extensive posterior synechiæ, resulting from an iritis 18 years previous. One week before the doctor saw her, she was attacked with severe neuralgia, especially in right side of head. Twenty-four hours later, the right eye became tender to touch and very painful, lachrymation profuse and hot, pericorneal and conjunctival injection; pupil dilated sluggishly and irregularly under the action of Atropine; face flushed. Rhus tox. and afterwards Merc. corr. were given without avail. Aconite[3] gave almost immediate relief, and in ten days the patient was well. For one and a half years she had occasional attacks, which became less frequent, and the trouble finally disappeared under the influence of Aconite. During some attacks both eyes were affected, but the right was much worse than the left. (Atropine was used.)—W. P. FOWLER.

Of use in the earlier stages of violent acute inflammation of the deep structures of the ball, when it becomes sensitive to touch and feels as if it were protruding (rarely, if ever, called for after the exudative stage is reached).

The following case illustrates the good effects of Aconite in asthenopia:—A middle-aged man was employed to sort railroad tickets, to run through columns of figures and do other fine work by a dim light; in eight days he began to have a spasmodic closure of the lids and heavy feeling over the eyes; then his eyes would get very hot—"felt as though they could set a match on fire," or as after a lash with a whip. The conjunctiva of the lids was intensely red, with constant winking and closing of the lids; could hardly force them open. The heat was always dry, and temporarily relieved by cloths wet in cold water; vision normal; refraction normal. Aconite relieved these symptoms magically, and allowed the man to continue his work (which he was obliged to do) till time enabled him to change his occupation.—T. F. A.

In a case of paralysis of the ciliary muscle of one day's standing, caused by sleeping near an open window, the accommodation was wholly restored within forty-eight hours after using Aconite[30].

AGARICUS.

Objective.—The lids are half-closed, swollen, especially towards the inner canthus; *twitchings of the lids*, with contracted fissura palpebrarum, without swelling. Twitchings of the ball, often painful; twitching of the ball while reading (especially the left); very little appearance of inflammatory action.

Subjective.—Pressure and heaviness in the eyes, especially painful on moving them or exerting them by lamp-light—with left-sided headache and involuntary twitching of the facial muscles. The bitings, itchings and jerkings about the brow and in the lids are very numerous in the provings. In the eyeball the sensations are mostly pressive and aching; the ball is sensitive to touch. Vision dim, as through a veil, with flickering; reads with difficulty, as the type seems to move. Short-sightedness.

Clinical.—Agaricus is of the greatest service in spasmodic affections of the lids and muscles of the ball. Its value can hardly be overestimated in *morbid nictitation* or chorea-like spasms of the lids, with general heaviness of them, especially if the *spasms occur on waking*, or are relieved temporarily by washing with cold water. Four drop doses of the tincture, two or three times a day, will often relieve when the higher attenuations have no effect.

An interesting case of anæmia of the optic nerve, retina and choroid, with general tendency to chorea, has been cured by this drug.—T. F. A.

Benefit has been obtained from Agaricus in myopia, dependent upon spasm of the ciliary muscle, especially if complicated with twitchings of the lids.

Its usefulness in nystagmus is illustrated by the following case:—A school girl, æt. 14, was unable to read, owing to spasms of the orbicularis and oscillation of the globes. The motion was circulatory in both eyes and continual, whether eyes were fixed at near or far points; it caused much pain, indistinctness of vision and occasional attacks of vertigo. In three month's treatment with Agaricus, 3d trit., a powder three times daily, and gymnastic exercises of the ocular muscles, the globes were so far controlled as to cease oscillating when the vision was fixed upon near objects. Improvement continued.—W. H. WINSLOW.

That its action upon the muscles is not confined to spasms is shown in the following case of weakness of the internal recti:—A lady suffered from muscular asthenopia, consequent upon uterine disorders and spinal anæmia. The spine was very sensitive to touch between the shoulders. She could not fix the eyes long even upon distant objects; could not converge the eyes (weak internal recti). She had sudden jerks in the ball itself; twitches of the lids, and at times in other parts of the body; the lids seemed heavy, as if stuck together, but were not; she had been given prisms (which, although allowing binocular vision without effort, gave nature no chance of recovery herself), and had been under various forms of general and local treatment. After Agaricus the change was marvelous; within a week the eyes could be fixed on objects at ten feet without conscious effort; the unpleasant sensations had entirely vanished, and the patient was enabled to begin systematic gymnastics for the eye (initiated by fixing the eyes on a white object while it is moved slowly right and left). The eyes have steadily improved, but the old pain returned in the spine; relieved only temporarily by applications of cold water. —T. F. A.

ALLIUM CEPA.

Lachrymation excessive, especially of the left eye, with redness of the eyeball after frequent sneezing. *Lachrymation (not excoriating) with coryza.* The lachrymation is for the most part in the evening, in a warm room; the left eye weeps more and is more sensitive to the light. Sensation as if something were under the lid, which causes a gush of tears to wash it out.

Clinical.—Of use in acute catarrhal conjunctivitis, associated with a similar condition of the air-passages, as in hay-fever; the lachrymation is not excoriating, though the nasal discharge is (reverse of Euphrasia).

ALUMEN EXSICCATUM.

Clinical.—This substance, first recommended by Dr. Liebold, has been employed with great benefit in *trachoma*, by dusting the crude powder upon the inner surface of the lids, allowing it to remain about a minute, more or less, and then washing off with pure water. At the same time the lower preparations are given internally. As a saturated solution in glycerine it may also be used with great benefit in trachoma and pannus.

ALUMINA.

Objective.—The upper lids are weak, seem to hang down as if paralyzed, especially the left lid; the lashes fall out; small pimples or incipient styes on the lids. Twitching of the lids, especially right upper. Redness and inflammation of conjunctiva, worse in right eye and aggravated in the evening.

Lachrymation, hot or even acrid, may be present, but absence of lachrymation predominates. Squinting of the eyes.

Subjective.—Burning and dryness in the lids every evening, with pain in the internal canthus of left eye and much dry mucus in the morning on waking. Morning agglutination; the eyes burn on being opened, with photophobia; itching in the canthi; dryness and excoriation in the internal canthi. In the eye in general the sensations are: Burning; burning dryness; burning on waking, especially on looking up; pressure on the eyes (and eyeballs), cannot open them; also photophobia.

Vision.—Dim vision which obliges her to wipe her eyes continually, thus giving relief, with a sensation as if the lids would adhere in the corners. Dim vision as through a fog, or as if hairs or feathers were before eyes. In the evening the vision is dim and eyes dry, so that she cannot use them.

Clinical.—Alumina is indicated in chronic inflammation of the lids in which there is dryness and smarting without much destruction of tissue (ulceration), and without great thickening of the lids.

Nictitation, dependent upon enlarged papillæ of the conjunctiva, has been relieved.—J. H. BUFFUM.

Some cases of chronic granular lids, or loss of power in the upper lids, met with in old dry cases of granulations, yield only to this drug. The evening dryness and dimness of the eyes, with inability to use them, have been verified in cases of chronic dry catarrh.

Dr. A. Wanstall recommends Alumina very highly for both acute and chronic catarrhal conjunctivitis, especially the latter, and sends me this case illustrating its action:—Miss A., æt. 18, artist, for a year or more has been unable to use her eyes at night. Hm. $\frac{1}{30}$. Eyes inflame after using; palpebral conjunctiva especially inflamed, with rough appearance on lower lids (follicular); dry scurfs on lashes. The patient declined to wear glasses. Alumina was prescribed, and in one week she reported, "I can now read with more ease at night;" and in six weeks she was entirely cured. A slight relapse eighteen months later was speedily relieved by the same remedy.

A very remarkable case of "amaurosis," cured by metallic Aluminum[200], was reported in the *A. H. Z.*, Vol. 54, by Bœnninghausen:—The history details an inflammation attacking the eyes after childbirth, treated allopathically till "amaurosis" (*sic*) destroyed the left eye and began to affect the right.

The eye (vision) was most obscured in bright sunlight, and she could only make her way about the streets in the twilight; no colors before vision; everything black and dark; constant headache, worse towards evening and on motion; sweats easily. Bellad. was first given to arrest progress of disease in right eye, which it did decidedly; then Conium, "which acts markedly on the left eye"; then Bellad. again, with the effect of stopping the clouds which began to reappear over the right eye. She became pregnant, and other complaints interfered with the eye treatment. In three months she complained of a yellow spot before the eye if she looked at white objects; this soon disappeared after a dose of Ammon. carb. After confinement she had various remedies and other treatment for a time, under which she became *stone blind*. She again improved under Sulphur, Calc., Caust. and Sepia, so that she could see her way about, but vision was very dim; the sleep disturbed by dreams; constipation and headache, were complications. Having just received Alumin. met.[200], he dissolved some in six spoonfuls of water and ordered a spoonful night and morning for three days. The result was astonishing; complete restoration of vision (as good as formerly) and relief in other respects.

Alumina should be one of our most important remedies for loss of power of the internal recti (compare Conium and Natr. mur.) and for paralytic squint.

AMMONIUM CARBONICUM.

Eyes weak and watery, especially after reading. A large black spot floats before vision after sewing.

Clinical.—Ammon. carb. is especially serviceable in cases of muscular asthenopia, from overstraining the eyes by prolonged sewing, etc. (compare Ruta, Natr. mur.). On referring to Bœnninghausen's case under Alumina, it will be seen that he cured "yellow spots on looking at white objects" with Ammon. carb. So far as we know, this is a clinical symptom, but seems to have been one on which Bœnninghausen relied.

AMYL NITRIT.

Under the ophthalmoscope the veins of the disc were seen to become enlarged, varicose and tortuous; the arteries small, but not abnormally so. Conjunctiva bloodshot. Protruding, staring eyes. Sight hazy.

Clinical.—Amyl nitr. is one of the two remedies most frequently indicated in a form of ciliary neuralgia with acute conjunctivitis, dependent upon disturbances in the vaso-motor system. Its sphere of action is illustrated in the following case:—Patrick A., twenty-three years of age; left eye had been inflamed three weeks before he was seen. For two weeks the pain had been quite severe, very sharp in character and extending through the left eye to the back of the head; always worse at night. The conjunctiva was very red with deep ciliary injection; the pupil was contracted, but could be dilated regularly, though slowly, by Atropine. He was treated as an out-patient for five days, with Atropine externally and Merc. protiod. or Merc. corr. internally. As he appeared to be growing worse he was taken into the N. Y. Ophthalmic Hospital, put to bed, a cotton pad applied to the eye, Atropine instilled, and Bryon.[30] given internally. Only slight temporary relief seemed to follow the use of the Bryon., and various remedies were given for three weeks with no permanent benefit. Terebinth cleared up the urine, which at one time was quite dark, though it produced no change in the eye. Cedron gave relief from pain for several days, but nothing permanent. As no benefit was obtained from Atropine and no tendency to adhesion of iris to lens was observed, its use was discontinued. It was noticed that when the Atropine was stopped for only a few hours, the pupil would rapidly contract. The tension was frequently tested and found to vary, even in a short time, sometimes being greatly diminished, and again normal. Most of the time, however, it was decreased; vision hazy. The left side of the face was flushed, and its temperature higher than the right; tongue coated and appetite poor. Amyl nitr.[30] was then given. Amelioration of the pains was noticed within twenty-four hours, while the redness of the eye and the other abnormal symptoms began gradually to disappear; in a week he was discharged, cured.

This drug has been found of great service in some cases of exophthalmic goitre; one case of which has been completely cured by the olfaction of Amyl nitrit. alone.—T. F. A.

ANTIMONIUM CRUDUM.

Small humid spots in the external canthus which are very painful if sweat touches them ; mucus in the canthi mornings with dry crusts on the lids. Eyes red and inflamed, with itching and agglutination nights and photophobia mornings; lids red with fine stitches in eyeballs. Itching in the canthi.

Clinical.—This drug has cured, or assisted in curing, some obstinate cases of *blepharitis*, in which the lids have been inflamed, swollen and moist, with pustules on the face; especially when occurring in cross, peevish children. (Compare Graphites.)

Marked success has been observed by Dr. Wanstall, from the use of this remedy in scrofulous ophthalmia characterized by pustules on the cornea or conjunctiva, with profuse mucous discharge and lachrymation; lids swollen, red, excoriated and bathed in the secretions; accompanying which will be found pustular eruptions on the face, moist eruptions about and on the ears, soreness of anterior nares, swollen upper lip, etc.

APIS MEL.

Objective.—*Lids much swollen, red and œdematous; often everted; the upper lid hangs like a sac over the eye.* Erysipelas of the lids; they are dark bluish-red, and so swollen as to close the eye, following severe pains; the swelling extends around the eyes and down over the cheek. The conjunctiva becomes congested, puffy, œdematous and full of dark red veins. Lachrymation hot, spirts out of the eye. Lachrymation with burning in the eyes, and with photophobia; with pains in the eyes on sewing, evenings; with pain on looking at bright objects; with severe burning and sensation of a foreign body in the eye.

Subjective.—Burning, *stinging* and sensation of swelling around the left eye in the superciliary ridge. Soreness of the lids and canthi, with agglutination; burning of the edges of the lids, causing lachrymation. Stinging or itching in the internal canthi, or smarting of edges of lids. *Stinging in the ball* and pain across the forehead; aching pressing in the lower part of the left eyeball. Fulness inside the ball, with flushed head and face. Violent shocking pains over the right eye, extending down to eyeball. Smarting and sensation of burning in the eyes, with bright redness of the conjunctiva; very sensitive to light. *Stinging pains*; pains on sewing; most dreadful pains shoot through the eye in inflammations; pains throbbing and burning; pains aggravated on moving the eyes; photophobia; eyes pain and are easily fatigued on exertion.

Clinical.—The clinical record of this drug is important, verifying nearly all its symptoms. It is especially adapted to *œdematous conditions of the lids or conjunctiva*, particularly non-inflammatory; inflammations with burning, biting pains; inflammations following eruptive diseases; inflammations with severe shooting pains, heat of the head, red face, cold feet, etc.; erysipelatous inflammations of the lids, with adjacent smooth swelling of the face, especially with chemosis.

It is also indicated in various forms of blepharitis with thickening or swelling, such as incipient phlegmon, with great puffiness and stinging pains. The following case by Dr. C. R. Norton shows its use in acute inflammation of the lids:—Lids much swollen, red and blue, cannot open them, lachrymation, much pain, restlessness at night, cold water gives great relief. Grew worse under Acon.³. Apis²⁰⁰ cured speedily. Chronic blepharitis with thickening of conjunctival layer, so that the lower lid is everted.

Ulceration of the margins of the lids and canthi with stinging pains may require this remedy.

Illustrative of its action in syphilitic ulceration of the lids is the following case:—Mrs. H., æt. 42, for three months had suffered from ulceration of the lower lid of the right eye. The history of syphilis was clear. Massive doses of iodide of potassium had arrested an extensive ulceration of the soft palate, but the ulcers on the lid appeared immediately afterward. There were two ulcers; one extending from the inner canthus along the margin of the lid to the centre, and the other, smaller, near the external canthus. They were dark red at the base with ragged edges; lids œdematously swollen and red. There was much pain of a sharp, stinging character. Merc. was given with no benefit; then Apis³, under which the pain almost immediately ceased, the swelling of the lids subsided, and in three weeks the ulcers had entirely healed. No return of difficulty to present time, five years.—W. P. Fowler.

Occasionally of service in acute catarrhal conjunctivitis, if there is bright redness of the conjunctiva and chemosis, with stinging pains; also in ophthalmia neonatorum with great swelling of the lids and adjacent cellular tissue.

Various and severe forms of keratitis have been cured by Apis, although I believe its sphere of usefulness in diseases of the cornea is very limited. Keratitis, with dreadful pains shooting through the eyes, with swollen lids and conjunctiva, with photophobia and hot lachrymation gushing out on opening the eyes (see Rhus). Pustular keratitis with chemosis, dark red conjunctiva and swollen lids. Ulceration of the cornea, vascular, with photophobia, lachrymation and burning pain; lids everted and often ulcerated on the margins.

An interesting case under my care in the N. Y. Ophthalmic Hospital shows that Apis may be of service in parenchymatous keratitis:—A boy, 11 years of age, was brought to me with the right cornea densely infiltrated, moderate redness and photophobia. Inflammation was just commencing in the left eye. The history of hereditary syphilis was tolerably clear. There was an exostosis on inferior maxilla; the joints were en-

larged and painful, so that he could not walk; high fever and
loss of appetite. He was taken into the hospital, and several
remedies given with no avail. Both corneæ became worse,
were infiltrated and inflamed, until vision was nearly lost in
both eyes. His fever also increased and was accompanied
with drowsiness and thirstlessness. Apis[1] was given, with immediate relief of the drowsiness, fever and inflammatory
symptoms of the eye. Under its influence the cornea began
at once to clear and a complete cure was the final result.

A case of hydrops retinæ, with pressive pain in the lower
part of the ball, with flushed face and head, was partially
relieved by Apis, but not cured.—T. F. A.

Asthenopic troubles, especially affections from using the
eyes at night, causing redness of the eyes, with lachrymation
and stinging pains, may call for this remedy.

The character of the pains will usually serve to distinguish
the Apis from the Rhus cases, which are objectively very similar. Apis does not seem to control suppurative inflammations
of the deep structures of the eye as does Rhus, though the
puffiness of the lids might seem to indicate it; these cases are
at first generally painless, and the external swelling is not
bright red, as are the local and external troubles of Apis.

The burning hot lachrymation calls to mind Arsen., but the
discharges are not acrid and excoriating in Apis, though they
feel burning hot; besides the Arsenicum cases usually present
a well marked cachexia.

ARGENTUM METALLICUM.

Margins of lids very thick and red. Violent itching in the
canthi.

Clinical.—This remedy has proved useful in some cases of
blepharitis, relieving the severe itching of the lids and angles
of the eye. One case of stricture of the lachrymal duct improved very rapidly under its use until lost sight of.—T. F. A.
(Compare the violent itching of this drug with Zinc. in which
it is very marked in the internal canthus.)

ARGENTUM NITRICUM.

Objective.—Ophthalmia, often with intense pain, abating in the cool and open air, but intolerable in a warm room. *The conjunctiva, both ocular and palpebral, becomes congested, and infiltrated,* with scarlet redness. The *caruncula lachrymalis is swollen* and looks like a lump of red flesh; clusters of intensely red vessels extend from the inner canthus to the cornea. *Profuse mucous discharge* in the morning on waking, with dulness of the head, especially in the forehead and root of the nose. The margins of the lids are thick and red; the canthi red and sore. Opacity of the cornea.

(From the local application of this drug, most violent inflammation of the conjunctiva of the lids and eyeballs ensues, with profuse muco-purulent discharge which is not excoriating to the lids.)

Subjective.— Heaviness over the eyes, which open with difficulty. Boring above the left eye. Infra-orbital neuralgia. Burning, biting and itching in the eyes, especially in the canthi; heat and pain in the ball on motion and touch; aching pain, deep in eye, early in the morning.

Vision.—She is only able to read by holding the page which she is reading at a distance from her eyes. The letters become blurred before the eyes; her sight vanishes when reading or writing. Vanishing of sight. Obscuration of sight with anxiety; heat in the face and lachrymation; gray spots and bodies in the shape of serpents move before the vision.

Clinical.—Nitrate of silver has been very freely employed as an empirical remedy for various diseases of the conjunctiva and cornea; it is now, however, quite going out of fashion and being replaced by preparations of copper.

It is useful in blepharitis if the lids are very red, thick and swollen, especially if complicated with granulations, conjunctivitis or some deeper inflammation of the eye. In one case of ciliary blepharitis with entropion, caused by being over a fire, and ameliorated in the cold air or by cold applications, it effected a cure.

Acute conjunctivitis resulting from bathing, with profuse

discharge and dark redness of the conjunctiva has been relieved.

Nitrate of silver is not homœopathic to granular lids in the
later stages, but is the appropiate remedy in the early stages
of acute granular conjunctivitis, in which the conjunctiva is
intensely pink or scarlet-red, and the discharge is profuse and
inclined to be muco-purulent. Although these may be confounded with Euphrasia cases, there is a wide difference, more
easy to recognize than to describe. In Euphrasia the profuse
discharge causes soreness of the lids and more or less swelling;
the character of the inflammation is more acute and short
lived and, as a rule, the redness is much less brilliant. In
Nitrate of silver cases we may, indeed, have very little discharge, except, perhaps, flakes of mucus when the patient complains of itching and biting in the eyes, and a dry burning
sensation without real dryness. (Cantharis has intense heat
and real dryness; Sulphur is very often indicated in these dry
conjunctival catarrhs, especially if there be sharp sticking
pains under the lids as if splinters were sticking into the eyeballs. Compare also Alumina, Graphites and Natr. mur.)

The greatest service that Argent. nitr. performs is in *purulent conjunctivitis.* With large experience in both hospital and
private practice, not a single eye has been lost from this disease when seen before the cornea has been destroyed, and most
of them have been treated with Nitrate of silver either used
internally alone or combined with the local application of a
solution of the first, third or thirtieth potency. The most intense chemosis, with strangulated vessels, most profuse purulent discharge, even the cornea beginning to get hazy and looking as though it would slough, have been seen to subside
rapidly under the internal administration of Argent. nitr. I
do believe there is no need of cauterization with it, *except in
the gonorrhœal form of purulent conjunctivitis.* The subjective
symptoms are almost none; their very absence, with the *profuse
purulent discharge* and the swollen lids, swollen from being distended by a collection of pus in the eye or swelling of the sub-
conjunctival tissue of the lids themselves (as in Rhus or
Apis), indicates the drug.

It has also relieved and contributed to the cure of diseases with destruction of tissue, as ulceration of the cornea; in one case with pains like darts through the eye mornings, better evenings; in another case there were small ulcers on the upper part of the cornea with much inflammation, burning pain and profuse discharge.

It has also been useful in kerato-iritis, with violent congestion of the conjunctiva; the cornea was vascular and eroded, with terrific pains from the vertex into the eye and with burning heat in the eyes.—T. F. A.

Coldness of the eye with boring pain in the head and a sensation as if the scalp was drawn tightly, has been removed by Arg. nitr.—T. F. A. (Fluor. ac. has a sensation of cold air blowing into the eye.) In the Arg. nitr. cases we sometimes meet with trembling of the whole body and headaches.

A case of retino-choroiditis was successfully treated by this remedy.—W. H. WOODYATT.

Arg. nitr. has greatly improved two cases of atrophy of the optic nerve; in one increasing the vision from $\frac{10}{100}$ to $\frac{20}{200}$.—C. M. THOMAS.

Dr. Woodyatt was the first to call attention to Arg. nitr. as a remedy for weakness or paralysis of the accommodation. Since then it has been found of great service in many cases of this kind, especially if dependent upon errors of refraction, in which the asthenopic symptoms on using the eyes are not relieved after correction with the proper glasses.

A very interesting case, illustrative of the optical illusions of this drug, is reported by Dr. C. Th. Liebold:—A young man was totally blind from cerebral disease, associated with loss of virility; was perfectly sane, but constantly complained that he seemed to see trees, people and green fields, but *everything was covered with snakes*, writhing and twisting in every form; snakes over his body, over his food; snakes of all sizes everywhere; he would sit for hours and contemplate these snakes he seemed to see; sometimes he saw bugs. Dr. Liebold found in Berridge's Repertory, under "tortuous bodies," Arg. nitr., among other remedies; it at once removed the snakes but did not restore vision.

ARNICA.

The margins of the upper eyelids, along their lines of contact with the eyeballs, internally, are painful when the lids are moved, as if they were too dry and a little sore. Cramp-like tearing or pressure in the eyebrow (left).

Clinical.—Arnica has been employed with marked success in a variety of eye troubles resulting from blows and various injuries; sometimes applied locally (tincture diluted with water) and sometimes given internally. It seems to be better adapted to contused than lacerated wounds, and to injuries before inflammatory symptoms have become prominent, although benefit has been derived from its use in inflammations of the lids, conjunctiva, and even of the whole globe, when of traumatic origin. (Acon., Calend.)

In hastening the absorption of extravasations of blood in the conjunctiva, aqueous humor, retina, or other ocular tunics, especially if resulting from injuries or the straining in whooping-cough, Arnica often acts well; it seems also, sometimes, to correct the relaxed condition of the blood-vessels and the too fluid condition of the blood, which predisposes to sub-conjunctival hæmorrhages in whooping-cough. (Hamamelis is more frequently useful in hæmorrhages into the anterior chamber; and Ledum in sub-conjunctival ecchymoses.)

In two cases of traumatic detachment of the retina, Dr. Hunt has observed the retinæ become re-attached under the influence of Arnica[30].

A case of traumatic mydriasis recovered very rapidly under this remedy.

Paralysis of the muscles from trauma has been cured, as in the following case of partial paralysis of the left superior oblique:—A man, æt. 25, after violent muscular exertion and injuries, saw double on looking down. There was an injury of left upper eyelid and a corresponding ecchymosis of the ball. Patient suffered from diplopia and vertigo; he carried his head forward and to the right; was fearful of his balance, the ground seeming to waver under his feet; relieved by closing his left eye. The muscle recovered completely under Arnica.—Payr.

ARSENICUM.

Objective.—*Eyelids swollen and œdematous*, first the upper and then the lower (this swelling is mostly non-inflammatory and painless); the œdematous lids are firmly and spasmodically closed, and look as if distended with air. Blepharadenitis ciliaris and ulcerosa; edges of lids very red. Continual trembling of the upper eyelids, with lachrymation. Conjunctiva inflamed; extreme *redness of the inner surface of the eyelids. Lachrymation and discharges from the eye excoriate the lid and cheek.*

Subjective.—Sub-orbital pain on the left side with prickings as with needles, sometimes quite severe. Extreme redness of the inner surface of the eyelids, with an uneasy sensation rather than pain, often obliging one to rub the eyes. Pain in the margin of the eyelids on moving them, as if they were dry and rubbed against the eyeballs, both in the open air and in the room. *Burning on margins of lids.* In the evening a feeling as of sand in the eyes, obliging him to rub them. *Burning in the eyes;* eyes hot, with burning, sore pain in the balls. Pulsative throbbing in the eyes, and with every pulsation a stitch; after midnight. Photophobia. She appeared to be sensitive to light and often kept her eyes closed.

Clinical.—Only by concomitant symptoms can we distinguish between Arsenicum and Apis for *non-inflammatory œdematous swelling of the lids*, as both are indicated in this condition.

Blepharitis, following erysipelas ten years previous, with scaly condition of edges of the lids and dry, smooth, scaly skin, was cured by this remedy.—J. H. Buffum.

Its value in croupous conjunctivitis following ophthalmia neonatorum was illustrated in a child three weeks old. The discharge was moderately tenacious, stringy and yellow-white in color. The lids were slightly œdematous. The right cornea was clear, but the palpebral conjunctiva (especially lower lid) was covered with shreds of exudation, loosely attached but easily removed, leaving a bleeding surface and hypertrophied papillæ. On the lower half of the left cornea was a large ulcer which had perforated, and the remainder of the cornea was opaque. The conjunctiva of the lower lid was covered with a dense, white, semi-transparent, fibrinous exudation which could not be removed without much force. A similar membrane was present on the upper lid, but not as dense nor as firmly attached. After Arg. nitr., Bromine, and chlorine water had failed to improve, Arsen.[30] was given on account of the restlessness after midnight and desire to nurse often and little. A solution of alcohol (℥j ad ℥ij) was used locally at the same time. The membrane rapidly disappeared and the ulcer healed, leaving a slight purulent discharge which Arg. nitr. controlled.

Arsenicum may be called for in chronic trachoma, in which the internal surfaces of the lids are inflamed, painful, dry and rub against the ball, especially if there are *intense burning pains and excoriating lachrymation.*

In scrofulous ophthalmia this remedy has been frequently employed with success, especially in ulcers of the cornea, with soreness of the internal surface of the lids, which are swollen and spasmodically closed, so that opening them causes intense burning, sticking pains, worse at night, excessive photophobia and acrid lachrymation; tears gush out on opening the eyes; eyes can be opened well in the cool open air, but not in the house, even in a dark room; eyes feel as if they had no room in the orbit; throbbing, pulsating in the eyeballs and around the orbit, with general ulceration of the cornea recurring first in one eye and then the other, especially in young people who are anæmic (in one case when the eyes were better the feet were swollen); ulcer on outer side of cornea with elevated edges, pain like the pricking of needles, excoriation of the external canthus, burning and sticking pains. The following case shows still further the action of Arsenic in ulceration of the cornea :—A woman, æt. 35, had ulcers of the cornea with chronic trachoma, with a blepharitis which dated some years from the suppression of an eruption on the scalp, which she described as scaly and very itchy. The cornea had become dim and dotted with small white scars from old ulcers; she had no lashes left; the lids were very sore on the inner margins; she had photophobia and various neuralgic pains. On the 12th of May she received one dose of Sulphur[200]. In a week the right eye was somewhat better, but the left was much worse. The head is getting sore, with an itching, moist eruption which forms a dry scurf; she complains of pains and restlessness at night; there is twitching of the eyes as if they were drawing into the head, with burning heat, hot lachrymation and photophobia, with tearing pains around the eyes on looking at the light. Arsen.[82m], one dose, was prescribed. In twelve days she reported wonderful improvement; no heat, no pains, no twitching; since the ulcers had healed the photophobia vanished; she received Sac. lac., and continued to improve for three weeks, when a slight return of the photophobia necessitated a repetition of the dose; each dose acted about four weeks. She gradually recovered nearly perfect vision, with disappearance of the granulations and perfect cure of the eruption.—T. F. A.

Vascular elevations on the cornea resulting from ulceration, aggravated by opening and closing the eyes, with violent, burning pains every afternoon, have been benefited.

Parenchymatous keratitis may require the use of this remedy, as, for example, the following case occurring in my clinic and treated by Dr. Charles A. Boyle:—Mrs. J., æt. 30, had suffered from an inflammation of the eyes for eleven weeks. Both corneæ were very hazy, densely infiltrated, and vision nearly lost, especially in the right eye. There was deep ciliary injection and commencing vascularity of the cornea; much photophobia and lachrymation; *burning pain in the eye and over the brow, worse about four* A.M.; shooting pain in the ball, over the head and down in the cheek; sensation like pins and needles sticking in the eyes, worse at night. Pupil dilated slowly under Atropine. No specific history. For one week Cinnab.[3] and Aur. mur.[3], with Atropine externally, were prescribed with only an aggravation of the symptoms. Arsen.[3] was then given with almost immediate amelioration of pain and rapid diminution of the inflammatory symptoms. One week later the 30th was prescribed. In about four weeks the haziness of the cornea had so nearly disappeared that with correcting glasses vision was $\frac{20}{30}$.

Several cases of kerato-iritis with burning pains over the orbit, worse at night, and with profuse acrid lachrymation have been cured.

Benefit has been derived from its use in syphilitic iritis and also in idiopathic iritis, characterized by burning pains in the eye, worse at night, especially after midnight, with great restlessness and much thirst.

Arsen. cured a progressive choroiditis disseminata which alternated with bronchial catarrh; when the eyes were better the chest was worse, and vice versa. There was heat in the eyes and burning in the chest, with dyspnœa and a whole train of Arsenic chest symptoms.—T. F. A.

The favorable results obtained from the use of Arsen. in retinitis albuminurica are sometimes very gratifying, as shown in the following case:—Miss M. P., æt. 20; retinitis albuminurica fully developed in both eyes. L. V. counts fingers at two feet. R. V. $\frac{20}{70}$. Right ventricle hypertrophied; appetite variable; bowels regular; great thirst for small amounts; occipital headache of a pricking character; tongue large, dry and yellowish; menses too often, and venous; breath oppressed and pulse irregular. Cured in two months by Arsenicum 3d and 30th, and Sulphur[30]. Last report; no albumen; R. V. $\frac{20}{20}$; L. V. $\frac{10}{50}$.—W. S. SEARLE.

Both Arsenicum and Rhus are often indicated in scrofulous cases, but the paroxysmal character of the pains, the extreme prostration often present, the burning, sticking pains and the excoriating discharges will distinguish Arsenic. The brilliant red inner margins of the lids, and the dryness of the inner surfaces are very marked indications for its use in trachoma. The nervous irritability associated with the symptoms of Arsenic is a very pronounced anæmic hyperæsthesia.

Arsenic cases are generally relieved by warm applications. They are very frequently periodic in their occurrence, commencing every fall, and often alternating from one eye to the other.

ARUM TRIPHYLLUM.

Clinical.—A brilliant cure of catarrh of the lachrymal sac, with *desire to bore into the side of the nose,* was made by this drug.—C. A. BACON.

ASAFŒTIDA.

Severe boring pain above the brows. Tearing pain in the forehead; dull pressure at the external border of the left orbit. Troublesome dryness of the eyes. Periodic burning in the eyes and pressing together of the lids, as if overcome with sleep. Burning in the ball from within outward.

Clinical.—Asaf. is very useful in *ciliary neuralgia,* and from its power of relieving the intense boring, burning pain in the brows, especially at night, has arisen its very beneficial action in certain forms of deep-seated inflammation of the eyeball attended by these ciliary pains and turbidity of the humors, as in iritis, kerato-iritis, irido-choroiditis and retinitis, especially if of syphilitic origin. The pains are usually throbbing, beating, boring or burning in character, either in the eye, over or around it; they are often intermittent, extend from within outwards and are ameliorated by rest and pressure (reverse of Aurum).

Asaf. has relieved a sharp pain extending through the eye into the head, upon touching.

ASARUM.

Clinical.—Asthenopia, accompanied by congestive headaches, has been cured. The eyes were worse morning and evening, when outdoors in the heat and sunlight; were better in the middle of the day and from bathing them in cold water.—T. F. A.

ATROPINE.

About 9 P. M., eyelids felt heavy and difficult to keep open. Sharp pain under the right eye, with slight pain in the temples. Neuralgic pains, commencing under the left orbit, and running back to the ear, lasting perhaps ten minutes at a time, and then disappearing for fifteen or twenty; these have been noticed for several hours.

Clinical.—In addition to the extensive use of Atropine for dilating the pupil, its use for the purposes of lessening the intraocular blood pressure in inflammatory diseases of the internal structures of the eyeball, and also in inflammation of the cornea and even conjunctiva, has lately come into vogue.

Its wholesale and empyrical application for therapeutic purposes is unwise and often unsafe, since we have few accurate data upon which to base a prescription of Atropine to cure (it should never be used when Belladonna is indicated, since Atropine does not comprise Belladonna).

It is a very happy provision that the local application of Atropine to a healthy eye, almost always spends its whole drug power upon the peripheral nerve fibres of the iris and ciliary muscle; and that very seldom do any constitutional symptoms arise. The instances of such marked drug affinity for accessible portions of the human body are, indeed, rare, or, at least, rarely recognized. We have then a mechanical agent, as it were, for treating diseases of the iris. Neither Bell. nor Atrop. are often indicated remedies in iritis. Is then the use of Atropine to be commended? The necessary conditions for the successful treatment of iritis are above all :—First, rest of the organ affected; second, isolation as far as possible from contiguous structures, in order to avoid adhesions of the iris to the surface of the lens. Rest of the iris can be approximately obtained by placing the patient in a perfectly dark room, and keeping him in a recumbent position. But we still have to deal with emotional effects as well as the irritating action of the inflammatory process. Darkness favors the dilatation of the pupil and consequent withdrawal of the margin of the iris from the lens capsule, but the inflammatory process supplies the stimulus or irritation which was banished with the light, and so but little has been gained. We cannot keep the patient constantly in the dark without detriment to his general health. Attempts of this kind have been attended with considerable damage to the patient. In several years experience we have seen no single bad effect from the use of strong (4 grs. to the ounce) solution of Atropine for dilating the pupil in order to examine the fundus; it is well, however, to avoid its use in all stages of glaucoma, as cases are reported of most violent inflammation following its use in that disease (though Belladonna does not seem to be at all homœopathic to glaucoma, as the action of Atropine is probably mechanical).

If an attack of iritis could be promptly recognized and met at the very beginning, before the exudative stage is reached (that is, within twenty-four hours), there might be no need of Atropine; but if exudation has taken place, and the inflammation is violent, use immediately a strong solution of Atropine, a drop every one to four hours; it will not materially interfere with the action of remedies; it is, however, *in all cases, the safest plan*, for if adhesions take place, an iridectomy will usually be required. For sub-acute cases a much weaker solution, one-quarter to one-eighth of a grain to the ounce, may be sufficient to dilate the pupil. In severe cases, in which the congestion of the capillaries is enormous, and the iris, being so full of blood, cannot dilate, Aconite may be employed in frequent doses to reduce the hyperæmia; in rare cases of this kind even cupping of the temples may be justifiable as a temporary expedient, to enable us to obtain a dilated pupil; this being accomplished, remedial measures may be resumed and continued.

Its use is recommended for the relief of ciliary neuralgia.

AURUM.

Objective.—Redness and swelling of the lids. Redness of the sclerotic; constant lachrymation; morning agglutination.

Subjective.—Burning, stitching, drawing and itching in the inner canthus of eyes and in the lids. Sensation, upon using the eyes, as of violent heat in them. Pressure in the eyes and constant feeling of sand in them. Pressive pain in the right ball from above downwards, also from without inwards, worse on touch. Pain in the eye from blowing the nose.

Vision.—Hemiopia, *the upper half of the field of vision seems covered by a black body,* the lower half visible. He cannot distinguish anything clearly, because he sees everything double, and one object is seen mixed with the other, with violent tension in the eyes.

Clinical.—In considering the clinical application of Aurum in ophthalmic diseases, no distinction will be made between metallic gold and the muriate, for experience has not yet demonstrated that there is any practical difference between these two preparations. It has been my practice to use the muriate when the administration of a low potency is desired, and the metallic if a high attenuation is required.

In blepharitis it is rarely useful, though may be called for, especially in syphilitic patients after the abuse of mercury, if the lids are red, swollen and ulcerated.

For *trachoma, with* or without *pannus* (especially with), there is probably no remedy oftener indicated than Aurum. Its characteristics are not well marked, as its usefulness has been confirmed in a variety of cases; there is commonly much photophobia, lachrymation and pain, burning or dull in character, compelling one to close the lids, usually worse in the morning and ameliorated by the application of cold water; although one or more of these symptoms may be absent without necessarily contra-indicating this remedy.

For ulcerations and pannus-like thickening of the outer layer, Aurum is of great service, especially in the cases of scrofulous ophthalmia with ulcerations and vascularity of the cornea, with great irritability of the patient; great sensitiveness to noise; photophobia; profuse, scalding lachrymation; sensitiveness of the eyes to touch; swollen cervical glands; pains from without inward, worse on touch (reverse of Asaf.).

No remedy has given greater satisfaction in the treatment of *interstitial keratitis* than Aurum muriaticum, and many cases of this sluggish form of inflammation have yielded promptly to its use. Its sphere of action does not seem to be closely circumscribed, for rapid improvement has followed its use in cases of a scrofulous origin, as well as in those which can be traced to *hereditary syphilis.* The *cornea is more or less opaque* and may be very vascular or not. Tne degree of ciliary injection, photophobia and pain is variable. An example of the speedy cure which may be effected by this drug, is found in the following:—A boy, seven years of age, had been suffering from inflammation of the eyes and loss of vision for two weeks. There was diffuse haziness of both corneæ, with dense points here and there, moderate redness and photophobia; no pain. The vision was reduced to counting fingers at two feet. Child scrofulous. Under Aur. mur.[3], in four weeks, right vision $\frac{2 0}{7 0}$, and left vision $\frac{2 0}{4 0}$. Two weeks later there was only slight haziness of the cornea remaining. Its verification in cases dependent upon hereditary syphilis, is of frequent occurrence.

In several cases, it has hastened the absorption of deposits in the cornea, and cleared up opacities remaining after ulceration or infiltration.

In low forms of episcleritis in which the cornea is becoming infiltrated from the sclera, with moderate redness, pain and photophobia, benefit has been derived from Aurum.

Favorable results have followed its use in iritis and kerato-iritis, particularly the syphilitic variety, and after the abuse of mercury. There is usually much pain around the eye, which seems to be deep in the bone and to extend from without inward; aggravated by touch. In one case recently under my care in which the improvement and cure was remarkably rapid under Aur. mur.[3], there was great swelling of the iris, extensive posterior synechiæ, large *gumma on iris*, haziness of aqueous, with deposits on posterior surface of cornea, tending to extension into the parenchyma, together with much pain and soreness around the eye; worse at night.

It is almost a specific for exudative chorio-retinitis with exudations in the vitreous.—T. F. A.

Choroiditis with injection of sub-conjunctival vessels, slight iritis, photophobia, pains in the hip, great craving for coffee, and general feeling of malaise, was cured by this remedy.— H. GILBERT.

Hemiopia, in which the right half of objects is invisible, has been helped, though not cured. But the form of hemiopia to which Aurum is especially adapted is when the patient can see nothing above the median line, as the following case will illustrate:—Some years ago a gentleman, who had taken large quantities of iodide of potash, complained that the vision of the left eye had been failing for a year and a half; he could not see the upper half of a room, or any large object, though the lower half was clear; no pains in the eye; objects seem smaller and more distant; has some black spots before vision; is always worse as the day progresses, and better in the morning; twitching in the upper lid. On inquiry it was found that he had syphilis ten years ago, but had not been recently troubled with any secondary symptoms, except that a large bursa-like swelling on the wrist had persisted a long time. Vision was $\frac{5}{200}$. Upon ophthalmoscopic examination there was found chorio-retinitis (chronic) with an accumulation of fluid beneath the retina, which settled to the lower portion of the eye and caused a large *detachment of the retina. Vitreous hazy from infiltration.* Right eye normal; refraction normal. Knowledge of the pathological condition here gave no clue to the remedy, and we were obliged, this time at least, to rely upon the symptomatology (as one should always be ready to do). The remarkable symptom of not seeing anything in the upper half of the field of vision is of course the most prominent. In addition to the Aurum symptom, we may find, under Digitalis, "as if the upper half of the field of vision were covered by a dark cloud evenings on walking." Digitalis, moreover, covers the pathological point, having been found curative in fluid exudations of various kinds. The symptoms are also worse in the evening, while those of Aurum are usually worse in the morning. Still, taking the history of the case into account and the previous dosing with iodide of potash, Aurum[200] was given, under which he steadily improved; the haziness of the vitreous almost entirely disappeared; the inflammation of the retina subsided and in one year the vision rose to and remained at $\frac{1.5}{100}$, beyond which it would not go, for the retina was partly disorganized and could not be repaired with retinal tissue.—T. F. A. Since then several cases of retinal disease have been successfully treated with Aurum, though in some cases no improvement followed and the remedy only served to arrest further progress of the malady (compare Gelsem.). Aurum cases will usually be found to follow overdosing by potash or mercury, and perfect vision can never be expected from the nature of the tissue changes.

One singular case of a man, forty years old, was sent for advice. A large black sub-choroidal tumor was found in the fundus just behind the lens growing from the inner side. He suffered no pain, but the symptoms of vision were those of Aurum. The whole disease had only lasted about six weeks. Vision $\frac{5}{200}$. After taking Aurum[200] a week, vision rose to $\frac{5}{80}$, and in eight weeks more to $\frac{5}{60}$; since which time he has not been seen. It was probably an exudation tumor, and may have been absorbed.—T. F. A.

Its reported benefit in paralysis of the muscles from syphilitic periostitis seems reasonable, though I have not yet had occasion to verify its action.

BADIAGO.

Bluish purple margins of lids. Headache, extending to the eyeballs. Pains in the eyeballs, extending into the temples, aggravated by turning them in either direction. Slight aching pains in the posterior portion of both eyeballs and in the temples (with headache from 2 P. M. till 7 A. M.). The left eyeball quite sore, even upon closing it tightly.

Clinical.—This variety of sponge has been useful in some cases of exophthalmic goitre and should always be thought of in this disease.

It may be of service in kopiopia hysterica with aching pains behind the eyeballs. (Cimicif., Ledum.)

BARYTA CARBONICA.

Redness of the conjunctiva, with swollen lids. Itching of the eyes. Sensation as of a gauze before the eyes, in the morning and after a meal.

Clinical.—Dr. Dudgeon advises its use in scrofulous inflammations of the eye characterized by phlyctenules and ulcers on the cornea, especially when associated with glandular swellings.

BARYTA IODATA.

Clinical.—Up to the present time no proving has been made of this substance, so that its sphere of action is hypothecated from its composition; clinically, it has proved a great addition to our armamentarium. It was first introduced to notice as an ophthalmic remedy by Dr. Liebold, who says that it is especially adapted to diseases, occurring in scrofulous subjects, in which there is great swelling of the glands, particularly of the lymphatics, "which feel like a string of beans everywhere between the muscles, down to the spinal column; they can be felt of all sizes and all degrees of induration; some may be suppurating, while others have healed with an ugly scar." It has been used very successfully in chronic recurrences of phlyctenular keratitis and conjunctivitis found in the above subjects.

Dr. Woodyatt has reported a cure of specific interstitial keratitis of both eyes, in which vision had decreased so that fingers could not be counted at more than four feet, complicated with enlargement of the cervical glands which were hard and painful on pressure. Since then I have verified its usefulness in one case of parenchymatous keratitis.

BELLADONNA.

Objective.—The eyes are protruding, staring and brilliant. The eyes become distorted, with redness and swelling of the face; spasms of the eyes; the eyes are in constant motion. Lids puffy, red and congested; inflammatory swelling of the lower lid near the inner canthus, with throbbing pains, etc. Conjunctiva red, tumefied. Lachrymation, with great photophobia. Total absence of lachrymation; motion of the eyes attended with a sense of dryness and stiffness; the conjunctival vessels fully injected. Pupils (at first, or from large doses) dilated;

(afterwards, or from minute doses) contracted. *The optic disc greatly deepened in tint, and the retinal arteries and veins much enlarged, the veins most markedly so.*

Subjective.—*Eye dry, motion attended with a sense of dryness and stiffness.* Pain and burning in the eyes. Feeling of heat in the eyes; it seems as if they were surrounded by a hot vapor. Burning heat in the eyes. The surface of the ball became quite dry, which caused a very disagreeable and uncomfortable sensation, which could not be relieved by winking or continued closing of the eyes. Pressive pain deep in the ball when she closed the eyes; feeling as if the eyes protruded.

Vision.—Dimness of sight or actual blindness. Every object in the room, both real and spectral, had a double or at least a dim outline, owing to the extreme dilatation of the pupils. *Everything* he looks at *seems red.* A large halo appears round the flame of the candle, partly colored, the red predominating; at times the light seems as if broken up into rays. Occasional *flashes of light before the eyes;* sparks of electricity before the eyes, especially on moving them; large bright sparks before the eyes. Retina insensible; he is quite blind. *Photophobia.*

Clinical.—The use of this drug in inflammatory diseases of the eye, is much more limited than is generally supposed.

Erythema and erysipelatous inflammation of the lids often require the administration of Belladonna.

It may be of service in some forms of conjunctivitis (especially catarrhal in the early stages) with dryness of the eyes, thickened, red lids and burning pains in the eyes, though not as frequently called for as Aconite. Its use may be necessary in acute aggravations of various chronic diseases, as in granular lids, when, after taking cold, the eyes become *sensitive to air and light,* with dryness and a gritty feeling in them; or in chronic forms of keratitis in which the eye suddenly becomes intensely congested, with excessive photophobia, heat and pains which may be throbbing or sharp, shooting through the eyeball to the back of the head.

Idiopathic iritis has been aborted in the early stages by this remedy, but it is not often indicated. Two cases, however, of *simple plastic iritis, resulting from a cold on the eighth day after a cataract extraction,* in which the *pains were severe and of a throbbing character in and above the eye, worse at night,* were promptly relieved under Bell.[30], after Atropine, cold and warmth externally, and Rhus., Merc. and Bry. internally had been given a faithful trial for several days with no improvement.

Mydriasis resulting from nervous headache has been relieved.

In diseases of the fundus, Belladonna has been a most valuable remedy. It has been employed with great advantage in hyperæmia of the choroid and also in inflammation, especially the disseminate form of choroiditis. There will usually be found accompanying these cases much headache, congestion of the head and considerable photophobia.

Bell. has relieved temporarily the severe pains of glaucoma, though I have never seen any permanent benefit from its use. (Glaucomatous eyes are exceedingly sensitive to the action of this drug, and atropine should never be used if possible to avoid it.)

It is often the remedy for *hyperæsthesia of the retina* dependent upon some anomaly in refraction, or due to reflex irritation, as illustrated in a case of hyperæsthesia of the retina with neuralgic dysmenorrhœa, by Dr. Fowler (Trans. O. and O. Soc., '79):—Miss F., æt. 22, had not been able to use her eyes for three months on account of the pain and dazzling whenever there was light enough to enable her to read or sew. On awakening in the morning, the light produced intense pain, not only in the eyes but in the head. Sometimes the headache continued all day; evening and darkness alone relieving it. Complained of "sparks" and flashes of light before the eyes; also of a feeling of heaviness in the eye-balls. Her general health was poor, "felt tired all the time"; menses regular, but very painful; sleep restless; mood despondent; complexion pale; appetite poor. Examination of eyes showed nothing abnormal. After Nux. v. had failed to benefit, Bell.[3] was given; in three weeks she could use her eyes about as well as ever and had no pain at menstrual period. There had been no further trouble of the kind two years later.

In *hyperæmia of the optic nerve and retina* this remedy has been especially efficacious, particularly if dependent upon cerebral congestion and accompanied by aching pain in the eye, aggravated by any light; also, in chronic forms of hyperæmia, if a red conjunctival line is very marked along the line of fissure of the lids. In some of these cases, as well as in some acute inflammatory affections, retinal photopsies are present, such as red sparks, flames, bright spots, lights, etc.

Its usefulness is not, however, confined to simple congestion of the optic nerve and retina, as it is one of our chief remedies in inflammation of these tissues. The following cases will show the sphere of action in inflammation of the optic nerve and retina:—Optic neuritis, in which the papilla was very much swollen, veins large, flashes of light before the eye and pains in the head. Bell. cured speedily.—Retinitis, occurring in a young lady who was subject to congestive headaches always worse in the afternoon. The retina was very hazy and œdematous, appearing as if covered with a bluish-gray film; outlines of disc ill-defined; vessels large and tortuous. Under Bell.[30] a rapid disappearance of the above symptoms took place.—Neuro-retinitis. Edith G., æt. 5, had suffered from "chills and fever," which had been relieved without quinine. Six weeks previous to my seeing her, and immediately after the chills had been stopped, it was first noticed that her sight was poor but variable; sometimes she seemed to be nearly blind, while again would distinguish medium-sized objects with comparative ease; complained very often of headache, especially every afternoon, when the head would be quite hot and the face flushed. She was more irritable and cross than formerly. The condition at the time was reported as follows: "Child has a full face, light complexion and red hair; is bright and smart. Her vision is very poor; does not seem to be able to count fingers, though, owing to her age, her statements are unreliable; sight is markedly better in right than left eye; nothing abnormal is to be seen externally, with the exception of a slight convergent strabismus in left eye. Ophthalmoscopic examination after dilatation of both pupils with Atropine. Right eye: Optic disc very much swollen, and outlines ill-defined; its edges, as well as the surrounding retina, are so infiltrated that it is only by tracing the retinal vessels that the optic nerve entrance is discovered. The arteries are about normal in size, but they, as well as the veins, which are large and tortuous, are veiled here and there by the infiltration. In the macula lutea bright white patches are seen, of a triangular shape, and extending more towards the nerve than outwards from the macula (are somewhat similar to the stellated arrangement usually found in retinitis albuminurica). Left eye: The same swollen condition of the optic nerve and surrounding retina is perceived as in the right eye, though mingled with the infiltration into the retina are spots of exudation of an opaque character. The retinal vessels are enlarged, especially the veins which are full and tortuous; they are hidden at points by the exudation into the retina; while along their course, especially on the nerve entrance and immediately around, small points of extravasation of blood are noticed. The changes in the macula lutea are similar to those in the right eye, though the white patches are more marked and divided into many, by fine lines or interspaces. A careful examination of the urine shows not the slightest trace of albumen." Bell.[3] was given. In three days vision was better. In two weeks no hæmorrhages were to be found in the retina, the swelling of optic papilla and retina were decidedly less, and the headache was relieved. In one month the vision was very good, both nerves somewhat atrophic and the points of exudation in the retina could scarcely be distinguished, though no perceptible change could be seen in the white patches in the macula lutea.

A case of apoplexy of the retina, with suppression of menstruation, occurring in a girl, æt. 18, is reported by Payr:—She was subject to cerebral congestions, sudden heat of head, vertigo, burning and throbbing frontal pain, noises in the ear and illusions of vision, while the rest of the body was cold and shivering. Headache increased, pulsation of the carotids became more severe, photopsies and then sudden blindness. Numerous apoplectic spots were found in the macula lutea, no change of papilla, pulsation of central vein, much active

4

cerebral congestion and great photophobia. Under Bell. complete recovery of vision and absorption of the hæmorrhages took place.

Convulsive movements of the eyeball in the light, with terrible, pressive pain extending through the whole head, ameliorated in a dark room, have been cured by Bell.; hence its use has been recommended in strabismus due to spasmodic action of the muscles, or when resulting from brain affections. In orbital neuralgia, especially of the infra-orbital nerve, with red face and hot hands, it is a valuable remedy.

Some cases of amaurosis and amblyopia will require this drug, especially if they are congestive in form and accompanied by the headache and other characteristic symptoms.

BRYONIA.

Objective.—Puffiness of the right upper lid. The conjunctiva is dark-red and swollen, with some discharge of pus. Morning agglutination and frequent lachrymation.

Subjective.—Pressive pain above the left eye. Pressure from within outward over the right orbit into the brain, which changes to a pressure on the eyeball from above downward. Pain deep in the right orbit, aggravated by pressure upon the eyeball. Drawing together of the left upper lid, with a sensation of heaviness therein; aching pains in the eyes. Severe burning and lachrymation of the right eye. Very *sensitive pressive* pain (coming and going) in the left eyeball, *especially violent on moving the ball*, with a feeling as if the eye became smaller and retracted in the orbit.

Vision.—Dim vision; on reading, the letters seem to run together; *appearance of all colors of the rainbow;* every object seems covered with these colors; photophobia.

Clinical.—It is found that Bryonia is rarely indicated in diseases affecting the external tissues of the eye, although in one case of acute inflammation of both the ocular and palpebral conjunctiva, worse in the left eye and towards the outer canthus, with marked *soreness to touch or upon any motion of the eyes,* and with a sticking sensation as of hairs in the eyes; a speedy cure resulted under Bryonia.

It's great sphere of usefulness is, however, in diseases of the uveal tract.

Favorable results frequently follow its use in iritis caused by a cold, especially in rheumatic subjects, in which there is *sharp shooting pain through the eye into the head, aggravated by motion* and relieved by pressure; or if the pain is a steady aching in the posterior portion of the eye extending through to the occiput, worse at night and on motion.

It is also often indicated if the inflammation has extended to the choroid, as was shown in a case of acute irido-choroiditis of the left eye in which there were present opacities in the vitreous, tremulous iris, great ciliary injection, pus in the anterior chamber, soreness in eyeball on moving it, and darting pains from the eye through the head, with heaviness of the head afternoons. Bryonia speedily relieved.

In the serous variety of choroiditis it is an important remedy, as one would be led to suppose from its relation to serous inflammation in general. Experience has also verified its usefulness in this disease.

Glaucoma appears to have been checked in its progress by Bryonia, when the eyeball has seemed too full, as if pressed out, with sharp shooting pains in the eye and head, worse at night; also in a case in the prodromal stage, in which the symptoms were as follows:—The vision of the left eye had been failing three months, and especially for one week; there was heavy pain over the eye, worse at night; halo around the light for one day; cupping of the optic disc, and T. +. The patient was rheumatic and nervous. Under Bryonia[30], all the symptoms were relieved with the exception of the excavation of the nerve.

A case of hyperæmia of the optic nerve and retina was immediately relieved by this drug; a bluish haze appeared before the vision (vision $\frac{20}{60}$); with severe pain over the eye as from a *needle going through the eye* and head (compelling her to go to bed); with heat through the whole head, aggravated by stooping.

Ciliary neuralgia often requires Bryonia, especially if the pains are sharp and severe, even making the patient scream out; the pains are aggravated by opening the eye and by any motion of the eyeball; the eyes must be kept closed and at rest. The pains, when this remedy is indicated, are usually *sharp in character, passing through the eye into the head, or from the eye downward into the malar region and thence backward to the occiput; the seat of pain becomes as sore as a boil, and the least exertion, talking, moving or using the eyes, aggravates the trouble.* The following symptoms have been reported as cured by this drug, though not found in any proving; some have been repeatedly verified and seem to direct the choice of the remedy. They are mostly variations of sensation in different persons, dependent upon the great characteristics of the remedy—aggravation on motion and amelioration on pressure. Pressing, crushing pain in the eyes, worse on motion; soreness and aching of the eyes on moving them; scalding in the corners of the eyes, aggravated at night; dull pain and soreness, especially in the left eye, worse in the morning and relieved by pressure.

CACTUS GRAND.

Clinical.—From its action on the heart, cases of exophthalmic goître have been improved. Angell advises its use in hyperæmia of the eye, especially of the fundus.

CALCAREA CARBONICA.

Objective.—Swelling and redness of the lids, with nightly agglutination; during the day the eyes are full of mucus, with a hot sensation, smarting pain and lachrymation. Redness of the conjunctiva. Lachrymation on writing.

Subjective.—Painful sensation as if a foreign body were in the eye. Pressure and itching in the eyes, worse in the evening. Itching, burning and stitches, especially on the margins of the lids and in the inner canthi.

Vision.—Farsightedness. Only one side of objects visible, with dilated pupils. Dimness of the eyes after getting the head cold. Halo around the light. Flickering, sparks and black spots before the eyes. Photophobia.

Clinical.—The clinical record of this drug, in superficial inflammations of the eye, is very full.

It has been found especially curative in various forms of blepharitis, occurring in unhealthy, "pot-bellied" children inclined to grow fat, and who sweat profusely about the head; lids red, swollen and indurated; inflammation of the margins of the lids, causing loss of the eye-lashes, with thick, purulent, excoriating discharge and burning, sticking pains; blepharitis with great itching in the lids.

Indurations remaining after styes and tarsal tumors have disappeared under its use.

Simple inflammation of the conjunctiva may call for this remedy, as in the following instance of acute conjunctivitis *caused by bathing:*—There was moderate redness and lachrymation; eyes felt hot and feverish, with a sensation as of sand in them. Acon.³ failed to relieve; Calc.³⁰ cured quickly.

The discharges from the eye are often profuse, and therefore this drug has been used with advantage in purulent ophthalmia, especially in that form found in new-born children, characterized by profuse yellowish-white discharges, great swelling of the lids and ulceration of the cornea.

Conjunctivitis trachomatosa, with pannus, much redness and lachrymation, caused from working in the wet, has been speedily relieved.

A marked illustration of the curative action of the drug in affections caused by working in water is shown by the following case:—A boatman, suffered for years from repeated attacks of sore eyes, *caused by getting wet and cold.* Pterygium developed and grew rapidly. Calc. c. speedily checked the progress of the disease, and when last seen, the cornea had cleared and but little thickness remained in the internal canthus.—T. F.A.

Favorable results have followed the use of this preparation of lime, in various forms of *inflammation of the cornea, caused from getting wet or aggravated in damp weather* (Rhus). It is, however, particulary in scrofulous inflammations of the cornea and conjunctiva, characterized by pustules and ulcers, that Calc. c. proves so beneficial. The following cases afford a good illustration of the prominent features of this drug:—A man was attacked with phlyctenules on the conjunctiva, after a severe cold, caused by working at night washing carriages. There were severe, sharp, shooting pains from the eye up into the head, worse from two to three in the morning and ameliorated on closing the eyes. Sulph. failed to benefit, but Calc. c.^{30} gave immediate relief.—Keratitis phlyctenularis, with much redness and photophobia; pain at night which wakes the child from sleep, with cold perspiration; was cured under Calc. c.^{30}.— Keratitis pustulosa, with profuse lachrymation, excessive photophobia and sticking pains; lids closed, red and swollen, with painful itching in them; agglutination mornings; head scurfy; cervical glands swollen, also the upper lip; acrid discharge from the nose; eruptions that burn and itch; abdomen distended and hard; skin pale and flabby. After the administration of Calc. the above symptoms were promptly relieved and the eye restored. It will be observed that the photophobia and lachrymation are usually excessive, but cases sometimes occur in which they are absent or present only in a moderate degree, though the general indications lead us to prescribe this remedy. The pains are more commonly sharp or sticking in character (Sulph.), though they may vary greatly. Another form of ulceration of the cornea, in which Calcarea is frequently indicated, is when an ulcer or pustule appears in the center of the cornea with more or less haziness of the corneal tissue around it, no vascularity of the cornea, very little or no ciliary injection, and a variable amount of photophobia and lachrymation. (Compare Puls. and Sil.)

It has seemed to hasten the absorption of the exudation into the cornea in interstitial keratitis, especially after the inflammatory symptoms have, in a measure, subsided. Benefit has also been derived from its use in opacities of the cornea, resulting from various forms of keratitis. Dr. C. M. Thomas writes me: "I have lately treated three cases of transverse calcareous band of the cornea; in two of which a complete clearing of the cornea followed a six to twelve weeks' use of Calcarea carb., preceded by a number of doses of Sulph. The third and least marked of the three resisted all treatment."

The following symptoms found in asthenopia have been

verified:—Pain in the eyes after using them, worse in damp weather and from warmth. Burning and cutting pains in the lids, especially on reading, or sticking pains in the eyes, with dull hearing. Dim vision after fine work, like a cloud before the eyes, objects run together, with desire to close the eyes. Red and green halo around the light.

The selection of Calcarea will, in the majority of cases, depend mainly upon the general condition (cachexia) of the patient, since the eye symptoms are very often too general to individualize the remedy. The reverse may be said of Euphrasia and other remedies exhibiting no general dyscrasia.

CALCAREA HYPOPHOSPH.

Clinical.—The hypophosphite of lime has proved to be a remedy of the first importance in severe cases of abscess or ulceration of the cornea. It is especially adapted to those cases, in which the patient is in a very low state of general health, and does not seem to have vitality sufficient to resist the ulcerative process. We meet with this condition not unfrequently in sloughing ulcers of the cornea, and also in that dangerous form of ulceration, the crescentic, in which, although it may not primarily be dependent upon a debilitated state of the general system, the health usually becomes impaired from the severity of the ulcerative process and blennorrhœa of the conjunctiva, which commonly accompanies this condition. In some of these cases pus will be found in the anterior chamber (hypopyon) or the iris will become inflamed and so increase the intensity of the symptoms.

CALCAREA IODATA.

Clinical.—The provings of this preparation of calcium give no clue to its sphere of action in diseases of the eye. But it is found by clinical observation to be an important remedy in scrofulous inflammations of the eyes and lids, as in chronic cases of blepharitis, complicated with enlargement of the tonsils.

It is, however, chiefly useful in pustules and ulcers, particularly of the cornea, marked by great photophobia, acrid lachrymation, sticking pains and spasm of the lids; upon forcing open the lids a stream of tears flows down the cheek; also in erysipelatous swelling of the lids, chiefly of the upper, which is shining and red (compare Rhus). The inflammation of the eyes is always worse from the least cold, to which these cases are very susceptible. It is chiefly indicated in pale, fat subjects who sweat much about the head, with enlargement of the tonsils and cervical glands.

In several cases, benefit seems to have been obtained from the use of iodide of calcium, in checking the progress of both conical cornea and staphyloma; in one marked case of progressive staphyloma of the cornea, the sequela of trachoma and pannus, the bulging of the cornea was checked and the infiltration into its parenchyma absorbed under the use of Calc. iod.

CALCAREA PHOSPHORICA.

Eyes red; capillary vessels visible in streaks from corners to cornea. Sensation of something in the eye; always felt if it is mentioned. Cannot read; light hurts, particularly candle-light.

Clinical.—Valuable results have been obtained from the use of Calc. phos. in parenchymatous keratitis, especially if occurring in patients of a scrofulous diathesis; in one case, in which the haziness of the left cornea had been present two weeks and had extended from above downwards, the vision was almost wholly lost. On account of enlargement of the tonsils, Dr. C. A. Boyle prescribed Calc. phos.[3], under which rapid improvement took place, and six weeks later only a slight macula remained; vision $\frac{20}{30}$. The photophobia has been well marked in all cases of corneal inflammation successfully treated with Calc. phos.

In checking the progress of cataract, it has appeared to be of decided service. The range of usefulness of this drug in ophthalmic disorders is, no doubt, much more extended than here given, but further experience is necessary to demonstrate its proper sphere of action.

CALENDULA.

Clinical.—The most marked success which has attended the use of Calendula, has been observed in injuries of the eye and its appendages, especially cut wounds.

In wounds of the lids and brows which have been badly treated by plasters until suppuration has taken place, the local application of Calendula is the remedy.

After all operations upon the eye or lids, this drug is useful in preventing any undue amount of inflammation and in hastening recovery. Its action is not, however, limited to the prevention of inflammation, as it has been of service in various forms of traumatic inflammation of the eye.

Benefit has been derived from this drug in blennorrhœa of the lachrymal sac.

In the practice of Dr. W. P. Fowler, good results have been obtained from Calendula, in a large number of cases of pustular conjunctivitis, especially if there was little or no photophobia but much redness. He has given the third potency internally and applied a solution of the tincture locally, twenty drops to two drachms of water.

Only occasionally has this drug been used internally; its most marked results having been obtained from its local application. A solution of the tincture—from ten drops to two drachms to the ounce of water—may be employed, but a decoction, made from the leaves, is the best preparation which can be used upon the eye.

CANNABIS SATIVA.

(Under this drug the symptoms of Cannabis indica will be included, but designated by *, as the clinical application of the two remedies is apparently the same.)

Objective.—*Injection of the vessels of the conjunctiva. *The vessels of the conjunctiva of both eyes are injected in a trian-

gular patch extending from the internal canthus to the cornea; worse at night. *The cornea becomes obscured.* *Lachrymation.

Subjective.—*Heat in the eyes. Sensation of spasmodic drawing in the eye; as if sand were in the eyes. Pressure from behind the eye forward.

Vision.—*While reading the letters run together. *Twinkling, trembling and glimmering before the eyes. *Sensitiveness of the eye to light.

Clinical.—Cannabis deserves to be employed more extensively in ophthalmic troubles than it has hitherto been, especially in affections of the cornea and conjunctiva. I would suggest its use in pterygium, though have not, at present writing, given it a trial.

The following case will illustrate its action in pustular keratitis:—Colored man, æt. 28, duration of disease two days. There was a large pustule on the inner margin of the left cornea, with excessive injection of the conjunctival vessels, commencing in a broad base at the internal canthus and terminating in the pustule which forms the apex of a triangle, similar to a pterygium. He was entirely cured in three days under Cannabis ind.—A. WANSTALL.

Both varieties of Cannabis have been used with benefit in vascular conditions of the cornea. Some cases of pannus have yielded to its influence, though more valuable results have been obtained from its use in parenchymatous keratitis, as a case recently under treatment will illustrate:—A boy, æt. 7, was brought to me on December 24th for treatment of an interstitial inflammation of the right cornea, of two weeks duration. The history of hereditary syphilis was fairly clear. Under Aurum mur.³, the eye was nearly well on January 20th, when the left eye became inflamed, and continued to grow worse until March 2d, notwithstanding the use of Aurum, Con., Arsen., etc. internally, and the instillation of Atropine in the eye. On March 2d, the *cornea was densely opaque and vascular,* so that the iris could not be seen through it. The epithelial layer was a little rough, but there was no superficial ulceration. There was *'profuse lachrymation and intense photophobia;* the child not being able to open his eyes in any light. He complained of some pain. Cannabis sativa[3], had been given for four days with no relief; the tincture, ten drops in two-thirds of a glass of water, one teaspoonful every hour, was now prescribed. Immediate improvement followed its use, and on March 8th the child could open the eye well, had no pain and the vascular infiltration into the cornea had diminished. The cornea continued to clear for a month or more, when, only a very moderate amount of haziness remaining, other remedies were given for other symptoms.

CANTHARIS.

Inflammation of the eyes. Lachrymation. *Burning in the eyes and glowing heat as from coals.* Biting sensation as if salt were in them.

Clinical.—Has proved efficacious in inflammations of the eye caused by burns, as in the case of a young man who had had a hot iron thrust into the eye, burning the conjunctiva and thus producing quite severe conjunctivitis with burning pain in the eye. Canth. quickly relieved the pain and cured. In another case, in which the cornea was inflamed as the result of a burn from fireworks, with some ciliary injection, great photophobia and moderate pain, a speedy cure was effected under Cantharis[30], after Aconite and Atropine had failed to relieve.

CARBO VEGETABILIS.

Subjective.—A heavy weight seemed to lie upon the eyes, so that he must make a great exertion when reading or writing in order to distinguish letters. The muscles of the eye pain when looking up. Itching in the margin of the lids and about the eyes.

Vision.—He became short-sighted after exerting the eyes for some time. Black floating spots, flickering and rings before the eyes.

Clinical.—This drug has been too little employed in eye diseases, and its clinical history is extremely scant.

From its symptomatology we are led to recommend its use

in cases of myopia, accompanied by posterior staphyloma, in which it ought to relieve the unpleasant symptoms and prevent the increase of the staphyloma, though I do not imagine that it would in any degree diminish the amount of myopia.

In asthenopia, as the verified symptoms indicate, it has proved beneficial.

CARBOLIC ACID.

Very severe orbital neuralgia over the right eye. Slight pain over the right eyebrow; the same kind of pain, but in a milder degree, under the right patella, both of short duration.

Clinical.—In conjunctivitis trachomatosa, with or without pannus, remarkable success has often followed the use of Carbolic acid and glycerine as a local application. I have used it in the proportion of six drops to the ounce, and in many cases it has acted much better than tannic acid or other astringents.

As indicated by the above verified symptomatology, it has proved of service in some cases of supra-orbital neuralgia.

CAUSTICUM.

Objective.—Inflammation of the eyes, with burning and pressure in them and agglutination in the morning. Visible twitching of the lids and in the left eyebrow. Lachrymation even in a warm room, but worse in the open air. Pupils dilated.

Subjective.—Burning and stinging as with needles in the eyes, with dryness and photophobia, especially in the evening. *Pressure in the eyes as if sand were in them.* Pressive pain in the eye increased by touch. Biting and pressure in the eyes, which seem heavy, with redness of the lid. Itching of the eyes, especially in the lids; disappears on rubbing. *Inclination to close the eyes;* they close involuntarily. *Sensation of heaviness in the upper lid* as if he could not raise it easily, or as if it were agglutinated to the lower lid and could not be easily loosened.

Opening of the lids is difficult. Itching on the lower lid and on its inner surface, with burning as soon as he touches the eye or moves it.

Vision.—Photophobia; constantly obliged to wink. Flickering before the eyes, as from swarms of insects. If he winks, he sees sparks of fire before the eyes, even on a bright day. The eyes become dim, and the *vision indistinct;* it seems as though a thick cloud were before the eyes. Obscuration of the vision, as if a veil were drawn before them; transient obscuration on blowing the nose. Farsightedness; unable to read without glasses.

Clinical.—From the symptomatology given above and the many verifications, it will be readily seen how important a remedy Causticum must be in ophthalmic diseases.

It has been employed with benefit in some cases of blepharitis (especially if ameliorated in the fresh air—Liebold), and in certain forms of tumors of the lids, particularly warts on the lids and brow.

Simple acute conjunctivitis, with a *sensation of sand in the eye* and dull pain in the eyeball as if sore, has been relieved under Caust.[200]. It is not, however, often the remedy for external inflammations of the eye, though as an intercurrent, in scrofulous inflammations and trachoma with pannus, it has been of decided service, if called for according to indications in the above symptomatology.

The action of Caust. upon the lens is probably as pronounced as that of any remedy in our materia medica, and several *cases of cataract have been arrested in their progress* and even the sight improved, where before its administration they were rapidly going on to complete blindness.

The following case will illustrate its action:—A man appeared for treatment with well-marked hard cataract, which was rapidly increasing. (Had been told by celebrated oculists of the old school that he would soon be blind and that he then could be operated upon.) He complained of the following symptoms: a sensation as if there was a substance in the eye too large, causing a kind of heaviness and distension, only in the evening, also a feeling as if there was something moving in the eyes in the evening; could not retain his urine, and could not feel the urine passing through the urethra. Under the influence of Caust. the progress of the cataract was immediately checked, and one year afterward the vision was found somewhat improved, though the white striae in the lens underwent no appreciable change. After seven years his vision remained fully as good as when he began treatment.—T. F. A. That this remedy has checked the progress of cataract and improved the vision has often been demonstrated to my satisfaction. A case of an old lady, sixty-five years of age, with immature hard cataract in both eyes, in which the vision improved in three months under Caust., from V. $\frac{20}{100}$ o. u., + 14 V. $\frac{20}{70}$, to R. V. $\frac{20}{70}$ L. V. $\frac{20}{50}$, + 16 R. V. $\frac{20}{70}$ L. V. $\frac{20}{40}$, is only one case out of many found on my record books. It must not be supposed, however, that I believe cataract can be cured by internal medication, for I have never seen any change in the opaque striae found in the lens, but only a clearing of the diffuse haziness which often accompanies this condition.

But its principal sphere of action is in *paralysis of the muscles,* and here it is the remedy "par excellence." It has been used more often with advantage in paralysis of the ciliary muscle, external rectus, levator palpebrae superioris, or orbicularis, though indicated in paralysis of any of the muscles, particularly if caused from exposure to cold. In cases of paralysis following diphtheria it has also been of service. Selected from a number of cures are the following, which will serve to illustrate its action:—A girl, eleven years of age, had complained of her vision gradually failing for near objects, for a week; supposed to be due to a cold. V. $\frac{20}{30}$ improved by + 24 to $\frac{20}{30}$. Could only read 3½ Snellen, at the distance of two or three feet, or, with + 24 glasses. The eyes were perfectly normal, pupils not dilated, and the action of the other muscles good. The diagnosis was paralysis of the accommodation in both eyes. Caust.[200] was prescribed. Three days later, when next seen, she had fully recovered the power of accommodation and reported that two hours after first taking the medicine the vision began to improve, and on the next day she could read as well as ever.—A lady, thirty-two, after being over-heated by dancing, took cold and was attacked in the night with severe tearing pains in the left half of the face; afterward she saw indistinctly; diplopia followed with inability to turn the left eye outward (paresis n. abducentis sin.). Caust. removed the paresis entirely in fourteen days.—Payr.

For paralysis of the muscles brought on by getting wet, Rhus is more often called for than Caust., as the latter is especially indicated in those cases resulting from exposure to cold.

CEDRON.

Pain across the eyes from temple to temple. *Severe shooting pain over the left eye.*

Clinical.—The sphere of usefulness for Cedron, so far as experience has taught us, is confined to neuralgic affections of the eye, particularly when involving the supra-orbital nerve; and in *supra-orbital neuralgia* it is among the first remedies to be thought of. *The pains are usually severe, sharp and shooting,* starting from one point over the eye (more often over the left), and then extending along the branches of the supra-orbital nerve up into the head; in some cases the pains would come and go suddenly and would be worse in the evening or upon lying down, though these may not be characteristic. One case of pressing frontal headache of long standing, occurring in a woman troubled with chronic disseminate choroiditis, with sharp pains extending from above the eyes back to the temples and occiput, and always worse before a storm, was very quickly and permanently relieved by a few doses of Cedron[3].

The severe supra-orbital pains found in iritis, choroiditis and other deep inflammations of the eye, are often speedily controlled by this drug.

CHAMOMILLA.

Objective.—The eyelids are swollen in the morning and agglutinated with purulent mucus; much discharge of pus or blood. Conjunctiva swollen and dark red. Lachrymation.

Subjective.—Burning and sensation of heat in the eyes; pressure in the eyes which are inflamed and full of mucus in the morning. Violent pressure in the orbital region; sensation in the eyeball as if it were compressed from all sides, with momentary obscuration of vision. Stitches in the orbital region and soreness in the canthi.

Clinical.—Chamomilla is especially adapted to superficial inflammations of the eye, occurring in children, being rarely, if ever, useful in diseases of the deeper tissues.

It is an excellent remedy in ophthalmia neonatorum, characterized by the usual symptoms (even if the cornea has been attacked), if the child is very fretful and wants to be carried all the time. It should also be thought of in inflammations of the eye in which the congestion is so great that the discharges are bloody as well as purulent (Nux).

Cham. has proved very serviceable in scrofulous ophthalmia occurring in *cross, peevish children during dentition,* and it will often relieve the severity of the symptoms, even though it does not complete the cure. The symptoms which call for this drug are usually severe; the pustules and ulcers are chiefly situated on the cornea, and are attended with great intolerance of light, considerable redness and lachrymation.

CHELIDONIUM MAJUS.

Objective.—Twitching and blinking of the lids. The white of the eye is of dirty yellow color. Redness of the conjunctiva, especially of the lower lid. Lachrymation.

Subjective.—Tearing pain in and above the eyes. Neuralgic pain above the right eye, especially in the evening when reading by artificial light. Pressive pain above the left eye, which seems to press down the upper lid. *Aching or pain in the eyeballs on looking up* or moving the eyes.

Vision.—Dimness of vision. A blinding spot seems to be before the eyes, and if he looks at it, the eye waters.

Clinical.—At one time remarkable success was claimed to have followed the use of this drug in a variety of eye troubles, as inflammations, opacities of the cornea, intermittent ciliary neuralgia, etc., but later observations have failed to verify much of its vaunted success.

The pain in and over the eye upon looking up has occasionally led to its employment with favorable results; as for instance in a case of acute aggravation of chronic trachoma, in which the right eye had been very red and inflamed for five days, with much pain all night and a hard, sharp pain on turning the eye upward. Under Chel.[30] the pain was at once relieved and the acute condition had entirely subsided in three days.

This remedy may be of service in affections of the muscles, as suggested by the following case :—A lady (age 40) reported that her eyes had been growing weak for three days, from no apparent cause. She complained of distant objects being blurred and that upon attempting to fixate an object, two were seen. Near vision was not affected. Examination showed decided weakness of the right external rectus muscle. Chel.[200] relieved all the symptoms in two days.—T. F. A.

CHIMAPHILA UMBELLATA.

Clinical.—A large number of cases of pterygium have been treated by this drug, a few of which have been improved, while others have exhibited no good results from its use.

CHINA.

Motion of eyes painful, with sensation of mechanical hindrance. Lachrymation, with crawling pains in the eyes and in the inner surface of the lids. Dimness of vision.

Clinical.—The clinical application of China in ophthalmic disorders has been varied, according to the reports in our literature, though it is a remedy not often called for in ophthalmic therapeutics.

It is especially adapted to those diseases of the eye which are of a malarial origin, or in which the pains are of an intermittent type; also to those affections in which there is impairment of tone from loss of vital fluids.

5

CHININUM MURIATICUM.

Clinical.—This form of quinine, in appreciable doses, has been used with great success in controlling the severe neuralgic pains occurring in iritis and various other diseases of the eye. In some cases it does more than control pain, as it exercises a very beneficial influence over the progress of the disease. This is especially so if malaria complicates the trouble and the *pains are intense and intermittent in type.*

Favorable results have been observed from its use in trachoma with or without pannus.

In ulceration of the cornea it is of service if the iris has become involved and there is severe pain, either in the eye or above, periodic in character, especially if accompanied by chills; also in ulceration of pannoused corneæ, with much pain in the morning. The intensity of the pains and their intermittent character will furnish our chief indications.

CHININUM SULPHURICUM.

Disc and retina both very anæmic. Pupils dilated. Neuralgic twinges in the supra and infra-orbital nerves, generally periodic in character.

Vision.—Dimness of vision as from a net before the eyes, and as from a dark fog. Great sensitiveness of the eye to the light, with lachrymation in the full glare of light. Bright lights and sparks before the eyes. Black spot, size of pins' head, about eighteen inches from right eye and moving with eye for some weeks.

Clinical.—From the physiological action of quinine upon the eye, it should prove a valuable remedy in affections of the optic nerve and retina. It has not, however, been employed to any extent, although cases of optic neuritis are said to have been cured by its use.

An interesting case of intermittent strabismus, occurring in a child and continuing for some time (would squint one day and be entirely well on the next), was cured by the use of this remedy in the hands of an empiric.

CHLORALUM.

Clinical.—The hydrate of chloral has a marked action upon the eye, in some persons producing injection of the conjunctiva, weakness of the eyes, paleness and congestion of the optic nerve, dimness of vision, etc. The clinical verifications of these symptoms have not, however, been made.

Dr. Buffum reports that he has cured with Chloral. hyd.[6], the following symptoms in asthenopia:—"Burning, smarting, itching; lids gummed in the morning; lids heavy, droop at night and after use; eyeballs feel too large; lids puffed; all symptoms brought on by use; eyes feel better in cool air."

CICUTA VIROSA.

Objective.—Eyes staring; she stares with unaltered look at one and the same place and cannot help it. Pupils dilated and insensible. Pupils first contracted then dilated.

Vision.—When she attempts to stand she wishes to hold on to something, because objects seem now to come nearer, and now to recede from her. Objects seem double (and black).

Clinical.—It is in spasmodic affections of the eye and its appendages, that this remedy is especially indicated. Thus we find it very valuable in strabismus, particularly if periodic and spasmodic in character; many cases of which have been cured (this, of course, excludes that form of periodic squint dependent upon an anomaly of refraction). Strabismus occurring after a fall or blow has been relieved.

CIMICIFUGA.

Eyes congested during headache. Pain over the eyes, extending from them to the top of the head. Pain over the left eye, extending along the base of the brain to the occiput. Pain in the centre of the eyeballs, and also sensation as if pain were situated between the eyeball and the orbital plate of the frontal bone, worse in the morning. *Aching pain in both eyeballs.* Black specks before the eyes.

Clinical.—Cimicifuga is not often required if there has been much tissue change, unless it be to control the pains which arise in the course of the disease, as for instance in occasional cases of ulceration of the cornea in which the pains are sharp, extending through the eye into the head.

It may be indicated in asthenopic troubles, as in a case of accommodative asthenopia in a myope of one-sixth, with aching in the eyeballs and shooting pains back into the head, aggravated at the menstrual periods. Cured by Cimicif.—J. H. Buffum.

In certain forms of ciliary neuralgia its value has been frequently demonstrated. It is indicated by aching pains in the eyeball or in the temples extending to the eyes, so severe, especially at night, that in some instances it seems as if the patient would go crazy; also if the pains are sharp or shooting, extending either from the occiput through to the eyes, from the eyes to the occiput or from the eyes to the top of the head; these pains are generally worse on the right side, in the afternoon and at night, and are ameliorated on lying down.

Macrotin, a resinoid from Cimicifuga, has often been employed in place of the whole drug, especially in ciliary neuralgia. Its action upon the eye is very similar to Cimicifuga, and, by some, it is usually given in preference to the latter. Angell highly recommends it for hyperæsthesia of the retina. A case of hyperæsthesia of the retina with retroversion of the uterus, characterized by much pain in and above the eyes, intense photophobia and profuse lachrymation is reported cured under Macrotin[3].—W. F. Fowler.

CINA.

Pulsation of the superciliary muscles; a kind of convulsion. A slow stitch extending from above the upper orbital margin deep into the brain. Pupils dilated.

On rising from the bed all becomes black before the eyes, with dizziness in the head and faintness; he totters to and fro; relieved on lying down. Yellow vision.

Clinical.—Cina or Santonine may be of service in strabismus or other ophthalmic disorders depending upon helminthiasis, if the child has a pale sickly look, with blue rings around the eyes, pain about the umbilicus, boring of the nose, etc.

Santonine has been used with favorable results in asthenopia caused by anomalies in refraction. The second decimal potency was employed.—W. H. Woodyatt.

CINNABARIS.

Inflammation of the eye. Aching soreness of eyes, worse in the evening. *Pain from inner canthus of left eye across eyebrows.* Weakness and sleepiness in the eyes about noon; could scarcely keep them open. *Drawing sensation from right inner canthus across the malar bone to the ear.* Shooting pains in inner canthus of right eye, with a burning and itching. *Pain from right lachrymal duct around the eye to the temple.*

Clinical.—This form of Mercury is an important remedy in ophthalmic therapeutics, and the indications for its use are generally very clear.

In various forms of blepharitis, conjunctivitis and keratitis even when severe ulceration of the cornea has occurred, it has proved especially serviceable, if accompanied by that characteristic symptom of *pain above the eye, extending from the internal to the external canthus, or a pain which runs around the eye, usually above but sometimes below;* this pain may vary greatly in intensity and character, being sometimes sharp, stinging or stitching, at other times dull or aching, and may extend into the eye or up into the head. The photophobia and lachrymation are usually very marked as well as the redness. The lids frequently feel so heavy that it is with difficulty they are kept open, especially in the evening.

Keratitis parenchymatosa and scleritis, in which there has been more or less pain over the eye, have been benefited by Cinnabar.

In iritis and kerato-iritis it is often called for, especially in the syphilitic variety and if gummata are present in the iris.

The chief indication will be found in the characteristic pain over the eye, although, in addition to this, there may be shooting pains through the eye into the head, or soreness along the course of the supra-orbital nerve and corresponding side of the head. *The pains are worse at night,* usually in the evening, though in one case the aggravation was from one to three in the morning.

Asthenopia, with pain extending from the inner canthus around the eye, and soreness over the exit of the supra-orbital nerve, worse in the morning; also with pain around the right eye, aggravated in the evening and upon using the eyes; has been relieved by this remedy.

Cinnabar is a very valuable remedy in certain forms of ciliary neuralgia, as indicated by the symptoms already mentioned. The pains are not sharp and lancinating, radiating from one point in various directions as in Spigelia, neither do they follow the course of the supra-orbital nerve as do the pains of Cedron. Kali bichrom. has a similar pain, on the left side.

CLEMATIS.

Inflammation of the white of the eye with lachrymation. Pain in the eye. Burning in the eyes, as if fire were streaming out of them, with sensation of dryness.

Clinical.—This remedy has been most useful in iritis or kerato-iritis, in which there has been much dryness and burning heat in the eyes with great sensitiveness to cold air, light or bathing.. In one case of chronic syphilitic iritis of two months' standing, with deep ciliary injection, slight pain, especially at night, and posterior synechiæ, a cure followed the use of Clematis[1] for ten days, after both homœopathic and allopathic treatment had failed to relieve him.

COLOCYNTHIS.

Painful pressure in the eye-balls, especially on stooping. Pain in the eyes; a sharp cutting in the right eye-ball.

Clinical.—It is chiefly serviceable in controlling the pains of iritis and glaucoma, with severe burning, sticking or cutting, extending from the eye up into the head and around the eye; or else an aching pain going back into the head, usually worse on rest at night and on stooping, and *ameliorated by firm pressure* and walking in a warm room; a sensation on stooping, as if the eye would fall out is also sometimes present. The lachrymation is profuse.

COMOCLADIA.

The eyes feel very heavy, larger than usual, painful and pressing out of the head, as if something was pressing on top of the eye-balls, moving them downward and outward. *Right eye very painful, feeling much larger and more protruded than the left.* The eyes feel more painful when near the warm stove. Right eye-ball very sore, worse on moving the eye. Eye-balls feel worse on moving them.

Clinical.—Ciliary neuralgia, from asthenopia, iritis and a variety of ocular diseases, has been relieved by Comocladia when indicated by the above symptoms.

CONIUM MACULATUM.

Objective.—Whites of the eye yellow. Affected with a weakness and dazzling of the eyes, together with a giddiness and debility of the whole body, especially the muscles of the arms and legs, so that on attempting to walk one staggers like a person who had drunk too much liquor. Partially paralyzed condition of the external muscles of the eye; he could hardly raise the eyelids, which seemed pressed down by a heavy weight, and was disposed to fall off to sleep. Pupils dilated.

Subjective.—Pressure in the eyes, while reading., Burning in the eyes and on the inner surface of the lids. Aching pain across the eyebrows and mistiness of vision.

Vision.—Weakness of vision. Double vision. *Sluggishness of accommodation*; vision good for fixed objects, but when an object is put in motion before the eyes, there is a haze and dimness of vision producing vertigo.

Clinical.—In superficial inflammations of the eye, Conium is a remedy of the first importance; but when the deeper structures have become invaded, not as much benefit has been derived from its use.

Indurations of the lids have been removed, and ptosis has been benefited by Conium.

It is, however, in inflammatory conditions of the cornea (ulcers and pustules) that this remedy is chiefly useful, especially if the *inflammation is superficial, involving only the epithelial layers*, and caused either from an injury, cold, or scrofulous diathesis; the latter of which is most frequently the case. The indications for its use are generally very clear and well marked; thus, the *photophobia*, which is the most prominent symptom, *is excessive*, so that it is with great difficulty that we are enabled to open the spasmodically closed lids, and when they are opened a profuse flow of hot tears takes place (Rhus). Upon examination of the eye we usually find *very slight, or no redness*, not sufficient to account for the great photophobia, which is out of all proportion to the amount of trouble. The discharge of mucus or pus is rarely profuse, but intimately mixed with the tears. The pains vary greatly, but are generally worse at night (eye aches on lying down to sleep) and in any light, relieved in a dark room, and sometimes by pressure. Hence it appears that Conium is chiefly adapted to those cases in which the nerves are in a state of hyperæsthesia, or when only the terminal filaments are exposed by superficial abrasion of the epithelial layer.

Hyperæsthesia of the retina frequently calls for this drug. The following instructive case, in which hyperæsthesia of the retina was a prominent symptom, came under my care about three years ago:—Jessie H., æt. 20, had been subject to severe headaches, often with nausea, all her life. Seven weeks previous to my seeing her, upon waking in the morning, she found she could see only dimly, with great photophobia and loss of color perception. She had been perfectly well (no headache or pain in the eyes) the day before, and inter-

ested in obtaining a situation which she desired. This condition
of the eyes continued, without change, until I saw her, although
she had suffered from a mild attack of pneumonia during the
interval. There was some leucorrhœa, but no other uterine
symptoms. Upon examination found *photophobia so intense that
she could not open the eyes*, even in a moderately darkened
room, without the aid of blue glasses. She could not see print
of any size, not even No. 200, Snellen, though could count
fingers at twenty feet. *All colors appeared white.* External and
internal examination of the eyes revealed nothing abnormal.
There was constant headache in the forehead, somewhat in
occiput, worse after 4 P. M., and in the morning, relieved by
tying the head up. ᵥConium[1] was given. Upon the next
day, when in church, she was attacked with intense pain in
both eyes, followed by headache, after which she could distinguish colors. Ten days later, the sensitiveness to light had
nearly disappeared, the headaches had been relieved, and her
perception of colors was good. Vision $\frac{18}{200}$, but with convex
40, vision $\frac{20}{20}$. Could not read without glasses, but with convex 60 could read at usual distance. Under the use of Ruta
grav.[2] for about six weeks, both near and distant vision became
perfect without glasses (vision $\frac{20}{20}$).

By reference to the symptomatology, it will be seen that it
must be an important remedy in paralysis of the muscles, especially weakness of the accommodation, in which it has often
been of great service. The following case, rapidly cured with
Conium, illustrates its use in asthenopia :—Can read only a
few seconds before the letters run together; burning pain deep
in the eyes, with hot flashes; cannot bear either light or heat,
is worse in a warm room, and better in the mornings, and on
a cloudy day ; black spots are seen on closing the eyes ; distant
objects appear more distant; objects are surrounded by prismatic colors, out of doors; eyes perfectly normal in appearance.—T. F. A.

CROCUS SATIVUS.

Objective.—Visible twitching of the lids, with a sensation
as if something must be wiped from the right eye. Inclined to

press the eyes tightly together from time to time. Pupils dilated.

Subjective.—Sensation of soreness in the lids. Feeling in the eyes as though he had wept very violently. After reading a while (even during the day) the eyes pain, with a sore burning and some dimness, so that he was frequently obliged to wink. Feeling as of biting smoke in the eyes. Feeling as though water were constantly coming into the eyes, only in the room, not in the open air.

Vision.—The light seems dimmer than usual, as if a veil were between the eyes and the light; is frequently obliged to wink and wipe his eyes, as though a film of mucus were over them. •

Clinical.—The use of Crocus has been chiefly limited to the relief of individual symptoms, arising in the course of various diseases, as indicated by the verified symptomatology.

The chief benefit has been observed from its use in asthenopic troubles, in which the above symptoms are especially found.

The feeling in the eyes as from violent weeping, especially if complicated with the sensation as if something were alive in the abdomen, is well marked and has been relieved by Crocus.

The following clinical symptoms have also disappeared under the use of this drug:—Pain in the eye to the top of the head (Cimicif., Lach.). Pain in the left eye darting to the right. A sensation of cold wind blowing across the eyes (Fluoric acid). Constant winking with suffusion of the eyes in tears.—J. T. O'Connor.

CROTALUS HORRIDUS.

Yellow color of the eyes. Blood exudes from the eye. Pressure and oppression above the eyes.

Clinical.—The chief sphere of action for Crotalus, in common with the other snake poisons, as suggested by Dr. C. Th. Liebold, is to be found in intraocular hemorrhages. It has appeared to hasten the absorption of extravasations into the vitreous, though more favorable results have been obtained from its use in *retinal hemorrhages*. It has been of service in the extravasations into the retina, dependent upon various forms of retinitis, but it is especially adapted to those cases which result from a degeneration of the vessels and are non-inflammatory in origin, in which it is more frequently indicated than Lachesis. The latter is, however, very similar to Crotalus in its action upon intraocular hemorrhages, and general indications must decide between the two.

CROTON TIGLIUM.

Inflammatory redness of the conjunctiva. Copious lachrymation.

Violent pains in the eye. *Tensive pain above the right orbit.*

Clinical.—Croton tigl. may be called for in pustular eruptions upon the lids, either with or without corneal or conjunctival complication, especially if accompanied by vesicular eruptions upon the face or head. (Ant. crud., if pustules are confined to the margins of lids.)

That it is an important remedy in herpes zoster ophthalmicus was illustrated in the case of a child, in which a vesicular eruption, with much redness of the surrounding integument, appeared along the course of nerves on the right side of the forehead after very severe pain. The pain continued after the appearance of the eruption and was so violent the child could not sleep at night. Some of the vesicles were filled with pus. Crot. tigl.[30] gave immediate relief, after Rhus[30] had proved of no avail.

In phlyctenular keratitis and conjunctivitis it has been employed with benefit, especially if associated with the characteristic eruption upon the face and lids; the eyes and face feel hot and burning, the photophobia is marked and ciliary injection deep, with considerable pain in and around the eye, usually worse at night.

It is not, however, confined to pustular inflammation in its first stage, but is useful when the pustules have terminated in ulcers, and also in real ulceration of the cornea, especially if there is much pain in the supra-ciliary region, and an eruption on the face. In one case there was always much pain in the eye whenever a movement from the bowels occurred. Crot. tigl. immediately relieved.—T. F. A.

CUNDURANGO.

Clinical.—This drug has been very useful in superficial ulceration of the cornea, with varying amount of redness, photophobia and pain, if accompanied by sores or cracking of the corners of the mouth.

CUPRUM ACETICUM.

Clinical.—The acetate of copper has proved beneficial in insufficiency of the external recti muscles.—J. H. Buffum. The following case of paralysis of the left nervus abducentis is reported by C. Heinigke in *H. Kl.*:—A young man, æt. 29, was suddenly taken, on leaving the cars after several hours of railroad ride, with indistinct and double vision. The above diagnosis was fully confirmed, and electricity with iodide of potash was used for three months with no change. No other symptoms were present, with the exception of slight frontal headache, of which the patient had been suffering for years. Sulphur and Rhus did little good. Cuprum acet., first 3, then 6, and afterwards 30, in repeated doses and at gradually increasing intervals, cured the case within a few months.

CUPRUM ALUMINATUM.

(The preparation of aluminate of copper most commonly employed, is the so-called "Lapis divinus," which is composed of equal parts of sulphate of copper, nitrate of potass. and alum.)

Clinical.—The aluminate of copper has been successfully used to a great extent in trachoma, to which condition it seems especially adapted. The results obtained are usually more satisfactory than those found from the sulphate of copper, which is the main reliance of the old school in the treatment of this disorder.   It is used locally by application of the crystals to the granulations; at the same time giving the remedy in the potencies internally.   Cuprum al. has been of service in conjunctivitis pustulosa with inflammation of the lids, though it cannot be often indicated in this affection.

Benefit has been derived from its use as a local application to opacities of the cornea.   Its irritative action serves to stimulate the absorption of the new cells in the cornea, which result from inflammation.

CUPRUM SULPHURICUM.

Clinical.—The sulphate of copper is one of the most efficient local applications employed by the old school in many superficial troubles of the eye, chief among which may be mentioned granular lids, although it has also proved beneficial in both catarrhal and purulent conjunctivitis.

DIGITALIS.

Pupils dilated.   Objects seem green or yellow.   In the evening while walking it seemed as though the upper part of the field of vision was covered by a dark cloud.—Digitalin.

Clinical.—This remedy is reported to have been beneficial in some cases of superficial inflammation of the eye, but I have never had occasion to confirm its usefulness in ophthalmic inflammations.

Some benefit has seemed to follow the use of Digitalis in detachment of the retina, especially in relieving such disagreeable symptoms as wavering before the eyes and the appearance as if everything were green.

DUBOISIA.

(The sulphate of Duboisin is more commonly used than the whole plant, Duboisia, but as the two are so similar in action, both will be considered under the above heading.)

Objective.—Lids slightly œdematous.   Agglutination of lids in the morning.   Dilatation of the pupil.   *Vessels of the optic* *disc much enlarged and tortuous,* so as to be easily visible. *Disc red and outline indistinct. Retinal veins dilated and tortuous.* Retinal arteries diminished. *Fundus of eye generally very hyperæmic.*

Subjective.—Eyes hot and dry. Eyes feel tired as if over-worked. *Pain in eyeball, just beneath brow. Sharp pain in the upper part of the eyeball.*

Vision.—Complete *paralysis of the accommodation;* could not read at any distance and could not look at food while eating, on account of pain. Can read better, and the print looks blacker atdouble the usual distance. Paralysis of the accommodation takes place before dilatation of the pupil, and continues after the latter has recovered.

Clinical.—From a very valuable paper upon the clinical and physiological action of Duboisin, by Dr. Charles Deady in the *Trans. of the Am. Hom. Oph. and Otol. Soc.,* 1880, the following conclusions upon its usefulness in diseases of the cornea and conjunctiva are cited:—"The results obtained in the cases of ulcer of the cornea, in which it has been used, are sufficiently good to warrant a trial in cases which prove intractable under other remedies. So far as we have been able to observe, it seems to be adapted to a slow form of ulcer, more or less deep, and *without* severe photophobia and lachrymation; in cases of superficial ulceration, or in which much photophobia was present, we have thus far obtained no benefit from its use.

"The drug has been successfully used in several cases of *chronic hyperæmia of the palpebral conjunctiva,* involving to some extent the borders of the lids. The symptoms calling for its use in this condition strongly resemble those of Aconite, viz., bright redness of the palpebral conjunctiva, with heat and dryness of the eye. The difference between the two drugs consists in the fact that the hyperæmia which Duboisin cures is a *chronic affection,'* such as is found in hyperopes, and which is not always relieved by the use of glasses."

In diseases of the fundus, especially of the optic nerve and retina, Duboisin has proved, as might be expected, an important remedy. Its value in *hyperæmia of the retina associated with weakness of the accommodation* is well illustrated in the following cases by Dr. Deady:—"May 17th, Mrs. C. Ophthalmoscope shows retinal veins very much swollen and tortuous; arteries about normal; fundus in other respects normal. There is much frontal headache; sharp pain through upper part of eyeballs from front to back, very much aggravated by artificial light; eyes feel hot and dry; conjunctiva of lids hyperæmic; sight has been growing dim for last two months; $V.=\frac{20}{30}$; $IIm.=\frac{1}{60}$, with which $V.=\frac{20}{20}$. Accommodative asthenopia; print blurs when held as near as eight inches. R. Duboisin[3], three hours.

May 20th. Better in every respect; no headache; no pain in eyes; ophthalmoscope shows fundus to be normal; conjunctiva normal; can read without any discomfort.

Case II.—Lady, aet. 21. May 18th. Cannot read by gaslight; dry, disagreeable feeling in eyes, pain and burning; lids swollen so as to almost close palpebral aperture; conjunctiva of lids very hyperæmic; lids very œdematous, look like two bags of water. These symptoms would all be brought on by reading one half hour in a room artificially lighted, or would come on without reading if she remained in the room an hour. Print blurred when read from eight to ten inches; ophthalmoscope shows a marked hyperæmia of fundus; hyperæmia of conjunctiva of the lids so great, that it had been diagnosed by former physician as granular lids. $V. \frac{20}{30}$; $IIm.=\frac{1}{60}$, $V. \frac{20}{20}$. R. Duboisin[3], four times a day.

May 21st. Very much better; eyes look well; lids normal; $V.=\frac{20}{20}$; fundus normal.

May 25th. Eyes normal."

In *optic neuritis* and retinitis Duboisin is, no doubt, often indicated, for several cases have yielded promptly to its influence, as the following will illustrate:—A man, aet. 42, had suffered from attacks of vertigo for three months. There was a history of syphilis twenty years, and of a blow on the head seventeen years, before. When first seen he complained of sleeplessness day and night, severe headache from the back of the neck over the head to the eyes, worse at night, and eyes painful as if the balls were being pressed into the head. V.

$\frac{20}{20}$ o. u., with difficulty. The ophthalmoscope revealed a typical picture of "engorged papilla" in each eye, marked enlargement of vessels on the disc, and extravasations on the right optic papilla and in the retina immediately around it. Bell.[3] was given for ten days with slight change in the symptoms, except that hemorrhages were found on both discs, pain above the eyes with constant aching in them, and heavy pressure on the vertex, worse in the morning. Within two weeks under Duboisin[3] the pain in the head had been relieved, the hemorrhages in the nerves and retinæ had disappeared, and the inflammation was decidedly less. V. $\frac{20}{20}$ o. u. There were one or two slight aggravations after this, but not important, when the patient was lost sight of.

True weakness of the accommodation may call for this remedy, as already suggested by the symptomatology, and the cases of hyperæmia of the retina (compare Ruta, Con., Arg. nit.). I use the term "true weakness," for I believe many of the so-called cases of asthenopia are dependent upon an "irritable weakness" of the accommodation, which is controlled by Jaborandi or one of that class of drugs.

ELECTRICITY AND GALVANISM.

Clinical.—Dr. John Butler, in his work on Electro-therapeutics, shows the homœopathicity of electricity to various ophthalmic affections. It is without doubt a valuable aid in the treatment of many affections of the eye, but the marvellous power ascribed to it by some writers cannot be verified in practice.

Many well authenticated cases of exophthalmic goitre have been cured by galvanization of the sympathetic, and although I have never used it to any great extent, I have no hesitation in recommending it as a valuable aid in this disease.

The use of the constant galvanic current in the production of *electrolysis of strictures of the lachrymal duct*, has been especially advocated by Dr. J. H. Buffum in *Trans. Am. Hom. O. and O. Soc. for* 1879. It is very useful in some cases, and is especially adapted to chronic strictures associated with blennorrhœa of the lachrymal sac. The beneficial results are not confined to the solution of the strictures, as an improvement in the blennorrhœa is usually soon observed.

It is, however, *in paralysis of the muscles* and weakness of the internal recti (asthenopia muscularis) that electricity proves itself chiefly efficacious. Cases of paralysis, both complete and partial, of all the ocular muscles have been restored by the aid of electricity or galvanism, though usually some remedy has been employed at the same time internally as, Caust., Rhus, Euphras., etc. It is usually applied by placing one electrode (some say the positive and others the negative) over the affected muscle, while the other is passed lightly over the corresponding brow, or in some cases placed at the back of the neck; it should be applied regularly every day or two for about three minutes at each sitting. *

Ciliary neuralgia, particularly if occurring in nervous subjects and not dependent upon any pathological changes in the eye, is often quickly relieved by a weak current of electricity through the painful region. This has been especially remarked in cases of kopiopia hysterica in which there have been a great variety of pains due to reflex irritation.

EUPATORIUM PERFOLIATUM.

Soreness of the eye-balls.

Clinical.—As an intercurrent remedy in various affections in which excessive soreness of the eye-balls has been a prominent symptom, this drug has been very useful.

EUPHRASIA.

Objective.—*Redness and swelling of the margins of the lids,* with at times an itching burning in them, and increased watery discharge. Margins of lids red, with dry sensation. The lids are swollen and red. Injection of conjunctival vessels. Lachrymation profuse; *tears acrid and burning.*

Subjective.—Burning and pressure in the eyes, with much lachrymation. Biting in the eyes at times; biting water runs

---

* Much use is now being made of reverse currents by most eminent electricians.

6

from them.   Burning biting in the eyes, obliging frequent winking.   Itching of the eyes on going out, obliging frequent winking and wiping of the eyes, with increased lachrymation in the afternoon.   Burning in the margins of the lids, with distressing sensation of dryness.   The lids are sensitive and swollen.   *Feeling as though the cornea were covered with much mucus; it obscures his vision and obliges him to frequently close and press the lids together.*   Vision somewhat dim, as through a veil, in the evening.   Eyes sensitive to candle-light.

Clinical.—The indiscriminate use of Euphrasia in all cases of ophthalmia, as prescribed by many practitioners, is not to be imitated, for although it is a remedy of great importance, especially in superficial diseases of the eye, still its sphere of action is well defined.

The results of many cases have proved its value in blepharitis.   When indicated, the lids will be found red, swollen and covered with a *thick, yellow, acrid discharge, together with profuse, acrid, burning lachrymation, which makes the lids and cheek sore and excoriated;* firm agglutination of the lids in the morning is also present, and fluent coryza often accompanies the eye symptoms.

The cases of catarrhal and strumous inflammation of the cornea and conjunctiva, which speedily respond to this drug, are to be counted by scores, for it is in these cases that Euphrasia is especially efficacious.   It is useful in both the chronic and acute form of inflammation, but especially in the latter, as follows:—Catarrhal inflammation from exposure to cold ; catarrhal inflammation of the eyes and nose in the first stage of measles; papillary trachoma with or without pannus; pustules on the cornea and conjunctiva; superficial ulceration of the cornea (sometimes accompanied with pannus), though is rarely indicated in the deep form, except, perhaps, as a palliative in the first stage.   In all the·above cases we usually find much photophobia, though it may be nearly absent.   The lachrymation is profuse, acrid and burning as is also the thick, yellow, muco-purulent discharge, which is usually present excoriating the lids, making them red, inflamed and sore, as well as giving the cheek an appearance as if varnished. The conjunctiva may be quite red, with chemosis. The pains are not characteristic though usually smarting, sticking or burning, from the nature of the discharges. Fluent coryza often accompanies the above symptoms.

The blurring of the eyes, relieved by winking, so often found in superficial inflammations of the eye, and due to the secretions getting upon the cornea, thus interfering with vision, and then carried away by the movement of the lids in winking, is a simple symptom, which is almost invariably relieved by Euphrasia.

Purulent ophthalmia has been benefited, particularly that form found in new-born children (ophthalmia neonatorum). The condition of the lids and nature of the discharges, already given, which indicate its choice, will be found more often in the later stages than at the beginning of the disease.

Dr. Dudgeon reports, in *Brit. Jour. of Hom.*, two cases of rheumatic iritis cured by this drug, in which there was great ciliary injection, photophobia, dimness of the aqueous, discoloration of the iris, posterior synechiæ and constant aching with occasional darting pain in the eye, always worse at night.

The following case indicates that it may be useful in paralysis of the muscles:—A man, æt. 52, appeared for treatment, with total paralysis of the oculo-motor nerve, even to those filaments which supply the iris and ciliary muscle, which came on rapidly after exposure in the cold and wet. Electricity was applied every day or two for about five weeks, and either Rhus or Caust. given internally at the same time, with no benefit. At the end of this time, on account of some slight catarrhal symptoms, Euphrasia[30] was given and the electricity continued. After taking two doses of Euphrasia the upper lid could be slightly raised, the pupil began to contract and the eye to turn inward; within four weeks a complete cure was effected.

Euphrasia is very similar to Mercurius in the character of its discharges, only that in Merc. they are thin and excoriating, while under Euphrasia they are thick and excoriating. Arsenicum also has acrid secretions, but they are usually thin, not as profuse as in the above remedies and are accompanied by much burning pain and photophobia. Rhus, like Euphrasia, has profuse lachrymation, but it is not as excoriating. In paralysis of the muscles, caused by exposure to cold or wet, Euphrasia may be compared to Caust. and Rhus, the remedies upon which we chiefly rely in these affections, but it seems especially called for when a catarrhal condition of the eye is, at the same time, present.

FERRUM.

Sticking pain over the left eye, coming suddenly and lasting a short time only.

Clinical.—The iodide of iron has been used by Dr. Liebold with benefit in exophthalmic goitre. In one case, occurring in a woman after suppression of the menses, and characterized by protrusion of the eyes, enlargement of the thyroid gland, palpitation of the heart, and excessive nervousness; the menses soon reappeared, the nervousness diminished, and all the symptoms improved after the administration of Ferrum iodatum. Another similar case, occurring in a colored woman, was relieved by the acetate of iron.

FLUORIC ACID.

Sensation as if the eyelids were opened by force and a *fresh wind were blowing on them*; after that, sensation like sand in the eyeball, which had the same feeling as if the eyes were inflamed.

Clinical.—A case of lachrymal fistula on the left side, of one years duration, with a clear, yellow scab on the cheek, near the inner canthus which is but slightly red and painful to pressure. Every three or four days it begins to itch, grow moist, then heads again; it is sometimes painful before it opens. Fluoric acid[30] cured.—C. HERING.

The symptom, *as if cold wind were blowing in the eye*, has been frequently verified in various ophthalmic diseases.

GELSEMIUM.

Objective.—*Drooping of the eyelids.* Eyelids half closed, with apparent inability to move them. Lids close on looking steadily at anything. *Great heaviness of the lids.* Pupils dilated.

Subjective.—Soreness of the eyeballs. Drawing over the eyes. Dull full feeling (attended with some aching) in the whole of the orbits. Bruised pain above and back of the orbits.

Vision.—Dimness of vision. *Dimness of sight and vertigo. Smoky appearance before the eyes, with pain above them.* Objects appear double. Diplopia which can be controlled by an effort of the will. Diplopia when inclining the head towards either side, but vision single when holding the head erect.

Clinical.—Gelsemium is rarely found of benefit in superficial affections of the eye, but is especially adapted to diseases of the fundus and paralysis of the nerves.

Its action upon the uveal tract is very marked, especially in the serous form of inflammation, either when it involves the iris, ciliary body and choroid separately or all three at the same time. In serous iritis, the hypersecretion and cloudiness of the aqueous humor, together with moderate ciliary injection and varying amount of pain in the eye and head, will be our chief indications. (Compare with Kali bichrom., which is the remedy for descemetitis, improperly classed by some authorities under serous iritis.)

In *serous choroiditis* Gelsem. is a remedy of the first importance. According to Dr. W. A. Phillips in a paper read before the Am. Hom. Ophth. and Otol. Soc., in 1881, the symptomatic indications for its use in serous choroiditis are:—"1. A dull pain in or about the eye, extending all of the time, or periodically, or finally, to the back of the head, and ameliorated by hot applications, but not by cold. 2. Impairment of vision gradually developed and not characterized by sudden changes, either for the better or the worse. 3. Heaviness of the lids. 4. Inability to accommodate the eye quickly for varying distances. 5. The asthenopic symptoms not marked by great irritability of the eye, but resulting from an evident want of tone or energy of the muscular structures—in other words, a passive asthenopia rather than active. 6. In general, a feeling of depression and lassitude, which are not relieved by food or stimulants." In addition to the above it will usually be found that the *haziness of the vitreous* is very fine, the tension tends to increase, the pupil to dilate and the eyeball to become sore to touch, with aching pain over and in the eye. The impairment of vision is not necessarily constant, as it may vary greatly, being one day very dim and the next quite bright. Many cases, illustrative of the marked benefit to be obtained from this drug, could be given, but I will only briefly report, on account of certain peculiar symptoms present, the first case[*] in which it was employed. Mrs. T., æt. 56, of dark complexion and bilious temperament, had been suffering from a serous inflammation of the choroid for nearly three months. The vitreous was so hazy that the fundus could not be seen. The vision was so nearly lost that she could hardly count fingers. The eyes were somewhat red and irritable, the pupils slightly dilated and T + (?). There was constant sore, aching pain in the eyes and around, with sharp sticking pain on moving the eyes. Bryonia, as well as several other remedies, had been used with temporary relief at times. At last, in addition to the above symptoms, small transparent points, elevations of the epithelium, made their appearance on the right cornea, looking like the swollen ends of nerve filaments; they were excessively sensitive to touch or any movement of the lids, and would come and go suddenly, often in the same day; after two days they became permanent and were very painful. Gelsem.[30] was given, when they gradually disappeared, the vitreous cleared and the vision was completely restored within two weeks.

Its usefulness in serous inflammation of the whole uveal tract (irido-choroiditis) is sufficiently illustrated in the following two cases:—A woman, æt. 32, had complained of the eyes being weak for two months, but worse recently. Right vision $\frac{20}{100}$ with difficulty. Left vision, counted fingers at 20 feet. Ophthalmoscope showed serous inflammation of the iris and choroid, deposits on the membrane of Descemet, aqueous and vitreous hazy in both eyes, and left pupil dilated and sluggish. There was a sensation of pressure over both eyes and headache in the temples. She was a seamstress and would not take proper

---

[*] Reported in detail in Hahnemannian Monthly, Nov., 1875.

rest. ℞. Gelsem.[30]. Two weeks later she reported that she began to improve immediately on taking the above powders, had taken no other medicine and had used the eyes all the time for sewing. Right vision $\frac{20}{30}$ with difficulty. Left vision $\frac{20}{20}$ with difficulty. Eyes appeared perfectly well, with the exception of a few small points on the posterior surface of the cornea, and slight dilatation of the left pupil, which eventually disappeared.—Chas. O'C., æt. 22, irido-choroiditis serosa, o. s. Duration, four weeks. Right vision $\frac{20}{20}$. Left vision $\frac{20}{200}$. With concave 20, left vision $\frac{20}{70}$. Examination of the left eye showed deposits on the lower posterior portion of the cornea, pupil dilated, vitreous hazy with floating opacities, moderate ciliary injection and no pain. Headache. Under Gelsem.[30] the vision began to improve, and two months later left vision $\frac{20}{20}$.

From its value in serous inflammations and from some temporary benefit derived from Gelsemium in glaucoma, it is recommended for this disease, especially if dependent upon increased secretion.* Dr. F. Park Lewis reports that it has been of use to him in "one case of glaucoma after iridectomy. Notwithstanding a large coloboma in both eyes, the sight began to diminish and pain and tenderness to come back in head. Gelsem.[1] relieved the pain and somewhat benefited the sight."

This remedy has been of service in some cases of disseminate choroiditis and chorio-retinitis—in one case there seemed to be a bluish snake before the vision.—T. F. A. Dr. C. M. Thomas writes me,—"in disseminate choroiditis and retino-choroiditis with no outside symptom, the good effect of Gelsem. is undoubted and it is used by me almost to the exclusion of other remedies."

A case of retinitis albuminurica, in which the dimness of vision came on suddenly during pregnancy and was worse after delivery, was cured under Gelsemium. There were white patches and extravasations of blood throughout the retina, while the outer part of the optic nerve appeared whiter than usual. There was no pain, only an itching of the eyes. —T. F. A.

Another great sphere of usefulness for this drug is to be

---

* Glaucoma is probably usually due to obstruction in excretion.

found in *detachment of the retina*. Dr. F. H. Boynton first reported, in the *American Observer*, a case cured under Gelsem., in which the detachment had been present three weeks and was dependent upon an injury. It was accompanied with diffuse haziness of the vitreous and serous inflammation of the choroid and retina. In one month, under Gelsem.[30], the vision improved from perception of light to $\frac{20}{70}$, and the retina became completely re-attached. Since then similar results have been obtained from its use in detachment of the retina, from myopia, severe attacks of neuralgia, etc. (compare Arnica and Aurum). It is no doubt the most commonly indicated remedy in this affection. (A most efficient aid in the treatment of these cases, which should never be neglected, if possible, is rest in bed.)

In paresis or paralysis of any of the ocular muscles, decided benefit has often been derived from the use of this remedy. It has been of service in paralysis following diphtheria (Buffum), and when associated with paralysis of the muscles of the throat, although often when indicated there is a complete lack of all subjective or objective symptoms, with the exception of the impairment of the muscle.

In asthenopia dependent upon weakness of the external recti muscles, Gelsem. was highly recommended by Dr. W. H. Woodyatt. As a remedy for clearing up troublesome asthenopic symptoms, even local irritations, such as blepharitis and conjunctival hyperæmia, due to refractive errors, Dr. C. M. Thomas has found it more serviceable than any other drug.

In paralysis of the nerves, compare Gelsem. with Caust., Conium and Rhus; and in serous choroiditis, compare with Bryonia. The condition which indicates Gelsemium is usually one of stolid indifference to external irritants, in which respect it stands in marked contrast to Conium, whose paralytic symptoms are characterized by great reflex irritability, photophobia, etc.

GRAPHITES.

Objective.—A stye on the lower lid, with drawing pain before the discharge of pus. Red, painful inflammation of the

lower lid and inner canthus. *Very inflamed margins of the lids.
Inflammation of the external canthus. Dry mucus in the lashes.*
Agglutination of the eyes in the morning. Redness of the
whites of the eyes, lachrymation and photophobia. Lachrymation.

Subjective.—Sensation of dryness in the lids, and pressure.
Heaviness of the lids. Heat about the lids. Heat, burning
and biting in the eyes.

Vision.—Vanishing of sight during menstruation. Intolerance of light, with redness of the eyes. *Great sensitiveness of
the eyes to daylight.*

Clinical.—There are few remedies in the materia medica so
commonly indicated in inflammatory conditions of the lids,
conjunctiva and cornea as Graphites, especially if occurring in
scrofulous subjects, with eczematous eruptions, which are
moist, fissured, bleed easily, and are situated chiefly on the
head and behind the ears.

It is particularly indicated in the *chronic form of blepharitis,*
or in eczema of the lids, though sometimes called for in acute
attacks, especially if complicated with such affections of the
cornea as ulcers and pustules. In chronic ciliary blepharitis,
in which Graphites is useful, *the edges of the lids will usually be
found slightly swollen, and of a pale red color; the inflammation
may be confined to the canthi* (blepharitis angularis), *especially to
the outer, which have a great tendency to crack, and bleed easily*
upon any attempt to open the lids; the margins may be ulcerated; *dry scurfs are usually present on the ciliæ*; there may be
burning and dryness in the lids, and biting and itching, which
cause a constant desire to rub the eyes. (Compare with Antimon. crud., which is adapted to pustules on the margins of
the lid.)

In one case of slight roughness of the integument of the
lids, with intense itching, which had been present for a year
or more, quick and permanent relief was obtained from Graphites.

It is of service in preventing the recurrence of successive
crops of styes. It is also valuable in eczema of the lids, if the
eruption is moist and fissured, while the margins of the lids
are covered with scales or crusts.

In catarrhal ophthalmia Graphites has been employed with benefit, and in scrofulous ophthalmia characterized by ulcers and pustules it is second to no other drug in importance. It has cured deep ulcers of the cornea, even with hypopyon, but it is more particularly adapted to superficial ulcerations, especially if resulting from pustules, often with considerable vascularity of the cornea. The pustules which have been removed under the influence of Graphites have been of various kinds and accompanied by various symptoms; they may be either on the cornea or conjunctiva, but especially on the former; the attacks may be acute or chronic, but it is particularly called for in the chronic recurrent form.

The following case illustrates very markedly the action of this remedy:—A boy had been troubled for a long time with chronic pustular inflammation of the cornea; no sooner would he recover from one attack before another would appear; there was great photophobia so that he could not open his eyes to see his way, profuse lachrymation, burning and aching in the eyes, sneezing upon opening them, *external canthi cracked and easily bleeding*, both corneæ pannoused, thin acrid discharge from the eyes, and *nose sore and surrounded by thick moist scabs.* Under the influence of Graph. a rapid and permanent cure was effected.

The *photophobia is usually intense* and the lachrymation profuse though in some cases nearly or entirely absent; it is generally worse by daylight than gaslight and in the morning, so that often the child cannot open the eyes before 9 or 10 A. M. The redness of the eye is generally marked and the discharges of a muco-purulent character, constant, thin and excoriating. The pains vary and are not important, being sometimes sticking, burning, aching or itching in character. The lids are red, sore and agglutinated in the morning or else covered with *dry scurfs*, and the *external canthi are cracked and bleed easily* upon opening the eye. A thin acrid discharge from the nose often accompanies the ophthalmias of Graphites.

Graphites is somewhat similar to Hepar and Sulphur in scrofulous inflammation of the eyes. Under Graphites, however, the discharges from the eyes and nose are thinner and more excoriating, and there is a greater tendency towards cracking of the external canthi ; the latter symptom is also sometimes observed under Hepar, but is not as marked, and the discharge is not as excoriating, though the lids are more swollen, eyes redder and ulceration deeper. The Sulphur patient is more restless and feverish at night, and complains of occasional sharp sticking pains in the eye; though the face and body may be covered with eruptions, they differ in character from those of Graphites.

HAMAMELIS VIRGINICA.

Clinical.—A spontaneous eversion of the upper lid during the course of a severe conjunctivitis, was relieved by the application of dilute "Ponds Extract."—W. S. Searle.

This remedy has been employed with decided success in inflammation of the conjunctiva or cornea, even in ulceration of the latter, if caused by a burn or an injury.

The action of Hamamelis in injuries of the eyeball is very similar to that of Arnica and Calendula, although it seems to be of more service than either of the above in *hastening the absorption of intraocular hemorrhages.* Illustrative of this point is a case which came under my observation this day. A colored boy was brought to my clinic two days ago, on account of an injury of the left eye received two days previously. The cornea was abraded, there was some blood in the anterior chamber and the vitreous was so dark from hemorrhage into it, that the fundus could not be illuminated. There was only perception of light. Hamamelis virg.[3] was given internally and the tincture, 10 drops to the ounce, used externally. To-day (after two days) his vision is $\frac{20}{30}$ and only slight haziness of the media remains.

Traumatic iritis with hemorrhage into the iris, and traumatic iritis with great pain at night and hemorrhage into the interior of the eye, have been speedily relieved by this drug.

HEPAR SULPHUR.

Objective.—*Redness, inflammation and swelling of the upper lid,* with pressive pain. The lids are closed in the morning on waking, so that she cannot open them for a long time. Inflammation and swelling of the eye, with redness of the white.

Subjective.—Smarting pain in the external canthus, with accumulation of hardened mucus. Pains in the eyes from the daylight. *The eyes are very painful in bright daylight if he attempts to move them.* Pressure in the eyes, especially on moving them, with redness. Eyes sore, agglutinated at night; secretion of hardened mucus. Pressive pain in the eyeballs, and a feeling as if beaten when touched.

Vision.—Obscuration of vision while reading. The eyes become dim and he cannot see well in the evening by candle-light. Feeling of blindness before the eyes on rising and standing up after sitting bent over.

Clinical.—In dacryocystitis and orbital cellulitis Hepar is a remedy of importance, especially if *pus has formed and there is great sensitiveness to touch, with throbbing pain.* It may prevent the formation of pus or accelerate its discharge; it also seems useful in controlling the discharge after the canaliculus has been opened.

Hepar may be called for in chronic ciliary blepharitis if complicated with swelling of the meibomian glands, or ulcers and swellings on the margin of the lid, which are painful in the evening and upon touch, though its chief sphere of action in palpebral diseases is in acute phlegmonous inflammation of the lids, which tends toward suppuration. The inflamed lids will be swollen, tense and shining, as if erysipelas had invaded them, with *throbbing,* aching, stinging pain and sensitiveness to touch; *the pains are aggravated by cold and relieved by warmth.*

Eczema of the lids, in which thick honey-comb scabs are found both on and around the lids, with nocturnal agglutination, etc., is especially amenable to Hepar.

Palpebral tumors have frequently disappeared under its use.

It is sometimes useful in simple catarrhal conjunctivitis after the inflammatory stage has passed, and also in some cases of purulent conjunctivitis characterized by profuse discharge and excessive sensitiveness to air and touch. Pustules on the conjunctiva may require its use, but not usually, unless the cornea has become involved.

For the severer forms of strumous ophthalmia, in which the pustules and ulcers invade the cornea and are marked by great intensity of the symptoms, there is probably no remedy more frequently indicated than Hepar. Its value in *ulcers and abscesses of the cornea*, especially the deep sloughing form of ulcer complicated with hypopyon, is undoubted. It has proved curative in some torpid ulcers, in which general symptoms have pointed to its use, but there is usually *intense photophobia, profuse lachrymation, great redness of the cornea and conjunctiva*, even chemosis, and *much pain* of a *throbbing*, aching, shooting character, which is *relieved by warmth*, so that one constantly wishes to keep the eye covered, and is worse on any draught of air (Sil.), at night or in the evening; the lids are often swollen, spasmodically closed and very *sensitive to touch*, or may be red, *swollen and bleed easily upon opening*.

It has been successfully employed in acute aggravations of pannus which tends toward ulceration, especially if occurring in mercurialized subjects.

In keratitis parenchymatosa it often serves to promote resorption after the disease has been checked by Merc., Aurum, Calc., or other remedies. It may, however, be of service in arresting the progress of the disease, as is well illustrated in the following case:—Mary A—, 33 years of age. For three months the left cornea had been so hazy that the iris could only be seen with difficulty, and for two months the right cornea had gradually become involved from the periphery toward the centre. Both corneæ were wholly opaque and vision lost. There was considerable pain in the eyes and head, with iritis. The ciliary injection was great and the dread of light excessive; lachrymation marked. There was no history of syphilis, but she suffered severely from rheumatic pains, particularly in the shoulder. Various remedies, high and low, had been given for two months with no avail. Under Hepar[30] rapid improvement took place; in a month she was discharged with fair vision and only moderate haziness of the corneæ.

"Hepar is the main remedy for keratitis punctata."—Payr.

It sometimes seems to be useful in clearing up opacities of the cornea.

Kerato-iritis frequently requires the use of this remedy, especially if characterized by ulceration of the cornea, hypopyon, sensitiveness to air and touch, and such other marked symptoms, as illustrated in the following case:—A man was attacked with severe inflammation of the cornea and iris of the left eye. Examination showed superficial ulceration of the cornea, much ciliary injection, contraction of the pupil, sluggishness of the iris, and great photophobia and lachrymation. There was much pain extending from the eye into the corresponding side of the head, worse at night, especially about two or three A.M., and the seat of pain in the head, as well as in the eye, was quite sore to touch. The lids were considerably swollen and the discharge from the eye was slight. A cure was quickly effected under Hepar.

For *hastening the absorption of pus in the anterior chamber* (hypopyon) there is no better remedy than Hepar. On this account it has been employed with benefit in iritis with hypopyon, or associated with small abscesses in the iris (suppurative iritis). It has also appeared to exert a very beneficial influence in purulent capsulitis after cataract extraction, either used alone or in alternation with Rhus.

Inflammation of the ciliary body, in which the sensitiveness to touch is excessive, sometimes yields to this drug.

From its usefulness in suppurative inflammation in general, it has been administered with benefit in suppurative choroiditis or panophthalmitis.

An interesting case of anæsthesia of the retina, of two months' duration, the result of looking at an eclipse, has been reported to me by Dr. Chas. Deady. The patient complained of seeing a light spot in the centre of the field of vision, surrounded by a dark ring, and again by a lighter ring, all of which were constantly turning and changing into various colors, especially green; aggravated on coming into a room from the bright sunlight, and only relieved during sleep. There was also a feeling as if the eyes were pulled back into the head, with photophobia. V. $\frac{20}{100}$. Field of vision very much contracted. Under Hepar[200] the sensation of the eyes being pulled back into the head was at once relieved, and in twelve days the vision became $\frac{20}{50}$, and the field of vision much enlarged.

Ulceration of external parts of the eye, which bleed easily and are very sensitive to touch, most positively indicate Hepar. These cases usually have excessive photophobia, which is also very marked in Merc. protiod.; while Kali bichrom., though indicated in extensive destruction of tissue, and great sensitiveness of the eye to touch, lacks entirely the photophobia so marked under Hepar.

HYDROCOTYLE.

Clinical.—This remedy has seemed to be of benefit in some cases of tumors of the lid, especially in epithelioma.

HYOSCYAMUS.

Eyes look red, wild, sparkling. Squinting. Pupils dilated.

Obscuration of vision; objects seem indistinct; he is near-sighted and is obliged to hold the book nearer than usual when reading. Dimness of vision, as if a veil were before the eyes. Deceptive vision; the flame of one light seemed smaller, that of another larger, though both were of equal size. Illusions of vision; small objects seem very large.

Clinical.—A case of hemeralopia in a myopic eye, with shooting pains from the eyes into the nose and head, and accompanied by headache ameliorated on closing the eyes, was relieved by Hyos.—T. F. A.

HYPERICUM.

Clinical.—The benefit which has been observed from this remedy in relieving the pain in old cicatrices, led Dr. John L.

Moffat to its use in a case of pain and irritation of the eye, from an anterior synechia which resulted from an injury two or three years previous. The healthy eye was also irritable. Hypericum[3] relieved.

IGNATIA.

Pain extending from the head into the left eye, when the eyes began to burn and water. Pressure within the eye as from sand. Sensation as if a particle were in the left external canthus. Pain in the inner surface of the upper lid, as if it were too dry, in the evening.

Unable to endure the glare of light. Zigzag and serpentine, white flickering at one side of the field of vision.

Clinical.—The following case of exophthalmus is from Dr. A. Wanstall:—Colored girl, æt. 17. Has always been very nervous and restless at night, walking and talking in her sleep. There has been "swelling of the eyes," lachrymation and pain in the eyes, with headache for six months, after having had a tooth drawn. A moderate amount of exophthalmus was present, together with palpitation of the heart; pulse 120, and congestive headaches but no enlargement of the thyroid gland. Menses regular. Under Ignatia[3], in one week the exophthalmus was scarcely perceptible, and all the other symptoms were relieved.

Morbid nictitation, with spasmodic action of various muscles of the face, has been relieved by this drug.

Catarrhal conjunctivitis with a sensation as of sand in the eye and great dryness, may require this remedy, as in the following:—A lady, artist, of dark complexion and so excessively nervous that she started at the slightest noïse, had been working late at night. She complained of one eyelid feeling as if sand were under it, with great dryness. Diagnosis, conjunctivitis palp. ac. Ignatia, 3d dec., one dose, removed the feeling in half an hour.—F. PARK LEWIS.

Dr. J. H. Buffum reports the following:—Two "chipping ulcers" at upper margin of right cornea, accompanied by periorbital pains, sharp sticking, generally in one spot in supraciliary ridge, temple or side of head. The sleep was disturbed and digestion poor. Ignatia[6] cured in four days.

In the *Trans. Am. Hom. Oph. and Otol. Soc.*, 1879, Dr. W. P. Fowler reports a case of "hyperæsthesia of the retina with hysteria," characterized by intense photophobia and ciliary neuralgia with general nervous symptoms, which was cured in ten days under Ignatia[3] and proper hygienic measures.

A case of ciliary neuralgia, in a woman, was cured very promptly by this remedy; the pains were very severe, extending from the eye to the top of the head, producing nausea, and often alternated with swelling in the throat (globus hystericus); the pains would begin very slightly, increase gradually until they became very severe and would only cease when she became exhausted.

From a study of the clinical application of Ignatia it will be seen that its usefulness is confined almost exclusively to those ophthalmic affections which may be found in nervous hysterical patients.

IPECACUANHA.

Inflammation of the eyes. On opening the right lids, which were swollen, there was a copious gush of tears. The conjunctiva of the bulb was injected and infiltrated. *The cornea was dim as if infiltrated; on close examination there was noticed a number of small depressions.* Intense tearing or tensive pains in the eyes. *Great photophobia.*

Clinical.—My attention was first directed to Ipecac., as a remedy for pustular inflammation of the cornea and conjunctiva, by Dr. A. Wanstall, who was led to its use from an article of Jousset's recommending it as a remedy for pustular conjunctivitis. W. says, "In my hands it has been as near a specific as can be, and certainly I have never handled any one drug that will cure as many cases." It is no doubt a very valuable remedy for *phlyctenular ophthalmia*, as I have had occasion to verify in many cases. It is adapted to both phlyctenules and ulcers of the cornea or conjunctiva, especially if there is *much photophobia.* The cornea may be vascular. The redness of the conjunctiva, lachrymation and pain are variable, though are usually well marked. Nausea occasionally accompanies the above symptoms. (Compare Conium, Hepar and Merc. protoiod.)

JABORANDI.

Contraction of the pupil. Tension of the accommodative appara-
tus of the eye, with approximation of the nearest and farthest
points of distinct vision. *Everything at a distance appeared*
hazy, and although he could read moderate-sized type at one foot, at
two feet it was indistinct. The state of vision is constantly
changing, becoming suddenly more or less dim, every few mo-
ments.

Clinical.—In 1878, after a study of the physiological action
of Jaborandi upon the eye, I determined to test its value, according to the law of similia, in *spasm of the accommodation.*
The results in many cases exceeded my most sanguine antici-
pations.

Selected from a large number of cases are the following,
which will illustrate its sphere of action:—

CASE I.—*Hyperopia et spasmus musc. cil.* James L., æt. thirty-
two, complained of everything becoming black before the eyes
on stooping, aching of the eyes on reading and spots before the
vision. V. $\frac{20}{30}$. With concave 42, V. $\frac{20}{20}$. Ophthalmoscope
showed slight hyperopia. R. Jaborandi[3]. Three days later
all the symptoms were relieved; V. $\frac{20}{20}$.

CASE II.—*Hyperopia et spasmus musc. cil.* Edw. D., aged 17.
For four or five weeks the eyes have pained constantly, even
upon using for distance. Has been using convex 24 on ac-
count of hyperopia. R. V. $\frac{20}{20}$. L. V. $\frac{20}{20}$. Concave 60, L. V. $\frac{20}{20}$.
Jaborandi[3] relieved in three days so that he could even read
without trouble and Hm. was $\frac{1}{40}$. Convex 18 was afterwards
given for latent hyperopia.

CASE III.—*Spasmus musc. cil.* Maggie M., æt. 22. V. $\frac{20}{50}$ but
variable, changing suddenly to less degree. In one week under Jaborandi[3] the vision became $\frac{20}{20}$.

CASE IV.—*Spasmus mus. cil.* Mr. M., æt. 32. V. $\frac{20}{30}$. Concave
42, V. $\frac{20}{20}$. For nine months had had spots before the vision
and aching of the eyes upon using. In three days under

Jabor.[3] vision had become $\frac{20}{40}$, and the muscæ volitantes had disappeared.

CASE V.—*Myopia cum spasmus musc. cil.* Mr. R., æt. 28. For seven years had been writing in a poor light all day. He thought his nearsightedness had appeared within one or two years. He complained of the myopia increasing and the eyes tiring on using them one and one-half hours. Fundus normal. V. $\frac{20}{70}$ o. u. Concave 40, V. $\frac{20}{40}$. Three weeks after using Jaborandi[3], he reported that he had used his eyes more than usual and had experienced no trouble. V. $\frac{20}{50}$. Concave 50, V. $\frac{20}{40}$.

CASE VI.—*Myopia cum astigmatismus myop. ex spasmus musc. cil.* Mrs. ——. R. V. $\frac{20}{200}$. L. V. $\frac{20}{40}$. With—30° $\bigcirc$ — 40°, axis vertical, R. V. $\frac{20}{40}$ difficulty. With—30° $\bigcirc$ — 40°, axis horizontal, L. V. $\frac{20}{40}$ difficulty. After giving Jaborandi[3] for three days, the test showed that both the spherical and cylindrical glasses, required to make the vision perfect, were of not more than one-half the above strength. Entire relief of the symptoms was afterwards obtained under the same remedy.—CHAS. DEADY.

CASE VII.—*Hyperopia cum asthenopia.* Miss S., æt. 40. For many months had not been able to read more than five minutes without the eyes tiring. *Nausea was always produced on looking at objects moving.* Jaborandi[3] relieved the nausea in twenty-four hours, and in a week she could read three-quarters of an hour without inconvenience.

CASE VIII.—*Cataracta dura immat. et asthenopia.* Mrs. D., æt. 52. For four years the eyes had been weak, worse for four months; she could not use them even a few minutes without smarting and pain in them, with nausea. The pain and nausea were also experienced when looking steadily at a distance. There was much vertigo, as if the head were too light, especially on moving or looking at objects. Dull pain in the eyes was constantly present, with occasional sharp pain. Jaborandi[3] relieved in three days all the nausea, vertigo and pain in the eyes.

The following symptoms observed in various anomalies of refraction have also been speedily relieved by this drug:—Blur before the eyes at times, especially on looking in the distance. Eyes tire easily and are irritable, especially on moving them.

Heat and burning in the eyes upon using. Headache upon using the eyes. Smarting and pain in the globes on use. Dim vision, twitching of the lids and pain in the eyeballs.

From the above it will be seen that Jaborandi is of the greatest importance in *spasm or irritability of the ciliary muscle*. In explanation of its usefulness in so-called asthenopia, I am inclined to believe that a large number of these cases are not dependent upon true weakness of the accommodation, but upon an *irritable weakness*, and that Jaborandi relieves by virtue of its power to control irritation. This is also further demonstrated in its ability to relieve reflex symptoms, as in cases VII and VIII, in which *nausea and vertigo due to reflex irritation from the eyes*, were at once cured by this drug. Thus far these two reflex symptoms have been valuable and characteristic indications.

The following case by Dr. J. H. Buffum, indicates that it may be of service in affections of the retina:—" *Torpor retinæ.* John W., æt. 14. One year ago after constant and close application in doing fine work on cardboard, he observed that retinal images were retained for several minutes. No other symptoms of discomfort or pain. Vision soon began to diminish, until for three months past he was unable to use the eyes at all for work. To-day, April 13th, R. V. $\frac{20}{30}$. L. V., fingers at eighteen feet. Convex 42, R. V. $\frac{20}{20}$. Insufficiency of each internal rectus. Has sharp pains in the eye shooting back into the head, with general dull ache of the head. Light is painful. Ophthalmoscope gives negative results. R. Jaborandi[3], three hours. One week later he reports that pain has lessened very rapidly and the headache is very slight. V. $\frac{20}{20}$ o. u. R. same, four a day and Dyers exercise. After twenty-two days treatment with Jaborandi, he returned home able to use the eyes for two hours at a time, without glasses and without discomfort. He has continued well for nearly a year."

From examination into the general sphere of action of Jaborandi it should be suggested to our minds as a remedy for serous choroiditis, and in one case it has improved the vision somewhat.

Its action upon the ciliary muscle seems to extend to a

limited degree to the internal recti. It is, therefore, recommended for periodic convergent squint, for strabismus of recent date not dependent upon weakness of the opposing muscle in which for one reason or the other it is necessary to postpone the operation, and for the tendency to recurrence of squint after an operation. Illustrative of the latter is the following:—*Strabismus convergens ex hyperopia.* Louis L., 9 years of age. Squint for seven years, especially in the left eye. R. V. $\frac{20}{30}$. L. V. $\frac{20}{50}$. Convex 36, R. V. $\frac{20}{20}$. Nov. 22.—Made tenotomy of both internal recti. Nov. 23.—There was crossed diplopia at the distance of one foot, but the eyes were apparently straight. Dec. 3.—Slight but marked convergence again. Prescribed convex 40 for constant use. Dec. 27.—No improvement. R. Jaborandi[3]. Jan. 11.—Eyes perfectly straight. March 20.—No convergence and had not used glasses.

Jaborandi is very similar to Physostigma and Agaricus in its action upon the accommodation, though it has been of more service to me in spasmodic affections of the ciliary muscle, than either of the two latter remedies. It is opposed to Duboisin in its action; the latter being indicated in *true* weakness of the accommodation, while Jaborandi is called for in *irritable* weakness.

KALI BICHROMICUM.

Objective.—Margins of the lids very red. Eyelids slightly granular. Inflammation of the eyes, with yellow discharge and agglutination in the morning. Inflammation of the eyes. Redness of conjunctiva, with lachrymation. Conjunctiva both of bulb and lids injected. Appearance of small white pustules in the conjunctiva. Pustule on left cornea, with surrounding indolent inflammation. Lachrymation. Lachrymation, with burning pain in the eyes.

Subjective.—Itching and burning in both eyes, lachrymation and photophobia. Heat and pressure in the eyes. Burning in the eyes. Violent shooting pains from the root of the nose along the left orbital arch to the external angle of the eye exactly, with dimness of sight like a scale on the eye.

Clinical.—The local application of a saturated aqueous solution of bichromate of potash to large acute granulations of the lids, has often caused their disappearance. It is, however, also serviceable as an internal remedy in trachoma and pannus, as shown in the following case:—"A man, æt. 27, had granular lids, complete pannus of right eye, so he could barely count fingers, and partial pannus of the left eye; there was considerable discharge and everything appeared slightly red to him; eyes' seemed to feel better when lying on his face. Under Kali bichr. the pannus entirely cleared, leaving a slight opacity behind, but could read No. 3 Snellen's test type easily with the right eye."—T. F. A.

Kali bichr. is of great value, and especially indicated in mild cases of croupous conjunctivitis (a condition midway between purulent and genuine croupous inflammation), in which the false membrane is loosely adherent, easily detached, and has a tendency to roll up and separate in shreds which come away in the discharges, giving them a stringy appearance. The discharges are profuse and the conjunctiva very much inflamed; even chemosis. The lids are swollen and the cornea, may be hazy.

Its usefulness in polypi of the conjunctiva is shown in the following case:—"A lady, æt. 52, had a large polypus springing from the conjunctiva of the upper lid. She was advised to have it removed by operation, but objected. A saturated aqueous solution of Kali bichr. was applied to the growth every other day for two weeks, and during that time the third potency of the same remedy was given internally. Under this treatment the polypus disappeared."—W. P. FOWLER.

It is of especial importance, however, in chronic indolent forms of inflammation of the eye, particularly of ulcers and pustules on the conjunctiva or cornea, in which no active inflammatory process is present and therefore characterized by *no photophobia and no redness* or very little, not as much as might be expected from the nature of the disease; the pains and lachrymation are also usually absent. Corneal ulcers which have a tendency to bore in without spreading laterally, indicate Kali bichr. The eye may be quite sensitive to touch and any secretions are of a *stringy character.*

Opacities of the cornea have been cleared under this remedy; sometimes used internally alone, and again both externally and internally.

For *true descemetitis*, characterized by fine punctate opacities in the membrane of Descemet, especially over the pupil, with only moderate irritation of the eye, there is no remedy so frequently called for as Kali bichr. If a serous inflammation of the iris accompanies the changes in the membrane of Descemet, Gelsemium should be suggested to our minds.

KALI CARBONICUM.

Objective.—Inflammation of the lids of the right eye, with pain in the eyes and inability to read by the light. *Swelling between the eyebrows and lids, like a sac.* Redness of the white of the eye, with many vessels in it. Lachrymation.

Subjective.—Pressure above the eyes. Sharp tearing in the right orbit and in the eye at night. Soreness of the external canthus with burning pain. Burning, biting and pressure in the eyes. The eyes are painful on reading. Stitches in the middle of the eye. Smarting pain in the eye. Weakness of vision. Photophobia.

Clinical.—Œdema of the lids, especially if accompanied by sticking pains and heart indications, often subsides under the use of Kali carb.

It may be occasionally of service in small round ulcers of the cornea with no photophobia.

Pannus always worse after a seminal emission was improved by this drug.—T. F. A.

The verified symptoms indicate its usefulness in asthenopic troubles.

KALI IODATUM.

Swelling of eyelids. Injection of the conjunctiva. The conjunctiva of one or both eyes is often seen to be affected; the attack commences by a more or less general and more or less rapid vascular injection, to which is speedily added a tumefaction of the mucous membrane, and an infiltration, generally well marked, of the submucous cellular tissue, which give rise to considerable chemosis of the eye and œdema of the eyelids.

Vision dim and foggy; she sees objects only indistinctly.

Clinical.—The iodide of potassium is of the greatest importance in the treatment of many *syphilitic affections of the eye.* It seems to antidote the syphilitic poison, and there should be no hesitation in employing it in material doses.

Periostitis of the orbit will often require this remedy, especially if of syphilitic origin, though cases in which there has been no trace of syphilis, have been benefited. There will be more or less swelling extending even to the temple, with œdema of the lids. The pain may be intense or absent entirely.

Tumors of the orbit have disappeared under the use of material doses of Kali iod., as in the following:—"A colored woman, with a history of syphilis, had several tumors on the entire upper border of the left orbit, firmly adherent to bone and appearing to extend into the orbit. The growths were very hard and encroached considerably upon the upper lid, especially at the inner corner; were painless and presented no signs of inflammation or softening. Entirely disappeared under the iodide of potassium in material doses."—A. WANSTALL.

It is sometimes useful in stricture of the lachrymal duct.

Its action in pustules of the conjunctiva and cornea, is very similar to bichromate of potash, and it has been used with benefit in similar cases.

In *syphilitic iritis,* Kali iodatum is of great value. It is especially indicated if the inflammation is very severe and unyielding to the influences of atropine. The inflammatory process in the iris is so high, that the pupil tends to contract, notwithstanding the frequent instillation of the strongest solutions of atropine. *The iris is much swollen and the aqueous more or less cloudy. The ciliary injection is very marked and of a bright angry appearance.* The pain may be severe, but is worse at night. The photophobia and lachrymation are variable.

Kali iodatum is a very prominent remedy in the treatment of acute or chronic irido-choroiditis, and disseminate choroiditis, especially if of syphilitic origin. In one typical case of syphilitic choroiditis, recently under treatment, in which the chief symptom was an *excessive and variable amount of haziness of the vitreous*, the vision improved from R. V., counts fingers (held to outer side of the field) at two feet and L. V. $\frac{10}{200}$, to normal, under the use of fifteen grains of the iodide of potash a day. Its special indications are not known, though its effects are often marvelous, even when the disease is non-syphilitic in origin, as the following case of disseminate choroiditis will illustrate:—A young lady had for a long time complained of loss of vision and severe headaches. There was no history of syphilis. The fundus of the right eye showed extensive white patches (atrophy of the choroid) and deposits of pigment over its whole extent, optic nerve hyperæmic, and slight haziness of the vitreous. Commencing atrophic spots in the choroid of the left eye and hyperæmia of the nerve could be detected by the ophthalmoscope. R. V. $\frac{20}{200}$. L. V. $\frac{20}{20}$. She was directed not to use the eyes more than was necessary, and Bell. was given for three or four weeks with no marked improvement, with the exception that the headaches were not quite as frequent. Kali iod. was now prescribed and the eyes rapidly began to grow stronger, the hyperæmia of the fundus disappeared and the headaches ceased entirely. Six months after using Kali iod., R. V. $\frac{20}{30}$. L. V. $\frac{20}{20}$, though the atrophic spots in the choroid, of course, underwent no change.

In paralysis of any of the muscles dependent upon syphilitic periostitis, the iodide of potassium is the remedy most frequently called for. The following case of paralysis of the left nervus abducens will show its action:—A man, 40 years of age, ten days previous to his appearance for treatment, awoke in the morning with dizziness, and afterwards had three similar attacks. Had had a severe cold. For two days had noticed a blurring of vision and diplopia which had been steadily increasing and was only noticed on looking to the left. Examination showed only slight action of the left external rectus. R. Caust.[30]. Two days later the paralysis of the muscle had become complete. It was found that he had had syphilis. R. Kali iod., eight grains a day. In two days decided improve-

ment was observed, and in two weeks the muscle had regained
its normal power.

KALI MURIATICUM.

Clinical.—The recommendation by Schüssler, of Kali mur.
for the stage of exudation in inflammations, suggested its employment in parenchymatous keratitis, especially since we
know that the Kalies are adapted to indolent forms of inflammation, which this form of keratitis usually assumes. The
following case will give its sphere of action in *parenchymatous
keratitis:*—Mr. L., aet. 35. For three months there had been an
infiltration into the right cornea, which commenced at the
outer side and extended over the whole cornea. He could
only count fingers. There was occasional pain, moderate photophobia and redness. The pupil dilated slowly and incom-
pletely, though regularly, under atropine, and contracted
quickly. Aurum mur., Cinnabar and other remedies, with
atropine externally, had been used with no benefit, except
some relief of pain. Under Kali mur., 6th dec., the inflammation was soon arrested and the cornea gradually cleared. In
three months R. V. $\frac{30}{30}$. The improvement has continued.

The benefit which has been derived from the muriate of
potassium in a case of chorio-retinitis indicates that it may be
a valuable remedy in intra-ocular troubles. "Chorio-retinitis:
—Mr. D., aet. 36. Noticed two years ago such dimness of the
right eye that he could not read a newspaper. Had observed
no previous trouble. After a month's treatment he could read
again, but suffering a relapse, the same treatment for a year
proved ineffectual and the case was deemed hopeless. No
history of syphilis. Examination showed cornea, iris and
pupil normal. No external redness. By ophthalmoscope;
vitreous rather hazy, with some black shreds suspended in it,
having very limited motion on rotating the eye. This would
indicate that the vitreous was not fluid. Optic nerve and
bloodvessels normal. Inside the disk, a large, irregular,
atrophic spot, involving the choroid and retina, surrounded
by several small ones; edges irregular and pigmented; the

sclerotic seen white through their centres; adjacent choroid congested and thickened; some vessels lost in the infiltrated part to appear on the other side ; a dull pain, occasionally, in the eye and over the brow, with an ill-defined feeling of contraction around the eye. V. $\frac{20}{200}$. Snellen 11, slowly deciphered. Prescribed Kali mur., 6th dec., four times daily. At the end of a month vision rose to $\frac{20}{50}$ and Snellen 3 was read at five inches. A year afterwards the man could read Snellen $2\frac{1}{2}$, distant vision $\frac{20}{70}$, but under Kali mur. for a week it was again $\frac{20}{50}$. The patient's business engagements prevented longer treatment."—W. H. WOODYATT.

KALMIA LATIFOLIA.

Sensation of stiffness in the muscles around the eyes and of the eyelids. Pain in the eyes, which makes it painful to turn them. Glimmering before the eyes.

Clinical.—From its action upon the muscles we are led to give it in asthenopia and with good results, especially if there is present a *stiff drawing sensation in the muscles* upon moving the eyes.

Sclero-choroiditis ant., in which the sclera was inflamed, vitreous perfectly filled with exudation, and glimmering of light before the eye, especially on reading with the other, was cured by this drug.—T. F. A.

Kalmia was prescribed in a case of retinitis albuminurica, occurring during pregnancy, on account of the characteristic pains in the back; it was continued for a long time, during which the white patches gradually became absorbed and recovery took place.—T. F. A.

KREOSOTUM.

Burning and redness of the conjunctiva. Smarting in the eyes. The tears are acrid like salt water.

Clinical.—Kreasote has been of service in acute aggravations of chronic keratitis, in which there was excessive, hot, smarting lachrymation; also in blenorrhœa of the conjunctiva,

with moderately profuse discharge, and much smarting in the
eyes.—T. F. A.

LACHESIS.

Subjective.—The eyes feel stiff. Aching of the eyes, especially of the left. A sticking, drawing pain in the right eye
extending up to the vertex. Pressure in the eyes. Stitches as
from knives in the eyes, coming from the head. Pains near
the eyes.

Vision.—*Dimness of vision; much black flickering before the
eyes,* that seems very near; it frequently makes reading difficult. A fog before the eyes; in the evening a bluish-gray
ring, about six inches in diameter, around the light. Eyes
sensitive to light. *Flickering before the eyes.* Flickering
and jerking in the right eye, with violent congestion to the
head. Flickering before the eyes, as from threads, or rays of
the sun. Flickering in peculiar angular zigzag figures, with
congestion to the head and headache. A beautiful bright
blue ring about the light, that was beautifully filled with fiery
rays.

Clinical.—A case of orbital cellulitis, following an operation for strabismus was effectually and rapidly cured under
this remedy. The symptoms were a marked protrusion of the
eye, and chemosis, with a purulent discharge, and sloughing
at the point of tenotomy, with a black spot in the centre of
the slough; the retina was hazy and congested.—T. F. A.

Lachesis is sometimes useful in phlyctenular keratitis, especially the chronic recurrent form, in which the surface of the
cornea may be ulcerated, with moderate redness of the eye.
The chief characteristic, however, has been the marked *photophobia, which is always worse in the morning, and after sleeping.*
The various pains in the eyes and head are also subject to the
same aggravation.

As already referred to in the article upon Crotalus, *intra-
ocular hemorrhages* will often call for Lachesis. Many cases
might be given to illustrate its usefulness in this respect, but
little would be gained by so doing, for the eye indications, with

the exception of the hemorrhages, have usually been unimportant or absent altogether. It may be said, however, that hemorrhages into the anterior chamber, into the vitreous, into the retina, and into the choroid, whether of spontaneous origin or dependent upon various diseased conditions, have all been seen to speedily disappear under the use of this remedy. The general indications are of more value in the selection of this drug, than those relating only to the eye. The brilliant results often observed from its employment in retinitis apoplectica, do not seem to be confined to the absorption of the hemorrhages, as it also appears to control the inflammatory symptoms and diminish the tendency to retinal extravasations.

Its value in relieving asthenopic symptoms is suggested by the following case:—Mr. M., æt. 24, had complained of his eyes a year or more. Had been using convex 48, which neutralized his hyperopia, and were correct. He was very nervous, and had a variety of pains and sensations in and around the eyes, especially the left, all of which were worse upon thinking of his eyes, upon using them, and upon waking in the morning. These pains were experienced even when using his glasses. There was no weakness of the internal recti. After the failure of several remedies Lachesis[30] was given, with permanent relief in four weeks.

LACTIC ACID.

Clinical.—Hyperæsthesia of the retina, with steady aching pain in and behind the eyeball, was quickly relieved by a few doses of Lactic acid.—T. F. A.

LEDUM PALUSTRE.

A pressure (or dull pain) behind the eyeball, as if it would be forced out.

Clinical.—Ledum has proved chiefly beneficial in contusions or wounds of the eye and lids, especially if accompanied by extravasations of blood.

In a case of complete ptosis (right eye) from an injury by a piece of wood striking the eye, in which there was *ecchymosis of the lids and conjunctiva*, a complete restoration of power to the upper lid took place in five days under Ledum externally and internally, after Arnica had been used for two days with no benefit.

Ecchymoses of the conjunctiva, either of traumatic or spontaneous origin, are often quickly absorbed by the use of this remedy, and in many cases more promptly than when our usual remedies, Arnica or Hamamelis, are employed. (It should be used in the same manner as Arnica.)

A case of *hemorrhage into the anterior chamber*, after an iridectomy, which had resisted both Hamamelis and Arnica for two weeks, was absorbed in four days under this drug, used externally and internally.

It is the remedy in asthenopia, if there is dull pain behind the eyeball, as if it would be forced out.

LILIUM TIGRINUM.

Lachrymation. Burning feeling in the eyes after reading or writing; eyes feel very weak. Blurred sight with heat in the eyelids and eyes.

Clinical.—Favorable results have been obtained from Lilium in the relief of so-called asthenopic symptoms, which were in all probability dependent upon spasm of the accommodation. The cases were as follows:—"Mr. B., æt. 45, teacher. Has been wearing convex 36 for his old sight, selected at an optician's; latterly has been using the microscope a good deal, and has been annoyed some by fatigue of the eyes. Test: V. $\frac{20}{30}$, Am. concave 24°, axis horizontal, V. $\frac{20}{20}$, A. 9″ to 24½″. Prescribed Lilium tigr.[30] four times a day. In seven days V. $\frac{20}{20}$ clearly. A week later, A. 7″ to 29″. One week later, A. 5½″ to 31″. Examined a month later after the medicine had been stopped and found the condition unchanged. Had abandoned his glasses entirely."—W. H. WOODYATT.

"Miss P., æt. 17. Has a dry, scaly blepharitis, appearing and disappearing from time to time, according to the use she gives her eyes, and complains of general asthenopic symptoms. Letter test shows the following: L. E. V. $= \frac{20}{30}$?—60° axis 180°, V. $= \frac{20}{20}$. R. E. V. $= \frac{20}{20}$??—48° axis 180°, V. $= \frac{20}{20}$. No. 1 Snellen read at 3″ and 17″. Lilium tigr.[30] was given four times daily. In five days the lids looked better and the letter test was unchanged; but in five days more the lids seemed well and vision was emmetropic with each eye."—W. H. WOODYATT. (*Trans. Am. Hom. O. and O. Soc.*)

Mrs. K., æt. 45. Pr. $\frac{1}{48}$. Kopiopia hysterica. Burning and smarting of lids, except in bright light. Insufficiency of each internal rectus 2°. Eyes always feel better when in open air. Lachrymation on looking down; no trouble with lachrymal conduits. Has crawling sensation in vertex, with stabbing pains in occiput. Cured by Lilium tigr.[6], after various other remedies had failed."—J. H. BUFFUM.

LITHIUM CARBONICUM.

Eyes pained during and after reading, as if dry. Uncertainty of vision and an *entire vanishing of the right half of whatever she looked at;* or if two short words occurred in succession, that on the right hand was invisible.

Clinical.—A brilliant cure of hemiopia with Lithium[30] is reported by Dr. Dunham, in which only the left half of an object was visible with the right eye and nothing at all with the left. In two or three other cases of hemiopia, in which only the left half of objects was visible, no benefit was derived from this remedy.

It may be of service in some cases of asthenopia.

LYCOPODIUM.

Objective.—Swelling and painfulness of the lids, with nightly agglutination of the canthi. Styes on the lids, towards the inner canthus. *Ulceration and redness of the eyelids;* the water which flows from the eye smarts and bites the cheek. Inflammation of the eyes, with itching in both canthi, redness and swelling of the lids of the right eye; distressing pain, as if they were dry, with nightly agglutination.

Subjective.—Eyelids dry, with smarting pain; they cannot be opened even on rubbing, in the morning. Smarting and burning of the lids. Dryness of the eyes, in the evening and at night. Dryness beneath the lids, as from dust, in the morning on waking. Eyes dry and dim. Eyes dry, difficult to open, with smarting pain, in the morning. Severe burning and itching in the eyes. Pressive pain in the eyes, as if dust were in them. Stitches in the eyes. Itching in the canthi.

Vision.—Vision weak, is unable to distinguish small objects as well as formerly. *The evening light blinds him very much; he cannot see anything upon the table.* A veil and flickering before the eyes, after the afternoon naps. Hemiopia; he sees only the left half of an object; same with one eye as with both, but worse with the right. Sensitiveness of the eye to daylight. Floating black spots before the eyes at a short distance.

Clinical.—External diseases of the eye are not commonly amenable to this drug, as its chief remedial power has been exhibited in the disorders of nutrition and function of the deep seated structures.

Ciliary blepharitis and hordeola occasionally call for the use of Lycopodium.

The progress of cataract has been arrested by this remedy, when prescribed for chronic dyspeptic symptoms.—T. F. A.

Opacities of the vitreous have occasionally been known to disappear during the administration of Lyco.

Hemiopia, in which the right half of the field of vision was obscured, has been improved.

In *Hemeralopia* its great value as an eye remedy becomes apparent, for no other drug in our Materia Medica has cured such a large number of cases as Lyco. There seems to be no marked indication for its use, with the exception of the night blindness coming on in the early eve, though in some instances it was found that the patient could see better at a distance than near at hand, yet in other cases this indication was wanting, so it cannot be considered important. If black spots, floating before the eyes, accompany the night blindness this drug is particularly called for.

LYCOPUS VIRGINICUS.

Clinical.—This remedy is noticed here on account of its reputed power in the treatment of exophthalmic goitre (morbus Basedowii). In my hands, however, it has failed to benefit in every case in which it has been given.

MERCURIALIS PERENNIS.

Objective.—Blinking of the eyes in the open air and sunlight. Twitching of the upper lids, especially of the left eye. Watery eyes. Pupils dilated.

Subjective.—On waking at night she was unable to open the lids immediately; they seemed paralyzed and could not be opened until she had rubbed them. Weakness of the upper lids, so that at times she could not completely raise them. *Lids heavy and dry. Dryness of the eyes.* Burning in the eyes. *Pain in the eyes while reading and writing.*

Vision foggy. Weakness and sensitiveness of the eyes to bright and artificial light. Blinking of the eyes, while sewing or reading by the light. *Letters run together while reading.*

Clinical.—Hyperæmia of the conjunctiva after using the eyes, with heaviness of the lids, will often find its remedy in Mercurialis.

In a case of conjunctivitis trachomatosa with pannus, Mercl.[30] seemed to act very promptly in relieving all the symptoms. The pannus was slight and the boy complained of feeling very sleepy. There was lachrymation and blurring of the vision in the morning.

Our attention should be more frequently directed toward this drug in the treatment of asthenopia. It is especially indicated if the patient complains of a sensation of dryness in the eyes and heaviness of the lids (compare with Alumina). The sensations as of a mist before the eyes in the morning, and a burning pain in the left eye worse in the evening and after using, occurring in cases of asthenopia, have also been relieved. Also the hyperæmia of the conjunctiva, already noted, should suggest this remedy in these cases.

8

MERCURIUS CORROSIVUS.

Redness of both ocular and palpebral conjunctiva. *Inflammation of the eyes.* Pupils insensible to light.

Eyes painful. Burning in the eyes. Tearing as if in the bone above the left eye, near the root of the nose, and in other parts of the bone. Pain behind the eyeballs as if they would be forced out. *Photophobia.*

Clinical.—The corrosive sublimate is more often indicated in severe inflammatory conditions of the eye, especially superficial, than any other form of mercury.

In certain forms of blepharitis it is frequently very valuable; as in inflammatory swelling of indurated lids; inflammatory swelling of the cheeks and parts around the orbits, which are covered with pustules, or in scrofulous inflammation of the lids, which are red as in erysipelas. In these cases the lids are usually *very red and excoriated by the acrid lachrymation, and the pains are very severe, particularly at night.*

Chronic catarrhal conjunctivitis, tending toward trachoma, with redness and excoriation of the lids, and a dull feeling, with itching in the eyes in the evening, has been cured under this remedy.

Merc. corr. is usually more useful in strumous ophthalmia than Merc. sol. It is chiefly called for if phlyctenules, ulcers, or even deep abscesses are formed in the cornea, for then the severity of the symptoms would lead us to its selection, as this remedy is especially indicated in the erethistic form of inflammation. The eye is usually very red and the cornea vascular and ulcerated. The cornea may have become so weakened from the inflammation as not to be able to resist the normal intraocular pressure, and so commencing staphyloma may be noticed. The *photophobia is excessive,* and *the lachrymation profuse* which together with the *ichorous discharges are acrid, excoriating the lids and cheek.* The pains vary in character, though are generally very severe and not confined to the eye, but extend into the forehead and temples; always worse at night. The lids are much swollen, erysipelatous, œdematous or indurated; are red and excoriated from the acrid discharges, and are spasmodically closed, rendering it almost impossible to open them, and they often bleed easily upon attempting to do so. There are also usually present, pustules on the cheek around the eye, soreness and excoriation of the nose, enlargement of the cervical glands, coated tongue, etc.

It has been employed with benefit in ophthalmia neonatorum in which the discharges were thin and excoriating, especially if the mother has gonorrhœa or syphilitic leucorrhœa.

Episcleritis, with *much pain in and around the eye at night*, requires Merc. corr.

For kerato-iritis it is one of our chief remedies.

In *iritis*, especially the syphilitic variety, it no doubt surpasses any other remedy in frequency of indication, and by some it is even considered a specific, providing Atropine is used at the same time locally. The severity of the symptoms, and the intensity of the pains at night over the eyes and through them, through the head and in the temples, are our chief indications. *It is no less useful in the other forms of plastic iritis*, as every-day experience fully verifies.

It seems to act beneficially in some cases of posterior synechia, causing them to soften so that Atropine can tear them, and it sometimes appears to absorb them entirely, if recent.

Hypopyon, occurring in the course of abscess of the cornea or iritis, has been frequently absorbed under its use.

If the inflammatory process has extended to other portions of the uveal tract (cyclitis, choroiditis, iridocyclitis. or iridochoroiditis(, this remedy still deserves special prominence.

In retinitis albuminurica, no remedy has been employed with better success in such a large number of cases; the inflammatory process is often seen to rapidly subside, and the exudations into the retina disappear, under the influence of this remedy. The prescription is chiefly based upon the pathological changes, as the symptoms are so few in this disease.

In retinitis hemorrhagica or apoplexia retinæ, Merc. corr. is of great value in hastening the absorption of extravasated blood and in toning up the walls of the vessels so as to successfully resist further blood pressure. A case now under treatment, in which there was no marked inflammation, but profuse hemorrhages throughout both retinæ, improved rapidly under Merc. corr.[2] after other remedies had been given three months with no benefit. Within two months V. had improved from $\frac{15}{100}$ to $\frac{15}{30}$, most of the hemorrhages had absorbed and no new hemorrhages were occurring.

In superficial inflammations of the eye, Mercurius closely resembles several remedies, as Graph., Euphras., Arsen. and Sulph., but the severity of the symptoms and nightly aggravations are much more marked under Merc. than either of the above. Under Graphites the discharges are also acrid and excoriating, and the photophobia often intense, but the pains are not usually so severe as under Merc. Besides, we usually find the external canthi cracked, and a moist eruption on the face and behind the ears, when Graph. is indicated. The acrid discharges of Euphrasia are generally thick, while those of Mercurius are thin. The character of the pains and general cachexia will serve to distinguish it from Arsen. and Sulph.

MERCURIUS DULCIS.

Clinical.—Ciliary blepharitis associated with phlyctenular ophthalmia, and accompanied by eruption on the face, soreness of the nose and swelling of the upper lip, is often amenable to Merc. dulc.

Calomel has been employed for many years by the old school, in scrofulous ophthalmia, and even to this day it is considered by them as one of their most important remedies, though not a specific as was formerly supposed. Dusting the fine powder in the eye is the manner in which it is used by them.

We also, as homœopaths, find it adapted to certain forms of *strumo.,s ophthalmia*, though given in a different manner, in different doses and upon different principles. We use it only internally and for the general cachexia, as the following case will illustrate:—A little girl, æt. 6, light complexion, pale skin, muscles soft and flabby, glands enlarged and general strumous diathesis. Upon examination a very deep ulcer of the left cornea was seen, which had so nearly perforated that the membrane of Descemet had begun to bulge; small ulcers and pustules were present at the border of the cornea. In the right eye pustules and maculæ of the cornea were also found. There was *considerable redness and great photophobia.* Various remedies, chiefly the anti-psorics, had been given with no benefit. Merc. dulc.², three doses daily, was administered; improvement soon began and went rapidly on to recovery, leaving only a macula behind.

Benefit has also been derived from the use of Merc. dulc. in deeper forms of inflammation of the eye, as in irido-choroiditis, especially if dependent upon a scrofulous diathesis, and the general cachexia of the patient suggests the remedy.

MERCURIUS IODATUS FLAVUS.

Clinical.—Dacryocystitis blenn. may call for this remedy, though it is not often indicated.

In some cases of blepharitis of syphilitic origin, favorable results have been obtained from Merc. prot., if the concomitant symptoms point to its use.

It has been of service in uncomplicated granular lids, but is more particularly adapted to trachoma with pannus. It may be indicated in all stages of pannus, but especially in acute aggravations after the first, or Aconite, stage has passed. In these cases it often exerts a marked beneficial influence upon the trachoma itself. (Special indications will be given after ulceration of the cornea.)

Merc. iod. flav. has been useful in pustular inflammation of the cornea and conjunctiva, but its principal sphere of action is in *ulceration of the cornea,* especially in that form of ulceration which commences at the margin of the cornea, and *extends, involving only the superficial layers, either over the whole cornea or a portion of it, particularly the upper part,* which appears as if chipped out with the finger nail, the so-called serpiginous form. Also in cases of *ulceration occurring in the course of pannus and granular conjunctivitis,* it is excelled by no other remedy in frequency of indication.

In all these cases there is usually present excessive photophobia and redness, though sometimes these may be nearly absent. The pains are generally of a throbbing, aching character, *worse at night;* the pain often extends up into the head which is sore to touch. In nearly every case we have the *thick yellow coating at the base of the tongue,* and swelling of the glands in various parts of the body, which are so prominent under this drug.

In the *Trans. of Am. Hom. Oph. and Otol. Soc.* for 1880, Dr. A. Wanstall describes a peculiar sclero-corneal formation, in a colored boy, in which the entire sclero-corneal margin was occupied by a slightly elevated opacity, of little width, and upon which was situated a chain of very minute vesicles. The pericorneal subconjunctival tissue was profusely injected with very fine vessels, through which was also distributed a large quantity of pigment, forming a zone as striking in appearance as the one occupying the limbus corneæ, into which it imperceptibly merged. The opacity of the cornea was sharply defined. Under Merc. prot.[3] the pericorneal injection rapidly disappeared, and the proliferation of tissue passed over into a macula.

Benefit has been derived from this preparation of Mercury in syphilitic iritis, although it is not as frequently required as Merc. corr.

In intraocular troubles, Dr. Woodyatt has observed very favorable results from the use of the iodide of mercury, as in opacities of the vitreous and in irido-choroiditis, as the following will illustrate:—"Miss L., aged 26. Eight years ago she noticed a drooping and heaviness of eyelids. After two years she found sight of left eye imperfect, and when this dimness appeared, the drooping of both eyelids ceased. No redness, pain nor photophobia; but black spots and flashes of light were sometimes seen. A year later the right eye was affected and rapidly grew worse than the left. Two years ago the sight failed entirely. Examination of right eye: No external redness; anterior chamber shallow; iris discolored and crowded forward by a swollen opaque lens, to the capsule of which it was attached all around the margin of a contracted pupil. Not even quantitative sight existed. Left eye: Anterior chamber shallow; iris dimmed and discolored; pupil moderately dilated and mobile. Ophthalmoscope revealed pigment spots on the lens capsule; vitreous hazy throughout; lying in it, near the retina, were three greenish-blue spots a little larger than the optic nerve, probably hemorrhagic effusions undergoing degeneration. $V.=\frac{20}{50}$, Snellen 1½ read slowly at 3 inches; irregular dilatation of pupil under Atropine. Patient in fair health and only complains of black spots in the visual axis, inability to bear strong light and to use her eyes continuously. Prescribed Mercurius iod., 3d dec., four times a day; to use protective glasses and to abstain from near work.

Twenty days later $V.=\frac{20}{30}$, Snellen 1½ read at 8 inches. During the menses, two days after this record, there was hemorrhage into the vitreous. For one day sight was only quantitative, but it rapidly cleared. For ten days, $V.=\frac{20}{20}$, emmetropic. Résumé: Duration of treatment, 60 days; left eye, from $V.=\frac{20}{50}$ to $\frac{20}{20}$."

Cases of paralysis of the oculo-motor nerve, of syphilitic origin, have been cured by this preparation of mercury, as is markedly shown in the following case:—A young man appeared for treatment, with complete paralysis of all the fibres of the third pair of nerves of the right eye. It was probably of syphilitic origin, as fifteen months previously he had had a chancre which was followed by pain in the bones worse at night, sore throat, etc. Kali iod., in material doses for three weeks and Rhus. tox.[1] for one week, together with electricity all the time, failed to improve. After three days use of Merc. iod. flav.[30] and electricity, the power began to return to the muscles, so that he could raise the upper lid somewhat, and in less than a month he was fully restored.

MERCURIUS IODATUS RUBER.

Clinical.—The action of this form of mercury is very similar to that of the yellow iodide, and by some is used instead of the latter.

Its usefulness has been especially verified in trachoma and pannus, though the points of difference between the two iodides in this affection are not known.

MERCURIUS NITROSUS.

Clinical.—The nitrate of mercury has been successfully employed, both externally and internally, in various forms of blepharitis with no particular indications.

As a caustic in syphilitic ulceration of the lids, there is none better.

This preparation of mercury is more often indicated than any other, in *pustules and ulcers of the cornea*, particularly the former. It has been especially used by Dr. Liebold, with remarkable success in a large number of cases, without regard to symptoms. Severe cases as well as mild, chronic cases as well as acute, and superficial as well as deep (even with hypopyon), have yielded to its influence; also in some cases there has been much photophobia, in others none at all; in some, severe pain, especially at night, while in others it has been nearly absent, and thus we might go through a variety of other symptoms, differing as much as the above, in which this drug has been curative. It has usually been employed both externally and internally at the same time, and in the lower potencies; about the first potency ten grains to two drams of water (or even stronger) as an external application, to be used in the eye two, three or more times a day, and the second or third potency to be taken internally. It may, however, be given internally alone with success. Atropine is sometimes used with it, especially if there be much photophobia.

MERCURIUS PRÆCIPITATUS FLAVUS.

Clinical.—Dr. W. P. Fowler writes of this remedy as follows:—"The yellow oxide of mercury is a remedy from which I have obtained very favorable results in marginal blepharitis. It has proved most beneficial in cases where the edges of the lids were red, covered with fine crusts, and slightly thickened. Where there is ulceration of the lids of an indolent nature, it is also efficacious. I have prescribed this remedy in the 6th trit. and applied it locally, prepared according to the formula:

R. Hydrarg. oxyd. flav., gr. xii.
Cosmoline ℥i.

Every night a little of the ointment should be applied with a camel's hair brush to the roots of the lashes. Before making the application, the margins of the lids should be thoroughly washed with warm water, all the crusts removed and the lids then carefully dried. Unless this precaution be taken, little, if any, benefit will follow." Dr. C. M. Thomas also says, "I find the yellow oxid. of mercury (1 gr. to ʒi cosmoline) far more effectual than Graphites or Merc. nitr., in blepharitis." The latter prescription of Merc. præc. flav. I have also found especially beneficial in ciliary blepharitis.

MERCURIUS PRÆCIPITATUS RUBER.

Clinical.—The red precipitate of mercury, so often used by the old school, has been too little employed by us, as we have no symptomatology, but are guided in its selection simply by clinical indications.

In scrofulous ophthalmia it has proved beneficial. There is commonly bright red swelling of the conjunctiva; the lids may be everted and granular; the cornea is superficially ulcerated and covered with red vessels; the discharges from the eye are copious and purulent, forming crusts upon the lids which are firmly agglutinated in the morning; the photophobia is usually great; the symptoms are aggravated by working over a fire.

Benefit has been derived from its use in ophthalmia neonatorum.

In trachoma with pannus it is a valuable remedy. It is rarely of much service in the acute stage, for it is especially adapted to old chronic cases, in which the cornea is covered with pannus of high degree, with considerable redness, discharge and photophobia; granulations may be present, or may have been already removed by caustics.

MERCURIUS SOLUBIS.

Objective.—*The upper lid is thick and red*, like a stye. Great swelling, redness and constriction of the lids, which were very sensitive to touch. Eyelids agglutinated in the morning. He is unable to open the eyes well, as if the eyeballs were agglutinated (to the lids). Inflamed swelling in the region of the lachrymal bone. Inflammation of both eyes, with burning pain, worse in the open air. The eyes were forcibly drawn together, as if long deprived of sleep. Lachrymation.

Subjective.—A sensation as of a cutting substance beneath the left upper lid. Heat, redness and pressure in eyes. Heat in the eyes, and lachrymation. Burning in the eyes. Burning and biting in the eyes, as from horse-radish.

Vision.—If she attempts to look at anything she cannot distinctly recognize it, and then the eyes are almost always involuntarily drawn together; the more she tries to restrain the contraction the less able is she to prevent it; she is obliged to lie down and close the eyes. A fog before one or both eyes. Dimness of vision. The eyes cannot tolerate the firelight or daylight. *Firelight blinds the eyes very much, in the evening.* Things like black insects or flies constantly float before the vision.

Clinical.—Mercurius solubis has for many years, been one of the most prominent remedies in ophthalmic practice, and even now it may be considered one of the polychrests.

Inflammation or blennorrhœa of the lachrymal sac should suggest this remedy, if there is considerable swelling and pain at night, or if the discharge is thin and acrid in nature, providing the general condition of the patient at the same time calls for it. For fistula lachrymalis, with external ulceration resulting from syphilis, it has also proved useful.

In blepharitis there is no better remedy if the lids are *red, thick and swollen* (particularly the upper) *and sensitive to heat,* cold or touch. The lachrymation is *profuse, burning and acrid,* making the lids sore, red and painful, especially worse in the open air or by the constant application of cold water. The *symptoms are all worse at night in bed and by warmth in gen-*

eral, also from the glare of a fire, which is unusually painful. It is especially indicated in ciliary blepharitis, caused by working over fires or forges, or by gaslight.

Ophthalmia neonatorum, marked by acrid discharge (usually thin) which makes the cheek sore, and particularly if caused from syphilitic leucorrhœa in the mother, is more quickly relieved by this drug than any other.

In superficial inflammations of the cornea and conjunctiva, either ulcerative, phlyctenular or catarrhal, Mercurius has proved especially serviceable. We are led to its use by the following symptoms, which have been collected from a large number of cases: In inflammatory conditions dependent upon syphilis, either hereditary or acquired, it is one of the first remedies to be thought of. The ulcers of the cornea are usually quite vascular, though they may be surrounded by a grayish opacity and complicated with existence of pus between the layers of the cornea (onyx). The redness of the conjunctiva is variable, though more frequently of high degree; in some cases chemosis. *The dread of light is generally very marked*, in some cases so intense that the eyes can hardly be opened, even in a darkened room, and is more often *aggravated by any artificial light, as gaslight or glare of a fire*. The *lachrymation* is profuse, *burning and excoriating*, and the muco-purulent discharges are very *thin and acrid*. The pains are generally severe and varying in character, but are more frequently tearing, burning, shooting or sticking, and are not confined to the eye, but extend up into the forehead and temples; are *always worse at night* especially before midnight, from heat, damp weather or extreme cold, and are often ameliorated temporarily by cold water. The lids may be spasmodically closed, are thick, red, swollen, even erysipelatously, *excoriated by the acrid discharges, and are sensitive to heat*, cold or contact; there is usually biting and burning in the lids, sometimes a feeling as if there were many fiery points in them; worse in the open air. The general aggravations in the evening by gaslight and at night after going to bed, are of the first importance. At the same time the concomitant symptoms of soreness of the head, excoriation of the nose, eruptions on the face, condition of the tongue, offensive breath, night sweats without relief, and pain in the bones especially at night, would lead us in its selection.

Keratitis parenchymatosa, dependent upon hereditary syphilis, very frequently calls for Mercurius, which has proved extremely valuable in this affection. It may also be of service in interstitial inflammation of the cornea, if traceable to acquired syphilis, as was verified in a case recently under treatment.

Kerato-iritis, both with and without hypopyon, has been cured with Merc.; it is indicated by the pains and nightly aggravation; in one case in which benefit was derived, the pain was very severe at night, the eye feeling as if it were a ball of fire, the lachrymation was hot and hypopyon was present.—T. F. A.

In the treatment of episcleritis it should be considered with Thuja, as the following case will illustrate:—A woman, æt. 35, had been troubled for a long time with inflammation of the eyes; the corneæ were covered with scars from old ulcerations; the scleral vessels were injected, especially between the insertion of the recti muscles, where the sclera was slightly bulged and thinned, so that the dark color of the choroid shown through; she complained of a steady aching pain in the eye all the time, worse at night. Merc.[30] was given, which relieved the pain within a few hours and a rapid recovery ensued. In another case similar to the above in its pathological changes, the pains were pricking in character, especially on turning the eye outward, with a "dizzy" pain and beating over the eye and in the temple at night. Merc.[30], with Atropine, cured in four days.

Mercury has always been and probably always will be the principal remedy for *iritis*. The solubis has been employed with great success in many cases, though it is not as commonly useful as the corrosivus. It is especially called for in the *syphilitic* variety and when gummata are present in the iris, though its sphere of usefulness is not confined to this form, as it may be indicated in the rheumatic or any other form of iritis, in mild cases as well as severe, when hypopyon is present and when it is absent. The usual symptoms of iritis—contraction, discoloration and immobility of the iris, ciliary injection, haziness of the aqueous, etc., are of course found, but the characteristic indications are to be looked for in the pains, which are usually of a *tearing, boring character, chiefly around the eye, in the forehead and temples, which are often sore to touch;* with this there may be throbbing, shooting and sticking pains in the eye; all of which are always *worse at night.*

In retinitis or in choroiditis, particularly if dependent upon syphilis, this remedy has been employed with benefit. In these cases the retina is often very sensitive to the glare of a fire. It is the great remedy for *diseases of the optic nerve and retina occurring in workers in foundries.*

In a case of ciliary neuralgia, in which the pain was very severe in character, shooting from the eye to the occiput, worse at night, with vertigo, and soreness of the head and arm to touch, prompt relief was obtained by Merc. sol.[30], after Sulph. had failed.

MEZEREUM.

Obstinate jerking of the muscle of the left upper lid. Lachrymation, with biting in the eyes. Eyes hot, inflamed, on rising in the morning; the conjunctiva of the ball very much injected, dirty red, especially in the vicinity of the external canthus; most in the left eye; with pressive pain, and a sensation of dryness. Much pressure in the eyes, with a sensation of dryness, as if the conjunctiva of .the lids were very much inflamed. Smarting in the eyes, compelling to rub them. Pressive pain above the left eye. Itching, biting on the margin of the lids and skin near the nose.

·**Clinical**.—In eczematous affections of the lids, face and head, characterized by *thick hard scabs from under which pus exudes on pressure,* Mezereum is especially useful. It has been given with benefit in blepharitis, pustular conjunctivitis and abscess of the cornea, chiefly when these symptoms have been present.

Ciliary neuralgia, especially after operations upon the eye, has been relieved by this drug.

MURIATICUM ACIDUM.

Clinical.—The following symptom, found in a case of muscular asthenopia, was speedily relieved by Muriatic acid: Sharp burning pain extending from the left to the right eye in the morning, ameliorated by washing.

NATRUM CARBONICUM.

He could hardly open the lids; they involuntarily closed. Small ulcers about the cornea, with stinging pains in the eye, so that she was obliged to shade it from every ray of light. Needle-like stitches in both eyes, after dinner. Heaviness of the upper lids.

Eyes dim; he was constantly obliged to wipe them. Black, floating spots before vision, while writing. Blinding lightnings before the eyes, on waking.

NATRUM MURIATICUM.

Objective.—Redness of the margins of the lids; in the morning the eyes were agglutinated with scabs. A catarrhal affection of the margins of the lids developed; *they became red, with burning, especially in the evening while reading;* secreted mucus and were agglutinated in the morning on waking, and covered with thick scabs. Spasmodic closure of the lids. Irritability of the margins of the lids, and their conjunctiva. Lachrymation in the open air. *Acrid lachrymation, which makes the canthi red and sore. Redness of the white of the eyes, with lachrymation.* Redness and inflammation of the white of the eye, with a feeling as if the balls were too large and compressed. Inflammation of the eyes, and lachrymation, in every slight wind. *Giving out of the eyes. The eyes give out on reading;* with a pressure in the right eye, extending into the head, disappearing on walking about the room. *The eyes give out on writing.*

Subjective.—Slight pressive pain above the eyebrows. Sensitive dry sensation in the eyes, as after weeping a long time, while riding in a carriage. Pain as from a foreign body in the eye. Burning in the eyes, with increased secretion of mucus; the lids are agglutinated in the morning, with great sensitiveness to lamplight. Violent burning in the eyes in the evening. Pressure in the eyes. *Pressure in the eye on looking intently at anything.* Sticking in the right eye. Sensitiveness of the eyes. Smarting pain in the eyes. *Sensation as if sand were in the eyes, in the morning.* Itching in the eyes. Itching in the inner canthi, and lachrymation. Violent itching of the left inner canthus.

Vision. Eyes dim and weak. Vision not as clear as usual; the eyes seem misty all day. Objects seem covered with a thin veil. On looking at anything, especially on sewing, sudden darkness before the eyes; she could see nothing till she directed the eyes to another object, at 6 P.M., with sleepiness. *Unsteadiness of vision; objects become confused on looking at them. Letters and stitches run together,* so that she cannot distinguish anything for five minutes. Small fiery points before the eyes wherever she looks.

Clinical.—Natrum mur. has been successfully employed in a variety of ophthalmic affections, both superficial and deep. It is better adapted to chronic diseases than to those which are more acute in their course.

Well authenticated cases of morbus Basedowii are reported to have been permanently relieved by this remedy. It is, therefore, mentioned in this place, though my own experience has not verified the indication.

Stricture of the lachrymal duct, fistula and blenorrhœa of the lachrymal sac, in which the diagnosis cannot be questioned, have been benefited by this remedy.

It is very useful in certain forms of blepharitis, in which the thick inflamed lids smart and burn, with a sensation of sand in the eye, and acrid lachrymation which excoriates the lids and cheek, especially if caused from caustics.

Entropion, resulting from caustic treatment of granular lids, has been cured under Natr. mur.

Dr. F. H. Boynton first called attention to Natrum mur. as a valuable remedy for follicular conjunctivitis. It is useful

in this form of inflammation of the conjunctiva, in which the
follicular formations are chronic and chiefly confined to the
oculo-palpebral folds. It has also been of service in these
cases when complicated with true trachoma.

Old cases of granular lids, with or without pannus, may require this remedy, especially if they have previously been
"much treated" with caustics and are accompanied by acrid,
excoriating lachrymation.

In pustules and ulcers of the cornea much benefit is frequently derived from the administration of Natrum mur.,
especially *in chronic recurrent cases*, though the symptoms
which lead to its selection are not particularly characteristic.
There may be itching and burning in the eyes or a feeling as
from sand in them, usually worse in the morning and forenoon. The pains vary in character, though are not severe,
with the exception of a *sharp pain over the eye on looking down.
The lachrymation is acrid and excoriating, making the lids red
and sore; the discharges from the eye are also thin, watery and
excoriating* (Merc., Arsen.). The photophobia is usually well
marked and the lids are spasmodically closed. *The skin of
the face, around the eye, is often glossy and shining, while the lips
may be sore and the corners of the mouth cracked.*

Hyperæsthesia of the retina has been relieved, in which
there was much lachrymation and burning in the morning,
with some conjunctival injection; also in cases in which, on
looking at a bright light, there was great photophobia, severe
sticking in the temples and, on reading, objects seemed to
swim before the sight. It is especially indicated in chlorotic
females.

*In asthenopia, particularly muscular, and dependent upon over-
use of the eyes, in either ametropia or emmetropia*, Natrum mur.
is a most important remedy. By reference to the verified
symptomatology of this drug, it will be seen how closely indicated it is in a large majority of asthenopic troubles. In
addition to which many clinical indications have been observed, as follows: *Drawing, stiff sensation in the muscles of the
eyes on moving them* (this is very characteristic of Natr. mur.).
Pain, burning and smarting of the eyes on attempting to use them

and after using them. *Heat* and a feeling as though there was
a rush of blood to the eyes. *Pain on looking steadily at distant
or near objects.* Severe pain over the right internal rectus
muscle (Buffum). Use of the eyes brings on *heaviness* and
drooping of the lids; causes letters or sketches to blur, and if
continued, produces aching in the balls; lamplight is particularly troublesome; retinal images are retained; right lower lid
twitches a great deal (Woodyatt). Lids smart and feel heavy
on slight use of eyes, with desire to rub them; sharp shooting
pains in the globe; blurred vision; constant dull aching pain
in the globes; photophobia, especially to gaslight (Woodyatt).
Headaches coming on in the morning, often before rising, beginning in one eye with a sensation as if the eye would be
pressed out, accompanied by nausea and vomiting; when
looking down, objects appear larger than when looking forward (Buffum). Together with the above symptoms, marked
weakness of the internal recti muscles will usually be found,
though in some cases the weakness of the ciliary muscle will
be more pronounced. A corresponding decrease in the acuteness of vision is frequently observed and remedied by the use
of Natr. mur. The following case very well illustrates its action:—F. H. G., æt. 28, book-keeper, overstrained his eyes,
working with various colored inks, writing very fine and un-
interruptedly from twelve to fifteen hours. The general health
was good. The refraction was normal, emmetropic, but considerable weakness of the internal recti prevented reading.
The eye was hyperæmic and there was moderate photophobia,
and constant inclination to close the eyes firmly. Touch was
unbearable, but hard pressure relieved. He experienced a
sensation as if something sharp and sticking was in the eye.
He said: "My eyes itch and burn just like chilblains; I must
wipe them often and pull at the lashes." The eyes were very
painful on turning them either in or out. Natrum mur.[200]
promptly cured.—T. F. A.

The asthenopic symptoms of kopiopia hysterica, due to reflex irritation from the uterus, will not uncommonly call for
this remedy.

When the weakness of the internal recti muscles has be-

9

come sufficient to produce divergent strabismus, benefit has been derived from Natr. mur., as shown in the following case: —"Divergent strabismus had existed from childhood in a patient, 20 years of age; it followed inflammatory rheumatism. One week after taking Rhus tox.[6] the eyes were parallel for one day, then the squint came on from fatigue. Squint had always been more marked in hot weather and worse in winter. Entirely cured by Natr. mur.[30] and [200].—J. H. BUFFUM.

NATRUM SALICYLICUM.

Clinical.—The salicylate of soda, although an empirical remedy, often renders valuable service in relieving *severe pain in and around the eye.* In severe cases of iritis and other diseases, it may not only relieve the ciliary neuralgia, but also have a beneficial influence over the progress of the disease. Its use has been particularly noted for the relief of the pain of iritis following severe operations, as cataract extraction. From three to five grain doses repeated from one to three hours or even oftener in some cases, will usually be found necessary.

NATRUM SULPHURICUM.

Both eyes agglutinated in the morning, with photophobia.

Clinical.—As a local application in maculæ of the cornea, it has seemed to hasten the absorption of the new elements and clear the cornea.

NITRICUM ACIDUM.

Yellowness about the eyes, with red cheeks. Difficulty in opening the eyes and raising the upper lid, in the morning.

Burning, biting and stitches in the eyes.

Vision.—Double vision of horizontal objects at some distance. Obscuration of the eyes while reading. She can clearly distinguish nothing at night, and everything seems double. Shortsighted; objects at a moderate distance were indistinct. He was obliged to stop reading in the twilight sooner than usual.

Clinical.—Nitric acid is of especial importance in diseases of the eye of syphilitic origin, or if the patient has been over-dosed with mercury or potash.

In one case of gonorrhœal ophthalmia, in which the discharge was profuse and cornea ulcerated, with burning pain, favorable results were obtained from Nitric acid[3] internally and a weak solution externally.

More benefit has been derived from this remedy in *syphilitic iritis* than in any other ophthalmic disease. It seems to be adapted to those cases which are chronic in their course and unaccompanied by the customary nightly pain, or the pain is very mild in comparison with the usual iritic pains; sometimes the pain may be more severe during the day than at night. Posterior synechiæ, often very firm, will usually be found when these patients appear for treatment.

NUX MOSCHATA.

Blue rings around the eyes.

Sensation of dryness in the eyes; reading by artificial light was difficult; the *eyes would close from sleep;* the head and forehead were dull, in the evening.

Everything looks too large.

Clinical.—Dr. D. J. McGuire sends me the report of a "case of episcleritis in a delicate girl of ten years, involving both eyes. The nodule over each external rectus was very large and very painful, had existed two weeks and was growing worse daily. The child was very sleepy, with dry lips and tongue, and had a tired sleepy expression. Gave Nux mosch.[30] every three hours the first day, then three times daily. After three days, as she was much relieved, gave blank powders for two days, during which time the patient became worse. Returned to Nux m., with prompt relief and a cure in twelve days."

NUX VOMICA.

Objective.—Twitching of the eyelids. Blinking of the eyes. Canthi purulent. Swelling of the eyes, with red streaks

in the whites and pressive-tensive pain. Inflammation of the
eyes. The eyes run water, as in a moist inflammation of the
eyes or as in stopped coryza. Painless injection of the whites
of the eyes. While yawning, in the morning, the eyes stand
full of water, with lachrymation.

Subjective.—The margin of the lid is painful, as if rubbed
sore, especially on touch *and in the morning.* Pressure in the
upper lids, especially *in the morning.* The inner canthus is
painful, as if sore and rubbed. The canthi are painful, as if
sore. *A smarting dry sensation in the inner canthi, in the morning,
in bed.* Biting in the eyes, especially in the external canthi,
as from salt, with lachrymation. Itching in the eyes, relieved
by rubbing.

Vision.—Vision extremely sensitive. *Vision cloudy. Intolerance of the daylight, in the morning,* with obscuration of vision.
Photophobia.

Clinical.—The power of Nux vomica to relieve nervous
irritability, has led to its beneficial use in diverse affections of
the eye, as the following clinical record will show.

In dacryo-cysto-blennorrhœa good results have been' obtained from its use.—A. WANSTALL.

In ciliary blepharitis, with smarting and dryness of the lids,
especially in the morning, our remedy will be found in Nux
vom. It is also indicated in ciliary blepharitis dependent
upon certain forms of gastric disturbances.

From its action in spasmodic affections, we are led to its use
in blepharospasmus or morbid nictitation, in which it has
been given with benefit, though is not so frequently indicated
as Agaricus.

As a remedy for conjunctivitis, it is not as often called for
as when the cornea becomes involved, though in both catarrhal
and scrofulous inflammation of the conjunctiva benefit has
been derived, especially if there is marked *morning aggravation*
and the usual concomitant symptoms. In acute conjunctivitis
with hemorrhages in the conjunctiva it is also sometimes indicated.

Good results were obtained from its use in ophthalmia neonatorum, in which the lids were much swollen, bled easily

and the child was troubled with vomiting, constipation and flatulent colic.

Old cases of trachoma, especially if complicated with pannus, and if they have had much treatment, are often benefited by this remedy. It is, however, frequently of use, either to commence the treatment or as an intercurrent remedy in trachoma with or without pannus, though it rarely effects a cure unassisted by any other drug. It has been of service in trachoma and follicular conjunctivitis occuring only in the summer and worse in the morning (compare Sepia).

Nux. vom. is frequently indicated in *ulcers* and pustules of the cornea, especially the former, *with excessive photophobia.* An important point regarding the photophobia, as well as the other symptoms, is the *morning aggravation*, which is rarely absent. In addition to this we usually have much lachrymation and a variety of pains, none of which, however, can be said to be very characteristic, though the following are a few which have been relieved: Sharp darting pains in the eye and over it, in some cases extending to the top of the head, and always worse in the morning. Burning pain in the eyes and lids. Tearing pain in the eye at night, awakening from sleep. Eye feels pressed out whenever she combs her hair. Sensation as of hot water in the eye. Pain in the lower lid as if something were cutting it. Burning pain when looking at a light, darting upward above the eyes, with pain in the eyebrow on going to bed. *Pain in the eye in the morning.* Sometimes relief from the pain is obtained by bathing the eyes in cold water. Cases that have been overdosed by external and internal medication particulary call for this remedy.

It has proved useful in iritis, as in one case of the syphilitic variety, with moderate ciliary injection, some photophobia, hot lachrymation, morning aggravation and great sensitiveness to the air, though it cannot be often indicated.

Even after the deeper structures have become inflamed, benefit has been derived from Nux. vom., as in a case of chorio-retinitis, in which there was much throbbing pain, especially in the left eye, and in the morning, ball sore to touch, upper part of the sclera bright red, burning pain in the eye not relieved by bathing, and aggravation of the symptoms on lying down.

In choroiditis disseminata it is a prominent remedy, especially if occurring in persons addicted to the use of stimulants; its special indications do not vary from those already given in writing of other diseases.

Hyperæsthesia of the retina, with frequent pains in the top of the head, sleepless nights and awakening cross in the morning, was promptly relieved by Nux vom.

Of late years strychnia has been employed very extensively by the old school, in the treatment of atrophy of the optic nerve and various forms of amblyopia. It is used chiefly by hypodermic injection, and in many cases with marked success. We also often find Nux vom. useful in atrophy of the optic nerve, checking the progress of the disease, and in many cases restoring the vision to a limited extent, though it is, of course, impossible to restore the sight wholly if genuine atrophy has once commenced. Illustrative of its action in atrophy of the optic nerve is the following:—Mr. T., æt. 60, dark complexion, dyspeptic; is a smoker but does not drink. For three or four months vision had been failing. V. $\frac{20}{200}$ o. u. With convex 36, V. $\frac{20}{50}$, great difficulty. Ophthalmoscope showed white atrophy of the outer halves of both optic papillæ. Under Nux vom., 3d, 30th and 200th, the vision improved in three months to $\frac{20}{40}$, great difficulty, and with convex 30 was $\frac{20}{20}$ difficulty.

In *amblyopia potatorum*, or impairment of vision due chiefly to the use of intoxicating drinks or even to dissipation in general, no remedy will more frequently restore to power the function of the benumbed nerve than this. Many confirmations of this assertion could be given, but the following was particularly marked:—J. N., æt. 53. Diagnosis, amblyopia potatorum et atrophia nerv. opt. Three months previous to my seeing him, he had noticed that his sight was failing. At that time he was drinking much and regularly, and was an inveterate smoker. The vision had grown worse until he entered the Inebriate Asylum on Ward's Island, in which he had been for several weeks. During this time he had received no treatment, only discontinuing the use of liquor; no improvement of vision took place. The ophthalmoscope showed decided white atrophy of both optic papillæ. R. V., fingers at four feet. L. V., fingers at five feet. Nux vom. 30th and 200th was given for ten days with no benefit, when Nux v.[1] was administered. Within six days he could count fingers at ten feet, and in two months and a half his vision became $\frac{16}{30}$ nearly, and with convex 14, could read three and a half Snellen slowly. The smoking was not stopped.

Tobacco amaurosis or amblyopia will often be benefited by the use of Nux, as can be seen from the following remarkable case: —J. W., æt. 18, of a nervous temperament, had been smoking excessively from early in the morning till late at night, and inhaling the smoke. One morning, three days before he was seen, on reading Greek, noticed a blur before the vision and on covering the right eye found he could not see with the left. The vision had nearly returned in the afternoon, but was again lost the next morning, and did not again return. He had not used alcoholic stimulants. R. V., $\frac{20}{20}$ difficulty. L. V., fingers at six feet. No improvement with glasses. The ophthalmoscope showed no change in refraction, media or fundus, only some sensitiveness to reflected light, which caused a stinging pain in the ball. No subjective symptoms of any kind, except the loss of vision. Two days later, having stopped the tobacco and given Nux v.[30], the vision in left eye had fallen to counting of fingers at one and a half feet. Under Nux v.[1], the vision at once began to improve, and in three weeks was $\frac{20}{20}$ in each eye.

Its action upon the muscles should not be overlooked, for though it is not often called for in strabismus, still it has benefited some cases, periodic in character, especially aggravated by mental excitement, or when caused by an injury.

For paralytic affections of the muscles it may sometimes be useful, especially when *caused or made worse by stimulants or tobacco*. In a case recently under treatment, not of this character, it was also of service:—A man, æt. 53, had noticed double vision for one week, followed by drooping of the left upper lid and complete paralysis of all the filaments of the third pair of nerves for three days. *Dull frontal headache in the morning.*

Supposed to be due to exposure in a draught, though had had
syphilis 23 years before. Causticum was given for over three
weeks with no improvement, when, on account of headache,
nausea and bad taste in the mouth in the morning, Nux
vom.[3] was given. Headache was at once relieved, and he soon
began to open his eye. After eighteen days of slow improvement, Nux[1] was prescribed, and in a month the action of all
the muscles was good.

Very favorable results have followed the use of this drug in
asthenopia, especially when the symptoms are more pronounced in the morning; also when aggravated by stomach
derangements.

In *U. S. M. & S. J.*, Dr. W. H. Woodyatt reported: "In
various forms of trouble I have been led to give Nux. vom.
for a blurring of sight by overheating, and nearly every time
with benefit."

Strychnia has sometimes been employed in preference to this
drug, though no apparent advantage has been gained by the
substitution.

OPIUM.

Pupils contracted.

Eyes dry and weak, with burning, and a sensation as if dust
were in them.

Clinical. The use of this drug in ophthalmology has been
very limited, except as an anodyne.

Two very interesting cases are, however, presented, in which
Opium acted very favorably:—A woman, æt. 35, had been
troubled with her eyes for six weeks. Upon examination, total
paralysis of the accommodation with impaired sensibility of
the retina of the right eye, and partial paralysis of the accommodation of the left eye, was found. It was supposed to be
due to the use of a cosmétic, which probably contained carbonate of lead. The other symptoms present were as follows:
almost constant frontal headache, vertigo with darting pains
from the occiput to the forehead, distressing feeling of empti-
ness in the stomach especially in the morning, bowels con-

stipated, and a sensation of pain and constriction as of a band encircling her chest in the line of the pleura. Nux vom.[2] failed. Opium[3] cured.—W. A. PHILLIPS.

The second case was one of embolism of the central artery of the retina. The arteries were bloodless, veins engorged and stagnant, and hemorrhagic spots on the disk. Came on after a severe attack of neuralgia. The face was very red, numb and drawn to the right side; tongue protruded to the right side; speech was imperfect, nearly voiceless, except with effort; pain in the back. All the pains were on the right side. Under the use of Opium alone, he gradually recovered not only his vision but also power over the paralyzed parts.—T. F. A.

PARIS QUADRIFOLIA.

Some stitches through the middle of the eye. Jerking and twitching of the right upper lid. The eyeballs seem too large.

Clinical.—This drug produced a permanent cure of paralysis of the iris and ciliary muscle, supposed to be due to an injury received two years previous. There was pain drawing from the eye to the back of the head, where there was a sore spot; even pressure with the finger would cause her to cry out. Many black floating specks before the vision were present.

The following symptoms have also been relieved by Paris : *Pain in the eyes as if pulled into the head.* Double vision. Headache worse in the evening, with confusion of the whole forehead, and sensation as if skin of the forehead were drawn together and the bones scraped sore, with inflamed lids, red margins and sensation *as if threads drew from the eye into the middle of the head.* Tension around the brow, as though the skin were thick, and difficult to wrinkle. "Feeling of contraction in the internal canthi."—DEADY.

PETROLEUM.

Objective.—An inflamed swelling, as large as a pigeon's egg, in the inner canthus, like an incipient lachrymal fistula, together with dryness of the right side of the nose. Lachrymation. Conjunctivitis and blepharadenitis.

Subjective.—Burning and pressure in the inner canthus. Itching and dryness of the lids. Burning in the eyes and pressure, with dimness on exerting them. Itching and sticking in the eyes.

The visual power is weak.

Clinical.—In disorders of the lachrymal apparatus, especially blennorrhœa of the lachrymal sac, decided benefit has been derived from Petrol.; its choice depends mainly upon the concomitant symptoms.

Within the last few years the purified preparations of petroleum, cosmoline and vaseline, have been used to a great extent and with much benefit as external applications in cases of blepharitis; they prevent the formation of new scabs and the agglutination of the lids, besides seeming to exert a beneficial influence over the progress of the disease. At the same time the use of Petrol. internally, is highly recommended, especially if indicated by the characteristic occipital headache, rough skin, etc. Cases, in which ciliary blepharitis has resulted from conjunctivitis granulosa, also when it has been a sequela of small pox, with smarting and sticking pains in the inner canthus, have been cured by this drug.

It is sometimes indicated in trachoma with pannus, especially when occurring in a scrofulous habit, with considerable white discharge from the eye and roughness of the cheek.

It may be called for in scrofulous ophthalmia, with mucopurulent discharge from the eyes, inflammation of the lid margins and burning, itching or sticking in the eyes and lids.

Iritis, with dull pulsating pain in the occiput, may require Petroleum.

PHOSPHORICUM ACIDUM.

Clinical.—*The headaches of school children dependent upon overuse of the eyes* (asthenopia) are frequently amenable to Phos. ac.

PHOSPHORUS.

Blue rings about the eyes. Eyes sunken. Pupils contracted. Stiffness and heat in the eyes.

Vision.—He sees more distinctly in the morning, in the twilight, than during the day. Giving out of the eyes while reading. She was obliged to hold objects near in order to see distinctly; at a distance everything seemed enveloped in a smoke or mist; she could see better when the pupils were dilated by shading the eyes with the hand. Cloudiness or dimness of vision. Everything seems in a mist. A green halo about the candlelight, in the evening. Flickering before the eyes and roaring in the head. Sparks before the eyes, in the dark. It seems as though a black veil were before the right eye. Black floating points before the eyes. Dark objects and spots before the eyes.

Clinical.—Very little successful use of Phosphorus has been made in external affections of the eye. Its greatest sphere of action is to be found in diseases of the fundus, especially when the optic nerve and retina are involved.

In both disseminate and serous choroiditis benefit has been derived from the use of Phos. In these cases there will usually be found *photopsies or chromopsies;* in one case of choroiditis disseminata, the latter were *red in color.* The following rapidly progressing case of chorio-retinitis was reported in the *N. Y. Jour. of Hom.* by Dr. T. F. Allen:—"The gentleman had been writing in a cellar by poor light for several months, and using tobacco to excess. Examination disclosed atrophic spots in the choroid very marked, surrounded by areolæ of active inflammation; the retina hazy, blurred; the optic disk red, somewhat swollen, with an indefined margin; the vitreous slightly turbid, with floating opacities. He complained of a mist before vision, of pinkish globules before vision, especially after a bright light; the outlines of objects seemed uneven and wavering (trembling); *on reading the letters looked red,* especially by gaslight, and flashing of lights before vision. The patient was weak and perspired very easily, but otherwise in good health. Phosphorus[200] removed first the red appearance of letters, and very speedily all traces of acute progressive disease, leaving only the atrophied spots, which will, of course, always remain. His vision rose from $\frac{1}{10}$ to $\frac{1}{8}$, where it remains."

There seems to be no question that Phos. is a valuable remedy in clearing up the vision and relieving many subjective symptoms in old cases of glaucoma after an iridectomy has been made, as illustrated by the following cases:—In a case of glaucoma after an iridectomy, the patient suffered from a pulling as if something were pulled tight over the eye, with spangles (white) around the gas and a boring in the eye extending into the head. Phos. relieved the pulling sensation and headache, and cleared up the vision.—T. F. A.

Case II.—Glaucoma simplex: W. C., colored, æt. 31. Duration of disease: Left eye, four years; right eye, two years. Vision failed gradually. A greater portion of the iris in the left eye had been removed by operations eighteen and six months previously and that which remained was dilated to a rim; a large segment of the iris of the right eye had also been removed sixteen months previously. The corneæ were slightly anæsthetic. The right anterior chamber was shallow, the left normal. T. normal. The ophthalmoscope revealed "both optic papillæ almost totally white and most completely and exquisitely cupped; arteries reduced, veins not over normal in calibre; no pulsation." R. V., fingers at eight feet. L. V., fingers counted only in close contact with the eye. The field of vision of the left eye was contracted inwards, downwards and outwards nearly to the point of fixation, while the field of the right eye was concentrically contracted, especially inwards and upwards. After using Phos. 1st or 3d for six months the test of vision showed: R. V. $\frac{20}{70}$. L. V. $\frac{20}{200}$.—A. WANSTALL.

In both hyperæmia and inflammation of the retina, favorable results have been obtained from this remedy. In one case it relieved very quickly a congestion of the retina, in which the balls were sore on motion, no photophobia, pains extending from the eyes to the top of the head.—T. F. A.

It may be called for in various forms of retinitis. It is especially indicated in retinitis nyctalopia. From its pathogenesis we are also led to believe that it will prove a valuable addition to our list of remedies for retinitis albuminurica, and some experience seems to corroborate this view. The *degenerated condition of the blood-vessels found in retinitis apoplectica* not unfrequently requires the use of Phos. It not only seems to aid in restoring the proper tone to the vessels but also appears to hasten the absorption of the hemorrhages. (Compare with Crotalus and Lachesis.) The hemorrhages may be confined to the different layers of the retina or (as has occasionally been the case) may have extended into the vitreous. The inflammatory symptoms are not usually prominent, the impairment of vision and hemorrhages into the retina constituting the chief symptoms. A hemorrhagic diathesis will often accompany the eye indications (especially hemoptysis).

The symptom of "*cherry red color before the vision*," found in optic neuritis and other diseases of the fundus, has been frequently relieved by this remedy.

In amaurosis and amblyopia, conditions in which "the patient sees nothing or very little and the doctor also sees nothing," the sight has often been greatly improved and even entirely restored under the influence of Phosphorus. In one case of complete loss of vision in the left eye, in which the sight became normal under Phos.[30], a marked symptom was, that she could *see better in the evening by candlelight*. If the cause of the impairment of vision can be traced to sexual excesses this remedy should be first suggested, though it is often called for when no cause of the disturbed function can be discovered.

Benefit has been observed from its use in stopping the progress of cataract, as in the case of an old lady, with incipient and progressive hard cataract, in whose lens were hard, white, convergent striæ with diffuse haziness; she complained that on reading the *letters seemed as if printed in red ink*, although the paper looked white and natural. V. $\frac{5}{30}$. Under Phosphorus the haziness disappeared, no more striæ appeared, and in six months the vision improved to $\frac{13}{70}$.—T. F. A.

Rapidly increasing myopia has been checked in its progress by this drug.—T. F. A.

The value of this remedy in paralysis of the muscles (so highly recommended by some) I have not had occasion to verify, though can readily understand that it may be useful, especially when general indications point to its use.

The following symptoms, observed in an excessively hypermetropic person, were quickly relieved: Mistiness before the vision with attacks of vanishing of sight; eyes so weak must close them; balls seem large, difficult to get the lids over them; lids agglutinated.—T. F. A.

In weakness of the internal recti muscles it has been found indicated, as in a case of asthenopia muscularis, in which there was pain and stiffness of the eye-balls on moving them and at times a feeling of heat in the eyes as after looking at a fire (Nat. mur.).—T. F. A.

PHYSOSTIGMA.

Twitching of lids. Drawing, twisting sensation in the eyes. Sharp shooting and drawing sensation in the right eye. Eyes are sore, and give pain when moved from side to side. Eyes smart; lids feel sore. *The musc. internus seems not to do its work rightly, and the axis of the eyes differs in each.* Felt film over the eyes, and blur; objects mixed; after which dull pain over the eyes, and between the eyes. Eyes feel weak. Pain in the eyeballs.

Contraction of the pupils. Spasm of the accommodation, which may be irregular, producing astigmatism. Myopia. Muscæ volitantes. The accommodation recovers before the pupil.

Clinical.—Calabar bean, being one of our most prominent myotics and antagonistic in its action to Atropine, has been often employed to overcome the ill effects of Atropine when used for purposes of examination, etc. Its action, however, is so short that frequent instillations are necessary to thoroughly counteract the effects of the mydriatic.

It has been used as a mechanical aid in tearing adhesions of the iris, especially to the cornea, and in cases of deep ulceration of the cornea when at the periphery, so that if perforation occurs the pupillary edge of the iris will not be drawn into the opening.

It has also been of service, used locally, in paralysis of the accommodation and dilatation of the pupils consequent upon loss of power of the oculo-motor nerve.

Its usefulness is not confined to its mechanical power, for when given internally upon physiological principles and according to the law of "similia" it is valuable.

Twitching of the lids should direct our attention to this drug, especially if combined with spasm of the ciliary muscle. In one case in which there was twitching around the eyes, patient could not read at all without much pain, frontal headache aggravated by any light, Physostigma gave quick relief.

Dr. W. H. Woodyatt, adopting the theory, that myopia in a great majority of cases is due to spasm of the ciliary muscle or at least that its increase depends upon this cause, gave Physostigma 2nd dec., in several cases with excellent results, often reducing the degree of myopia very perceptibly, and even in some cases restoring the vision entirely. The *symptoms of irritation, pain after using the eyes, musci volitantes, flashes of light, etc.*, which might lead us to suspect spasm of the accommodation, were usually present and were soon relieved; while in other cases no symptoms of irritation were to be perceived, still the administration of Physostigma was followed by favorable results. The above observations have been frequently verified in practice, though hardly to the extent first reported by W. Its action in these conditions is very similar to Jaborandi, though I do not believe it to be as commonly indicated as the latter in irritability of the ciliary muscle.

It has been useful in paresis of the accommodation after diphtheria, and in muscular asthenopia.—J. H. Buffum.

Eserine, an alkaloid of Calabar bean, has of late been employed very extensively in ophthalmic practice.

Laqueur, of Strassburg, first recommended the instillations of Eserine in the treatment of glaucoma (*Archiv für Ophthalmologie*, xxiii., 3). Since then it has been used by most oculists, with varying success. There is no doubt that in some cases it may relieve the intra-ocular tension temporarily, if not permanently. Its action is chiefly, if not wholly, mechanical;

by acting upon the muscular tissue of the vessels, it causes a contraction in their calibre, or, as is more probable, by drawing away the iris from the angle of the anterior chamber, the filtration passages are opened and so excretion accelerated. It should not be substituted for iridectomy, however, but be reserved for exceptional cases, as, for instance, when the operation must be postponed for one reason or another, or when the tension increases after an iridectomy, or in some case of secondary glaucoma.

The following case, in which Eserine proved beneficial is of interest :—A woman had a cataractous lens dislocated into the anterior chamber by a blow on the temple, two days previously. There was conjunctival irritation, much photophobia and lachrymation, with severe throbbing pain in eye and right side of head. The tension of the eyeball was increased. "I decided to remove the lens at once, and succeeded, after some difficulty, in doing so. During the next twenty-four hours the tension remained normal and the wound tended to heal kindly. On the second morning following the removal of the lens she complained greatly of pain, which had kept her awake during the night and still continued. The upper lid was swollen and œdematous. The borders of the cut for a space of two or three lines were hazy and infiltrated, a slight stringy and mucous discharge had occurred and the tension of the eyeball had again increased. A solution of Eserine $\frac{1}{200}$, one drop every two hours, was instilled into the eye, and Eserine, the 3d trituration, a dose every two hours, was prescribed. In the course of twenty-four hours the tendency to sloughing had ceased, and a rapid recovery followed."—D. B. Hunt.

Eserine has been recommended by prominent specialists of the old school for a variety of ocular diseases, as conjunctivitis purulenta; keratitis, especially suppurative; kerato-conus; asthenopia, muscular and accommodative, etc.

PHYTOLACCA DECANDRA.

Eyelids agglutinated and œdematous. Reddish blue swelling of the eyelids, worse on the left side and in the morning. Eyes inflamed. Lachrymation.

Aching pain along the lower half of the right orbit. *Pressure around the eyes, in the afternoon, as if the eyes were too large.* Smarting and sandy feeling in the eyes. Lids feel as if granulated, and the tarsal edges have a scalded, hot feeling, as if raw. Photophobia.

Clinical.—There is a comparatively rare form of orbital cellulitis in which Phytolacca is a remedy of great value. The inflammation is slow in its course and not attended by severe pain. The infiltration into the cellular tissue of the orbit is very pronounced; *hard and unyielding to touch. The eyelids are reddish-blue, hard and swollen.* The eyeball is pressed forward and its mobility impaired or lost entirely. There is chemosis and more or less dull aching pain, lachrymation and photophobia.

It has been employed with some success in ameliorating, if not curing, malignant ulcers of the lids, as lupus and epithelioma.

A very interesting case of suppurative choroiditis (panophthalmitis) in the right eye of a child, after a needle operation for cataract, occurred in Dr. Liebold's clinic. The lids were enormously swollen, very hard and red, conjunctiva injected, chemosis, anterior chamber filled with pus and cornea tending towards suppuration; child pale, weak and restless. Phytolacca was prescribed, externally and internally. Rapid subsidence of all the inflammatory symptoms followed its use.

In orbital cellulitis and panophthalmitis Rhus tox. should be compared with Phytolacca. The former, however, more often corresponds to the symptomatology of these diseases, as the symptoms are more intense, pain more severe and inflammation more active under Rhus than under Phytolacca. The lids are also œdematously swollen and lachrymation profuse in Rhus while they are hard, bluish-red and swollen in Phyto.

PLANTAGO MAJOR.

Clinical.—*Ciliary neuralgia from decayed teeth* has been relieved by this drug. "In one case, there was a dull heavy ache in the left eye, with exquisite tenderness of the ball;

10

left upper incisor decayed. Plantago relieved promptly."— J. H. BUFFUM.

PRUNUS SPINOSA.

A sharp pain beginning in the right side of the forehead, shooting like lightning through the brain and coming out at the occiput. Pain in the right eyeball, as if the inner portion of the eye would be torn out.

Clinical.—As a remedy for ciliary neuralgia, whether originating from some diseased condition of the eye or not, there are few, if any, drugs more often called for than Prunus.

The character of the pains will furnish our chief indications; thus we have pain in the eyeball as if it were crushed or wrenched, or *pain as if pressed asunder*; again we often find the *pain of a sharp, shooting* character extending through the eye back into the brain, or this sharp pain may be seated above the eye extending into and around it or over the corresponding side of the head. Sometimes the pain will commence behind the ears and shoot forward to the eye, but, as already remarked, it is generally of this sharp piercing character. Motion usually aggravates, and rest relieves, the severity of the pains. The pains are occasionally periodic in character, and may be worse at night.

These pains, to which Prunus is adapted, are especially found in disorders of the internal structures of the eye, therefore it has been given in many of these cases with marked benefit. Particularly in sclerotico-choroiditis post. have good results been obtained in stopping the progress of the disease.

Dr. O'Connor, who first brought this drug into notice in ophthalmic affections, says he has used it with benefit in the following cases:—"Two cases of chorio-retinitis in myopic patients, with sclerectasia posterior, and fluidity of the vitreous with floating opacities in it (hemorrhagic). One case of irido-choroiditis, no fluidity of the vitreous and no floating opacities. Another case of irido-cyclitis with anterior synechiæ. Also once in an old lady, æt. 76, who had paralysis of the right side, and cornea nearly opaque, with excessive congestion of the superficial and deep vessels of the conjunctiva and sclerotic." In all these cases the pains were the chief indications.

Other cases of choroiditis, either with or without retinal complication, have been quickly relieved and the vision restored, so far as possible in the degenerated condition of the tissues.

The opacities and haziness of the vitreous occurring during the course of choroideal troubles, have been known to disappear under Prunus, when given in accordance with the usual indications.

PSORINUM.

Ophthalmia, with pressing pains, as if sand were in the eyes. Soreness of the eyes and burning, she has to close them constantly. The eyes become gummy. Lachrymation.

Burning, pressing pains in the eyes. Stitches in the eyes. Itching of the lids, especially in the canthi.

Vision blurred. Fiery sparks before the eyes.

Clinical.—As one of our antipsorics, this remedy occupies an important position in the treatment of many ophthalmic disorders, dependent upon scrofula.

Cases of ciliary blepharitis, especially if of a chronic recurrent nature, are often amenable to this drug; they are usually old chronic cases with no marked local symptoms to govern us in the selection of the remedy. Inflammation of the lids, of a more acute character, as when the internal surface has become much congested, and combined with great photophobia so that the child cannot open the eyes, but lies constantly on the face; has been cured.

In old recurrent cases of pustular inflammation of the cornea and conjunctiva, most benefit seems to have been gained. The chronic nature, recurrent form and scrofulous basis are our chief indications.

A case of serous choroiditis, occurring in a young lady, about twenty-one, was greatly improved under its use. There was some ciliary congestion, and great haziness of the vitreous so that the optic nerve was only discerned with great difficulty, and then was found decidedly hyperæmic, as was the whole fundus. Some headache was present, especially in the morning; also a profuse sweating of the palms of the hands all the time.

PULSATILLA.

Objective.—*The margin of the lower lid is inflamed and swollen, with lachrymation, in the morning. Stye on the lid, with inflammation of the white of the eye,* now in one, now in the other canthus, with drawing-tensive pains in the eyes on moving the muscles of the face, and with ulcerated nostrils. The inner canthus seems agglutinated with matter, in the morning. *The eyelids are agglutinated in the morning. Lachrymation in the cold open air.* The eyes are full of water in the wind. The eyes are full of water; they lachrymate; blear eyed. *A red (inflamed) spot on the white of the eye, near the cornea.*

Subjective.—Dryness of the lids. A biting pain and a sensation of soreness in the inner canthus. Pressive pain in the inner canthus. Violent sticking in the eyelids and canthi, in the evening. *Itching (biting) and burning in the lids, in the evening.* Itching in the inner canthi, like the healing of an ulcer, in the evening after sundown; after rubbing, there is a pressive, fine sticking pain. Dryness of the eye, and a sensation in the morning as if a foreign body were pressing in it. Dryness of the right eye, and a sensation as if mucus were hanging before the eye, that obscured the vision and that could be wiped away, in the evening. Pressure, as from sand, in the eye when reading. Pressive pain in the eyes, as if there were heat in them. Pressive pain in the left eye. A pressive-burning pain in the eyes. Pressive-burning pain in the eye, as if a hair were in it. *Burning and itching in the eyes, that provoke rubbing and scratching.* Itching-sticking in the eyes, that provokes scratching. Itching of the eyes.

Vision.—Dimness of vision. *Dimness before the eyes and lachrymation in the open air.* Weak vision. Dimness of vision, like a fog before the eyes. Obscuration of vision, with inclination to vomit and paleness of the face. Dizzy obscuration of vision after sitting, on rising and beginning to walk about. Obscuration of vision, like a fog before the eyes, on rising from a seat and walking. Transient obscuration of vision. It seems dark before the eyes, in the morning, on rising from bed. *During the menses it became black before the eyes, and she felt worse on going into a warm room.*

Clinical.—This remedy is very frequently indicated in a great variety of diseases of the eye, but in its selection we are governed in a great measure by the temperament and general symptoms of the patient. Those eye troubles, especially the superficial, found in the *negro race, as well as those occurring in the mild tearful female,* seem to be particularly amenable to Pulsatilla.

Its action upon the lachrymal sac is very decided. No remedy is more frequently needed in the *early stages of acute phlegmonous dacryocystitis* than Pulsatilla. It will, sometimes, abort the inflammation and prevent the formation of pus, even when the swelling at the inner angle of the eye is extensive, sensitive to touch and involves both lids. It may be useful throughout the whole course of the disease. For blennorrhœal inflammation of the lachrymal sac it is also valuable, especially if the *discharge is profuse, yellow-white, thick and bland,* and occurring in a Pulsatilla temperament. It has appeared to be particularly called for, in affections of the lachrymal sac found in children.

For blepharitis, both acute and chronic, it is a valuable remedy, especially, if there is inflammation of the glands of the lids, both meibomian and sebaceous (blepharadenitis); also in cases of blepharitis in which there is a great tendency to the formation of styes or abscesses on the margin of the lids. It is called for in blepharitis resulting from indulgence in high living or fat food, and if accompanied by acne of the face. The swelling and redness of the lids vary in different instances, as does also the discharge, though more frequently we find profuse secretions, which cause agglutination of the lids in the morning. The sensations experienced are usually of an itching, burning character, and are aggravated in the evening, in a warm room, or in a cool draught of air, but *ameliorated in the cool open air.*

If prescribed early in the treatment of *styes* (hordeola) it will, in the majority of cases, cause them to abort without the formation of pus. It is especially adapted to the attack *per se*, but may be of service in preventing the recurrence of successive crops.

In tarsal tumors, especially of recent origin, subject to inflammation, or when accompanied by a catarrhal condition of the eye, help has been derived from its use.

Spasmodic action of the lids, with lachrymation and photophobia, has been relieved.

Pulsatilla has been successfully employed in a great variety of conjunctival and corneal affections. It is often the remedy for simple catarrhal conjunctivitis, especially the acute form (though also useful in the chronic), either resulting from a cold, from bathing, an attack of measles, or other cause; if there is present, a variable amount of redness, even in some cases chemosis, *burning, itching or sticking pain in the eye; usually worse in the evening*, when out in the wind, and after reading, but *relieved in the cool open air*. The lachrymation may be profuse by day, with purulent discharge at night, though generally a moderately profuse muco-purulent discharge of a whitish color, and bland character, which agglutinates the lids in the morning, is to be found. Catarrhal conditions of the conjunctiva, dependent upon gastric disturbances, may also require this remedy.

In purulent ophthalmia, benefit will frequently be derived from this drug if the *discharge is profuse and bland*, and the concomitant symptoms also indicate its selection. The form of purulent *ophthalmia found in new-born children* (ophthalmia neonatorum), has been greatly benefited, even in some instances well marked cases have been cured without the use of any other drug. It seems, however, especially useful in this trouble as an intercurrent remedy during the treatment by Argentum nitricum, for often when the improvement is at a stand-still, a few doses of Pulsatilla will materially hasten the progress of the cure.

It has been employed with some success in trachoma, usually uncomplicated with pannus. The granulations are generally very fine; eye sometimes dry or may be bathed in an excessive secretion of bland mucus. There may also be soreness of the ball to touch, and itching or pain in the eye, worse in the evening, and better in the cool air or by cold applications. It is especially adapted to cases occurring in anæmic amenorrhœic females.

Another large class of superficial ophthalmic disorders, in which Pulsatilla is particularly useful, is to be found in scrofulous ophthalmia, phlyctenular conjunctivitis or keratitis. Here it has proved one of our sheet anchors in the treatment, especially *if the pustules are on the conjunctiva.* The dread of light is usually moderate in degree, though may be absent. The lachrymation is not acrid, but more abundant in the open air, while the other discharges may be very moderate or profuse, thick, white or yellow, and bland. The pains are more often of a pressing, stinging character, though vary greatly. The lids may be swollen, but are not excoriated, though *subject to styes.* The eyes feel *worse on getting warm from exercise, or in a warm room,* and generally *in the evening,* but are *relieved in the open air,* and by cold applications. The concomitant symptoms of ear disorders, thirstlessness, gastric derangement, and amenorrhœa, must be taken into consideration.

Pulsatilla has been successfully given in ulcers of the cornea, especially, if superficial and resulting from phlyctenules. Excellent results have also followed its use in those *small ulcers,* which prove so intractable to treatment, occurring *near the center of the cornea,* with no vascular supply, especially, if found in strumous subjects, with phlyctenules on the cornea or conjunctiva. The photophobia and pain are usually considerable in these cases.

In a case of conical cornea occurring in a colored girl, æt. 23, with occasional shooting pain through the right eye, fingers could only be counted at four feet with right eye and ten feet with left eye. Two months afterwards, under Puls.[30], she was able to count fingers at seven feet with the right eye and twenty feet with the left eye.

A case of episcleritis, circumscribed, situated between the superior and external recti muscles, was very promptly relieved by this remedy. It occurred in a man, highly myopic; the sclera was slightly bulged, and some itching-sticking pain in the ball, with dimness of vision. His eyes always felt much better in the open air.

This drug may occasionally be required in idiopathic iritis, especially in young girls with delayed and scanty menstruation. More often indicated in the colored race.

Its influence upon choroideal affections was illustrated in a case of hyperæmia of the choroid consequent upon hyperopia. The patient could not look long at any object; was subject to severe neuralgic headaches extending into the eyes; head felt full and congested; was a great tea drinker. Puls. effected a cure.—T. F. A.

Payr recommends this drug in sub-acute cases of choroiditis in persons subject to arthritis vaga, venous hyperæmia of the capillaries, pressing, tearing and throbbing pain in the head, with heaviness and vertigo, dull sight, photophobia, and fiery circles before the eyes. Females with mild and yielding disposition, scanty and delayed menstruation.

The value of Pulsatilla in hyperæmia and inflammation of the optic nerve and retina is not, I believe, fully appreciated. Its marvellous results and indications for selection are well illustrated in the following cases:—A clerk complained of a sensation, as of a veil before his eyes, especially in the bright light, together with *headache when in the store, relieved in the open air.* V. $\frac{12}{20}$, difficulty. The ophthalmoscope revealed decided injection of the retinal vessels, halo around the macula lutea and hyperæmia of the optic nerve, more marked in the right eye. Within a week, under Puls.[30], the hyperæmic ring around the macula, dimness of vision and headache were relieved.

The second case was of so much interest that it will be given in full as published in *Trans. of Oph. and Otol. Soc.*, 1879. *Neuritis N. O. (choked disc).* Carl H——, æt. 32, barber, applied to me at New York Ophthalmic Hospital November 26th, 1878, on account of loss of sight. Reports that his sight had always been good till five days ago, when it began to fail in his right eye; since then, has been rapidly growing worse, until now can see very little with this eye; within the last twenty-four hours has noticed a blur coming over the left eye. Has not been well for some time; four weeks ago had a "kidney trouble," though cannot tell what it was; also for five weeks has had an almost *constant pain in the forehead, which at times becomes most intense, seeming as if it would drive him crazy. This pain is always much better in the open air.* His appetite is good and he feels well in every other way. He is of a light comlexion and nervous temperament. *Status præsens.* R. V., fingers at four feet. L. V. $\frac{20}{20}$. Nothing abnormal externally. Media clear. R. E.—Optic papilla shows the characteristic appearances of "stauungs papilla;" disc very much swollen, reddish-gray and striated; outlines ill defined; veins engorged, and covered here and there by the exudation. Retina very little involved, and macula lutea apparently normal. L. E.— Similar changes beginning, swelling of nerve entrance, especially of inner two-thirds, veins enlarged, arteries about normal and partially hidden by the swelling. Examination of the urine gave a slight trace of albumen. Heart's action normal. Admitted him to the hospital, put him to bed and gave Bell.[3]

Dec. 3d.—Having found that his headache seemed to be increased while in bed, have allowed him to be up for the past two or three days and take exercise in the open air, which always relieves the severe pain in the head. The vision remains the same, as well as the ophthalmoscopic appearances. R. Puls.[30]

Dec. 5th.—R. V., fingers at ten feet. L. V. $\frac{20}{20}$. Swelling of optic disc decidedly less. Headache has been better, though had a severe attack this morning. Repeat.

Dec. 11th.—Only a very little swelling of nerve entrances. The headache is greatly improved, though seems to be moderately severe every second day. Vision not tested as it was dark when examined. Discharged from hospital. Continue medicine.

Dec. 13th.—R. V. $\frac{20}{30}$. L. V. $\frac{20}{20}$.

Dec. 18th.—R. V. $\frac{20}{40}$. L. V. $\frac{20}{20}$. Only slight haziness around the optic papilla. Continue.

Dec. 30th.—R. V. $\frac{20}{20}$. L. V. $\frac{20}{20}$. Headache only occasionally. No ophthalmoscopic appearances that would lead one to suspect that an engorged papilla had been present.

In a case of immature hard cataract with blurring of the sight, especially in the forenoon, and some conjunctival irritation, the progress was checked and vision improved under Puls.[200]—A. WANSTALL.

Accommodative asthenopia, with much aching sensation in the eyes after using; also darting pains in the eyes after sewing, in asthenopia from general prostration; have been cured. —T. F. A.

RANUNCULUS BULBOSUS.

Sensation of burning soreness in the right lower lid. Smarting and feeling of soreness in the outer canthus of the right eye. Smarting in the eyes. Sore smarting within the right eye. Smarting in the eyes, as from smoke. Violent pressing pains in the eyeballs, at times in one, at times in the other. Painfulness of the right eyeball. Mist before the eyes.

Clinical.—Ranunculus was found indicated in one case of herpes zoster supra-orbitalis, with bluish-black vesicles, high fever and the usual pains accompanying this disease. The success consequent upon the use of the drug was exceedingly brilliant.

RHODODENDRON.

Dilatation of the pupils. Periodical burning in the eyes without inflammation. Burning pain in the eyes; when reading or writing he has a feeling of heat in the eyes.

Clinical.—Very marked and satisfactory results were obtained from Rhod. in the following case:—A man, about 40, complained of gradual failure of sight, accompanied by periodically recurring pains of the most violent character, involving the eyeball, extending to orbit and head, *always worse at the approach of a storm*, and ameliorated when the storm broke out. The patient had a strongly marked rheumatic diathesis, otherwise general good health. On examination, the pupils were noticed to be somewhat dilated and sluggish. T. + 1 in both eyes. Pulsation of the retinal veins, but no excavation of the optic nerve. Field of vision not circumscribed. Hm. $\frac{1}{30}$. Vision improved by glasses, but could not be brought above $\frac{20}{30}$. The ability to use the eyes was greatly improved by convex 36, and afterward by convex 24, but the attacks of pain continued to recur and his vision suffered sensible impairment from every attack. These pains were promptly relieved under Rhod., so that within six months he was entirely relieved of the attacks, though he has continued to keep the medicine by him for several years. His vision has gradually improved, so that it is now fully $\frac{20}{30}$.—T. F. A.

In insufficiency of the internal recti muscles (asthenopia muscularis), benefit has been derived, as was well marked in a case, in which darting pains like arrows through the eye from the head, always worse before a storm, was an accompanying symptom.—T. F. A.

Ciliary neuralgia, in which the *pains are always aggravated before a storm*, will usually be relieved by Rhododendron.

RHUS TOXICODENDRON.

Objective.—*Inflammation of the lids.* A red, hard swelling, like a stye, on the left lower lid, toward the inner canthus, with pressive pain. *Great swelling of the lids.* The eyes are red and agglutinated with matter, in the morning. Relaxation of the eyelids, with puffiness of lids and hot flushed face. *Heaviness and stiffness of the lids, like a paralysis, as if it were difficult to move the lids.* Lachrymation in the evening, with burning pain. Weeping eyes. *Inflammation of the eyes.* The white of the eye is red in the morning, with burning pressure in it.

Subjective.—Drawing and tearing in the region of the brows and in the malar bones. *Very sore around the right eye.* Violent burning, itching and prickling in the swollen eyelids. Burning in the inner canthus of the right eye. Itching in the eyes, on exerting vision. Aching in the eyes. Her left eye felt enormously swollen and enlarged. Pressive pain in the eyes. Pressure as if dust were in the eye. Sharp pains run from the eyes into the head. Biting as from something sharp and acid in the right eye. Biting in the eyes; in the morning the eyes are agglutinated with matter. *When he turns the eye or presses upon it, the eyeball is sore, he can scarcely turn it.*

Vision.—Sensation of a veil before the eyes, she could not see well. Extreme confusion of sight. Great obscurity of vision. Objects were seen double.

Clinical.—The clinical application of this drug in diseases of the eye is extensive and merits careful consideration. It is of value in many ophthalmic disorders, but it seems especially adapted to the severer forms of the inflammatory process, in which there is a great tendency to suppuration, or even when the formation of pus has already taken place.

For *orbital cellulitis*, it is a remedy of the first importance, and will no doubt be oftener called for than any other drug, whatever may be the origin of the trouble (whether traumatic or not), as the picture of the disease corresponds very closely to the symptomatology of the drug, and experience has proven the truth of the assertion that it is *the* remedy for the treatment of this dangerous malady. Some alarming cases of this disease have been promptly arrested by this drug. In one case, one eye was entirely lost and had been operated upon with a view of providing free exit for the suppurative process, and the disease was making alarming and rapid progress in the other eye. Rhus[1] speedily arrested its progress.

Epiphora of long standing, with no apparent stricture of the lachrymal duct, was immediately relieved under Rhus[30].

It will be seen from a study of the symptoms which Rhus produces upon the palpebræ, that its curative power is chiefly exerted upon those symptoms of the lids which are dependent upon inflammation of the deeper structures. However, we may often find it a valuable remedy in uncomplicated blepharitis, especially of the acute form, if there is a tendency to the formation of an abscess and the *lids are œdematously swollen*, accompanied by *profuse lachrymation* and pains which are worse at night and relieved by warm applications.

We also occasionally find it useful in chronic inflammation of the lids, in which there is puffiness of the lids and face, enlargement of the meibomian glands, falling out of the ciliæ, itching and biting in the lids, sensation of dryness of the eyes and burning in the internal canthus, with acrid lachrymation in the morning and in the open air, or as is more commonly the case, constant profuse lachrymation which may be acrid or not.

Simple œdema of the lids has been relieved. (Compare Apis, Ars. and Kali carb.)

In erysipelas of the lids, of spontaneous or traumatic origin, it is a very important aid in the treatment, if there is œdematous erysipelatous swelling of the lids and face, with small watery vesicles scattered over the surface, and drawing pains in the cheek and head.

In any of these cases in which the lids are affected, there is frequently *spasmodic closure with profuse lachrymation upon opening them*, which more than ever points to the employment of Rhus.

Ptosis has been relieved under this remedy; it is probably adapted to that variety caused from exposure to cold or wet (Caust.).

Simple conjunctivitis caused from exposure to wet, or aggravated in damp weather (Calc.), frequently calls for Rhus, especially if there is much *chemosis* with some photophobia, profuse lachrymation and œdematous swelling of the lids.

In severe cases of conjunctivitis granulosa with pannus, the intensity of the symptoms may occasionally be relieved by the use of this remedy, and possibly a cure be effected.

Rhus may in rare cases be found serviceable in ophthalmia neonatorum, if the lids are red, œdematously swollen and spasmodically closed. There will also be restlessness at night and other concomitant symptoms.

In ulcers and pustules of the cornea, Rhus has been often employed with success, especially in the latter and superficial forms of ulceration, in which the *photophobia is very great*, so that the patient lies constantly on the face. *The lachrymation is very profuse, so that the tears gush out on opening the spasmodically closed lids*, which are usually much swollen, especially the upper. The conjunctiva is quite red; *chemosis*. The skin of the face around the eye is often covered with a Rhus eruption. The remedy is especially suitable to persons of a rheumatic diathesis. The symptoms are usually worse at night, after midnight, and in damp weather, therefore the patients are restless at night and disturbed by bad dreams.

Its action, however, is not confined to the superficial variety of keratitis, as great benefit has been observed from its use in *suppuration of the cornea, especially if consequent upon cataract extraction.*

In simple idiopathic or rheumatic iritis, this drug has proved serviceable, especially in those cases resulting from exposure to wet, or if the predisposing cause can be referred to a rheumatic diathesis.

Mydriasis from exposure to cold and dampness, has been relieved by Rhus.

Its grandest sphere of action is to be found in *suppurative iritis*, or in the still more severe cases in which *the inflammatory process has involved the remainder of the uveal tract* (ciliary body and choroid), especially if of traumatic origin as after cataract extraction. As a remedy in this dangerous form of inflammation of the eye it stands unrivalled, no other drug having, as yet, been found equal to it in importance in this serious malady. The symptoms of the drug will be seen to correspond very closely to a great majority of the cases. *The lids are red, swollen and œdematous, especially the upper, and spasmodically closed, with profuse gushes of hot tears upon opening them; sac-like swelling of the conjunctiva* and yellow purulent, mucous discharge; *pain in and around the eye;* swelling of the cheek and surrounding parts, besides the usual concomitant symptoms. For suppurative inflammation of a part or whole of the uveal tract of non-traumatic origin, Rhus has been known to restore the eye "ad integrum;" even if the formation of pus has already taken place, it may cause its absorption. We also think from experience that it serves, to a certain extent, to prevent suppurative inflammation after severe operations upon the eye, though do not by any means consider it a sure preventive.*

---

* NOTE —If most prompt results are not found from the higher potencies in a few hours, the first should be resorted to. This is a most important note to make, for not a moment can be lost in arresting the disease, nor can we afford to produce an aggravation in a sensitive subject with large doses.

In paresis or paralysis of any of the muscles of the eyeball, resulting from rheumatism, exposure to cold or getting the feet wet, this remedy is very useful and should be compared with Causticum in frequency of indication.

The symptomatology of Rhus and Apis are somewhat similar, but the latter is not as frequently indicated in severe inflammations of the deep structures, which tend toward suppuration, as the former. The Apis patient is drowsy and thirstless, while the Rhus patient is restless and thirsty (Arsen.).

Rhus radicans has been employed with great success in scrofulous ophthalmia, in which the same symptoms are present which have been given under Rhus tox.

RUTA GRAVEOLENS.

Cramp in the lower lid, the tarsal cartilage is drawn back and forth, and after this ceases water runs from both eyes for an hour and a half.

Subjective —Pressure deep in the orbits. Pain as from a bruise in the orbicular cartilages. Stitches in the left frontal bone, only while reading. *Pressure over the eye-brow.* Itching in the inner canthi and on the lower lids, that after rubbing became a biting, so that the eye filled with water. Burning beneath the left eye. *Sensation of heat and fire in the eyes, and aching while reading (in the evening, by the light).* Slight pain like a pressure in the right eye, with obscuration of vision, as if one had looked too long and intently at an object, which distressed the eye. Pressure on the inner surface of the left eye, with profuse lachrymation. *The eyes feel fatigued, as after reading too long.* Weary pain in the eyes while reading.

Vision.—*Vision very weak, as if the eyes were excessively strained.* Objects seem dim before the eyes, as if a shadow were flitting before it.

Clinical.—Ruta has been of service in a case of choroiditis in a myope, resulting from over-straining the eyes. There was much pain in the eyes on trying to look at objects, heat in the eye (though it seems cold) and twitching in the eyeballs. —T. F. A.

Under the use of this drug the vision has been restored, in amblyopia dependent upon over-exertion of the eyes in anomalies of refraction, or even when no cause has been apparent.

Its chief value is to be found in the relief of asthenopia, in which it is a remedy of the first importance. It is more often indicated in *weakness of the ciliary muscle* than of the internal recti. Such asthenopic symptoms as heat and *aching* in and *over the eyes*, feeling as if the eyes were balls of fire at night, blurring of the vision, letters seem to run together, and lachrymation, which are caused or always made worse by straining the eyes at fine work or too much reading; are often relieved by a few doses of Ruta.

We must, of course, remember that a great majority of these cases are dependent upon anomalies in the refraction or accommodation, which render the proper selection of glasses absolutely necessary before we can ameliorate the asthenopic symptoms.

In comparing the usual remedies employed in asthenopia, it will be found that Conium and Arg. nitr. are very similar in their action to Ruta; all three are especially called for in accommodative asthenopia. Conium has more photophobia and Arg. nitr. more tendency to catarrhal symptoms than Ruta. The asthenopic symptoms, which Nat. mur. relieves, are more commonly dependent upon muscular asthenopia.

SANGUINARIA.

Redness of the eyes in the morning. Lachrymation. Burning dryness in the eyes. Pain over the eyes. Dilatation of the pupils.

Clinical.—Benefit has been derived from its employment in blepharadenitis, with a feeling of dryness under the upper lid and burning in the edges of the lids, with accumulation of mucus in the eye in the morning.

Acute conjunctivitis, with excessive redness and numerous ecchymoses in the conjunctiva, tending towards trachoma, with moderate discharge and some pain in the eye, has been speedily cured by the local use of Sanguinaria (gtt. x: aq. c. ℥ j).

SECALE CORNUTUM.

Cataracts, both hard and soft. Eyes sunken and surrounded with a blue margin. Dilatation of the pupils. Dimness of vision.

Clinical.—Favorable results were obtained from Secale in a case of suppuration of the cornea, aggravated by warm applications.—C. A. BACON.

The unquestionable production of cataract by this drug, should suggest its use in checking the progress of this disease.

From a study of the general action of Secale it is recommended for retinitis diabetica.

SENEGA.

Weakness of the eyes, with slight burning and lachrymation. Weakness of the eyes when reading, with lachrymation on exerting them too much. When looking at an object intently or permanently, the eyes tremble and run. Aching pain over the orbits. Drawing and pressure in the eyeballs, with diminution of visual power.

Vision.—Weakness of sight and flickering before the eyes when reading, obliging one to wipe them often. Objects look shaded. While reading the eyes feel dazzled ; this makes reading difficult. Flickering before the eyes and weakness of sight, when continuing to read or write. When walking towards the setting sun he seemed to see another smaller sun hover below the other, assuming a somewhat oval shape, when looking down, *disappearing on bending the head backwards and on closing the eyes.* Flickering and running together of letters when reading.

Clinical.—The action of Senega upon the lids is very marked in the provings. This, together with its marked action upon general mucous surfaces, renders its use in catarrhal ophthalmia obvious, as also in blepharitis, in which there is smarting and dry crusts on the lids, especially in the morning.

Very marked improvement was observed from this drug, in an old case of opacities in the vitreous. Within three

11

months the vitreous had cleared to such an extent that the vision had increased from counting fingers at ten feet, to $\frac{10}{70}$, and was still improving under Senega[3].—A. Wanstall.

Senega is of great importance in promoting the *absorption of lens fragments* after cataract operations or injuries to the lens.

In addition to and corresponding with the general muscular laxity, we find remarkable symptoms of paralysis of the muscles of the eye. It has proved most brilliantly curative in paresis of the left oculo-motor nerve, with paralysis of the superior rectus muscle, in which the patient could only see clearly by bending the head backwards, as this position relieved the confusion of double vision which caused him to take missteps. The upper lid was very weak, falling half over the eye; difficult convergence; weak back; deficient muscular power; subject to bilious headaches. Senega[200], a dose every twenty-four hours, was given. Double vision was better in a few days. Cured in a few weeks.—T. F. A.

In paresis of the superior oblique it has also been of decided service.

SEPIA.

Objective. — *Lachrymation, morning and evening.* Lachrymation in the open air. Drooping of the eyelids, with the dull headache. Agglutination of the eyelids. A red herpetic spot on the upper eyelid, scaly and peeling off. *Pustules on the conjunctiva of the left eye.* A swelling in the eyes, burning, and a flow of tears which affords relief. Inflammation of the eyes, with redness of the whites; stitching and pressure therein. Redness of the white of the eye in the morning on awaking, with burning, smarting, and pressure. The eyes feel tired and look injected.

Subjective.—Eyelids heavy, with much frontal pain. Heat and dryness of the margins of the lids. The eyelids pain on awaking as if too heavy. Great itching of the margins of the lids. Both eyes feel heavy and the lids are inclined to close. Pain in the eyes several times, with headache and heat in the eyes. In the evening, after walking in the cold wind, I had a sore, rough, burning feeling in my eyes, aggravated by gaslight and on attempting to read. Eyes feel very sore, as if bruised. Dragging feeling in eyes. Pressure in the right eye, as from a grain of sand, aggravated by rubbing; felt most sensitively when pressing the eyelids together. Pressure in the eyes at night. Great burning and lachrymation of the eyes. Burning in the morning. Eyes hot and dry. Eyes feel like balls of fire, especially the left, which is much injected. A slight burning feeling in the eyes and a desire to close them; they feel sore to touch. Smarting pain in both eyes. *Smarting in the right eye, in the evening*, with inclination of the lids to close against one's wish. The eyes become fatigued from reading and writing. The candlelight fatigues the eyes when reading or writing, by causing a contractive sensation. Cannot bear reflected light from bright objects; annoyed by reflections from bright objects.

Vision.—Vanishing of sight. Vision is impeded by fiery zigzags before the eyes. Fiery sparks before the eyes, with great weakness. Flickering before the eyes when looking into light; he sees a zigzag circle of colors. Many black spots before the eyes. During the menses everything gets black and clouded before the eyes, in the evening, accompanied by great weakness, which passes off when lying.

Clinical.—Sepia is especially adapted to ophthalmic disorders dependent upon uterine troubles, and in prescribing this drug, great reliance should be placed upon these and other accessory symptoms.

The *aggravation morning and evening*, and the amelioration in the middle of the day, are almost always present.

In chronic ciliary blepharitis very favorable results have been obtained from Sepia. In addition to the scaly condition of the lid margin, *small pustules* (acne ciliaris) *will usually be found on the ciliary border* (Ant. crud.). The subjective symptoms will also indicate our choice, as, feeling of heaviness in the lids in the morning, or on waking at night; soreness or numb pain in the internal canthi; and scratching sensation in the eyes, worse at night and at any time during the day, upon

closing the lids, as they feel as if they were too tight and did
not cover the eye. The aggravation of the symptoms morning and evening will usually be noticed.

Tarsal tumors have been benefited by Sepia[30].

Acute catarrhal conjunctivitis, with *drawing sensation* in the
external canthus and smarting in the eyes, ameliorated by
bathing in cold water, and *aggravated morning and evening;* also
conjunctivitis, with muco-purulent discharge in the morning
and great dryness in the evening; have been quickly relieved
under this remedy.

In follicular conjunctivitis, or a mixed form of follicular
and trachomatous conjunctivitis, which is only observed *during the summer,* or always made worse by hot weather, Sepia is
especially indicated. In one case of a lady who had suffered
every summer for twenty years, from the beginning of the
warm weather in the spring, till its close in the fall, with severe
conjunctivitis, much enlargement of the papillæ, and marked
aggravation in the morning and usually in the evening; a
prompt cure resulted under Sepia[30]. It may be serviceable in
trachoma, with or without pannus, especially in tea-drinking
females. It is indicated if there is excessive irritability of the
eye to both use and light, particularly night and morning,
better through the day; lids close in spite of him, and sparks
may be flashing before the eyes.

It is sometimes indicated in phlyctenular conjunctivitis,
though not as frequently as when the cornea is implicated.

For keratitis phlyctenularis, especially in females suffering
from uterine disturbances, Sepia is of great value. The pains
are usually of a drawing, aching, or sticking character, aggravated by rubbing, pressing the lids together, or pressing upon
the eye. The light of day dazzles, and causes the head to ache;
with lachrymation, especially in the open air. The conjunctiva may be swollen, with considerable purulent discharge,
edges of lids raw and sore, and eruption on the face. The
usual time of aggravation is present.

Dr. C. Th. Liebold has used it with very favorable results in
keratitis parenchymatosa, complicated with uterine troubles.

At Dr. W. H. Woodyatt's suggestion, Sepia has been employed in several cases of cataract, especially in women, with manifest advantage, arresting the progress of the disease, and often improving the vision very decidedly. The concomitant symptoms will guide us in the selection of this remedy in diseases of the lens.

A case of astigmatism, resulting from granular lids, in which on reading black seemed gray, with improvement of the vision on looking out under the brows, and pain on using the eyes by artificial light, terminated in recovery under the use of Sepia.—T. F. A.

The asthenopic symptoms dependent upon reflex irritation from the uterus (kopiopia hysterica) will very frequently require this remedy. The indications will be apparent from a study of the verified symptomatology.

SILICEA.

Objective.—*Swelling in the region of the right lachrymal gland and lachrymal sac.* Lachrymation. Agglutination of the eyes at night, with smarting of the lids. Agglutination of the eyes in the morning. Twitching of the eyelids. Redness at first around the eyes, then also of the white of the eyes, with inflammation and lachrymation. Redness of the whites of the eyes. *Ulcer on the left eye.* Eyes weak.

Subjective.—Pressure in the upper lid, with violent stitches, as from a splinter, and vanishing of visual power. The eyes are painful, as if too dry and full of sand, in the morning. Tension in the eyes and forehead, with weakness of the body. Piercing-stinging pain in the left eye. Sudden piercing pain in the left eye. Tearing and burning in the eyes on pressing them together. Heat and smarting in the eyes.

Vision.—Vision indistinct, misty, with flickering before the eyes. She could neither read nor write; everything ran together.

Clinical.—Silicea is more commonly indicated in caries of the orbit, than any one remedy in the materia medica. Its value was very forcibly illustrated in the following case:—A girl, æt. 11, had for four months, a constant discharge and ulceration under the right lower lid, the result of a severe inflammation. Examination showed, over the right inferior orbital ridge, cicatrices which everted the lid, together with three openings, as found over dead bone, discharging a yellow white pus. On probing, caries of the lower orbital arch was found, extending over the malar and superior maxillary bones, and connecting by sinuses with the upper jaw, opening over the first molar tooth, through which opening the discharge escaped into the mouth. Silicea[30] was prescribed. At first occasional injections of a one per cent. solution of carbolic acid was used, but soon discontinued. Under Silicea a cure was effected, leaving only a slight scar which was not adherent, and the lid returned to its normal position.

In diseases of the lachrymal apparatus it is a remedy of prime importance. It is often indicated in inflammation of the lachrymal sac (dacryocystitis), characterized by all the prominent symptoms, swelling, tenderness, pain and lachrymation, especially if the patient takes cold easily or is very sensitive to a draught of air. Several cases, even though so far advanced that suppuration seemed inevitable, have been cured without breaking externally and without the aid of an operation. But, notwithstanding, experience shows how much may be sometimes gained from the administration of Silicea and other remedies, yet we would not advise delay in opening the canaliculus as soon as pus has begun to form.

Blennorrhœa of the lachrymal sac has quite frequently been controlled, and Sil. should be one of the first remedies thought of in connection with this trouble.

The treatment of acute lachrymal fistulæ by Sil. has been attended with favorable results, but chronic cases do not seem to yield to this or any other drug.

Blepharitis, either acute or chronic, caused or aggravated from working in a damp place or from being in the cold air, will often require Silicea (compare Calc.).

It has been useful in tarsal tumors, when indicated by concomitant symptoms.

Silicea is often the remedy for sloughing ulcers of the cornea, with or without hypopyon; for *crescentic ulcers;* for small round ulcers which have a tendency to perforate, and also for non-vascular ulcers centrally located. The pains, photophobia and lachrymation, are not particularly marked. The discharge is frequently very profuse, though it may be moderate in quantity. But there is almost always present in these cases, in fact in the majority of ophthalmic disorders which call for Silicea, a *great sensitiveness to cold and desire to be warmly wrapped, especially about the head.*

For hypopyon it is especially valuable.

The following case of sclero-choroiditis ant. was effectually relieved by this remedy: The conjunctiva and sclera were both injected, and a bluish irregular bulging around the cornea was present. The retina was hazy though no opacities were visible in vitreous. There were severe pains extending from the eyes into the head, relieved by warmth, also a severe aching in the back of the head on one side, corresponding to that eye which was worse; the severity of the symptoms alternated from one eye to the other.—T. F. A.

It has also proved useful in choroiditis in a myope, in whom upon any exertion of the eye, excessive pain extended to the head and ears.—T. F. A.

Irido-choroiditis, with great tenderness of the eye to touch, deep ciliary injection, contraction of the pupil, posterior synechiæ and excessive sensitiveness to a draught of air, will be found amenable to Silicea.

Many brilliant cures of cataract under this remedy are reported, though grave doubts are entertained regarding the correctness of the diagnosis. It may be serviceable, however, in checking the progress of cataract when indicated by concomitant symptoms, upon which chief reliance is placed in prescribing for diseases of the lens.

Ciliary neuralgia, characterized by *darting pains through the eyes and head upon exposure to any draught of air*, or just before a storm, has been speedily relieved by Silicea.

Silicea and Hepar should be compared with each other, as their actions are very similar. Both are indicated in ulcerations, are relieved by warmth and aggravated by cold. The ulceration of Hepar is, however, usually accompanied by more pain, redness, photophobia and sensitiveness to touch than that of Silicea.

SPIGELIA.

Objective.—Lids lax and paralyzed; they hang low down and must be raised with the hand, with dilated pupils. Redness and inflammation of the white of the eye; in the morning the lids are so heavy that he can scarcely·open them. Redness of the white of the eye. Lachrymation.

Subjective —Pain as if the upper lid were hard or immovable; he cannot raise it easily. Fine painful cutting on the margin of the left lower lid, like a knife. Sticking pressure under both lids. Pain as if the left orbit were pressed from above downward. *Tensive tearing pain in the forehead, especially beneath the left frontal eminence, extending towards the orbits. Thrust-like tearing pain in the forehead, worse in the right frontal eminence. A shoot of pain through the forehead. Burning pain in the right side of the forehead, extending to the eye, so that he could not turn it without pain. The eyes hurt on motion, as if too large for their orbits.* He could not turn the eyes in all directions without pain. *Violent burrowing stitch in the middle of the eye* and inner canthus, that does not prevent vision, but presses the upper lid downward. *Intolerable pressive pain in the eyeballs, still more painful on turning the eyes; on attempting to look with the eyes turned he became dizzy, so that he was obliged to turn the whole head.* Pressive pain in the eyeballs. A contractive burning pain in the right eyeball. *Constant sticking pain in the right eyeball, also on moving it.* Itching stitch in the right eyeball, that returned after rubbing.

Clinical.—Spigelia is especially applicable to severe neuralgic pains, arising in a great variety of ophthalmic troubles, particularly in rheumatic and arthritic inflammations. In all cases the character and intensity of the pains furnish the chief indications for the selection of this remedy.

Ptosis, as one would be led to suppose from the symptomatology, should often require the use of Spigelia. A case, occurring in a seamstress, after inflammation, with sharp stabbing pains through the eyes and head, and much hot, scalding lachrymation, was very favorably affected by its use. —T. F. A.

It is not a remedy which we would be liable to think of in inflammatory diseases of the conjunctiva or cornea, still it has been found beneficial in exceptional cases when accompanied by the characteristic sharp pains. Even in ulcers of the cornea, with considerable infiltration into the cornea around the ulcer, its employment has been followed by brilliant results, providing *shooting, radiating pains from the eyes into the head*, usually worse at night, have been present.

Excellent results have been obtained from this drug in iritis, especially in the rheumatic form, with severe pains around and deep in the eye. The following case will illustrate its action:—J. M., æt. 51, had suffered from rheumatic iritis in the left eye, with excessive ciliary neuralgia, for three weeks. There was much redness, deep ciliary injection and posterior synechiæ, with violent pain from 3 A.M. for two or three hours, continuing more or less until 3 P.M. Atropine was used externally and Sulphur internally. The adhesions were torn and the pain relieved on the first night. On the second night, although the pupil was widely dilated, the pain returned more severely than ever. The pain was as if the eye were being pulled forward and backward, with numb pain through the head, which woke him at 2 A.M. and continued the remainder of the night and all the forenoon; it seemed as if it would drive him crazy. Each attack of pain was accompanied by a chill. No change was made in the Atropine, but Spigelia[200] was prescribed, internally. There was only a little pain at about noon the next day, none afterwards, and within five days the eye was perfectly well.

The pains of glaucoma may indicate this remedy. Benefit has also been derived from its use in sclero-choroiditis accompanied by much pain.

In accommodative asthenopia, with slight retinitis and severe neuralgic headaches; also in asthenopia, with anæmia of the optic nerve and characteristic pains, dependent upon too great indulgence in tea; great benefit has been obtained from Spigelia.

It is, however, in ciliary neuralgia, intermittent or not intermittent, dependent upon some observable disease or arising
from some cause unknown, that the greatest power of Spig. is
exercised. The pains are various in character, though usually
sharp and stabbing, like a knife sticking through the ball back into
the head, or they may seem to start from one point and then radiate
in different directions; are generally aggravated by motion and at
night. The following variety of pains, as described by patients,
have been cured by Spigelia, in addition to those already
given : Pains around and deep in the eye. Severe pain on
moving the eyes, worse at night. Severe pressure extending
to the orbit after sleep, or as if the eye would ulcerate. Very
severe sharp pain in and around the left eye, seems as if it
would drive him crazy, wakes him at 3 A.M. and continues the
remainder of the night; also has a similar attack in the latter
part of the forenoon, always accompanied by fever and sweat.
Sharp pains through the right eye and corresponding side of
head, worse at night and relieved by warmth, accompanied by
excessive sensitiveness of the eyeball to touch. Burning or
sticking pains in the eye, and sensation as if the eyeball were
too large. Burning pains going to the bones. Sticking, boring pains extending to the bones around the eyes, especially
supra-orbital and temporal regions. Eye feels too large and
as if forcibly turned around in the orbit; the pain makes one
shut the eye, and on opening it, seem to see a sea of fire; with
the severe pain, hot tears run out of the eye, and the pains are
worse in the open air and at night. After long continued use
of the eyes, terrible pains every morning at six in the left eye,
as if the ball were too large and was forcibly pressed out of
the orbit, with violent aching, boring and severe stitches,
made worse by opening and moving the eye, often extending
to the forehead. The slightest touch excites the pains, which
disappear about noon. Severe boring pain deep in the eye,
aggravated on moving it; parts around the eye painful to
touch, and sparks before the vision. Sharp sticking pains
through the ball of the eye into the head on the right side,
worse at night; frontal headache and frequent winking.
Intolerable pain in the supra-ciliary ridge, worse on any

change of weather and in the wind. Severe pressing, jerking, sticking pains in the left eye, so hard as to cause her to cry out and lose consciousness; every few minutes they would extend to the muscles of the left upper arm.

SPONGIA.

Clinical.—The chief use which has been made of Spongia in ophthalmic therapeutics has been in Basedow's disease, as the following case will illustrate:—A woman, about 40. Eyeballs staring and perceptibly protruding; stitches in the balls and burning around the eyes, with lachrymation worse from any sudden light; often the eye feels as if twisted around; there is constant flashing of different colors, mostly deep red, figures of light, etc., even when the eye is closed, especially at night. The thyroid gland is considerably hypertrophied. The palpitation of the heart is very marked, which makes her uneasy, restless and easily frightened, especially at night. Spongia in the higher potencies effected a cure.—T. F. A.

SQUILLA.

The eyes seem swimming in cold water.

Clinical.—A man, 25 years of age, had been troubled with a large phlyctenule of the conjunctiva on the outer side of the cornea, for two weeks. He complained of a sensation as of cold water in the eye, whenever in a cold wind. Squilla[200] cured the phlyctenule and relieved the above sensation within two days.—Chas. Deady.

STANNUM.

Pustular swelling of the left inner canthus.

Pressure in the left inner canthus, as from a stye, with lachrymation. Itching in the inner canthus.

Clinical.—Ptosis from sympathetic paralysis, in which the disease returned every Tuesday, was cured by Stannum.—J. A. Campbell.

Stannum, first employed by Drs. Liebold and Hunt in blennorrhœa of the lachrymal sac, has now become one of our
most common remedies for this affection. It is often used
with advantage in controlling the profuse yellow-white discharge observed in this condition. There may be a tendency
to a more active form of inflammation, especially towards
night, and accompanied by sharp pain in the internal canthus.

STAPHYSAGRIA.

Subjective —Pain as if a hard substance were lying beneath
the left upper lid. Pressure in the upper lid all day, worse on
closing the eye. Itching on the margin of the upper lid in the
open air. *Itching of the margins of the lids.* Dryness of the
eyes. The eyes are dry in the morning on waking. The eyes
are dry in the evening, with pressure in them.

Clinical.—The clinical application of Staphysagria has been
chiefly confined to the lids. The form of blepharitis to which
it is adapted is characterized by dryness of the margins of the
lids, small hard nodules on the ciliary border and destruction
of the hair follicles, with much itching of the margins of the
lids.

Its greatest usefulness is in tarsal tumors, in which it is
quite commonly employed, as when the glands of the lids are
enlarged, with redness and tensive tearing pains, especially in
the evening, or more particularly if *little hard nodules are found
on the lids, resulting from styes,* also if crops of small tarsal tumors are constantly recurring.

Syphilitic iritis, with bursting pain in the eyeball, temple,
and side of face, worse from evening to morning and upon
using the eyes by any light, was promptly relieved by this
drug.—C. A. Bacon.

SULPHUR.

Objective.—An inflamed pimple above the left eyebrow.
Lachrymation in the morning, followed by dryness. Lachry-

mation and burning, in the morning. Swelling and pain in the eyelids, with lachrymation. Redness of the eyelids and conjunctiva. Eruption of pimples on the upper lid. *Aggluti-nated eyes, in the morning* (after burning, in the evening). Jerking in the lids. Eyes sunken, surrounded by blue rings. *Redness of the eyes during the day; violent itching in them in the evening.* A white vesicle on the white of the eye, close to the cornea. Much matter in the eye, in the morning. Purulent mucus in the eyes. Heaviness of the eyes. Dryness of the eyes.

Subjective.—*Much itching in the eyebrows* and in the tip of the nose. *Dryness of the inner surface of the lids.* Pressure in the eyelids in the evening. *Burning of the lids,* which are inflamed and red and tense on motion. Burning of the eyelids externally. Sticking and burning in the outer canthi. Burning in the edges of the lids, in the morning; cutting-burning pains in the borders of the eyelids, and especially in the external canthi, after dinner; very distressing burning in the outer canthi, and on shutting the eyes, a sensation as of a foreign body between the edges of the lids towards their external commissure, in the evening. In the forenoon, some burning on the edges of the lids. Smarting sore pain on the inner side of the lids after midnight, followed by a sensation of a rubbing dryness upon the inner surfaces. *Smarting pain as from dryness of the margins of the lids.* Smarting of the lids; inclination to rub them; the eyes can hardly bear the light in the evening. In the morning, slight sensitiveness of the edges of the lids. Rubbing, dry sensation (like sand) in the mucous surface of the eyelids. In the morning, on awaking, feeling of sand in the eyes, with raw pain on rubbing them. *In the morning, after awaking, painful rubbing dry feeling* in the borders of the right eyelids. *Itching of the eyelids, as if they would become inflamed.* Itching of the lids, obliging him to rest them every moment, in the afternoon; the eyes can scarcely endure the light at all in the evening. *Itching and burning of the lids, which are red and swollen in the morning.* Frequent itching, burning and smarting in the canthi, making him rub them. Itching in eyelids and burning in eyes. In the morning after awaking, itching, smarting, or feeling as of fine sand in the eyes. A sensation of prickling in both eyelids, causing him to scratch and rub them. In the afternoon, itching, burning and redness of the edges of the lids. Itching on the borders of the eyelids.

The eyeballs are painful on moving them. Pressure in the eyeballs on walking, in the open air. In the evening, dull aching and feeling of weight in both eyeballs, with loss of vision, as if a thick veil were before the eyes. Pain as from dryness of the eyeballs, and a sensation as if they rubbed against the lids.

Burning in the eyes, especially toward the external canthi, at various times of day. Burning and easy fatigue of eyes when reading. Burning of the eyes, without redness. *Burning of the eyes, with great sensitiveness to daylight.* Burning and pressure in the eyes; in the morning they were agglutinated and the whole face swollen. *Burning in the eyes, with redness of them. In the afternoon burning shooting beneath the lids of the left eye, as though sand had got into it.* Sensitiveness and burning in the eyes. Burning in eyes and feet. In the evening troublesome feeling of heat in the eyes. Burning heat in the eyes. Painful smarting of the eyes. Sensation of foreign body in the eyes. Sensation as if an inflammation of the eye were about to come on; in the morning on awaking, prickling, causing him to scratch; itching and smarting in the lids. *Violent pains in the left eye, as if it were rubbed against spiculæ of glass, and drawn in towards the pupil; he was obliged to close the eye five or six times involuntarily; this was followed by burning in the eye and flow of tears. Severe cutting in right eye.* Shooting in the left eye, preventing him from reading for several days; when he attempts to read he gets, immediately, violent *shooting pains* through the middle of the pupil deep into the eye. Biting of the eyes and lachrymation, every evening. A feeling as of sand in the eyes. *Stitches as with a knife in the right eye.* Itching and burning of the eyes.

Vision.—Dimness of vision, as from a fog, with the headache. Dimness of vision of both eyes, with great sensitiveness to bright daylight; great dimness of vision (on reading), as if the cornea had lost its transparency; at the same time a feeling of dryness (as from fine sand) between the eyelids. Dimness of vision and weakness of both eyes, with innumerable confused dark spots floating before the eyes. Since commencing my proving of Sulphur, I have observed a considerable weakness of vision and very often a feeling of heaviness and aching in the eyeballs; when reading or writing. I often feel as if a mist were before the eyes; I must cover the eyes with the hand, slightly press and rub them in order to read. *Sensation of a veil before the eyes, and dim vision for near and distant objects. Sensitiveness of the eyes to daylight.* Vision as through a veil. *Intolerance of sunlight.* Obscuration of vision while reading. Objects seem more distant than they really are. *Flickering before the eyes. Dark points and spots before the eyes.* Black flies seem to float not far from the eyes.

Clinical.—The clinical application of Sulphur in diseases of the eye has been more varied than that of any other remedy, though it will be seen that its sphere of action is usually well marked.

In blennorrhœa of the lachrymal sac it may be of service, though is not often indicated.

Blepharitis, particularly the chronic form, quite frequently calls for this drug, especially if occurring in children of a strumous diathesis, who are irritable and cross by day, and *restless and feverish by night.* The lids are swollen, red and agglutinated in the morning, or there may be numerous small itching pustules on the margins of the lids. There may be itching, biting, burning or sensation as if sand were in the eye, though the pains are usually of a sticking character. There is generally great aversion to water, so cannot bear to have the eyes washed. It is especially useful if the blepharitis appears after the suppression of an eruption, or if the child or adult is already covered with eczema.

Eczematous affections of the lids have been often controlled, when Sulph. has been given according to the indications for eczema in other portions of the body.

It has been of service in preventing the recurrence of successive crops of styes, and in accelerating the absorption, in some cases, of tarsal tumors.

In conjunctivitis catarrhalis, both acute and chronic, this remedy is often very useful. The degree of redness may vary greatly, be confined to one eye or involve both. The lids may be swollen, even puffy, or remain unaffected. But the *sharp darting pains, like pins sticking into the eye*, will furnish our chief indications (these pains are characteristic of the drug and may occur at any time of the day or night). There may also be pressing, tensive, cutting or burning pains, feeling as of sand in the eyes, tearing in the head, poor appetite and feverishness at night, with chills during the day.

Acute and chronic trachoma has been benefited by Sulphur. It is often called for as an intercurrent remedy, even if it does not complete the cure alone, especially if the pains are *sharp and sticking* in the morning and the lids are glued together so that it is with the greatest difficulty they can be opened. Water is not a favorite application and usually aggravates the trouble.

Sulphur has been employed with success in ophthalmia neonatorum, especially in chronic cases which have a great tendency to relapse.

It is, however, the remedy "par excellence" for pustular inflammation of the cornea or conjunctiva. As its sphere of action is very wide, it is adapted to a great variety of cases, especially if chronic, and occurring in scrofulous children covered with eruptions (among which the majority of these cases are found), or if the cause can be traced to the suppression of an eruption by external applications. The character of the pains may vary, though they are usually *sharp and sticking, as if a needle or splinter were sticking into the eye, or there may be a sharp, shooting pain going through the eye back into the head, from one to three A. M.*, awaking him from sleep; although besides these we have a variety of other sensations, such as smarting, itching and burning in the eyes, a feeling of pressure as from a foreign body, stinging burning in the eye especially from light and in the morning, burning as from lime, biting as if salt were in the eye, sensation as if there were a number of little burning sparks on the lids, which cause them to spasmodically close, painful dryness as if the lids rubbed the eye-

balls, bruised pain, etc., etc. The photophobia is generally
very marked and the lachrymation profuse, though in some
cases they may be almost or entirely absent. The redness varies greatly, but is usually considerable, especially at the angles.
The secretions also vary both in quantity and quality, being
often, however, acrid, corrosive and sometimes tenacious. Agglutination in the morning is commonly present. The lids
are often swollen ; burn and smart as if bathed in some acrid
fluid, or there is an itching sensation, compelling the patient
to rub them most of the time. The lids, as well as the surrounding integument of the head and face, are frequently covered with an eruption. All the symptoms are, as a rule, made
worse by bathing the eyes, so that the child cannot bear to have
any water touch them. Open air, especially on first going out,
usually aggravates.

The value of Sulphur in the treatment of ulcers and abscesses of the cornea is hardly less than in pustular inflammation. Its usefulness is not confined to any one species of
ulcer, as it has cured not only the *superficial variety*, but also
the deep sloughing form which tends towards perforation and
destruction of the whole cornea. In fact it should always be
thought of in ulceration or abscess of the cornea with hypopyon, especially if of an indolent type, with no photophobia
nor vascularity; as it has often produced absorption of the pus,
and exercised a beneficial influence over the destructive process going on in the cornea. The indications which lead us
to its selection are derived chiefly from the general condition
of the patient, while the eye symptoms are the same as those
given above for the phlyctenular form of inflammation, except
that in severe cases the pains may be more intense. There
may be severe pressing pains in the eye, besides the characteristic stitches. The other symptoms may also be proportion-
ately increased.

Pannus, resulting from various causes and occurring in patients of a strumous diathesis, has been frequently cured under
this remedy. In some instances there has been true pannus
crassum, the whole of the cornea presenting the appearance of
a piece of fresh raw beef, and yet vision has been restored by

12

the internal administration of Sulphur. It is especially useful in the so-called herpetic pannus, resulting from phlyctenular inflammation.

A case of keratitis parenchymatosa in a scrofulous subject; cornea like ground glass, photophobia, lids swollen and bleeding easily; was permanently relieved by this remedy. It will often be found to promote absorption of the infiltration, after the disease has been checked by other remedies.

In severe forms of inflammation of the cornea, the iris not unfrequently becomes involved (kerato-iritis), though this does not by any means contra-indicate the use of Sulph., even if hypopyon be present.

It has been employed with favorable results in inflammation of the sclera, with corneal and iritic complications, as well as in uncomplicated cases. There may be, in addition to the well known objective symptoms, only a feeling of fullness and largeness of the eyeball, worse from use or exposure to light, especially gaslight, or there may be great photophobia, acrid lachrymation and severe tearing pains in the supra-orbital and temporal regions, as well as in the eye itself, especially worse in the evening and at night, (Merc.).

In iritis, both idiopathic and syphilitic (especially the former), benefit has occasionally been derived from the use of this remedy, though it is not frequently indicated. It is especially adapted to chronic cases marked somewhat by drawing pains around the eye, but chiefly by *sharp, sticking pains* in the eyes, worse at night (Spig.) and towards morning. The eyeballs may be painful on motion, and the usual characteristic symptoms are present. It may be of service after iritis, in promoting the absorption of recent adhesions (posterior synechiae).

The hypopyon resulting from iritis, or in fact, pus found in the anterior chamber under any circumstances, will frequently disappear after the administration of a few doses of Sulphur. (Compare Hepar and Sil.)

Benefit has been derived from the use of Sulphur in inflammatory affections of the fundus. It has been successfully employed in chorio-retinitis and uncomplicated choroiditis, if accompanied by *darting pains*, and in one case in which hemer-

alopia was present. It is not, however, a frequently indicated remedy in any of the acute forms of intra-ocular disease,
though is sometimes useful, especially as an intercurrent; it
is particularly called for in chronic cases. Payr says, regarding its use in choroiditis, that it is frequently indicated in the
chronic form, especially when the trouble is based upon ab-
dominal venosity, stagnation in the portal circulation, habitual
constipation and cerebral congestion occasioned thereby; also .
in metastases of chronic or suppressed skin diseases.

Retinitis caused from over-study, with much congestion of
the optic nerve, outlines ill-defined and accompanied by pain
around the eye and itching in the internal canthi, has been
cured.—T. F. A.

Sulphur often acts very promptly in clearing up opacities
in the vitreous, resulting from choroideal exudations and old
hemorrhages.

The following case of sympathetic irritation of the right eye,
occurring in a young lady, was speedily relieved: The left eye
had been removed six months previous, on account of extensive staphylomatous bulging of the whole eye, by abscising
the cornea and evacuating the contents of the globe, thus leaving only the sclera and muscles intact. She now appeared,
complaining of sharp pain in the stump, extending in stitches
to the healthy eye in which there was considerable irritation
and photophobia, occasional obscuration of vision and commencing presbyopia. There was constant discharge from the
old stump, which was excessively sensitive to touch. Sulph.[200]
relieved in a few days.

Asthenopia, both muscular and accommodative, has been
occasionally benefited by Sulphur, when the character of the
pains has pointed to its selection. "Gaslight hurts more than
sunlight," a symptom not rarely found in these cases, has been
relieved.

Benefit was derived from this remedy in the following case
of paresis of the right nervus abducens:—A woman, æt. 40, had,
for three months, been troubled with double images to the
right and downward. There was no perceptible diminution
in the movements of the eye, and no cause for the paresis was

apparent. There was some pain in the eye on looking upwards; some headache, and restlessness at night. Various remedies were used for two months with no avail. Under Sulph.[30], a cure resulted in three weeks.

The *iodide of sulphur* has occasionally been employed in ophthalmic diseases with marked success, especially in strumous subjects with enlarged glands.

SYPHILINUM.

Clinical.—Very marked success has attended the use of this remedy in some cases of chronic recurrent phlyctenular inflammation of the cornea. When indicated, successive crops of phlyctenules and abrasion of the epithelial layer of the cornea will be found; the photophobia will be intense and the lachrymation profuse; the redness and pain will vary but will be usually well marked. It is indicated in delicate scrofulous children, especially if any trace of hereditary syphilis can be discovered.

TABACUM.

Clinical.—The following case consequent upon the use of tobacco may prove interesting:—The patient was amblyopic, vision $\frac{20}{100}$, refraction normal, divergence of one and a half lines behind a screen, diplopia in the distance. On leaving off tobacco for a time he improved and saw single, but within ten minutes after returning to its use the vision became dim, black spots floated before the eyes and he saw double. Stimulants only aggravated the difficulty.

(See cure of tobacco amaurosis under Nux v.)

TELLURIUM.

Clinical.—Tellurium has proved successful in conjunctivitis pustulosa, with eczema impetiginoides on the lids and much purulent discharge from the eyes, also an offensive discharge from the ear, to which the child was subject.

It is probably more often indicated in scrofulous ophthalmia than we are now led to suppose.

The offensive otorrhœa, smelling like fish-brine, is an important concomitant symptom.

TEREBINTHINA.

Clinical.—Terebinth is constantly assuming more and more importance as an ophthalmic remedy. Its eye symptomatology according to physiological provings furnishes no idea of its sphere of action, as all its clinical verifications have been obtained from prescriptions based upon characteristic constitutional symptoms.

In a comparatively rare form of ciliary neuralgia, with acute conjunctivitis, Terebinth is the remedy most frequently indicated. The injection of the conjunctiva is variable, sometimes being excessive and again very moderate, amounting to hardly more than a simple hyperæmia, but at no time commensurate with the severity of the pain. The redness is usually dark, especially in the later stages, though during the height of the inflammation may be bright. There may be chemosis and even infiltration into the cellular tissue of the orbit. Deep ciliary injection, swelling of the lids, photophobia and lachrymation may be present. The pupil is contracted, but dilates regularly, though slowly, under Atropine. The tension is changeable even within a short time, though is more frequently diminished than otherwise. The eyeball is sensitive to touch. The *pain is excessive* and always present; varies in character from a dull "grumbling," aching, beating sore pain to a severe, sharp, darting pain seeming as if it would almost drive the patient crazy; not only involves the eyeball, but is especially severe *over* and around the eye, extending through to occiput on corresponding side of the head, often following the course of the supra-orbital nerve; is always *worse at night*, and is frequently accompanied by severe paroxysms, particularly in the early morning hours (1 to 3 A.M.).. The corresponding side of the face is flushed. General disturbances will accompany the above, especially *scanty and high-*

colored urine, with pain in the back, which is always present when Terebinth is indicated. (Compare Amyl nitrit.)

A man, about 40 years of age, had been suffering from episcleritis in left eye for over three weeks. The eye was very red, especially at inner side of the cornea where there was a hard bluish-red elevation. *The pain in the eye and corresponding side of the head was intense, day and night.* The pupil reacted well. The urine was very dark. Atropine and various remedies of both schools had failed to relieve. Terebinth[1] relieved the pain in a few hours and a complete cure resulted in less than a week.

This remedy, first employed in iritis by Dr. Liebold, has proved a valuable remedy, especially in rheumatic iritis. The pains will be intense and the characteristic urinary symptoms —frequent desire, pressure and pain in the kidneys, burning in the urethra and dark urine—will be present. Also called for if there is a suppression of habitual transpiration of the feet.

Recent adhesions of the iris to the lens (posterior synechiæ) have also seemed to yield under its use.

The following interesting case shows that it may be useful in amblyopia potatorum :—"Mr. S., æt. 37 years; first seen August 17th, 1876. He had been intemperate for ten years or more. Eight weeks before consulting me, his sight began to grow dim. There was an almost constant, dull, aching pain in the region of the kidneys; urine dark colored and loaded with acid phosphates, sp. grav. 1028. On examination I found vision $\frac{5}{70}$ in both eyes; fundus normal in appearance. R. Nux. vom.[3]; continued it for two weeks with no benefit; then Terebinth[2] was given, a dose three times a day. Under this remedy, which was continued four weeks, all pain in the back ceased, the urine became normal in appearance and vision was restored, being $\frac{20}{20}$. Although the patient has only partially given up drinking there has been no return of the difficulty."—W. P. Fowler.

THUJA.

Objective.—Agglutination of the lids at night. Pimple on the margin of lower lid. Stye on the right eye. The white of the eye is very much inflamed and red. Weak eyes, pressure as from fine sand in them.

Subjective.—Tearing pain in the left eyebrow, disappearing after touch. Feeling as if the eyelids were swollen and a foreign body were in the eye. Burning and stinging in the edges of the eyelids in the evening. Feeling of dryness in the eyes. Feeling of sand in the eyes. Burning of the eyes. Burning and stinging in both eyes and eyelids, with injection of the cornea. Pressure in the eyes. A painful stitch through the centre of the left eye, commencing in the centre of the brain.

Vision.—Dimness of vision like a mist before the eyes, and pressure in them, as if they would be pressed out of the head, or as if they were swollen. Dimness of vision in the open air, like a veil, for near and distant objects, with confusion of the head for half an hour. The vision seems dim, with a feeling as if something were before the eyes. Muscæ volitantes. Great flickering before the eyes. Seeing of a luminous disk, shining like a firefly.

Clinical.—No remedy is more frequently indicated in *tarsal tumors* than Thuja, especially for verucæ and tumors that resemble small condylomata, though it is also useful in other varieties, not only in preventing their return after removal by the knife but in promoting their absorption without the employment of instrumental means. This can sometimes be done by simply using the drug internally, though it usually seems to act more rapidly if employed in the tincture externally at the same time.

"In two cases of what appeared undoubted epithelioma of the left lower eyelid, one of eight months, the other of three years standing, there was complete recovery under Thuja locally and internally."—C. M. Thomas.

Conjunctivitis trachomatosa, in which the granulations are large, like warts or blisters, with burning in the lids and eyes, worse at night, photophobia by day and suffusion of the eye with tears, would lead us to give Thuja with favorable results.

In chronic cases of large phlyctenules of the conjunctiva, which are very slow in progress, unyielding to treatment and which decidedly involve the sub-conjunctival tissue, Thuja will often be found to be the remedy.

It has occasionally been of service in inflammations of the cornea, especially in ulcerations of a syphilitic origin, even if hypopyon is present.

The action of Thuja upon the sclera is very marked indeed, probably more so than any other drug. It has been employed with excellent success in *episcleritis, scleritis,* sclero-choroiditis ant. and commencing scleral staphyloma, even when no characteristic indications were present. There will, however, usually be sensitiveness of the eyeball to touch and aching pain in and over the eye, with some heat. In some cases warmth relieves.

For syphilitic iritis, with *gummata on the iris*, it is a grand remedy. The pains are usually severe, sharp and sticking in the eye, worse at night, with *much heat* above and around the eye, or there may be a pain in the left frontal eminence, as if a nail were being driven in; in some cases the pain is described as a dull aching in the eye, and sometimes seems to be relieved in the open air.

Exophthalmus consequent upon a tumor behind the eyeball, has been relieved.—T. F. A.

In a case of amblyopia, with blurring of the vision, relieved by rubbing (Euphras.), black spots and bright sparks before the eyes, and dull aching above the eye to the back of the head, with nausea, the vision was restored by this remedy.—T. F. A.

The following symptom of vision was relieved by Thuya: "Flames of light before the eyes, mostly yellow."—T. F. A.

VERATRUM VIRIDE.

Subjective.—Aching in the upper part of the right orbit· Full, pressing, heavy feeling in eyes, with slight headache.

Severe shooting, suddenly-stopping pain in left eye. Pupils dilated.

Vision.—Dimness of sight. Cannot walk; if I attempt it, I am very faint and completely blind. Photophobia and vertigo, relieved by closing eyes and resting head. If I assumed the erect position for even a minute, dimness of sight and partial syncope supervened. Unsteady vision.

Clinical.—In erysipelatous inflammation of the lids, face and head, especially if of traumatic origin, Veratrum viride, as recommended by Dr. Liebold, has proved of great value. It is usually used locally as well as internally.

From the experience of Dr. D. J. McGuire it seems that Veratrum viride must be an important remedy in a certain class of ocular diseases; and, as the following cases are of such marked interest in illustrating the sphere of action of this remedy, they are given in full as reported to me by the doctor.

Case I. "April 14th, 1879. Mrs. ——, æt. 32, never had any previous eye trouble. Vision good for all distances. Has always suffered from dysmenorrhœa, with severe cephalalgia just before or after menstrual period, and for the last six years occasional epileptiform convulsions. All of which symptoms were interrupted during her only pregnancy and the subsequent period of lactation. The child died when nine months old, and with the reestablishment of the menstrual function, occurred the dysmenorrhœa, head pains and convulsions; the latter being more frequent than ever. The eye history as revealed at first visit was as follows: Eight weeks ago, sudden complete loss of qualitative vision of right eye, with contracted pupil; vision of left eye being only slightly disturbed. There was no pain or uneasiness until two days after the loss of vision was observed, when she had a severe attack of cephalalgia lasting one week, with unconsciousness, fainting and vomiting; objects appearing like balls of fire before the eyes. Had a subsequent similar attack three weeks later. Since which time has had aching pains in one or the other eye constantly, increased in the evening to sharp pains; also the appearances of stars, flashes of fire, etc. L. V. $\frac{15}{30}$. R. V. perception of light. The ophthalmoscope revealed a circumscribed patch of choroiditis (with beginning atrophy) about two and one half lines in diameter, situated some three lines externally from macula, with a strip of red elevated tissue extending up to and evidently involving the macula (thus causing the sudden loss of vision). The patient came under my care at menstrual period, at close of which she had the usual attack of head pain beginning at orbital regions and gradually extending backwards to base and cord. After a few hours there was marked opisthotonos, and the surface of limbs and body became highly hyperæsthetic, consecutively from above downward, following the course of the pain. A few hours later these parts became markedly anæsthetic. The muscles also showed decided atrophic changes, becoming soft and attenuated, particularly marked in those of the extremities; so much so, in fact, that it was more than three weeks before the patient could stand alone. Bell., Cimicif., Arn., Nux vom., were of no avail. The next monthly period presented the usual phases. Six hours after the headache began I saw her. The opisthotonos was already quite marked, and considerable hyperæsthesia existed. R. Veratrum viride, five drops in glass half full of water; dessertspoonful every half hour, until an impression was made. The patient remarked a sense of relief before the second dose was given, and five hours later, when I called, the patient was lying quietly, and almost free from pain. There was, however, well marked anæsthesia, less than in previous attacks, followed by wasting in muscles and inability to walk unaided for the next ten days. I may here add that the pulse at my first visit during this attack—and I believe it to have been a characteristic one for that stage—was feeble, that is about sixty per minute in frequency, soft and compressible, but under the Veratr. rapidly improved in character. The next attack followed the next menstruation, but the remedy was given at the beginning, with the effect of aborting it entirely. Subsequent attacks were controlled by the early administration of the remedy. The medicine was also given for from one to three weeks following these periods, in attenuations ranging from the 1st dec. to the 200th. August 14. R. V. $\frac{15}{30}$. L. V. $\frac{13}{15}$. Reads Snellen No. 4. R. E. p. 7″, r. 13″. L. E. p. 7″, r. 18″. The vision has, of course, reached this point by gradual stages, which I have not thought necessary to follow here. The patient now returned to her home, several hundred miles distant, but reports that she has had no return of the headaches or convulsions, and no longer suffers from dysmenorrhœa. The vision remained good, and probably improved over the above test.

Remarks.—The known influence (physiological) which this remedy exerts over the vaso-motor function, and the clinical results obtained in pelvic cellulitis[*] first led me to consider it in this class of cases, believing that the eye trouble was the result of sympathetic influence. In addition it will be found that the remedy corresponded very closely symptomatically with this case."

Case II. "Mrs. ——, æt. 21, brunette, always had good vision. Brown irides, good physique. Menses always infrequent and scant. Never pregnant. Hemiplegia, paraplegia and apoplexia have affected a number of her ancestors on both maternal and paternal sides. Six weeks ago she was attacked with violent pain in small of back and across hypogastric regions, with burning as if boiling water were being poured over the parts, pain and violent cramping in calves and feet with numbness and itching. Preceding these symptoms was violent cephalalgia, beginning in nape and base. The pains in all these parts still exist, are acute in character and much worse on lying down. Scalp sensitive. A written statement from the gynecologist in Boston who treated her during the first weeks of her illness, showed acute metritic cellulitis. The history of the eye trouble dates back only five days. Since when, she has had dull pain in the left eye, with gradual failure of vision, some heavy pain in the left side of head, ameliorated by pressure, aggravated by lying down, marked retrobulbar pain from lateral motion of or pressure on bulb. Pupil responds to light. R. V. $\frac{15}{20}$, with convex 40, $\frac{15}{13}$ L. V. $\frac{4}{70}$. Inspection of fundus of right eye showed the veins markedly

---

[*] A physical examination made by Dr. Phil. Porter showed the uterus to be enlarged in all diameters, canal lengthened and walls thickened, os being thick and indurated.

tortuous and dilated. (No vision disturbance noted by patient in this eye.) Left eye: A typical "stauungspapilla," papillary margins entirely obscured and presenting the characteristic gray woolly appearance. Both veins and arteries large and tortuous. R. Verat. vir., 1st dec., in water. May 12th. Visited patient at her residence. She thinks she suffers less pain but the vision of left eye is now only quantitative, while that of the right is to her perceptibly blurred. Continue Ver. v. May 13th. Cramps and head pains all relieved; retrobulbar pains and soreness much less; is able to lie comfortably in bed and slept well during the night. Ver. v. continued. May 15th. All pain and soreness gone. May 23d. The Verat. having been interrupted occasionally for twenty-four hours to meet some intercurrent condition, the ophthalmoscope showed in the left eye marked retrogressive changes. May 25th. Can get a small crescent at outer lower quadrant of disk; tortuosity of veins gone. The vessels of right eye appear normal and the sense of blurr is relieved. June 7th. R. V. $\frac{15}{13}$. IIm. $\frac{1}{36}$. L. V. distinguishes hand at upper part of field. June 20th. L. V. $\frac{15}{70}$. Letters seem small. Illness on my own part prevented later tests, but she reports vision good (probably not full value) and general health better than in years."

The doctor also says: "My experience with the remedy has been quite extended, and while I have found its principal sphere of usefulness in diseases of the fundus oculi to be confined to females, it has not been entirely so. In one case of white atrophy of the disk, in a gentleman who had gone through a severe business excitement, the head pains were always promptly relieved by it. In all cases, in which the fundus disease, whether of the choroid, retina or disk, could be traced to vaso-motor influence, the results have been most satisfactory."

ZINCUM.

Objective.—Agglutination of the inner canthus in the morning, with a pressing sore feeling. Inflammation and redness of the conjunctiva of the right eye; suppuration in the inner canthus; the eyes are most painful in the evening and night, as from sand, with frequent lachrymation; even the upper lid, towards the inner canthus, is red and swollen. During the menses inflammation of the eyes.

Subjective.—Burning of the left lid, as if too dry. *Feeling of soreness in the inner canthi.* Soreness of the outer canthus, with biting pain. Pressure on the margin of the left lower lid, near the inner canthus. Painful pressure in the right inner canthus, with redness of the conjunctiva. Biting in the right inner canthus, relieved by rubbing. *Itching and sticking pain in the inner angles of the eyes,* with cloudiness of sight. Feeling of dryness in the eyeball. Constant burning in the eyes, in the afternoon. Much burning in the eyes and lids, in the morning and evening, with feeling of dryness and pressure in them. Constant pressure in the left eye, in the evening. Burning and biting, with photophobia of the eye, which waters, especially in the evening, and is agglutinated in the morning. Tickling in the right eye, as from dust, frequently. Sore, painful biting in the eyes, towards evening, especially in the right eye. Violent itching of the left eye.

Vision.—Dimness of vision. A good deal of photophobia. Green rings before the eyes.

Clinical.—The indications for Zinc., in tarsal tumors, are well illustrated in the following case:—"A man, æt. 48, having sandy hair and blue eyes, consulted me November 8th, 1877. He complained of soreness and almost constant itching in the inner canthus of the right eye; also of itching in other portions of the body—back, hands and arms; there was an aggravation of all symptoms towards night. The right lower lid was literally filled with small tumors, and in the upper lid several were making their appearance. The caruncle was swollen and bright red, and the ocular conjunctiva congested towards the inner canthus. The margin of the lower lid was thickened, indurated, bright red, and somewhat everted. Patient stated that the difficulty had been coming on for about six months. Excision of the tumors was impracticable. R. Zincum[200]. In one week all soreness and itching had disappeared, and at the end of two months the case was discharged cured, the tumors having been completely reabsorbed."—W. P. Fowler.

It is not unfrequently called for in inflammation of the conjunctiva, especially if confined to the canthi,—more particularly the internal,—and accompanied by soreness, itching and sticking pains at the angles of the eye, with agglutination. It has also removed persistent redness of the conjunctiva, remaining after pustular keratitis, without any discharge, worse towards evening and in the cool air.

For pterygium it is a valuable remedy, as several well marked cases have been cured. In one case, reported by Dr. Carroll Dunham, the pterygium covered one half of the pupil and was growing rapidly; there was much conjunctival injection, lachrymation in the evening, discharge and photophobia, especially by artificial light, pricking pain and soreness, worse in the inner angle and in the evening, but particularly marked was a sensation of *great pressure across the root of the nose* and supra-orbital region. Zincum cured. In another case of pterygium, which nearly covered the cornea, there was photophobia and profuse lachrymation at night, external canthi cracked, much itching and heat in the eye at night, worse in the cold air and better in a warm room; she saw a green halo around the evening light, and had attacks of rushing of blood to the head, etc. Under Zinc.[200] the green halo first disappeared, then the lachrymation, aggravation nights, etc.—T. F. A.

The *sulphate of zinc* has sometimes been employed in place of the metal. "A case of dacryo-cysto-blennorrhœa; discharge profuse muco-purulent, integument adjoining inner canthus red and inflamed; was entirely relieved by Zincum sulph.[3]."—A. Wanstall.

The sulphate of zinc may occasionally be used with advantage locally in acute conjunctivitis. (See Conjunctivitis, Part 2.)

PART II.

OPHTHALMIC

THERAPEUTICS.

ORBIT.

PERIOSTITIS, CARIES, NECROSIS.

(Inflammation of the Periosteum, and Caries of the Walls of the Orbit.)

The general plan of treatment is very similar to that recommended for cellulitis, as we should at first endeavor to prevent destruction of tissue, but if that does occur give the pus free vent. If the bone should be diseased the opening must be kept open and injection of a weak solution of carbolic acid may be used with advantage. If any loose pieces of the bone are discovered they should be removed. The remedies described under cellulitis are also applicable to this disease; in addition to which we note the following:

Aurum.—For both periostitis and *caries* when *dependent upon, or complicated with a mercurio-syphilitic dyscrasia;* also useful in strumous subjects. The pains are tense, and seem to be in the bones, are worse at night, bone sensitive to touch and the patient is excessively sensitive to the pain.

Calc. hypophos.—In appreciable doses, has been used as a "tissue remedy" in scrofulous subjects, apparently with good results.

Kali iod.—This form of potash is one of the most important remedies we possess for periostitis. It is especially adapted to

13   (193)

the syphilitic variety, though useful when dependent upon other causes. The pain is usually marked, though may be absent entirely. The lids will often be œdematous. The crude salt has seemed to act more rapidly than the attenuations.

Mercurius.—As described under cellulitis, this remedy will be found very useful in both periostitis and caries, particularly when dependent upon syphilis, as the nocturnal aggravation is very marked under both the drug and disease. The different forms are employed according to general indications.

Silicea.—Its action upon diseased bone renders it especially valuable in caries of the orbit. The roughened bone and moderately profuse yellow-white discharge are the principal indications, though the weakened general condition, relief from warmth and other concomitant symptoms will be present.

The following remedies may be required: Asaf., Calc. carb., Fluoric acid, Hecla lava, Lyco., Mezer., Nitr. ac., Petrol., Phosphor. and Sulphur.

CELLULITIS.

(Inflammation of the Cellular Tissue of the Orbit.)

When this form of inflammation results from an injury, or the introduction of a foreign body, the latter should be first removed, and then cold compresses of Calendula solution, or ice bags, be employed to subdue the inflammatory symptoms. But if suppuration has already set in, poultices should be applied to promote the discharge of pus, which should be evacuated *at an early period*, by a free incision through the conjunctiva if practicable, if not, through the lid itself. Care should be taken that the pus has free vent at all times. Diet and rest should be prescribed according to the general tone of the patient and severity of the attack.

Aconite.—In the first stage, when the lids are much swollen, with a tight feeling in them; chemosis, with much *heat* and *sensitiveness* in and around the eye, and a sensation as if the eyeball were protruding, making the lids tense; associated with the general Aconite fever.

Apis mel.—Before the formation of pus. *Lids œdematously swollen, with stinging, shooting pains.* Patient drowsy, without thirst.

Hepar sulph.—Especially after pus has formed. Lids swollen and *very sensitive to both touch and cold.* The pains are usually of a *throbbing character.*

Lachesis.—Orbital cellulitis following squint operation, point of tenotomy sloughing, with a *black spot in the centre;* chemosis, and much discharge, with general Lach. condition.

Mercurius.—In the later stages after pus has formed, and even after it has discharged for some time and has become *thin* in character, especially if occurring in a syphilitic subject. There is often much pain in and around the eye, always worse at night.

Phytolacca.—Inflammation of the cellular tissue of the orbit without much pain, slow in its course and with little tendency to suppuration. The eye will be protruded and the infiltration into the orbit and lids will be hard and *unyielding to touch.*

Rhus tox.—This is a remedy of the very first importance in this form of inflammation, whether or not of traumatic origin. *The lids are œdematously swollen, as well as the conjunctiva,* and upon opening them, a profuse gush of tears takes place. The pains vary in character and may be greatly influenced by any change in the weather. Panophthalmitis is liable to complicate the trouble. See under Rhus. Other remedies may be thought of, as Ars., Bell., Bry., Kali iod., Sil., Sulphur.

MORBUS BASEDOWII.

(*Exophthalmic Goitre.*)

We are compelled to place our chief reliance upon internal remedies in the treatment of this disorder, though there are several measures which may be employed as adjuvants. Galvanization of the sympathetic in the neck has been followed by very good success in many instances, especially when combined with internal medication. Both tarsoraphy and tenotomy of the levator palpebræ superioris have been advised and employed in order to protect the partially uncovered globe.

These proceedings are, however, of very questionable utility. To promote a permanent cure, rest, especially in the country; freedom from all excitement, especially emotional; exercise in open air; a generous diet, and abstinence from all stimulants, are particularly required and should be insisted upon whenever practicable.

Amyl nit.—Cases have been entirely cured by olfaction of this drug alone. The eyes are protruding, staring, and the conjunctival vessels injected, as well as those of the fundus. Especially indicated when there are frequent flushes of the face and head, oppressed respiration, etc.

Badiago.—Exophthalmic goitre, with aching pains in the posterior portion of the eyeballs, aggravated on moving them, accompanied by tremulous palpitation of the heart, and glandular swellings.

Cactus grand.—When prescribed on the heart symptoms, cases of exophthalmic goitre have been improved.

Chloroform is said to have improved a case, occurring in a woman, which came on after the administration of chloroform.

Ferrum.—Both the iodide and acetate have been followed by favorable results, especially when the disease comes on after the suppression of the menses; protruding eyes, enlargement of the thyroid, palpitation of the heart, and excessive nervousness.

Lycopus virg.—Judging from its provings, it should be a valuable remedy in this disorder. But though experience is reported to have given some good results they are not as great as one would be led to suppose.

Spongia.—Exophthalmus, enlargement of the thyroid and palpitation of heart, great uneasiness and easily frightened, especially at night; stitches in the ball and burning around the eyes, with lachrymation in the light; the eye feels twisted around; chromopsies, especially deep red, and photopsies even when the eye is closed at night—all indicate this drug, which has proved serviceable.

Nat. mur. and *Baryta c.* are reported to have cured well marked cases. Other remedies which have been recommended are Bell., Brom., Calc., Iod., Phos., Sil., Sulph. and Veratrum alb. and viride.

TUMORES.

(Tumors of the Orbit.)

The most approved method of treatment of all tumors of the orbit is to remove them as early as possible, endeavoring to save the eye whenever sight is present, unless it be a malignant growth and there is danger of not removing the whole of the tumor without sacrificing the globe; in which case it is usually better to remove all the contents of the orbit. A careful diagnosis must be made before operating, in order to aid in the operation and prevent the opening of a vascular tumor.

Our remedies are the same as for tumors in other portions of the body, though we would especially mention *Thuja* and *Kali iodata*, which have been of service in some cases.

LÆSIONES.

(Wounds and Injuries of the Orbit.)

When a foreign body has penetrated the orbit it should be removed as soon as possible, after which cold compresses of Calendula in solution, or bags of ice, should be applied.

If there has been an effusion of blood into the orbit, as the result of any injury, or when spontaneous (as is rarely the case), causing the eye to protrude, a cold compress and a firm bandage will be found very beneficial. In emphysema of the orbit and lids a compress bandage will be required.

LACHRYMAL APPARATUS.

MORBI GLANDULÆ LACHRYMARUM.

(Diseases of the Lachrymal Gland.)

Affections of this gland, acute and chronic inflammation, hypertrophy, fistulæ, tumors, etc., are of rare occurrence, and the treatment does not vary from analagous diseases in other portions of the body.

DACRYOCYSTITIS PHLEGMONOSA.

(Phlegmonous Inflammation of the Lachrymal Sac.)

At the commencement of an inflammation of the lachrymal sac, before the formation of pus has begun, cold compresses (even ice) are advisable, which, together with the indicated remedy, may cause the inflammation to abort before an abscess has formed.

As soon, however, as pus has begun to collect in the lachrymal sac, our treatment must undergo a decided change. The first and most important step to be taken is the opening of the canaliculus into the sac and the evacuation of its contents, thus giving the pus free exit through the natural channel. This, as we have said, must be done as soon as suppuration is suspected, for if not attended to, an opening externally will be made, and a lachrymal fistula may be the result. But if the disease has so far advanced that perforation is inevitable, a free incision into the sac should be made externally, after which, and also in case the abscess has opened spontaneously, warm compresses may be employed for twenty-four or forty-eight hours, but must not be continued too long. After the subsidence of the inflammation this opening will usually close without trouble, though it may be necessary to open the nasal duct and establish a free passage for the tears before it closes. Probing of the nasal duct should be avoided, until the severity of the inflammation has subsided. Warm applications should be substituted for the cold as soon as suppuration has commenced. Among the best of those in use is a solution of Calendula. Internal medication during the whole course of the disease will form an important feature in the treatment. *Acon.*, *Puls.*, *Sil.* and *Hepar* are most commonly called for, but for special indications refer to "blennorrhœa of the lachrymal sac."

Under this treatment the inflammatory symptoms usually disappear, though a catarrhal condition of the lachrymal sac may remain behind, which requires further treatment.

DACRYO-CYSTITIS CATARRHALIS ET BLENNOR-RHŒICA; STRICTURA DUCTUS LACHRYMALIS.

(Catarrhal and Blennorrhœal Inflammation of the Lachrymal Sac; Stricture or Closure of the Lachrymal Duct.)

Since lachrymal diseases are frequently dependent upon nasal catarrh, treatment must be directed to this affection; if aggravated by the presence of nasal polypi, or caused by foreign bodies, these must of course be removed.

As in nearly all cases of blennorrhœa of the sac a more or less firm stricture of the lachrymal duct is present, this will require our special attention. Slight or moderate strictures (almost always dependent upon catarrhal inflammation) may be treated by appropriate medication, from which better results will be finally obtained than from probing. If there is a stricture in the canaliculus, as is often the case, at the entrance to sac, so as to prevent the collection of tears and diseased secretions in the sac from being readily pressed out, the canaliculus should be divided at once. If the stricture in the nasal duct is so great as to almost close it, or if there is closure, it is better to divide the stricture in four sections (Stilling's operation). The advisability of probing immediately after the operation is still a disputed point. If there is considerable catarrhal inflammation with tendency to heal quickly, especially in adults, I do not hesitate to use probes as large as possible, every day for a week or so, and then increase the intervals between their introduction according to the tendency of the stricture to contract. Bowman's silver probes are more commonly employed (from No. 1 to 8), although leaden probes have been used with advantage. If there is very little catarrhal inflammation, especially in children, it is not always necessary to probe after Stilling's operation. Gradual dilatation of strictures by using larger and larger probes has frequently been followed by favorable results, although the benefit is liable to be only temporary. Marked benefit has also been observed from electrolysis, and there is no doubt it should be more extensively employed.

In the treatment of the blennorrhœa, a free vent for the secretions through the opened or unopened canaliculus being present, the patient should be instructed to press out the matter several times a day. Also anything that tends to produce irritation, as cold winds and overexertion of the eyes, should be avoided. Mild astringent injections of boraccic acid, sulphate of zinc or the like may sometimes prove very serviceable.

Aconite.—Inflammation of the lachrymal sac, with great heat, dryness, tenderness, sharp pains and general fever.

Argentum nit.—Discharge very profuse, caruncula lachrymalis swollen, looking like a lump of red flesh; conjunctiva usually congested. *Argentum met.* has relieved a case of stricture.

Arum triph.—Catarrh of the lachrymal sac, with desire to bore into that side of the nose; nose obstructed, compelling to breathe through the mouth; nostrils sore, the left discharges continually.

Calendula.—As a local application in blennorrhœa of the sac, after the canaliculus has been opened, it has been found useful, especially in cases of great tenderness.

Euphrasia.—Much *thick, yellow, acrid discharge*, making the lids sore and excoriated. Blurring of the vision relieved by winking. Thin, watery *bland* discharge from the nose.

Hepar sulph. — Inflammation of the lachrymal sac after pus has formed or in blennorrhœa, with great sensitiveness to touch and to cold, with profuse discharge. Also useful in controlling the discharge after the canaliculus has been opened.

Mercurius.—Discharge thin and excoriating; acrid coryza; nocturnal aggravation.

Petroleum.—Discharge from the lachrymal sac, with roughness of the check, occipital headache, and other marked concomitant symptoms.

Pulsatilla.—One of the most important remedies for dacryocystitis, which may sometimes be cut short at its very beginning with it, and may be useful at any stage of the inflammation. It is also important in blennorrhœa of the sac if the *discharge is profuse and bland.* Profuse thick and bland discharge from the nose; especially beneficial in children.

Silicea.—Occasionally indicated in dacryocystitis characterized by the usual symptoms; even cases that have far advanced toward suppuration, have been checked. Blennorrhœa of the lachrymal sac often calls for it. The patient is particularly sensitive to cold air and wishes to keep warmly covered.

Stannum.—Very favorable results have frequently been obtained in controlling the yellow-white discharge from the lachrymal sac, itching or sharp pain in the inner canthus, especially at night.

Other remedies which have been recommended and proved useful are Bell., Calc., *Cinnab.*, Hydrast., Kali iod., Merc. prot., *Nat. mur.*, Nux, Sulph., and *Zinc. sulph.*

FISTULA LACHRYMALIS.

(Fistula of the Lachrymal Sac.)

The first point to be attended to, is to see that the passage is free into the nose. We must therefore slit up the canaliculus and divide any stricture found in the nasal duct, providing it is sufficient to interfere with the flow of tears; after which the canal should be kept open.

The fistula must now be healed, and if recent, this is best done by touching the edges with a stick of nitrate of silver. Packing it with alumen exsiccatum has also proved of advantage. If the edges of the fistula are healed and covered with smooth skin, it will be necessary to pare the edges and unite with a suture.

The following remedies have been advised and may have been of service in recent cases, though we doubt if any effect can be obtained in old chronic fistulæ: Brom., Calc., Fluoric ac., Lach., Merc., Nat. mur., Petrol., Sil., and Sulph.

LIDS.

ŒDEMA.

As this condition is usually dependent upon some constitutional cause or severe form of inflammation of the conjunctiva, cornea, or iris, it should be considered only a symptom which will disappear when the original trouble subsides. We are, however, called upon for relief of this troublesome and disfiguring symptom, when no special cause can be readily found. Our remedies are generally all we require for its removal, though a compress bandage may materially assist in some instances.

The chief remedies are: *Apis, Arsen., Kali carb.,* and *Rhus.* (See Part I for special indications.)

In *emphysema of the lids* use a compress bandage.

For *erythema of the lids* Bellad. or Apis will be most frequently required.

BLEPHARITIS ACUTA.

(Acute Phlegmonous Inflammation [Abscess] of the Lids.)

By a careful selection of our remedy in the first stage, we can often cause the inflammation to subside before suppuration has taken place. It is also possible to promote the resolution and discharge of pus already formed. Cold (iced) applications are recommended if the disease is seen at the outset; but if we suspect that the formation of pus has commenced, a change to hot applications (poultices) should be made.

As soon as fluctuation can be felt, a free incision into the swelling parallel to the margin of the lids should be made, in order to give free vent to the confined pus. After the escape of the pus, warm applications of Calendula and water (ten drops to the ounce) are advised. A compress bandage should also be employed if the abscess is extensive, so as to keep the lid in position and the walls of the abscess in contact, and thus hasten the union.

If it has already spontaneously opened, the perforation should be enlarged if it be insufficient and unfavorably situated; also if there be several apertures, they should be united by an incision, in order to leave as small a cicatrix as possible. A generous diet should be prescribed.

Aconite.—In the *very first stage*, when the lids are swollen, red, hard, and with a tight feeling in them; also when they are very *sensitive to air* and touch, with *great heat* and burning. There is hardly any lachrymation present. General febrile symptoms often accompany the above.

Apis mel.—Incipient stage before the formation of pus, if there is *great puffiness of the lids, especially of the upper, with stinging pains.* Much swelling of the lids of a reddish-blue color; temporary relief from cold water. There is often chemosis and the lachrymation is profuse, hot and burning (Rhus), though not acrid as under Arsenicum. Drowsiness and absence of thirst are often present.

Arsenicum.—When the inflammation of the lids is dependent upon, or associated with a general cachectic habit, great prostration, restlessness, especially at night, much thirst, etc. The lids may be œdematously swollen, especially the lower, though not usually very red. *The pains are of a decided burning character, and the lachrymation profuse, hot and acrid,* excoriating the lids and cheek.

Hepar sulph.—This is the remedy most frequently employed, especially after the first stage has passed, and *suppuration is about to, or has already taken place.* The lids are inflamed, as if erysipelas had invaded them, with *throbbing,* aching, stinging pains in them, and are very *sensitive to touch;* the pains are aggravated by cold and from contact, but *ameliorated by warmth.*

Rhus tox.—When there is a tendency to the formation of

an abscess; lids œdematously swollen (especially the upper), and accompanied by *profuse lachrymation;* there may be *erysipelatous swelling* of the lids with vesicles on the skin. *Chemosis* is often present. The pains are worse at night, and in cold, damp weather, but relieved by warm applications.

Silicea.—Indicated after suppuration has commenced. Silicea is more particularly called for in the carbuncular form, and especially if the patient is very nervous and the local symptoms are accompanied by sharp pains in the head, ameliorated by wrapping up warm.

Graph., *Puls.*, and *Sulph.*, are said to have been of service. The special indications are to be found under blepharitis ciliaris.

BLEPHARITIS CILIARIS.

(Inflammation of the Edges of the Lids.)

(Syn. tinea tarsi, ophthalmia tarsi, blepharitis marginalis seu tarsalis, blepharadenitis, etc.) Including, acne ciliaris, eczema palpebrarum and phtheiriasis ciliarum.

"*Tolle causam*" should be our motto in contending against this trouble; for, unless the causes are removed (and they are many) no headway can be made in the treatment.

First, we should, as a rule, examine the refraction of the patient, whether he be hypermetropic or myopic, for often we find this to be the chief cause (especially hypermetropia), particularly when there is only slight inflammation of the edges of the lids, giving them a red, irritable look, with little scurfs on the ciliæ. If any anomaly of refraction is discovered it must first be corrected by the proper glasses, which is sometimes sufficient to cure the whole trouble, though afterwards some external application or internal medication may also be needed.

In rare cases the presence of lice on the eyelashes may be the exciting cause (phtheiriasis ciliarum), when we should be careful to remove them, and apply either cosmoline or some mercurial ointment, which will destroy them, and prevent their recurrence.

Fungous growths in the hair follicles are also said to cause this disease, in which case the hairs should be extirpated, and either external or internal medication employed.

Blepharitis ciliaris is often developed secondarily after some other trouble of the eye, as conjunctivitis, keratitis, etc., besides being often found as a sequela of acute exanthemata, as small-pox, measles, etc.

In some persons there seems to be a pre-disposition to this trouble, for it will occur after almost any constitutional disturbance.

Another cause is frequently found in affections of the lachry-mal canal, particularly catarrh of the lachrymal sac, and stricture of the duct; in these cases the tears being hindered from flowing through their natural passage into the nose, collect in the eye, flow over the lids and down the cheek; thus the retention of the tears will cause an inflammation of the margins and eventually of the whole structure of the lids. Any other affection which will have the same result (flowing of the tears over the lids) will, of course, produce the same trouble, and this is often found in slight degrees of eversion of the lower lids (ectropion) which displace the puncta lachry-malis, and thus prevent the tears from passing into the sac. In all such cases, the first thing to be done is to open the canaliculus into the sac, and if necessary the nasal duct into the nose, so as to give a free passage for the tears into that organ, after which the treatment is the same as in uncompli-cated cases.

But the most common causes of ciliary blepharitis are expos-ure to wind, dust, smoke, etc., especially when complicated with *want of cleanliness*; it is for this reason we see this trouble so frequently among the poorer classes. As it is upon this point—cleanliness—that the success of our treatment depends to a great extent, we should impress upon the patient's mind the necessity of it, in terms as forcible as possible.

They should be directed to remove the scales or crusts from the margins of the lids *as soon as formed*, not allowing them to remain even a few minutes. This should not be done by rub-bing, as the patient is inclined to do on account of the itching sensation, for by so doing, excoriations are made, lymph is thrown out, and new scabs form, which only aggravate the inflammation. But they should be directed to moisten the crusts in warm water, and then carefully remove them with a piece of fine linen, or by drawing the ciliæ between the thumb and fingers; at the same time gentle traction may be made on the lashes, so as to remove all that are loose, as they act only as foreign bodies. Sometimes the scabs are so thick and firm, that moistening in warm water is not sufficient to remove them; in such cases, hot compresses or poultices should be applied for ten or twenty minutes at a time, until they can be easily taken away.

In the treatment of *chronic* inflammation of the margins of the lids, *external applications* are of great value and without their use a cure is often impossible. It is true that a careful attention to cleanliness, together with the internal administration of the indicated remedy, will cure a large proportion of our cases, but the duration of treatment will be usually much longer than if we employ local means at the same time we give internal remedies.

Cosmoline or Vaseline.—This unguent has been of great service in the treatment of ciliary blepharitis. It may be used alone or to form a base for the administration of other remedies. It prevents the formation of new scales and the agglutination of the lids, besides seeming to exert a beneficial influence over the progress of the disease. This, like all other ointments, should be used once or twice a day, or even oftener if the case is very severe. All scales or crusts should first be carefully removed; after which a very little of the ointment may be applied to the edge of the lids with the finger or camel's hair brush. The smallest amount possible to oil the ciliary margins of the lids should be applied, as an aggravation of the inflammation may result from its too free use.

Grapho-vaseline.—Graphites, as will be seen in the symptomatology, is more commonly indicated in ciliary blepharitis than any other one remedy. Many cures have resulted from its internal administration alone, when indicated, but more brilliant results may be obtained by employing at the same time locally the following collyrium :

R. Graphites, gr. ij.
Vaseline, 3ij.
Misce.

Mercury.—For years this has been a favorite local application in ciliary blepharitis. It seems to be better adapted to the severe forms of inflammation of the lids than Graphites, for there is more redness, more swelling, more secretion and more tendency toward ulceration. The two following prescriptions have been employed with the most favorable results, especially the yellow oxide:

R. Hydrarg. oxyd. flav., gr. ij.
Vaseline, 3ij.
Misce.
R. Liq. Hydrarg. Nitr., gtt. iij.
Ol Morrhuæ, 3ij.
Misce.

In some cases more of the mercury is used, in others less, according to the severity of the symptoms.

Various other ointments and washes have been used with variable success. The use of milk, cream, lard and simple cerate, to prevent the lids from sticking together have also been of aid, with internal medication.

Aconite.—Chiefly called for in the acute variety of this trouble, especially when caused from *exposure to cold dry winds. The lids—especially the upper—are red and swollen, with a tight feeling in them, while great heat, dryness, burning and sensitiveness to air are present;* the dry heat is temporarily relieved by cold water. The conjunctiva is usually implicated. Concomitant symptoms of fever, thirst and restlessness, are to be taken into consideration.

Alumina.—Chronic inflammation of the lids (particularly if complicated with granulations) characterized by burning and *dryness* of the lids, especially in the evening; *itching, dryness and excoriation at the canthi. Absence of lachrymation.* There is not usually much destruction of tissue nor great thickening of the lids.

Antimonium crud.—Obstinate cases in which the lids are

red, swollen and moist, with pustules on the face. Especially in cross children. *Pustules on the ciliary margins.*

Argentum nit.—*Lids sore, very red and swollen,* especially when complicated with granular conjunctivitis, or some other external trouble. There is usually *profuse discharge* from the eyes, causing firm agglutination in the morning. The symptoms are often *relieved in the cold air,* or by cold applications, and may be associated with headache, pain in root of the nose, etc.

Arsenicum.—Inflammation of the margins of the lids, which are *thick, red, and excoriated by the burning acrid lachrymation.* The cheek may also be excoriated. The lids are sometimes œdematously swollen and spasmodically closed, especially when the cornea is at the same time affected. The *characteristic burning pains* are important and usually present. The general condition of the patient decides us in its selection, as the great restlessness, aggravation after midnight, and thirst are commonly seen in scrofulous children.

Aurum.—Rarely useful in uncomplicated blepharitis, except when occurring in scrofulous, or syphilitic subjects, after the abuse of mercury. The lids may be red and ulcerated, with stinging, pricking or itching pain in them. Ciliæ rapidly fall out.

Calcarea carb.—Blepharitis occurring in persons inclined to grow fat, or in *unhealthy, "pot-bellied"* children of a scrofulous diathesis, who sweat much about the head. The lids are red, swollen and *indurated.* Inflammation of the margins of the lids, causing loss of the eyelashes, with thick, purulent, excoriating discharge, and burning, sticking pains. *Great itching* and burning of the margins of the lids, particularly at the canthi; throbbing pain in the lids. Most of the eye symptoms are worse in the morning, on moving the eyes, and in *damp weather.* Great reliance should be placed on the general cachexia of the patient.

Calcarea iodata.—Seems to act better than the carbonate in blepharitis found in those unhealthy children afflicted with *enlargement of the glands, and especially of the tonsils.*

Causticum.—Blepharitis, with warts on the eyebrows and

lids. The symptoms are ameliorated in the open air. *Feeling of sand in the eye.*

Chamomilla.—Of benefit as an intercurrent remedy, even if it does not complete the cure, in cross, peevish children who want to be carried. The local symptoms are not marked.

Cinnabaris.—Ciliary blepharitis, with *dull pain over or around the eye.* There may be dryness of the eye, or considerable discharge.

Croton tig.—When there is complicated with the blepharitis a *vesicular eruption on the lids and face.*

Euphrasia.—A valuable remedy, if the lids are red, swollen, and excoriated by the profuse, acrid, muco-purulent discharge, or even if ulcerated.

The *lachrymation is also profuse, acrid, and burning;* often accompanied by fluent coryza. The cheek around the eye is also usually sore and red from the nature of the discharges.

Graphites.—This is one of the most important remedies we possess for the chronic form of this disease, though may be indicated in acute attacks, especially if complicated with ulcers or pustules on the cornea. Particularly useful if the inflammation occurs in scrofulous subjects covered with *eczematous eruptions,* chiefly on the head and *behind the ears, which are moist, fissured, and bleed easily.* The edges of the lids are slightly swollen of a pale red color, and covered with *dry scales or scurfs,* or the margins may be ulcerated. The inflammation may be confined to the canthi, especially the *outer, which have a great tendency to crack and bleed, upon any attempt to open.* Burning and dryness of the lids are often present, also biting and *itching,* causing a constant desire to rub them. It is important in *eczema of the lids,* if the eruption is moist, with tendency to crack, while the margins are covered with scales or crusts.

Hepar sulph.—Especially adapted to acute phlegmonous inflammation, though also may be useful in certain forms of blepharitis in which the lids are inflamed, sore and corroded, as if eaten out, or if small red swellings are found along the margins of the lids, which are painful in the evening and *upon touch.* There is *general amelioration from warmth.* Often

14

called for when the meibomian glands are affected. For eczema palpebrarum in which the scabs are thick and honeycomb in character on and around the lids, it is very valuable.

Mercurius sol.—Very favorable results have been gained by this remedy in blepharitis, especially if dependent upon or found in a *syphilitic subject*, or if caused from working over *fires or forges. The lids are thick, red, swollen and ulcerated* (particularly the upper) *and sensitive to heat or cold and to touch. Profuse acrid lachrymation* is usually present, which makes the lids sore, red and painful, especially worse in the open air or by the constant application of cold water. *All the symptoms are worse in the evening after going to bed and from warmth in general,* also from the glare of a fire or any artificial light. The concomitant symptoms should receive special attention, as excoriation of the nose from the acrid coryza, flabby condition of the tongue, nocturnal pains, etc., etc.

Mercurius corr.—This form of mercury differs very little in its symptomatology from the above, and that is chiefly in degree, *as the pains are generally more severe* and spasmodic in character, *lachrymation more profuse and acrid, secretions thinner and more excoriating,* and inflammatory swelling greater than in any other preparation. It has proved curative in inflammatory swelling of indurated lids, inflammatory swelling of cheeks and parts around the orbits, which are covered with small pustules, and especially in *scrofulous inflammation of the lids.* Nocturnal aggravation of the symptoms is usually present.

Mezereum.—Blepharitis accompanied by tinea capitis; or *eczema of the lids* and head, characterized by *thick hard scabs,* from under which pus exudes on pressure.

Natrum mur.—Ciliary blepharitis, particularly if caused by the use of caustics (nitrate of silver). The lids are thick and inflamed, smart and burn, with a feeling of sand in the eye. The lachrymation is acrid, excoriating the lids and cheeks, making them *glossy and shining;* often accompanied by eczema.

Nux vom.—Chronic inflammation of the lids, with smarting and dryness, especially *worse in the morning.* It is particularly indicated in ciliary blepharitis dependent upon gastric disturbances.

Petroleum.—Has been of benefit in ciliary blepharitis, especially if combined with the use of cosmoline externally Great reliance should be placed on the occipital headache, rough skin, etc., generally found when this drug is indicated, though has been used with advantage when no marked symptoms were present.

Psorinum.—Old chronic cases of inflammation of the lids, especially when subject to occasional exacerbations. It has also been of service in the acute variety when the internal surface of the lids was chiefly affected, with considerable photophobia. Particularly indicated in a *strumous diathesis*, with unhealthy offensive discharges from the eyes.

Pulsatilla.—Blepharitis, both acute and chronic, especially if the glands of the lids are affected (blepharadenitis) or when there is a great tendency to the formation of *styes* or abscesses on the margin of the palpebræ. Blepharitis resulting from high living or fat food and when accompanied by acne of the face; also in cases in which the lachrymal passages are involved. The swelling, redness and discharges vary, though the latter are more often *profuse and bland*, causing agglutination of the lids in the morning. *Itching* and *burning* are the chief sensations experienced. The symptoms are usually *aggravated in the evening*, in a warm room or in a cold draught of air, but *ameliorated in the cool open air*.

Rhus tox.—Its chief use is in acute phlegmonous inflammation of the lids, and erysipelas; though may be of service in acute aggravations of chronic inflammation from exposure in wet weather or when worse at that time, with much *swelling of the lids* and *profuse lachrymation*.

Sepia.—Chronic inflammation of the edges of the lids with scales on the ciliæ and *small pustules on the lid margins* (acne ciliaris). Feeling as if the lids were too heavy, or as if they were too tight and did not cover the ball. *Worse morning and evening*.

Silicea.—Blepharitis from working in a damp place or being in the cold air. (Calc., Rhus.)

Staphisagria.—Blepharitis, in which the margins of the lids are dry with hard nodules on the borders and destruction of the hair follicles. Itching of the lids.

Sulphur.—A remedy called for, especially in the chronic form of this disease and when found in children of a strumous diathesis, who are irritable and cross by day and restless and feverish by night; also for blepharitis appearing after the suppression of an eruption or when the patient is covered with eczema. The lids are red, swollen and agglutinated in the morning, or there may be numerous small itching pustules on the margins. The *pains are usually of a sticking character,* though we may have itching, biting, burning and a variety of other sensations in the lids. There is generally great aversion to water so that *they cannot bear to have the eyes washed.* Eczematous affections of the lids, like eczema in other portions of the body, which indicate Sulphur, are often controlled.

Tellurium.—Eczema of the lids, especially if complicated with a moist eruption behind the ears and *offensive otorrhœa* smelling like fish brine.

In addition to the above, the following remedies have also proved serviceable: Ant. crud., Apis mel., Arg. met., Lyco., Merc. nitr., Merc. prot., Sang., Seneg.

ERYSIPELAS.

Externally, warm applications should be employed, either dry or moist, as may be most agreeable to the patient. If the chemosis is very great and firm, so as to endanger the nutrition of the cornea, incisions of the conjunctiva at different points are advisable. If pus has formed, a free incision must be made at once to allow it to escape, in order that the scar and contraction of the tissues may be as small as possible. Careful attention must be paid to the general hygienic condition of the patient. The diet must be generous, and stimulants may be employed with advantage.

Apis mel.—Erysipelatous inflammation of the lids, with adjacent smooth swelling of the face, especially if accompanied with *chemosis. The upper lid is particularly œdematously swollen* *and hangs like a sack over the eye.* The photophobia and lachrymation are often very marked. There may be *stinging*, itching, burning, or a swollen feeling around the eyes and in the brows; also *severe shooting pains* over the eye (right) extending into the ball. The patient may be drowsy and thirstless (reverse of Arsenicum), and is usually worse in the evening or forepart of the night.

Arsenicum.—Erysipelas of the lids, associated with the *general cachectic Arsenic condition*, great prostration, restlessness, thirst, etc. The lids are swollen and œdematous, especially the lower (though mostly non-inflammatory and painless). The pains are of a decided *burning* character, while the aggravations are periodic, especially after midnight. (Apis before midnight.)

Belladonna.—*Lids and surrounding tissues red, swollen and congested*, with throbbing pain in them. The integument may be bright red and shining, though has not the peculiar œdematous look found under Apis and Rhus. *Absence of lachrymation* predominates, in this respect differing from the other remedies mentioned. The inflammation is no more marked in one lid than in the other. Conjunctiva usually congested. The face is flushed and the headache severe, of a throbbing character.

Rhus tox.—Erysipelas of the lids, whether traumatic or not, if there is *much œdematous, erysipelatous swelling of the lids and face, with small watery vesicles scattered over the surface*, and drawing pains in the cheek and head. The lids are usually *spasmodically closed* and upon opening them a *profuse gush of tears takes place*. There is usually chemosis, and the aggravation of the symptoms is especially in the latter part of the night and in damp weather. Especially useful if resulting from exposure in the wet, getting the feet wet, or from change in the weather.

Terebinth has been successfully employed in some cases of erysipelas.

Veratrum vir.—Erysipelas of the lids and surrounding tissues, especially if traumatic in origin. It should be used externally as well as internally.

HORDEOLUM.

(Stye.)

We are not often called upon to prescribe for a single stye, but usually to prevent the recurrence of successive crops. If the case is seen at its very outset, especially if severe, cold compresses may be used with advantage, though usually more benefit is derived, especially after its commencement, from hot poultices. If pus has formed, as shown by a yellow point, a small incision can be made to permit its ready escape. If dependent, as it frequently is, upon impairment of the general health, proper hygienic measures must be advised.

Graphites.—Useful in preventing the recurrence of styes. (Compare general symptoms of patient.)

Hepar.—Indicated if suppuration has already commenced, with *throbbing pain, great sensitiveness to touch and amelioration by warmth.*

Pulsatilla.—This is an excellent remedy for styes of every description and in every stage of the disease. If given early before the formation of pus, it will often cause them to abort; if used later, relief from the pain and hastening of the process of cure is frequently produced, while as a remedy for the prevention of the recurrence of successive crops it is often of great value. It is especially useful if *dependent upon some gastric derangement,* as from indulgence in high living, fat food, etc., and if *accompanied by acne of the face;* also when found in amenorrhœic females or the peculiar Pulsatilla temperament.

Staphisagria.—Recurrence of styes, especially on the lower lid, which are inclined to abort and leave little hard nodules in the lids.

Sulphur.—To prevent the recurrence of successive crops, especially in a strumous diathesis, as shown by eruptions, boils, etc., in various portions of the body. Cannot bear to have the eyes washed and is restless and feverish at night.

Thuja.—Obstinate forms of styes, which seem to resist treatment and form little hard nodules on the margins of the lids.

The following remedies have also been recommended and

used with advantage: Acon., Arsen., Calc., Caust., Con., Electricity, Lyco., Merc., Pic. ac., Phosph. ac., Rhus, and Silicea.

ULCUS SYPHILITICA ET EXANTHEMATA.

(*Syphilitic and Exanthematous Affections of the Lids.*)

Syphilitic ulcers may involve all the tissues of the lids, including the palpebral conjunctiva. They are obstinate in their course, and may cause destruction of the entire lid; therefore require careful attention. The local use of caustics is often indispensable, and that which has proved most beneficial in my experience has been the *acid nitrate of mercury*. The remedies which have been found most efficacious are the following, prescribed according to general indications: Ars., *Apis,* Aurum, Cinnab., Hepar, *Kali iod., Merc.,* Nitric acid, and Thuja.

The various exanthematous affections of the lids in smallpox, scarlet fever, measles, etc., will not usually require especial attention.

Herpes zoster frontalis, a rare but painful disease, must be treated by internal medication. The remedies most useful are, Ars., *Croton tig.,* Electricity, Graph., Merc., Puls., *Ranunculus bulb.,* and *Rhus.*

EPITHELIOMA, LUPUS, SARCOMA.

(*Malignant Tumors of the Lids.*)

Cases of malignant tumor are reported to have been cured by our remedies, but owing, probably, to our limited knowledge, many cases prove very obstinate to internal medication. *Excision* is therefore advised, if the disease is circumscribed and moderate in extent; care being taken that all the morbid tissue is removed. The edges of the wound may be brought together by sutures, or a plastic operation may be made, bringing the integument from the temple or some adjoining point.

Various caustics have also been employed, chief among which may be mentioned, caustic potash, nitrate of silver, chloride of zinc, arsenic paste, and acetic acid. Electrolysis has been recommended.

If the disease is very extensive, involving the tissues of the face to such an extent that extirpation is impracticable, we then rely chiefly upon our internal remedies, using only such local applications as prove agreeable and of temporary relief to the patient. For instance, if the discharge is profuse and offensive, a weak solution of carbolic acid, salicylic acid, or some other disinfectant, proves of service. An application from which we have often seen excellent results is carbolic acid and linseed oil (4 grains to the ounce); it relieves the patient, and seems to exert a beneficial effect over the progress of the disease.

Apis.—Lupus non exedens, *sharp, stinging pains,* and tendency towards puffiness of the lower lids.

Hydrocotyle asiatica.—Has obtained a high reputation in the hands of Dr. Boileau as a remedy for lupus, and deserves our attention. (We have, however, failed to perceive any results from its use.)

Phytolacca dec.—Benefit seems to have been derived in relieving, if not curing malignant ulcers of the lids, when used both externally and internally.

Thuja.—Epithelioma of the lids.

TUMORES NON MALIGNI.

(*Benign Tumors of the Lids, Chalazion, Verucæ, Sebaceous, Fibroid, Fatty, etc.*)

Excision, as a rule, is the most satisfactory treatment of tarsal tumors, providing there is only one or two. But as it is usually tedious and painful to remove a small solid tumor, we may substitute for excision, pricking of the tumor with the point of a knife, and stirring up of its contents. This will cause a slight inflammation which will hasten absorption. It may have to be repeated several times, but as there will be little pain attending the operation, no objection will be made by the patient. This is also the most efficacious treatment in cases of multiple tumors. After opening, and at other times also, I usually apply locally the indicated remedy—especially the tincture of Thuja. In the case of cystic tumors the whole of the cyst wall should be removed; it may be destroyed by the use of a seton, but removal with the knife is usually more satisfactory. Many cases have been cured by internal medication alone, and remedies should always be employed, whether the knife is used or not, for they no doubt hasten the cure and serve to prevent recurrence.

Calcarea carb.—Tarsal tumors occurring in fat, flabby subjects.

Causticum.—Tumors, especially warts found on the lids and eyebrows.

Conium.—Indurations of the lids, remaining after inflammation.

Hepar.—Tarsal tumors that have become inflamed and are sensitive to touch.

Pulsatilla.—Tarsal tumors of recent origin that are subject to inflammation, or are accompanied by catarrhal conditions of the eye. The temperament and general symptoms will decide the choice.

Staphisagria.—An important remedy for tumors of the lid. Enlargement of the glands of the lids, which are red and accompanied by tensive tearing pains, especially in the evening. For little *indurations of the lids, resulting from styes*, or, for successive crops of small tarsal tumors, this drug is especially indicated.

Thuja.—This is one of the most valuable remedies for tarsal tumors, whether single or multiple, especially if they appear like a condyloma, either on the internal or external surface of the lid. We have seen them disappear by simply giving the drug internally, though it usually seems to act more speedily if we use, at the same time, the tincture externally. It is also recommended for the prevention of their return after removal by the knife, and for hastening their absorption after operation. For condylomata, or warty excrescences on the lids, especially if occurring in syphilitic subjects, this drug deserves attention.

Zincum.—Tumors of the lids with *soreness and itching in the internal canthi.*

Baryta carb. and iod., Graph., Lyco., Kali iod., Merc., Nitric acid, Sep., Sil. and Sulph. may be required.

PTOSIS.

(Drooping of the Upper Lid.)

This affection is usually associated with paralysis of one or more of the ocular muscles supplied by the same nerve—oculomotorius—though frequently only those twigs which supply the levator palpebræ superioris are involved, giving rise to simple drooping of the lid. In the treatment, chief reliance must be placed upon internal medication, though sometimes *Electricity* proves of great value, either used alone or in connection with the indicated remedy. If the disease resists all treatment—dependent upon irremediable causes—operative measures must be resorted to.

Alumina.—The upper lids are weak, seem to hang down as if paralyzed, especially the left. *Burning dryness* in the eyes, especially on looking up. *Absence of lachrymation.* Particularly useful for loss of power in the upper lids *met with in old dry cases of granulations.*

Causticum.—More benefit has probably been derived from this remedy in the treatment of ptosis than from any other. Its special indication is, *drooping of the lid resulting from exposure to cold* (Rhus, from damp cold). The symptoms in the provings very strongly point to Caust. as a remedy in this disorder, as, "inclination to close the eyes; they close involuntarily. Sensation of heaviness in the upper lid as if he could not raise it easily, etc."

Euphrasia.—If caused from exposure to cold and wet, and accompanied by catarrhal symptoms of the conjunctiva.

Ledum.—Ptosis resulting from an injury, with ecchymosis of the lids and conjunctiva.

Rhus tox.—Especially if found in a *rheumatic diathesis*, and if the cause can be traced to *working in the wet, getting the feet damp*, or to *change in the weather.* Heaviness and stiffness of the lids, like a paralysis, as if it were difficult to move them. There may be aching, drawing pains in the head and face or they may be absent. The concomitant symptoms will point to its selection, though it has proved useful when none are present.

Spigelia.—Ptosis, resulting from inflammation or other causes, in which *sharp stabbing pains through the eye* are present. Sometimes hot scalding lachrymation accompanies the above.

Gelsemium, Stannum and *Conium* have been favorably employed in this affection, especially the former. (Compare paralysis of the muscles.)

BLEPHAROSPASMUS.

(*Spasm of the Lids.*)

True spasm of the lids is usually dependent upon corneal troubles and is relieved with them. It may, however, be independent of such affections, when remedies must be prescribed for the spasm *"per se."* Division of the affected nerve may be necessary in aggravated cases.

Morbid nictitation is of frequent occurrence, especially in nervous and delicate persons. If there is any anomaly of refraction, it must first be corrected by the proper glass. The general health must be attended to.

Agaricus.—*Twitchings of the lids* with a feeling of heaviness in them, *relieved during sleep* and sometimes temporarily by washing in cold water. Spasms of the lids. It is very rare to meet a case of morbid nictitation which will not yield to this remedy. Four drop doses of the tincture two or three times a day will often relieve when the potencies fail.

Other remedies which have proved useful in individual cases are Alumina, Cicuta, Ignatia, Nux v., Physos., and Pulsat.

TRICHIASIS, DISTICHIASIS.

(*Ingrowing Eyelashes.*)

The treatment of distorted eyelashes is chiefly surgical, being rarely if ever amenable to internal medication. The most common method of dealing with them, if few in number, is to extract them as fast as they grow and irritate the eye. Frequent evulsions may in time cause the hair bulbs to atrophy, and thus cure the case, though usually this treatment is only palliative. To obtain a permanent cure operative measures must be resorted to, and a variety of these have been devised and employed with more or less favorable results. If the faulty position is limited to a few hairs the destruction of the hair follicles by galvano-cautery is the most appropriate treatment.

ENTROPIUM.

(*Inversion of the Lid.*)

The treatment of inversion of the lids varies according to the cause and duration of the disease. If the entropium is slight and recent, and of spasmodic or senile origin, (especially of the lower lid) a cure may often be effected by painting the parts with collodion or by the proper use of adhesive strips. The collodion, however, must be renewed every two or three days or oftener, in order to keep the lid in position. This method will not suffice, in an entropium of long duration or considerable degree; in which case surgical means must be employed. A variety of operations have been proposed, though the one most commonly made is simply the removal of a horizontal fold of integument, parallel and close to the margin of the lid, *including a portion of the orbicularis muscle;* after which the edges of the wound are brought together by three or four sutures. Canthoplasty is frequently beneficial either alone or combined with the previous operation.

Remedies may possibly be useful if the inversion is recent and only slight in degree. The following are suggested: Aconite, Argent. nit., Calc. and Natrum mur.

ECTROPIUM.

(*Eversion of the Lid.*)

In acute cases of eversion of the lids, consequent upon inflammation and hypertrophy of the conjunctiva, they should be replaced and retained in position for several days by the use of a compress bandage. This bandage properly and patiently applied is frequently all that is sufficient. Scarification or cauterization of the hypertrophied conjunctiva has been advised in acute cases, if the bandage alone is not all that is required.

Narrowing the palpebral fissure (tarsoraphia) may be useful in both the acute and chronic stage of the disease.

The operations (to which we must often resort) recommended for this affection are legion, and must necessarily vary in nearly every case, according to the cause, degree and position of the eversion.

Apis.—Is especially indicated in the first stage of this affection, in which the swelling of the conjunctiva is very great. ′

Argent. nit.—If the lids are swollen, inflamed, everted and the *puncta lachrymalia very red and prominent.* The discharge of tears and pus is profuse.

Hamamelis vir.—A dilute solution of "Pond's Extract" applied locally is said to have cured a case, occurring during the course of a severe conjunctivitis.

Little reliance must be placed upon internal medication in either entropium or ectropium, as operative measures are almost invariably necessary, except occasionally in the first stage.

LÆSIONES.

(*Wounds and Injuries of the Lid.*)

Immediately after contused wounds of the lids, cold compresses should be employed; they should be applied with a firm bandage which often proves of advantage in limiting the amount of ecchymosis.

Arnica, our great remedy for all contusions, deserves its extensive reputation for curing "black eyes" as there is no other drug better adapted to this condition. A solution of the tincture in water, ten drops to the ounce, is usually employed, though both stronger and weaker solutions are in vogue. Ledum used in the same manner has also proved of service.

Incised wounds are generally more serious in nature, though vary greatly according to situation, both in danger and results of treatment. The first object in view should be to bring to gether the edges, of the wound by means of *sutures*, adhesive strips or collodion; after which the application of a solution of Calendula, ten drops to the ounce of water, may be applied. If the tissues are very much bruised Arnica may be employed, though as a rule Calendula will be found more useful in cut wounds. If the wound is incised, without any contusion, and the edges are early brought accurately together, a dry dressing will often be found most beneficial.

Hamamelis and Ledum have both been recommended for wounds of the lids.

Burns and scalds must be treated as usual in other parts of the body, except that care should be taken to prevent the union of the lids (anchyloblepharon), by frequently opening them, and by inunction of the edges with simple cerate or cosmoline; also great attention should be paid to the prevention of a cicatrix (which causes ectropium), by keeping the skin on the stretch by a bandage, during the period of cicatrization. Cosmoline is especially recommended as an external application

When dependent upon the stings of insects, the sting should be removed and cold water dressings applied.

DEFORMITATES INGENITÆ.

(*Congenital Malformations.*)

Congenital malformations, as epicanthus and coloboma, can only be remedied by proper operative measures.

CONJUNCTIVA.

CONJUNCTIVITIS CATARRHALIS.

(Acute and Chronic Catarrhal Inflammation of the Conjunctiva.)

The first point in the treatment should be the removal of any exciting cause. To accomplish this the lids should first be everted and examined for the presence of a foreign body, which, if detected, should be removed. Should the conjunctivitis depend upon any anomaly of refraction, this should be corrected. If due to straining of the eyes in reading, writing, etc. (especially in the evening), or to exposure to wind, dust or any bright light, as working over a fire, directions to abstain from overuse, or to protect the eyes from the injurious causes, should be given. Should the case be very severe, the patient may be confined to his room, though this is rarely required in pleasant weather. As a local remedy in acute inflammation of the conjunctiva, the use of *ice* is especially recommended. It may be used in rubber bags made for that purpose or by wrapping it in a towel. If prescribed it should be used *constantly* for twenty-four or forty-eight hours or longer, according to the benefit derived. Great reliance should be placed upon the sensations experienced by the patient regarding the use of warm or cold applications, as the beneficial results obtained vary in different cases. Sometimes the same remedy that we employ internally is used with benefit externally. Cleanliness especially should be required. To prevent the formation of crusts on the lids, the edges may be smeared at night with a little vaseline, simple cerate, cream or the like.

In conjunctivitis after the acute symptoms have subsided we sometimes find the inflammation will come to a standstill, notwithstanding our most careful selection of remedies; in these cases a mild astringent will be found advisable, and the following recommended to me by Dr. Burdick, has proved most serviceable:

> R. Zinci sulph., gr. ij
> Sodium chlorid., gr. iv
> Aqua dist., ℥i.
> Misce.

Instill a few drops in the eye four times a day. Atropine should not be used unless there is iritic complication.

The attendants should be warned that the discharge is contagious, and that the sponges, towels, etc., used upon the patient should not be employed for any other purpose.

Aconite.—Is especially indicated in the *first stage of catarrhal inflammation*, prior to exudation, if the conjunctiva is intensely hyperæmic and œdematous, with severe pain in the eye, often so terrible that one wishes to die; or, as is more frequently the case, a feeling of *burning and general heat in the eye, with great dryness.* There may also be an aching or bruised pain, or a feeling as if the ball were enlarged and protruding, making the lids tense. The eye is generally very sensitive, especially to air. This is the first remedy to be thought of for conjunctivitis, dependent upon exposure to cold, dry air. For inflammatory conditions of the conjunctiva, resulting from the *irritant action of foreign bodies* in that tissue, there is no better remedy. (It is in the Aconite stage that ice is most valuable.)

Allium cepa.—Of use in acute catarrhal conjunctivitis, associated with a similar condition of the air passages, as in hay fever; the lachrymation is scalding, profuse and not excoriating, though the nasal discharge is so (reverse of Euphrasia).

Alumina. — Inflammation of the conjunctiva, usually chronic and affecting chiefly the palpebral conjunctiva, always aggravated from over-use of the eyes and accompanied by a sensation of dryness in them, with moderate discharge and a heavy feeling in the lids. ·

Amyl nit.—Acute conjunctivitis with much redness, severe ciliary neuralgia, flushing and heat of corresponding side of face.

Apis mel.—Especially called for in the acute form of conjunctivitis, when the conjunctiva is bright red and puffy, lachrymation hot and moderately profuse, and pains in the eye, burning, biting or stinging; sometimes the pains are very severe, darting through the eye, or possibly around the eye and in the brows. Photophobia may be present. The *œdematous condition of the lids*, especially the upper, which is usually present in the cases in which Apis is indicated, is an important symptom. There is generally aggravation in the evening and fore part of the night. Although the lachrymation is hot and burning, yet it does not excoriate the lids, as in cases in which Arsenicum is indicated. General symptoms of dropsy, absence of thirst, etc., would suggest this remedy to our minds.

Argentum nit.—Should be employed if the *discharge becomes profuse*, assuming the character of purulent ophthalmia. It may also be indicated in the chronic form of conjunctivitis, when the conjunctiva is scarlet-red and the papillæ hypertrophied. The inflammatory symptoms usually subside in the open air, and are aggravated in a warm room.

Arnica.—In conjunctivitis resulting from blows and various injuries Arnica is often beneficial.

Arsenicum.—Occasionally useful in acute conjunctivitis with chemosis, much hot, scalding lachrymation, *burning pains, especially at night*, and œdematous condition of the lids, particularly the lower lid. It is also indicated in the chronic form, if the *lachrymation and discharge from the eyes are acrid*, excoriating the lids and cheek; the balls burn as if on fire, especially at night.

Warm applications generally relieve. The attacks of inflammation are frequently periodic and often alternate from one eye to the other.

Belladonna.—The remedy in the early stages of catarrhal conjunctivitis, if there is great dryness of the eyes, with a sense of dryness and stiffness in the thickened red lids, and smarting, burning pains in the eyes. Photophobia is marked. Much dependence should be placed, however, upon the concomitant symptoms of headache, red face, etc., etc. It will be seen that Bell. is similar to Aconite, and that both correspond to the early stages of the disease. The dryness of the eyes exists equally under both drugs; but under Acon. we have much more heat and burning in and around the eye than under Bell.

Calcarea carb.—Occasionally useful in catarrhal conjunc-

15

tivitis caused by working in water. Eyes hot with feeling of sand in them.

Causticum.—Conjunctivitis with a *feeling of sand in the eyes* and dull aching pain.

Chamomilla.—Catarrhal conjunctivitis, occurring in peevish children during dentition. Conjunctiva so congested that blood oozes out.

Cinnabaris.—May be called for in conjunctivitis, especially with the characteristic symptom of *pain above the eye, extending from the internal to the external canthus* (usually above, though sometimes below).

Duboisin.—Chronic hyperæmia of the palpebral conjunctiva in hyperopes.

Euphrasia.—In this drug, we have a very valuable remedy for both acute and chronic catarrhal conjunctivitis, especially acute. It is useful in catarrhal inflammation of the eye, caused by exposure to cold, and also in that of the eyes and nose found in the first stage of measles. In the selection of this drug, we are guided chiefly by the objective symptoms as the subjective are not very definite, there being a variety of sensations. The conjunctiva is intensely red; even chemosis. The *lachrymation is profuse, acrid, burning, while the discharge from the eye, which is also quite profuse, is thick, yellow, muco-purulent and acrid, making the lids and cheek sore and excoriated.* (The secretion is also excoriating under Arsenic and Mercurius, but is thinner.) *Blurring of the vision relieved by winking,* dependent upon the secretion covering the cornea temporarily, is especially characteristic of this remedy.

Graphites.—Sometimes indicated, especially in the chronic form of catarrhal conjunctivitis, though it is more particularly the remedy for phlyctenular ophthalmia. The redness, photophobia and lachrymation are usually well marked, but may vary to a great extent. The discharges from the eye, if present, are thin and acrid, while the *nose is sore, excoriated* and often surrounded by thick, moist scabs. Dry scurfs are frequently found on the lids, while the *external canthi crack and bleed easily.*

Hepar sulph.—Another remedy more useful in strumous

ophthalmia; though it is sometimes employed with benefit in the catarrhal form, as when the conjunctiva is much congested, even chemosis, with considerable photophobia and lachrymation, while the lids are much swollen and very sensitive to touch. The discharge is of a muco-purulent character and often well marked. The pains are throbbing, aching or lancinating and relieved by warmth, so that one wishes to keep the eye covered most of the time.

Ignatia.—Has been successfully used in catarrhal ophthalmia in nervous hysterical subjects, when there has been a sensation as if a grain of sand were rolling around under the lid, with great dryness and lachrymation only when exposed to the sunlight.

Merc. sol.—In mercury we possess an important remedy for catarrhal conjunctivitis, and this preparation is most commonly required, though some other may be employed, if the concomitant symptoms so indicate. The redness and dread of light are usually well marked, especially in the evening, by artificial light. The *lachrymation is profuse, burning and excoriating and the muco-purulent discharges thin and acrid*, making the lids and cheek red and sore. The pains vary in character and are not confined to the eye but extend into the forehead and temples, *are always worse at night*, especially before midnight, in extreme heat or cold and in damp weather, and are often temporarily ameliorated by cold water. It is especially indicated in syphilitic subjects, and when the concomitant symptoms of soreness of the head, excoriation of the nose, nocturnal pains, etc., are present.

Nux vomica.—Is not very often called for in this variety of conjunctivitis. It would be suggested to our minds if there were much dread of light, marked *morning aggravation* and accompanying gastric symptoms.

Pulsatilla.—This is another of our standard remedies for catarrhal conjunctivitis, especially the acute form, though it is also useful in the chronic. It is particularly to be thought of in conjunctivitis occurring in the colored race, as well as in the mild, tearful female. Catarrhal inflammations resulting from a cold, from bathing, an attack of measles, stricture of the lachrymal duct, traumatic and various other causes, have been benefited. The redness is variable and may be accompanied by chemosis. The pains in the eye are burning, itching or lancinating, usually worse in the evening, when in the wind, and after reading, but *relieved by the cool open air.* The lachrymation is often profuse by day, with a purulent discharge at night; though generally a *moderately profuse muco-purulent discharge of a white color and bland character,* which agglutinates the lids in the morning, is to be found. Gastric and other concomitant symptoms if present will influence our choice.

Rhus tox.—Is the chief remedy for conjunctivitis caused by *exposure in water* (Calc.), especially if there is much chemosis, with some photophobia, *profuse lachrymation* and *œdematous swelling of the lids.* A rheumatic diathesis would especially suggest this remedy.

Sanguinaria.—Benefit has been derived from its use in catarrhal conditions of the conjunctiva, with burning in the edges of the lids, worse in the afternoon. Hemorrhages in the conjunctiva with tendency to trachoma; moderate discharge and pain.

Sepia.—Acute catarrhal conjunctivitis with drawing sensation in the external canthi and smarting in the eyes, ameliorated by bathing in cold water and *aggravated morning and evening.* Conjunctivitis with muco-purulent discharge from the eyes in the morning and great dryness in the evening.

Spigelia.—Rarely useful, though, according to Lippe, it has benefited a case occurring in the left eye with *severe lancinating pains* in the eye and left temple, worse at night, preventing sleep.

Sulphur.—This is one of our chief remedies in both the acute and chronic forms of catarrhal conjunctivitis. The degree of redness may vary greatly: it may be confined to one eye or may involve both. The lids may be swollen or remain unaffected. The *sharp, darting pains, like pins piercing the eye,* occurring at any time of the day or night, will furnish our chief indication. A severe pain darting through the eye back into the head, from 1 to 3 A.M., waking the patient from sleep, is also an important indication. A variety of other sensations may be present; as pressing, tensive, cutting or burning pains, a feeling of sand in the eyes, etc. The patients are usually *feverish and restless at night.*

Terebinth.—Great redness of the conjunctiva, usually dark in color, with *severe pain in the eye and corresponding side of head.* Some pain in the back, and *urine dark in color.*

Zincum.—Has been useful in conjunctivitis especially when confined to the *inner half of the eye,* with much discharge: worse towards evening, and in the cool air. Generally there is *itching,* and perhaps pain, *in the internal canthus.*

The following remedies have also been used with benefit or may be indicated in occasional cases: Chelidonium, Chloral, Cuprum al., Cuprum sulph., Digitalis, Kali bichr., Natrum mur., Senega, Silicea and Thuja.

CONJUNCTIVITIS PURULENTA.

(Purulent Inflammation of the Conjunctiva.)

Under this head we shall include gonorrhœal ophthalmia and ophthalmia neonatorum, which are only different forms of purulent conjunctivitis. If the attack is very severe, the patient may be confined to a darkened room, or even to bed; if only one eye is affected, the other should be hermetically closed, in order to prevent any of the matter coming in contact with this eye, for this discharge is very contagious, especially in the gonorrhœal form and in that found in new-born children. On this account great care should be exercised, both by the nurse and physician, to protect their own eyes and those of others by providing that the sponges, towels, etc., are used only by the patient; also that their hands are thoroughly cleansed before touching another eye, for often the physician and other patients have been inoculated and vision destroyed through carelessness on this point. If by accident any of the discharge should have got into a healthy eye, lukewarm water should be at once injected under the lids to wash it away; after which, drop in a solution of chlorine-water, or a weak solution of nitrate of silver (gr. ij. ad ℥j.). Fresh air and nourishing diet are important aids. But the special and primary point to be attended to in the treatment is *cleanliness*. To ensure this, the discharges should be often removed by dropping warm water into the inner canthus, until all the pus has been washed away, or by cleansing with the palpebral syringe. This should be done at intervals of from fifteen minutes to an hour during the day and occasionally through the night, according to the severity of the case.

In the inflammatory stage of purulent conjunctivitis, *ice compresses* will usually be found most valuable, often aborting the attack. Ice-bags may be used on the eye, or pledgets of lint laid on a lump of ice until quite cold and then rapidly changed to the eye.

The topical application of caustics and astringents is not usually necessary. The same remedy that is used internally may also be often applied locally with advantage. (See Argent. nit.) The use of chlorine water, boracic acid and the like is frequently of great service. Astringents, especially a weak solution of nitrate of silver (2–5 grains to the ounce), may be required. If the patient is seen shortly after inoculation with gonorrhœal virus, evert the lids, and brush with a strong solution of nitrate of silver (gr. xxx. ad ℥j.) washing it off with water.

When the cornea becomes ulcerated, some operative measure or the use of Atropine may be required according to the complication. Canthoplasty may be necessary to relieve the pressure upon the eyeball, if the lids are much swollen and very tense. •

Aconite.—May be indicated in the very first stage, according to the symptoms given under catarrhal conjunctivitis; or if there is great redness, chemosis and profuse purulent discharge, with swelling and redness of the lids and *much burning heat in the eye.*

Apis mel.—Is useful in violent cases of purulent conjunctivitis and ophthalmia neonatorum if there is *great swelling (œdematous) of the lids and adjacent cellular tissue.* The conjunctiva is also congested, puffy and full of dark red veins. The discharge is moderate, not profuse, though the lachrymation is well marked. The character of the pains, which are

•

stinging and shooting, is an important indication. There is usually much photophobia accompanied by hot lachrymation (Rhus). The symptoms are aggravated in the evening. Objectively the Rhus cases are similar to Apis; the character of the pains will usually serve to distinguish between the two.

Argentum nit.—This is the most frequently indicated remedy in the whole Materia Medica for any form of purulent inflammation of the conjunctiva. It is not necessary to obtain its caustic effects, except in the gonorrhœal form of conjunctivitis, as the most intense chemosis with strangulated vessels, most profuse purulent discharge and commencing haziness of the cornea, with a tendency to slough, have been seen to subside rapidly under this remedy internally administered.

The subjective symptoms are almost none. Their very absence, with the profuse purulent discharge and the swollen lids, swollen from being distended by a collection of pus in the eye or from swelling of the sub-conjunctival tissues and not from infiltration of the connective tissue of the lids themselves (as in Rhus or Apis), indicates the drug.

We are in the habit of using the third or thirtieth potency internally, and, at the same time, a solution of five or ten grains of the first, third or thirtieth trituration to two drams of water as an external application, all the time taking great care to ensure cleanliness; and we have yet to see the first case go on to destruction of the cornea, when seen in the early stage.

Calcarea carb.—The discharges from the eye, under this drug, are often profuse and therefore it has been used with advantage in some cases of purulent or infantile ophthalmia, characterized by profuse, yellowish-white discharge, œdema of the lids and ulceration of the cornea. It is specially indicated when the trouble arises from working in the water. It is, however, especially useful for the *results* of purulent ophthalmia, clearing up the opacities of the cornea, etc. In the selection of this drug, great reliance should be placed upon the general condition (cachexia) of the patient, as the eye symptoms are not very characteristic.

Calcarea hypophos.—Purulent conjunctivitis, with ulceration of the cornea, occurring in patients who are very much debilitated and who have little vitality.

Chamomilla.—Is often of service in ophthalmia neonatorum as an intercurrent remedy, even if it does not remove the whole trouble. It is indicated when the child is very fretful and wants to be carried all the time, and when the usual symptoms of the disease are present even though the cornea has been invaded. Sometimes the conjunctiva is so much congested that blood may ooze out, drop by drop, from between the swollen lids, especially upon any attempt to open them (Nux).

Chlorine.—Aqua chlorinii, as an external application, has proved a very valuable remedy in the various forms of purulent ophthalmia. Cases have been relieved by it when used alone, as well as with the indicated remedy given at the same time internally (which has generally been the case). The strong solution is sometimes employed, though we usually dilute it to one-half, one-third or still weaker.

Euphrasia.—Is useful, especially in that form found in new-born children, more often in the later stages of the disease than at the beginning, as can well be understood by examining the symptoms already given under catarrhal conjunctivitis, where the indications have been stated.

Hepar sulph.—May be indicated in any form of this disease, particularly when the cornea has become implicated and ulceration has taken place. The *lids may be swollen, spasmodically closed, bleeding easily upon any attempt to open them and very sensitive to touch.* There is much redness, *chemosis,* and the *discharge is considerable,* of a yellowish-white color. The *photophobia is intense,* lachrymation profuse and pain severe, of a throbbing, aching character, relieved by warmth; any draught of air aggravates the symptoms. When the *ulceration is severe* and *hypopyon* has taken place, Hepar is especially the remedy.

Kreosote.—Blennorrhœa of the conjunctiva; the discharge is moderately profuse, with much smarting in the eyes.

Mercurius.—Has been employed with benefit, particularly in ophthalmia neonatorum when the *discharges were thin, excoriating* and *caused by syphilitic leucorrhœa.* It is also one of our best remedies for gonorrhœal ophthalmia and for purulent conjunctivitis found in syphilitic subjects, whether it be acquired or hereditary. The discharge, as has been said, is thin and excoriating, making the lids and cheek sore and raw. The lachrymation and photophobia are usually marked and the pains severe, though variable in character and always worse at night. Is more commonly called for late in the disease, especially if the cornea has become involved. The concomitant symptoms are important aids in the selection. Mercurius corr., Mercurius sol. and Mercurius præc. ruber have all been successfully used; though the eye symptoms, we believe, vary little in these preparations, except perhaps being more intense under the corrosivus.

Nitric acid.—Is especially advised for gonorrhœal ophthalmia. Lids much swollen, red, hard and painful, conjunctiva hyperæmic, chemosis, cornea ulcerated, great photophobia and lachrymation, copious discharge of yellow pus, which flows down the cheek, pressing and burning pain in the eye worse at night. The cheeks are also usually much swollen and painful. A few drops of the first or third potency in water may be used locally at the same time it is given internally.

Pulsatilla.—This remedy stands high in the treatment of purulent conjunctivitis, when the *discharge is profuse and bland.* Benefit has been gained from its use in blennorrhœa of the conjunctiva, caused by the gonorrhœal contagion. It is, however, most frequently useful in ophthalmia neonatorum, characterized by the usual well-marked symptoms. Many cases of this form of conjunctivitis have been cured by this drug alone, though we believe that it is particularly called for as an intercurrent remedy, during the treatment by Argent. nit.; for, often when the improvement under the latter remedy is at a stand still, a few doses of Pulsatilla will materially hasten the progress of the cure. The symptoms are usually worse in the evening and ameliorated in the open air.

Rhus tox.—Ophthalmia neonatorum, and when the trouble arises from exposure in water. The *lids are red, œdematous* and spasmodically closed. The palpebral conjunctiva is especially inflamed, so that when the lids are opened a thick, red swelling appears, with a *copious, thick, yellow, purulent discharge;* or the discharge may be less and a *profuse gush of tears may take place.* The child is usually cachectic and restless; head hot. It has been used both externally and internally.

Sulphur.—Is not so useful in this variety of conjunctivitis as in the pustular or even the catarrhal form, though it has been of service more frequently in that form found in new-born children, especially when the trouble has become chronic and when not dependent upon syphilis. The symptoms observed are not characteristic, with the exception, perhaps, of the sharp sticking pains, as if pins were sticking in the eye. We rely, to a great extent, in selecting this drug, upon the general condition (scrofulous cachexia) of the patient.

Other remedies, as Cupr. al., Cupr. sulph., Eserine, Natrum mur. and Nux vom., may be required.

CONJUNCTIVITIS DIPHTHERITICA ET CROUPOSA.

(Diphtheritic and Croupous Inflammation of the Conjunctiva.)

Although these two forms of inflammation are wholly distinct from each other, they will be considered under the same section, as the treatment is not dissimilar in many points. If only one eye is involved endeavor to prevent the extension of the disease to the other eye by hermetically closing it, for the discharge is very contagious; though extension may take place through the general dyscrasia. *Cleanliness* is of the greatest importance, as in purulent conjunctivitis. It is better not to exercise any force in removing the false membrane as it only leaves a raw surface, upon which a new membrane forms, thus doing more harm than good; though all loose shreds should be carefully removed whenever the eyes are washed.

The application of caustics or strong astringents, especially in diphtheritic conjunctivitis, is always injurious. In the early stages of either form of inflammation *ice compresses* seem to exert a beneficial influence over the course of the disease and should be used. A solution of *alcohol* and water (℥j ad ℥ij) has been employed locally with some benefit in diphtheritic inflammation; also a one per cent. solution of *carbolic acid*. In croupous inflammation, *chlorine water* has been useful as an external application. Corneal complications require especial attention. Cold compresses must be discontinued as soon as the cornea becomes involved.

Acetic acid.—A remedy of the first importance in croupous conjunctivitis in which the *false membrane is dense, yellow-white, tough and so closely adherent* that removal is almost impossible. The lids are œdematously swollen and red. Although the membrane is closely adherent it is not in the tissue and so does not correspond to diphtheritic conjunctivitis.

Aconite.—Of importance in the first stage. For indications refer to catarrhal conjunctivitis.

Apis mel.—Croupous conjunctivitis, or very early in the diphtheritic before the lids have become firm and hard. Lids *red and œdematous*, especially the upper. Marked *chemosis* and severe pains, of a *stinging, shooting* character. Patient drowsy and thirstless.

Argentum nit.—Blennorrhœal stage of either form of inflammation. The discharge is profuse and purulent. Use both externally and internally.

Arsenicum.—Of service in weak cachectic children who are very restless and thirsty, especially after midnight. False membrane firmly attached in places, with ulceration of the cornea. Lids swollen, lachrymation and discharges excoriating, and burning pain in the eyes.

Hepar sulph.—Blennorrhœal stage, or if the *cornea is ulcerating*. Pains severe and relieved by warmth.

Kali bichrom.—Both croupous and diphtheritic conjunctivitis. Especially indicated when the false membrane is present, if *shreds or strings of it float loose in the eye. The discharge is of a stringy character* and mixed with tears. Non-vascular ulceration of the cornea. General symptoms will confirm the above local indications.

Lachesis.—A great tendency to hemorrhage upon removing any of the membrane or even without doing so.

Mercurius prot.—This form of Mercury will be more commonly called for than the other preparations. Indicated in all stages of the disease. Membrane on the conjunctiva, and cornea ulcerated. Cornea more vascular, pains, photophobia and other symptoms of a higher degree than Kali bichr. ' The nocturnal aggravation and characteristic appearance of tongue and throat are present.

Phytolacca.—Should be valuable in diphtheritic conjunctivitis with *firm hard swelling of the lids*.

Calc. c., Carbol. ac., Chlorine, Bromine, Iodine, Kali iod., Pulsat., and Rhus should be borne in mind.

CONJUNCTIVITIS TRACHOMATOSA ET FOLLICULARIS.

(Acute and Chronic Granular or Follicular Inflammation of the Conjunctiva—with or without Pannus.)

[Syn. Granular Lids, Trachoma.]

As this form of conjunctivitis is usually found among the lower classes or those who are constantly exposed to wind and dust, care should be taken that these exciting causes be removed as far as possible; cleanliness and proper hygienic measures being very important aids in the treatment of this affection.

It should be remembered that the discharges from granular lids are contagious and that whole families or a whole school may be inoculated from one member, by an indiscriminate use of towels, etc.; therefore strict attention should be paid to the prevention of its extension.

There is no reason why trachoma should not be cured by the internal administration of medicines alone, but owing to the present inadequate knowledge of our drugs in this affection, a majority of the cases we meet prove so extremely obstinate to treatment that both the patient and doctor become discouraged. If a cure can be effected by internal medication it seems to be more permanent than if total reliance is placed upon local applications, but I do not hesitate to use local remedies if .there is no particular indication for any special drug, or if the case proves very obstinate. In acute trachoma or acute aggravations of chronic granular lids, *ice compresses* will prove very agreeable to the patient and aid materially in controlling the intensity of the inflammatory process. In chronic granular inflammation of the conjunctiva, especially when complicated with pannus which is usually present, local treatment will be found of the greatest service. The following topical applications have been followed by more favorable results in my hands than any others:

R.   Carbolic acid, gtt. vi
Glycerine, ℥j
Misce.

R.   Tannin, gr. xv
Glycerine, ℥j
Misce.

They should be applied with a camels hair brush to the everted lids once a day. Other applications which have also proved beneficial in individual cases are alum used as a powder, in a saturated solution with glycerine and in the crude stick; Cuprum aluminatum and sulphuricum used in crystals; nitrate of silver in a weak solution (gr. ij — x ad. ℥j); and bichromate of potash in a saturated solution.

At the same time local treatment is employed the carefully selected internal remedy should be administered.

Aconite.—In the first stage of granular conjunctivitis, when the eyes are *inflamed, hot, burning and very painful.* There may be a sensation of great *dryness,* or moderate lachrymation. *Acute aggravation of granular lids and pannus, with excessive hyperaemia, heat* and dryness, especially if the aggravation be induced by overheating from violent exercise or by exposure to dry, cold air. Ice compresses are especially serviceable in Aconite cases.

Alumen exsiccatum.—This remedy may be of value in all forms of trachoma, whether complicated with pannus or not. It is employed by dusting the crude powder on the inner surface of the lids, allowing it to remain about a minute and then washing it off with pure water and, at the same time, giving the lower preparations internally.

Alumina.—Chronic granular lids in which there is marked

dryness of the lids and eye especially in the evening, with burning, itching and pressure in the eyes; agglutination mornings; the upper lids are weak, and seem to hang down as if paralyzed. The symptoms of loss of power in the upper lids are often met with in old dry cases of granulation; in these cases Alumina does good.

Argentum nit.—Especially serviceable in the early stages of acute granular conjunctivitis, if the conjunctiva is intensely pink or scarlet-red and the *discharge is profuse* and inclined to be muco-purulent.

Arsenicum.—Indicated in chronic granular lids, when the palpebral conjunctiva only is inflamed; the lids are painful, dry and rub against the ball; they burn and can scarcely be opened. Chiefly called for when the pains are intense burning, and the lachrymation very excoriating.

Aurum met.—Is the appropriate remedy for many cases of trachoma either with or without pannus (especially however, when pannus is present); there is probably no other remedy which has only been employed internally, that has cured more cases. Its use is highly recommended, though the local symptoms which lead us to its selection have not yet been found peculiar or characteristic. The pains may be burning or dull in character, compelling the patient to close the lids. They are usually worse in the morning and ameliorated by the application of cold water. For the corneal ulcerations found in pannus Aurum is of great value.

The *muriate of gold* is frequently employed, though the symptoms, as far as known, vary but slightly from those of the metal.

Belladonna.—As a temporary remedy in acute aggravations of granular lids may be beneficial. After taking cold the eyes become sensitive to air and light, with dryness and a gritty feeling in them.

Calcarea carb.—Conjunctivitis trachomatosa with pannus, caused by working in the water, with much redness and lachrymation, has been relieved by this drug. The general condition of the patient will, to a great extent, lead to its selection.

Carbolic acid.—Chronic trachoma, especially with pannus. Can be given internally at the same time it is used locally.

Chelidonium.—Trachoma, with pain in and over the eye upon looking upwards.

Chininum mur.—Marked improvement has been observed from the internal use of this drug in granular lids, with or without pannus.

Cuprum al.—The aluminate of copper has been successfully used to a great extent in trachoma, either with or without pannus. The results obtained are usually much more satisfactory than those from the sulphate of copper, which is the main reliance of the old school in the treatment of this disorder. It is employed locally by application of the crystals to the granulations, at the same time giving the remedy in the potencies internally.

Euphrasia.—Trachoma with or without pannus, if the eye is very red and irritable, with *profuse lachrymation and thick discharge, which excoriate the lids and cheek.*

Kali bichr.—Trachoma with pannus; much discharge; every thing appears slightly red; usually not much photophobia or redness of conjunctiva, though ulceration of the cornea may be present; eyes seem to feel better when lying on the face. A saturated solution applied to the granulations is often beneficial.

Mercurius præc. rub.—In trachoma with pannus it is a valuable remedy; rarely of much use in acute cases, but especially adapted to old chronic cases, when the cornea is covered with pannus of a high degree, with considerable redness, discharge and photophobia. The granulations may be present or may have been already removed by caustics.

Mercurius protoiod.—Especially if pannus accompanies the trachoma and the eye is quite *red and painful, with photophobia* and acrid discharges. *Tongue coated yellow at the base.* Is the remedy for *ulceration of a pannoused cornea, particularly if superficial.*

Natrum mur.—Particularly useful in follicular conjunctivitis, in chronic cases and when the lids have been already treated by caustics (especially the nitrate of silver). The pannus or the irritable condition of the eye resulting from, or kept up by the scarred palpebral conjunctiva found after cauterization, is often greatly relieved by this drug. The lachrymation is acrid and excoriating, as well as the discharges which are thin, watery, and make the cheek raw and sore. The pains are variable, though sometimes we have a sharp pain over the eye upon looking down, which is very marked. The skin of the face round the eye is often glossy and shining.

Nux vom.—Of service in old cases of trachoma that have had much treatment, especially when complicated with pannus. Nux is frequently of great benefit in commencing the treatment of granular lids with or without pannus; also as an intercurrent remedy for the morning aggravation, which is particularly marked under this drug and in the disease. It will rarely however, effect a cure, unassisted by any other remedy.

Pulsatilla.—The granulations are generally very fine (papillary trachoma); the eye is sometimes dry or there may be excessive secretion of bland mucus. There may also be soreness of the ball to touch, and itching or pain in the eye, which is worse in the evening and better in cool air or by cold applications.

Rhus tox.—Of value in relieving the intensity of the symptoms found in conjunctivitis granulosa with pannus. The eye is quite red, with *much photophobia and profuse lachrymation.* No remedy acts so powerfully as Rhus tox. in diminishing the profuse secretion of tears.

Sepia.—Follicular or trachomatous conjunctivitis which is only observed in, or always made worse by hot weather.

Sulphur.—Trachoma, acute and chronic, with or without pannus, has been benefited by this drug which is often called for as an intercurrent remedy, even if it does not complete the cure alone. It is especially indicated when the *pains are sharp and lancinating in character,* worse in the morning; and when the lids are glued together by the secretion during the night. The application of water is not agreeable to the patient and it often aggravates the disease.

Thuja occid.—Favorable results have been gained by the use of this remedy in conjunctivitis trachomatosa, when the granulations have been large, like warts or blisters, with burning in the lids and eyes, worse at night; photophobia by day, and suffusion of the eyes with tears.

The following remedies have also been employed with favorable results: Causticum, Cinnabaris, Conium, Cuprum sulph., Hepar, Mercurius, Petrol., Sanguinaria and Zinc.

OPHTHALMIA PHLYCTENULARIS.

(Phlyctenular or Pustular Inflammation of the Cornea and Conjunctiva.)

[Syn. Ophthalmia scrofulosa, Ophthalmia exanthem., Keratitis phlyct., Conjunctivitis phlyct., Pustular Ophthalmia, Herpes corneæ.]

It has been thought best to include under this head the various forms of pustular inflammation of the eye, whether affecting the cornea or conjunctiva, as the etiology, symptomatology, course and treatment vary little in either case; in fact those remedies which have been found useful when the cornea is invaded, are also our chief reliance in this form of inflammation of the conjunctiva.

The first points to be attended to are cleanliness and regulation of diet. The eyes should be bathed often in lukewarm water, and any little scabs which may have formed on the lids immediately removed, as they only prove a source of irritation. If there is considerable photophobia, and the child is rubbing the eye constantly, a compress bandage will prevent this, and, at the same time, by keeping the lids closed, will relieve the irritation to the eye-ball occasioned by their constant opening and closing; it also excludes the light, relieving the photophobia, soaks up the tears and so prevents their running over the cheek, making it sore and excoriated. The bandage if used, though it is not commonly necessary, should be removed every four or five hours and the eyes cleansed. External applications should not, as a rule, be employed, as we can usually cure better and quicker with internal remedies alone if we are careful in the selection of our drugs, although

16

sometimes they may be useful and necessary; thus, occasionally a case will be found which has proved very obstinate to treatment; ciliary injection great, photophobia intense and pupil a little sluggish—in which, a weak solution of *Atropine* dropped into the eye, once or twice a day, will be of great benefit.

Antimonium crud.—Pustules on the cornea or conjunctiva, especially in cross children who are afflicted with pustules on the face and moist eruptions behind the ears. The lids are red, swollen, and excoriated by the profuse mucus discharges and lachrymation. Excoriation of the nostrils, and swollen upper lip. (Similar to Graphites.)

Apis mel.—Pustular keratitis with dark puffy conjunctiva and œdematous lids. This puffy condition of the conjunctiva and lids is very important, especially when accompanied by burning, *stinging* or shooting pains in the eyes. The discharges are slight, with the exception of the tears, which are usually profuse and burning, with photophobia (Rhus). The aggravation is usually in the evening, and often concomitant symptoms, such as drowsiness and absence of thirst, are present. This remedy is not frequently called for, though useful when the above indications are present.

Arsenicum.—Especially useful when the cornea has become affected and the pustules have broken, leaving *superficial ulceration.* The *photophobia is usually intense* at all times, though it may be so relieved in the open air that the child will open its eyes easily. The lachrymation is profuse, *burning and excoriating, as are all the discharges from the eye,* which are also thin in character. The conjunctival redness is variable; chemosis. The pains are generally of a burning character and may be very severe; the eye often feels very hot. The lids may be œdematous and spasmodically closed or else red, inflamed and excoriated by the acrid discharges. The nostrils and upper lip are usually excoriated by the acrid coryza. It is especially indicated in low, cachectic conditions, and for the ill-nourished, scrofulous children of the poor. Great restlessness and thirst for small quantities of water are commonly noticed.

Aurum met.—Scrofulous ophthalmia with ulceration and

vascularity of the cornea. Photophobia severe, lachrymation profuse and scalding; eyes very sensitive to the touch. The pains are from without inward and worse upon touch (reverse of Asafœtida). The cervical glands are usually swollen; patient very irritable and sensitive to noise.

Baryta.—Both the carbonate and iodide have been employed in scrofulous ophthalmia, especially when complicated with *enlarged cervical glands*. We have obtained better results from the iodide than from the carbonate.

Belladonna.—Rarely useful except in acute aggravations in which there is great photophobia.

Calcarea carb.—Particularly indicated in phlyctenular keratitis, though it has also been successfully used in conjunctivitis. It is indicated when the disease can be traced to exposure to wet. We usually, though not always, find excessive photophobia and lachrymation (often acrid). The amount of redness is variable, as is also the character of the pain, though this is more commonly described as sticking than otherwise. The lids may be red, swollen and agglutinated in the morning. There is a general *aggravation of the eye-symptoms during damp weather*, or from the least cold, to which the patient is very susceptible. It is especially the remedy for pustular inflammation, occurring in *fat, unhealthy, strumous children* who have enlarged glands, distended abdomen, pale, flabby skin, eruptions on the head and body, which burn and itch, and cold sweat of the head. In fact, upon the concomitant symptoms we place our chief reliance, as the eye symptoms are not characteristic.

Calcarea iod.—The indications are nearly the same as for Calcarea carb., though it is preferable in cases in which we have considerable swelling of the tonsils and cervical glands.

Calendula.—Pustular conjunctivitis, with great redness, but no photophobia.

Cannabis ind.—Large pustules on the conjunctiva, with great vascularity.

Chamomilla.—Has proved very serviceable in scrofulous ophthalmia occurring in *cross, peevish children, during dentition*, and will often relieve the severity of the symptoms, even though it does not complete the cure. The cornea is usually invaded, and we have great intolerance of light, considerable redness and lachrymation.

Cinnabaris.—The cornea is generally implicated in the trouble, and the symptoms of photophobia, lachrymation, etc., are severe. *Pain from the inner canthus across the eyebrows*, or extending around the eye is a very marked indication for Cinnabaris.

Conium mac.—When the inflammation is chiefly confined to the cornea, and we have *intense photophobia and profuse lachrymation* upon any attempt to open the spasmodically closed lids. The pains are various, but are generally worse at night. With all this intense photophobia, there is *very slight, or no redness of the conjunctiva*, not sufficient to account for the severity of the symptoms.

Croton tig.—Phlyctenular keratitis and conjunctivitis, associated with a vesicular eruption on the face and lids; the eyes and face feel hot and burning, especially at night; the photophobia is marked; ciliary injection like iritis often present, and considerable pain in and around the eye, usually worse at night.

Euphrasia.—Phlyctenular ophthalmia, in which the *lachrymation is excessive, acrid*, and burning, or if there is a profuse, *thick, acrid, muco-purulent discharge, which excoriates the lids*, making them red, inflamed and sore; from this discharge the cheek may look as if varnished. Intolerance of light is generally present, though not always, and the conjunctiva may be red; even chemosis. The pains are not marked, though usually of a smarting character from the nature of the discharges. *Blurring of the eyes, relieved by winking*, dependent upon the secretions temporarily covering the cornea, especially indicates Euphrasia. Fluent, acrid coryza, often accompanies the above symptoms.

Graphites.—This is one of the most important remedies we possess for this disease, and its sphere of action is not limited to any special variety, for excellent results have been gained from its use in both the acute and chronic form, whether the cornea is involved or not; it is, perhaps, more often called for in phlyctenular keratitis of the chronic recurrent form. It is especially indicated in scrofulous subjects, covered with eczematous eruptions, chiefly on the head and behind the ears, which eruptions are glutinous, fissured, and bleed easily. The *photophobia is usually intense*, and the lachrymation profuse, though in some cases, nearly or entirely absent; generally worse by daylight than gaslight, and in the morning, so that often the child cannot open the eyes before 9 or 10 A. M. The redness of the eye is generally important (there may be pannus); the discharges are muco-purulent, constant, thin and excoriating. The pains are not important and vary; may be sticking, burning, aching, or itching. The lids are red, sore, and agglutinated in the morning, or else covered with dry scabs, while the *external canthi are cracked and bleed easily upon opening the eye.* We often notice a *thin, acrid discharge from the nose* accompanying the eye affection.

Hepar sulph.—Is most useful in the severer forms of pustular inflammation, especially when upon the cornea, and when ulceration has already commenced. The intensity of the symptoms suggests its use, as *intense photophobia, lachrymation, and great redness of the eye, even chemosis.* The pains are severe, generally of a *throbbing*, stinging character, *ameliorated by warmth* (so that one wishes to keep the eye covered), and aggravated by cold or uncovering the eye; also usually worse at night or in the evening. The lids are often swollen, spasmodically closed and very *sensitive to touch*; also may be *red, swollen, and bleed easily upon opening.* Particularly indicated in scrofulous, outrageously cross children who have eruptions and boils on various portions of the body.

Ipecac.—It is one of the most frequently indicated remedies in pustules and ulcers of the cornea and conjunctiva. There is *much photophobia.* The redness and pain is variable. Nausea may be present.

Kali bichrom.—Is adapted to phlyctenules on the conjunctiva or to chronic cases of low grade. The chief characteristics are *absence of photophobia and of redness*, or much less of each than would be expected from the nature of the disease. The pains and lachrymation are also generally absent or nearly so.

The eye is often quite sensitive to touch, and its secretions are of a stringy character. This form of potash has been more often employed than any other, though the iodide is also useful in similar cases.

Mercurius.—Mercury, in some form, is a frequent remedy for strumous ophthalmia, especially when the cornea has become involved. As the symptoms are similar in all the preparations, we shall first, under this general head, give those symptoms common to all forms and afterwards give the special indications for each. This is the first remedy to be thought of when this form of inflammation occurs in *syphilitic subjects*, whether the taint is hereditary or acquired. Especially useful when the cornea is invaded and the vascularity is great, though sometimes there may be a well-marked grayish infiltration around the pustule or ulcer. The redness of the conjunctiva is usually great; the dread of light is generally marked and often intense, so that the patients cannot open their eyes even in a darkened room, and it is more often *aggravated by any artificial light*, as gaslight, or the glare of a fire. The *lachrymation is profuse, burning and excoriating*, and the *muco-purulent discharges are thin and acrid*. The *pains are generally severe*, varying in character, though more often tearing, burning, shooting or lancinating and are not confined to the eye, but extend to the forehead and temples, seeming to lie deep in the bones; they are *always aggravated at night*, especially before midnight, by heat, extreme cold, and in damp weather and are temporarily relieved by cold water. The lids are often spasmodically closed, thick, red, swollen, excoriated from the acrid lachrymation and sensitive to heat or cold and also to contact. The concomitant symptoms of excoriation of the nose, condition of the tongue, eruption on the face, pain in the bones, etc., etc., are of the first importance in selecting this drug.

Mercurius corr.—Indicated in the erethistic form of inflammation, occurring in strumous subjects. The pustules are usually found upon the cornea, and hence the severity of the symptoms so marked under this preparation of mercury, which is more useful than solubilis in severe cases; the pains are more severe, photophobia more marked, lachrymation more profuse and excoriating, and all the symptoms more intense than under any preparation we have. Pustules on the cheek, enlarged cervical glands, coated tongue, excoriating coryza, etc., are usually present.

Mercurius dulc.—Calomel dusted into the eye has been employed for many years by the old school in scrofulous ophthalmia, and even now is considered one of their chief remedies. We also have found this remedy, given internally in the potencies, very useful in the severer forms of this inflammation, occurring in pale, flabby, scrofulous subjects. Nose sore and upper lips swollen.

Mercurius nit. — This remedy seems to be particularly adapted to this form of inflammation, and has been used, especially by Dr. Liebold, with remarkable success, in a large number of cases. Severe as well as mild, chronic as well as acute cases, superficial as well as deep ulcers have yielded to its influence; in some cases there has been *much photophobia*, in others none at all, in some *severe pain*, in others none. We might thus go through a variety of symptoms differing as much as the above, in which this drug has proved curative. It is commonly used externally and internally at the same time; the first potency, ten grains to two drachms of water (or even stronger) as an external application, to be used in the eye, two, three or more times a day, and the second or third potency to be taken internally. *Atropine* is sometimes used with it, especially if there is considerable photophobia.

Mercurius praec. rub.—This varies little from the general description given of mercury; it is used in strumous ophthalmia with great benefit.

Mercurius prot.—Not as often required as the other forms of mercury, unless there be quite extensive superficial ulceration of the cornea, with much photophobia and nocturnal aggravation. There is also, usually, swelling of the glands, and the tongue has a thick yellow coating at the base.

Mercurius sol.—Is very often employed in scrofulous ophthalmia; the indications correspond very closely in all points to those found under the head of Mercurius.

Mezereum.—Pustular conjunctivitis, accompanied by eczema of the face and lids, especially if characterized by thick, hard scabs, from under which pus exudes on pressure.

Natrum mur.—Especially useful in chronic cases and after the use of caustics (nitrate of silver). The eye symptoms are not particularly characteristic; there may be itching, burning and feeling as of sand in the eyes, worse in the morning and forenoon; the pains are not severe, except perhaps the sharp pain over the eye upon looking down. The lachrymation is acrid and excoriating, making the lids red and sore; the discharges from the eye are also thin, watery and acrid. The photophobia is usually marked, and the lids are spasmodically closed. The skin of the face, around the eyes, is often *glossy and shining*, while throbbing headache and other concomitant symptoms are generally present.

Nux vom.—Favorable results have been gained in *cases previously much medicated,* both externally and internally. Rarely of service when the conjunctiva only is affected, as the most characteristic indications are *excessive photophobia and morning aggravation of all symptoms,* which are indications that the cornea is implicated. The lachrymation is usually profuse and the pains vary as follows: sharp, darting pains in the eye and over it, in some cases extending to the top of the head and always worse in the morning; burning pains in the eyes and lids; a sense of tearing in the eye at night on awaking from sleep; eye feels pressed out whenever she combs her hair; sensation as of hot water in the eye; pain in the lower lid as if something were cutting it, etc. Sometimes relief from the pain is obtained by bathing the eyes in cold water.

Psorinum.—Especially adapted to *chronic cases of recurrent scrofulous ophthalmia.*

Pulsatilla.—This is one of our sheet anchors in the treatment of this disease, especially when the *pustules are confined to the conjunctiva.* It is particularly indicated in persons, especially amenorrhœic females, of a mild temperament and fair complexion, and is also very suitable to this class of ailments, occurring in the negro. When pain in the ear, otorrhœa and other aural symptoms accompany the eye disorder, this remedy would be suggested to our minds. The dread of light is often absent or quite moderate, and the redness varies. The lachrymation is not acrid, but more abundant in the open air, while the other *discharges are generally profuse, thick, white or yellow and bland.* The pains vary greatly, but are more often of a pressing, stinging character. The lids may be swollen, are not excoriated, but very *subject to styes.* The eyes feel worse on getting warm from exercise or in a heated room and generally in the evening, but are *ameliorated in the open air* and by cold applications. The concomitant symptoms of stomach derangement, amenorrhœa, etc., must be taken into consideration.

Rhus tox.—Useful in pustular inflammation after it has progressed to superficial ulceration of the cornea; for then we have present the *intense photophobia and profuse lachrymation* so characteristic of this drug. The conjunctiva may be very red, even *chemosis, and the lids œdematous, particularly the upper, and spasmodically closed, so that we are compelled to open them by force when a profuse gush of tears takes place.* The skin of the face, around the eyes, is often covered by a Rhus eruption; especially suitable in a rheumatic diathesis. The symptoms are usually worse at night, after midnight and in damp weather; the patients are restless at night, and disturbed by bad dreams. *Rhus rad.* has been employed with excellent results in scrofulous ophthalmia when the above symptoms were present. In what respect it differs from Rhus tox. remains to be shown.

Sepia.—Especially of value in pustular inflammation found in women, either *occurring with or dependent upon uterine troubles.* More often called for when the cornea is affected than when the inflammation is confined to the conjunctiva. The pains are usually of a drawing, aching, piercing character; aggravated by rubbing, pressing the lids together or pressing upon the eye. The light of day dazzles and causes the head to ache. The conjunctiva may be swollen, with agglutination of the eyes morning and evening, considerable purulent discharge, edges of the lids raw and sore, feeling as if the lids were too tight and did not cover the ball, eruption on the face, etc. *All the symptoms are worse in the morning and evening* and better in the middle of the day.

Sulphur.—This is the remedy, *par excellence,* for pustular in-

flammation of the cornea or conjunctiva. Its sphere of action
is very wide and adapts it to a great variety of cases, especially
chronic and occurring in scrofulous children covered with eruptions
(and the majority of cases are found in this class); also to
those cases which have been caused by suppressing an eruption
with external applications. The pains vary, though are usually of a *sharp, lancinating character, as if a needle or splinter were
piercing the eye*, and may occur at any time of the day or night;
we may have a *sharp, shooting pain going through the eye back
into the head, from 1 to 3* A.M., which disturbs the sleep of the
patients; although, besides these, there may be a variety of
other sensations, as smarting, itching and burning in the eyes,
feeling of pressure as from a foreign body; burning, as from
lime; stinging, burning in the eye, especially from light and
in the morning; biting, as if salt were in the eye; sensations
as if there were a number of little burning sparks on the lids,
which cause them to close spasmodically; painful dryness as
if the lids rubbed the eyeball, bruised pain, etc., etc. The
photophobia is generally very marked and the lachrymation
profuse, though in some cases they may be almost or entirely
absent. The redness varies greatly, but is usually considerable, especially at the angles; the secretions also vary both in
quantity and quality, being often, however, acrid and corrod-
ing, and sometimes tenacious. Agglutination in the morning
is commonly present. The lids are often swollen, burn and
smart as if bathed in some acrid fluid, or there is an itching
sensation compelling the patient to rub them most of the time.
They are frequently covered with an eruption, as well as the
surrounding integument of the head and face. All the symptoms are, as a rule, *aggravated by bathing the eyes, so that the
child cannot bear to have any water touch them;* also usually worse
in the open air.

Syphilinum.—Chronic recurrent phlyctenular inflammation, in scrofulous delicate children, especially if there is any
taint of hereditary syphilis. The epithelial layer of the cornea will be abraded. The photophobia will be intense and
lachrymation profuse.

Tellurium.—Has proved successful in phlyctenular conjunctivitis, with eczema impetiginoides on the lids and much purulent discharge from the eyes, complicated with an offensive otorrhœa, smelling like fishbrine.

Thuja.—Large phlyctenules which involve the subconjunctival tissue and are slow in yielding to usual remedies.

Zincum.—Favorable results have been obtained for the persistent redness of the eye remaining after pustular keratitis; especially if the redness is more marked at the inner angle and worse toward evening and in the open air.

The following remedies have also proved serviceable in scrofulous ophthalmia, though not so commonly called for as the above: Antimon. tart., Argentum nit., Caust., Cuprum al., Kali mur., Kreosot., Lachesis, Petroleum, Robinia, Squilla, Sulphur iod.

OPHTHALMIA TRAUMATICA ET ECCHYMOSIS.

(Traumatic Inflammation of the Cornea and Conjunctiva. Hemorrhage in Conjunctiva.)

The first point to which our attention should be directed is the removal of any exciting cause, as a foreign body. (See Injuries of Conjunctiva.)

Applications of cold water, ice compresses, or a solution of one of the following remedies are advised, unless due to some chemical injury.

A compress bandage sometimes seems to hasten the absorption of hemorrhages into the conjunctiva.

Aconite.—There is no remedy more frequently useful than this in *inflammatory conditions of the eye, resulting from the irritant action of foreign bodies,* as cinders, chips of steel, stone or coal, which produce a variable amount of redness and pain, with a sensation of *dryness, heat and burning* in the eye.

Arnica.—An important remedy for *traumatic conjunctivitis or keratitis, following blows and various injuries* of the eye. It is particularly called for *immediately* after the injury, before the inflammatory symptoms have really set in, though is also useful in the latter stages. Both spontaneous and traumatic hemorrhages into the conjunctiva have been promptly absorbed under the use of Arnica.

The relaxation of the blood-vessels and too fluid conditions of the blood, which predispose to these hemorrhages in whooping cough have seemed to be corrected by this drug.

Calendula.—Useful in traumatic inflammation of the conjunctiva or cornea, *following any operation* or resulting from a cut wound of any description.

Cantharis.—Ophthalmia traumatica, *caused from any burn*, as from the flame of a candle, explosion of fireworks, etc., especially if characterized by much *burning pain* in the eye.

Hamamelis virg.—Has proved very beneficial in traumatic conjunctivitis and keratitis, consequent upon burns or other injuries. It also seems to hasten the absorption of conjunctival hemorrhages. "Pond's Extract" may be used locally.

Ledum pal.—Is more commonly called for in both *traumatic and spontaneous ecchymoses of the conjunctiva* than any other remedy. It also often seems to correct the tendency to hemorrhage in these cases. Of value in inflammation of the conjunctiva in which extravasations of blood predominate.

Any of the above remedies, with perhaps the exception of Cantharis, should always be used locally as well as internally in the proportion of from ten to twenty drops of the tincture to the ounce of water. Compresses wet in this should be laid upon the eye.

Euphrasia, Hepar, Ignatia, Nux, Rhus, Silicea and other remedies may prove serviceable when special indications point to their use.

XEROPHTHALMIA.

(Dryness of the Conjunctiva from Atrophy.)

(Syn. Xerosis Conjunctivæ.)

The treatment can only be palliative, that is, ameliorate the excessive dryness which gives rise to so much heat and pain. Milk answers the purpose very well, or a weak solution of glycerine and water, to which one per cent. of salt should be added. Artificial serum is perhaps better still. "Cold expressed castor oil has also proved effectual."—Thomas.

PTERYGIUM.

(Hypertrophy of the Conjunctiva.)

This disease, considered by the old school as proof against internal medication, has yielded to the proper homœopathic remedy, though it is true that cases are often met, which prove very obstinate to treatment (probably owing to our incomplete knowledge of the Materia Medica); in which cases we are compelled to resort to operative measures. Numerous methods have been advocated, chief among which are excision, ligation and transplantation; for the description of these we would refer to any of the text books on the subject.

Calcarea carb.—Especially indicated in *pterygium caused from exposure to wet and cold.*

Chimaphila.—This drug has been used in many cases, in which no marked indications have been present, with some success, though it has also often failed to improve.

Zincum.—Zinc has been more frequently employed and with greater satisfaction than any other remedy, especially in that form of pterygium which extends from the inner canthus (as it usually does); for the majority of the eye symptoms are found at the inner angle as will be noticed by examination of the provings. The lachrymation is usually profuse and photophobia marked, especially by artificial light. The pains are pricking, with *itching and soreness in the inner angle* worse at night; also itching and heat in the eyes, worse in the cold air and better in a warm room; external canthi cracked; green halo around the evening light. There may also be present great *pressure across the root of the nose* and supraorbital region.

The following remedies are also reported to have been employed with advantage in the treatment of pterygium when suggested by constitutional symptoms or certain general characteristic eye indications: Argent. nit., Arsen., Cannabis, Psor., Ratan., Spig., and Sulph.

ANCHYLOBLEPHARON ET SYMBLEPHARON.

(Adhesion of the Edges of the Lids, and of the Lid to the Eyeball.)

Either affection is only amenable to operative interference, which must vary according to the position and extent of the adhesion.

TUMORES.

(Tumors of the Conjunctiva.)

They may be removed in some cases, according to the nature of the tumor, by the proper selection of our drugs based upon constitutional symptoms, though we are often compelled to have recourse to operative measures.

Calcarea.—Some benefit has been derived from its use in polypi of the conjunctiva.

Kali bichrom.—A saturated aqueous solution, used locally, has been employed with excellent success in polypi.

Lycopodium is reported to have cured polypi, but I have also seen it fail.

Lapis alb.—Slight improvement in a case of melanoma has been observed.

LÆSIONES.

(Injuries of the Conjunctiva.)

These may be of a mechanical or chemical nature. If mechanical they are usually dependent upon some foreign body which has lodged on the conjunctiva, therefore the first point to be attended to is its removal, which is generally easily effected. After which, directions should be given to bathe the eye in cold water or a weak solution of *Aconite*, Arnica or Calendula. This will usually suffice, though in severe cases it may be advisable to drop a little olive oil into the eye after removing the foreign body.

Chemical injuries, especially from lime, are, unfortunately, of frequent occurrence and very dangerous in their nature on account of the formation of deep sloughs, which have a great tendency to result in symblepharon. If seen early, we should endeavor to remove as much as possible of the lime and then drop into the eye either a little olive oil, oil of sweet almonds, milk, weak solution of vinegar or some substance which will unite with the lime and form an innocuous compound. Water should never be employed. Great care should be taken while the wound is healing that no adhesions between the lids and ball occur. If there is a tendency in this direction, the adhesions should be broken up once or twice a day by means of a probe.

When the injury is from strong acids, as sulphuric or nitric, the eye should be syringed out with a weak solution of carbonate of soda or potassa (∂j to $\bar{\mathfrak{z}}$vi aq. destil.) in order to neutralize the acid; afterwards olive oil should be dropped in.

CORNEA.

KERATITIS.

(Inflammation of the Cornea.)

[Under this heading is included Keratitis superficialis, Keratitis pannosa, Keratitis ulcerosa, Uleus corneæ (cum Hypopion), Abscessus corneæ and Keratitis suppurativa.]

Superficial inflammation of the cornea will not usually require local treatment, unless it is caused by granular lids (see conjunctivitis trachomatosa page 236) or by entropion, inverted lashes, etc., in which case the cause must, of course, be first removed. Severe cases, not dependent upon granular lids or traumatic causes, will be greatly improved by the use of a *bandage*. *Atropine* may be of service in rare cases, with much photophobia and deep ciliary injection, though is not commonly necessary under appropriate homœopathic treatment. If the palpebral aperture is much shortened and the eyelids thus press upon the eyeball, the outer canthus may be divided (canthoplasty) so as to relieve the increased pressure on the cornea. In obstinate cases of pannus, syndectomy or even inoculation of purulent matter may be thought of.

In the treatment of ulcers and abcesses of the cornea, local and dietetic measures are of great importance. If the ulcer is extensive, the patient should be directed to remain quiet in the house (in bed, if possible) that absolute rest may be obtained. As this disease is more often found in weak, debilitated subjects, a very nutritious diet should be prescribed, and it may even be necessary to use stimulants; in these cases the concentrated tincture of *avena sativa*, ten drop doses four times a day, or the use of *cod liver oil* will be found of great service.

As a rule *cold applications* are injurious, except occasionally in the first or inflammatory stage of superficial keratitis, or in ulceration of the cornea occurring during the course of pannus. *Hot poultices* also are not advised, except in indolent ulcers which are deep, non-vascular and have no tendency to heal, in which they may often be employed with advantage.

Bandaging upon the other hand is of the utmost importance in the treatment, even in some cases producing a cure alone. In all cases in which the ulcer or abscess is deep, or obstinate to treatment, a protective bandage should be immediately applied. It is usually sufficient to bandage only the affected eye (if one be healthy) unless the ulcer be very deep and extensive, when both eyes should be covered. The objects of the bandage are; to keep the eye quiet and protected by its natural coverings, the lids, from all irritating causes, such as wind, dust, etc., and to keep the eye warm, in order to promote local nutrition.

Atropine is not usually required in ulcers or abscesses of the cornea, unless the ulcer is central and has a tendency to perforate, or if iritis complicates the corneal trouble; then Atropine should be employed until full dilatation of the pupil is produced, which should be maintained. It may also be of service in relieving the great irritability and intense photophobia observed in some obstinate forms of corneal inflammation.

Eserine should be instilled if the ulcer tends toward perforation at the periphery or if the intraocular tension becomes increased.

External applications are rarely necessary, though sometimes good results have followed the external use of the same drug that is prescribed internally. *Aqua chlorinii* used locally, has proved beneficial in some cases, *especially in the crescentic form,* and when the discharge of pus has been profuse. It may be used pure or diluted one-half, one-third, or even more.

In those cases in which the ulcer is deep, with a great tendency to perforate, "*Sæmisch's incision*" is recommended. It consists in cutting through the ulcer into the anterior chamber, with a Graefe's cataract knife, which is entered in the healthy tissue on one side, and brought out in the healthy tissue on the other side of the ulceration, which is then divided by a sawing movement of the knife; after which Atropine is instilled and a compress bandage applied. The wound can be

17

kept open by the aid of a spatula or Daviel's spoon, for two or three days if desirable.

Paracentesis may also be resorted to in the above cases, though it has been nearly supplanted by "Sæmisch's incision" which, in the majority of instances, is far preferable. All ulcers should be closely watched, that we may detect any hernia of the cornea or prolapse of the iris as soon as they occur. If a prolapse has taken place, and is of recent origin, we should endeavor to replace it, either by dilating or contracting the pupil, according to its situation; if this proves inadequate, the protruding iris should be snipped off with a pair of scissors, Atropine instilled and a pressure bandage applied.

Aconite.—Superficial ulceration of the cornea, of *traumatic origin.* First stage of ulceration caused from exposure in the open air. Conjunctiva very red, chemosis, photophobia, and lachrymation; or, more commonly, the eye is *dry, hot, burning,* and very sensitive to air. Patient restless, feverish and thirsty.

Apis.—Ulcerations of the cornea, vascular, with photophobia, hot lachrymation, and burning, *stinging pains;* sometimes the pains are very severe, and *shoot* through the eye, with swollen, *œdematous condition of the lids* and conjunctiva. Patient drowsy and thirstless.

Argent. nit.—*Ulceration of the cornea, in new-born infants, or from any form of purulent ophthalmia, with profuse discharge from the eyes.* Ulceration with pains like darts through the eye, morning and evening. The pains are usually better in the cool, open air, and aggravated in a warm room. The lids are generally red, thick, and swollen; conjunctiva œdematous, and the *discharge of white-yellow pus profuse.*

Arnica.—Traumatic ulceration with much *hemorrhage into the anterior chamber.* (Superficial traumatic ulcerations generally yield more readily to Aconite.)

Arsenicum.—Especially when found in scrofulous, anæmic, restless children. The ulceration is chiefly superficial, and has a tendency to recur first in one eye, and then in the other.

The *photophobia is usually excessive,* and the *lachrymation hot, burning, acrid and profuse.* The pains are *burning, sticking;*

there may be throbbing, pulsating, or tearing, around the eye, *worse at night.* The *burning pains* predominate, and are worse *at night, especially after midnight,* when the child becomes very restless and cross. Bathing in cold water often aggravates, while warm water may relieve. Eyeballs sore to touch. Conjunctiva quite red; chemosis. Marked *soreness on the internal surface of the lids,* which are swollen externally (œdematous), spasmodically closed, and often *excoriated by the acrid discharges.*

Asafœtida.—Ulceration, accompanied by iritic pains which *extend from within outwards, and are relieved by rest and pressure.*

Aurum.—Ulceration of the cornea, especially occurring during the course of *pannus* or scrofulous ophthalmia. Cornea quite vascular, and the patient very irritable and sensitive to noise. Cervical glands often enlarged and inflamed. The *photophobia* is marked, *lachrymation profuse and scalding, and the eyes very sensitive to touch.* The pains extend from without inwards, and are worse on touch (reverse of Asaf.).

Belladonna.—Superficial ulceration of the cornea, with intense photophobia, and some throbbing pain, aggravated afternoon and evening.

Calcarea carb.—Particularly valuable for *corneal ulcerations found in fat, unhealthy children* with large abdomens, who sweat much, especially about the head, and are very susceptible to cold air; also in deep, sloughing ulcers, found in weak, cachectic individuals. The pains, redness, photophobia, and lachrymation are variable, and, though it is a prominent remedy for this disorder, there are no characteristic eye symptoms, and we are guided in its selection chiefly by concomitant indications.

Calc. hypophos.—This preparation of lime is most commonly called for in *deep sloughing ulcers,* or abscesses, found in weak, debilitated individuals. Especially indicated in *crescentic ulcers* following purulent conjunctivitis.

Calc. iodata.—Ulcerations in strumous subjects, with enlargement of the tonsils, and cervical glands.

Cantharis.—Superficial ulceration caused by burns, with burning pain and lachrymation.

Chamomilla.—Ulceration occurring in cross, peevish children during dentition.

Chinin. mur.—Ulceration of the cornea, of *malarial origin,* or dependent upon *anæmic conditions,* especially if the iris has become affected and there are *severe pains,* either in or above the eye, *periodic in character* and accompanied by chills. Ulcers found in the course of pannus, with much pain in the morning.

Cimicifuga.—Ulcers with *sharp, neuralgic pains through the eye into the head.*

Cinnabaris.—When accompanied by that characteristic *pain above the eye, extending from the internal to the external canthus, or running around the eye.* This pain varies greatly, both in intensity and character. Photophobia and lachrymation are usually present.

. **Conium.**—An important remedy in superficial ulceration in which the *surface* of the cornea only is abraded; thus, owing to the exposure of the terminal filaments of the nerves or to hyperæsthesia, there is *intense photophobia* and much lachrymation. On account of the great photophobia, the lids are spasmodically closed, and when opened, a profuse gush of tears occurs (Rhus). The discharges are usually slight and the pains variable, though aggravated by any light. But, notwithstanding all this photophobia, pain and lachrymation, we find upon examination, *very little or no redness of the conjunctiva,* not sufficient to account for the great photophobia, which is out of all proportion to the amount of trouble. Strumous conditions, enlarged glands, etc. would assist us.

(Conium[1] has sometimes cured when the high potencies have failed.)

Croton tig.—Ulceration, with marked pain in the supraciliary region at night, especially if accompanied by a *vesicular eruption on the face and lids.*

Cundurango.—Superficial ulceration, with sores or cracks at the corners of the mouth.

Duboisin.—Low form of ulceration, more or less deep, *without* photophobia and lachrymation.

Eserine.—Sloughing ulceration of the cornea, with tendency to increased intra-ocular tension.

Euphrasia.—Superficial ulceration (sometimes with pannus) may be relieved, though it rarely affects beneficially any extensive ulceration, except to palliate the symptoms in the first stage.

Photophobia is generally present, as well as *profuse, acrid, burning lachrymation,* together with *profuse, acrid, yellowish-white, muco-purulent discharge from the eyes,* which makes the lids red and excoriated, giving them and the cheek an appearance as if varnished.

The conjunctiva is quite red and the eyes smart and burn. *Blurring of the eyes, relieved by winking.*

Graphites.—A very valuable remedy in ulceration of the cornea, especially occurring in scrofulous children who are covered with eczematous eruptions, particularly on the head and *behind the ears;* eruptions are *moist, fissured and glutinous.* Is especially adapted to *superficial ulcerations, resulting from pustules,* though has also been useful in deep ulcers even with hypopyon. The cornea is more frequently found quite vascular, and conjunctiva much injected, though both may be slight in degree. The *photophobia is usually intense,* and the lachrymation profuse, but may be very moderate in amount. The pains are variable, and the discharges generally thin and excoriating. The lids are sometimes covered with *dry scales* (the edges) though are more commonly red and sore, with *cracking and bleeding of the external canthi* upon any attempt to open the eyes. Generally accompanying the above symptoms, we find an acrid discharge from the nose, which makes the nostrils sore and covered with scabs.

Hamamelis.—When dependent upon a blow or burn, especially when complicated with hemorrhage into the anterior chamber (hypæmia).

Hepar.—This is one of the most frequently indicated remedies for ulcers and abscesses of the cornea, especially for the *deep, sloughing form, and when hypopyon is present.* Also useful in acute aggravations of pannus tending towards ulceration.

Some torpid forms of ulcers and abscesses have been benefited, though usually the symptoms are well pronounced when this drug is indicated. There is *intense* photophobia, profuse lachrymation, and *great redness of the cornea and conjunctiva,* even chemosis. The *pains are severe and of a throbbing*, aching, stinging character, *ameliorated by warmth and aggravated by cold or uncovering the eye*, and in the evening. There is marked *sensitiveness of the eye to touch*. The lids may be red, swollen, spasmodically closed, and *bleed easily upon opening them*. *For the absorption of pus in the anterior chamber* (hypopyon), *there is no better remedy than Hepar*. Cases found in strumous, outrageously cross children, should suggest this drug. General symptoms of chilliness, etc., are important.

Ignatia.—Ulcers in nervous, hysterical persons, with various peri-orbital pains, especially at one point.

Ipecac.—Vascular ulceration of the cornea, with *much photophobia*.

Kali bichrom.—Especially of value in those cases of *indolent ulceration*, which prove so intractable to treatment; cases in which there is no active inflammatory process, only a low grade of chronic inflammation, therefore marked by *no photophobia and no redness*. The pains are generally slight and variable, and the discharge, if any, of a *stringy* character. Ulcers which have a tendency to bore in, without extending laterally.

Mercurius sol.—Mercury in some one of its preparations is a common prescription for ulcers and abscesses; and as the soluble mercury of Hahnemann is perhaps more commonly employed than any other, we shall describe this more in detail, and afterwards give simply the variations found in the other forms.

Is adapted to both superficial and deep ulceration, especially in *syphilitic* or strumous subjects. The cornea, at the point of ulceration, is usually quite vascular, though may be surrounded by a greyish opacity due to infiltration between its layers; the conjunctival redness is also marked. The *dread of light* is generally great, especially of artificial light, and the *lachrymation is profuse, burning and excoriating, while the discharges are thin and acrid* in character. The pains are often severe and vary in character, but are *always aggravated at night*, by damp weather or extreme cold, and ameliorated temporarily by cold water. The lids are thick, *red, swollen, and excoriated by the acrid discharges*, sensitive to extreme heat or cold and to contact, and are forcibly closed. The concomitant symptoms of excoriation of the nostrils, flabby tongue, night sweats, pain at night, etc., are usually present.

Mercurius corr. — Called for when the above mercurial symptoms are especially severe, particularly if the iris has become involved. The *photophobia, acrid lachrymation, discharges, pains, burning and excoriation of the lids, are excessive* (which are more often found in the scrofulous diathesis).

Mercurius dulc. — Deep or superficial ulcers or abscesses found in *pale, flabby, strumous children*, with enlarged glands and general scrofulous cachexia. Other symptoms vary little from Merc. sol.

Mercurius nitr.—Has been used empirically with excellent success in all kinds of ulceration, both in the acute and chronic, superficial and deep forms, whether accompanied by hypopyon or not, in cases in which there has been much photophobia, and in cases in which there has been none; where there has been much pain, and where there has been no pain. In fact, it has been successfully employed in all imaginable forms of the disease, but it seems to act better in those cases in which there is a tendency to the formation of pustules. It is generally prescribed both externally and internally at the same time, and in the lower potencies; the first potency in water externally, and the third internally. (Atropine may be used with it, especially if there is much photophobia.)

Mercurius præc. rub.—Ulceration of a cornea covered with pannus, lids granular and usual eye symptoms of mercury. Aggravation from working over a fire.

Mercurius prot.—*Serpiginous ulceration* of the cornea that commences at the margin and *extends over the whole cornea, or a portion of it, especially the upper part, involving only the superficial layers*. This form of ulceration is more commonly found during the course of *trachoma and pannus*, in which the proto-iodide of mercury has often proved its value. The *vascularity of the cornea and conjunctiva* is usually great, while the *photophobia is excessive*. The pains are the same as those given under Mercurius sol. Non-vascular central ulcer of the cornea with pain at night. A *thick yellow coating at the base of the tongue is generally present*.

Natrum mur.—Ulcers that appear *after the use of caustics*, particularly the nitrate of silver. Photophobia usually marked, so that a child will lie with the head buried in the pillows, *lachrymation acrid*, discharges thin and excoriating, lids swollen, eruption around the eye on face which is often *shining*, pains various, though often *sharp and piercing above the eye on looking down*, are the most prominent eye indications. Concomitants will decide our choice.

Nux vom.—*Superficial ulceration* of the cornea characterized by *excessive photophobia, especially in the morning*; during the day is often comparatively free from it. The amount of redness is not usually excessive, though varies, as does also the character of the pains. Lachrymation is profuse. To be thought of in cases that have been previously over-dosed with medicine, both externally and internally. Neuro-paralytic inflammation of the cornea has been benefited.

Pulsatilla.—Superficial ulcers following phlyctenulæ, especially in females of a mild temperament. *Thick, bland, white or yellow discharge from the eyes, and general amelioration of the symptoms in open air.* Small ulcers on the centre of the cornea with no vascularity and only moderate irritation of the eye.

Rhus tox.—*Superficial keratitis, with excessive photophobia and lachrymation, so that the tears gush out upon opening the spasmodically closed lids*; if a child, will often lie with its face buried in the pillows all day. *Profuse flow of tears* is a very important symptom under this drug, and benefit is frequently derived from its use in *superficial ulceration of the cornea with granular lids* in which this symptom is prominent. Keratitis caused from *exposure in the water*, often calls for Rhus (Calc.).

The redness of the eye is generally marked, with *chemosis. The lids are œdematously swollen, especially the upper.* An eruption may frequently be found around the eye, characteristic of the drug. The symptoms are *generally worse in damp weather and at night after midnight*, therefore the patients are restless at night and disturbed by bad dreams. A rheumatic diathesis would also influence our choice.

Silicea.—Adapted to *sloughing ulcers* of the cornea, and the crescentic form of ulceration; also to *small round ulcers* which have a tendency to perforate, especially if situated near the centre of the cornea and having no blood vessels running to them. Pain, photophobia, lachrymation, redness and discharges vary, though the latter are generally profuse in the sloughing form of the disease. Hypopyon may be present. The Silicea patient is usually *very sensitive to cold* and therefore wishes to keep wrapped up warm, especially about the head.

Spigelia.—Ulcers with sharp shooting pains through the eye, and into the head.

Sulphur.—Beneficial results have followed the use of this drug in all varieties of ulcers and abscesses, from the simple abrasion of the epithelial layer following the disappearance of a phlyctenule, to the most severe sloughing form of ulcers or abscesses we may see. Both acute and chronic cases have been relieved, though it is more often to be thought of in the latter form even in cases in which the destruction of tissue is great and *pus is present in the anterior chamber*, especially if the inflammation be indolent in nature, with no photophobia and but slight vascularity. Ulcerations occurring in, or dependent upon a *scrofulous diathesis*, as shown by eruptions, etc., suggest this remedy, as does also any case which can be traced to the suppression of an eruption. The most prominent eye indications which would lead us to its selection, are the pains, which are usually *sharp and sticking as if a needle or splinter were sticking in the eye, or there may be sharp, shooting pains through the eye into the head from one to three A. M.* (These severe pains through the eye into the head, during the day or evening, rarely call for Sulphur, but for Spig., Bry., Cimicif., or the like.) Again we may have a great variety of other sensations. The *intolerance of light is generally great* and the *lachrymation profuse*, though both are variable.

All the symptoms are, as a rule, *aggravated by bathing the eyes*, so that a child cannot bear to have any water touch them.

Thuja.—Ulcerations of a syphilitic origin, even when hypopyon is present, suffusion of the eyes and burning in them. Pain over the eye as if a nail were being driven in.

The following remedies have also been followed by favorable results in occasional cases: Alumina, Baryta carb. and jod., Cannabis, Caust., Chin. ars., Kali carb., Kali mur. and jod., Kreos., Nit. ac., Petrol., Sang., Secale, Seneg., Sepia and Vaccin.

KERATITIS PHLYCTENULARIS.

(Phlyctenular Inflammation of the Cornea.)

See Ophthalmia phlyctenularis, page 241.

KERATITIS TRAUMATICA.

(Traumatic Inflammation of the Cornea.)

See Ophthalmia traumatica, page 251.

KERATITIS PARENCHYMATOSA.

(Diffuse or Interstitial Inflammation of the Cornea.)

In the treatment of this variety of inflammation of the cornea, our main dependence must be placed upon constitutional treatment. Here homœopathy shows its great advantage over the old school, for we can often check the progress of the disease in a speedy manner, by the careful selection and administration of our drugs.

As the general health of these patients is not usually good, plenty of exercise in the open air, and a nutritious diet are to be especially advised.

No external applications should be prescribed, except in rare cases in which the ciliary injection is great and there seems to be iritic complication, when Atropine may be employed with benefit.

Iridectomy may be thought of as a last resort, or when there is increase of the intra-ocular tension.

Apis.—Corneæ densely infiltrated, with moderate redness and photophobia. History of hereditary syphilis, with exostoses, swelling of the joints, high fever, drowsiness and thirstlessness, may be present.

Arsenicum.—Interstitial keratitis, cornea, hazy with commencing vascularity. *Intense photophobia and profuse lachrymation, with burning pain in and around the eye, worse after midnight.*

Aurum mur.—The muriate of gold has been most commonly used, and in the lower potencies. It is especially important in all those cases in which the cause can be traced to *hereditary syphilis,* and as the majority of cases of genuine interstitial keratitis are of this origin, it can readily be seen how common a remedy this may be. It is also valuable in diffuse keratitis of strumous origin. We have seen it act speedily and permanently in both the vascular and non-vascular variety of the disease, though generally marked symptoms of an hereditary taint have been present, as shown by the character of the teeth, described by Hutchinson, as well as by the history of the case. The subjective symptoms are not prominent and may be absent, though usually there is some photophobia, irritable condition of the eye and dull pain in and around the eye, which often seems deep in the bone.

Baryta iod.—Interstitial keratitis, occurring in scrofulous subjects, *with great enlargement of the cervical glands,* which are hard and painful on pressure.

Calcarea phos.—Parenchymatous inflammation of the cornea, of strumous origin. The infiltration into the cornea may be dense. Photophobia is usually present. Enlargement of the tonsils, and other Calcarea symptoms will be found.

Cannabis.—Interstitial inflammation of the cornea from hereditary syphilis. Cornea densely opaque and *vascular.* The photophobia is intense, and lachrymation profuse.

Hepar.—Keratitis parenchymatosa in scrofulous subjects. Cornea opaque and vascular, with deep ciliary injection, severe iritic pains, excessive photophobia, profuse lachrymation, and great sensitiveness of the eyeball to touch. Of service in clearing the cornea after the inflammatory process has been checked.

Kali mur.—Diffuse infiltration of the cornea, with some pain, moderate photophobia and redness. The absorption of Atropine is very slow.

Merc. sol.—Especially indicated if the cause can be traced to either acquired or hereditary syphilis. The ciliary injection, pain, and iritic complication, are well marked, as well as the nocturnal aggravation, and general concomitant symptoms. The inflammation is more active than under Aurum.

Sepia.—Keratitis parenchymatosa, complicated with uterine disturbances.

Sulphur.—Indicated in strumous subjects, even if the inflammation is in an active stage. Especially useful, however, in promoting the absorption of the infiltration into the cornea, after the inflammation has been allayed by proper remedies.

Other preparations of Calcarea, Kali, and Mercurius, may prove of service in the treatment of this disease.

DESCEMETITIS.

(Inflammation of the Posterior Elastic Layer of the Cornea.)

The chief remedies will be *Kali bichr*. and *Gels*. For special indications refer to Iritis, page 274.

KERATO IRITIS.

(Inflammation of the Cornea and Iris.)

(Refer to *Iritis* and *Keratitis*.)

LEUCOMA, MACULA, ETC.

(Opacities of the Cornea.)

The prognosis of opacities of the cornea varies according to their duration and character. If they are dependent upon infiltration into the cornea, proper treatment will usually cause their absorption, but if they result from new scar tissue, as in extensive ulceration, the prognosis is not favorable. Time will, however, do considerable in clearing the cornea, especially in the opacities of children.

The application of irritants to the cornea to promote the dispersion of opacities is often of great advantage, if there is no vascularity of the cornea, nor other symptoms of irritation. The following have been found most efficacious, and should be applied directly to the opacity: Sulphate of soda, aluminate of copper, bichromate of potash, or carbolic acid and glycerine (gtt. vi. ad ʒj.).

In order to cut off the irregularly refracted rays of light, in some forms of opacities, stenopaic spectacles, either with or without convex or concave glasses, may be of advantage.

An iridectomy opposite a transparent portion of the cornea, is frequently advisable, if the opacity is too dense to be removed by remedies.

As there is usually a total lack of eye symptoms in these cases, we must chiefly rely upon the general condition of the patient, though the following are the drugs which have been found more commonly indicated: Aurum, *Calc. carb.* and *iod.*, Cannabis, *Cuprum al.*, *Hepar*, *Kali bichr.*, *Nat. sulph.*, Sil. and Sulphur.

KERATOCONUS, KERATOGLOBUS, STAPHYLOMA CORNEÆ ET IRIDIS.

(Conical Cornea, Spherical Bulging of the Cornea, Staphyloma of the Cornea and Iris.)

The progress of conical cornea can often be checked by the employment of the proper homœopathic remedy, though it is impossible to diminish the conicity of the cornea without instrumental interference.

The remedy must be chosen according to both local and constitutional symptoms, though *Calc. jod.*, *Eserine* and Pulsat. have thus far proved most serviceable. Suitable hygienic measures are of great importance, as this affection may be dependent upon a debilitated condition of the health. A pressure bandage may sometimes be used with advantage, but if the disease seems still to increase, in spite of medication, an iridectomy is required. Either stenopaic or concave glasses may improve the vision.

Various operations are recommended for the cure of conical cornea, as cauterization, removal of a piece from the apex, etc.

Staphyloma of the cornea may be total or partial, and either accompanied by protrusion of the iris or not. Our first aim should be, in the treatment of ulcers and other diseases of the cornea which tend toward this sad result, to endeavor to prevent it by bandaging and proper medicinal means. If, however, staphyloma is already present, we must have recourse to the knife, and here we find many operations advisable, according to the duration and extent of the staphylomatous bulging.

LÆSIONES.

(Injuries and Wounds of the Cornea.)

Foreign bodies in the cornea are of frequent occurrence and can usually be easily removed by the aid of a spud without fixation of the eye, though if the patient be very nervous and the foreign body imbedded in the cornea, it is better to use a stop speculum and then fix the eye with a pair of forceps, or employ an anæsthetic. If the foreign body has penetrated the cornea and lies partly in the anterior chamber, a broad needle should be introduced behind it, in order to prevent its being pushed backward in our attempt to extract it. Pieces of steel may be removed with a magnet. Chemical injuries have already been treated of under the conjunctiva.

The treatment of wounds of the cornea vary according to the complications which may arise. Our first endeavor should be to subdue the inflammatory symptoms, if seen early, by the use of *ice bags;* especially is this true if the iris and other tissues have also been injured. Cold compresses of *Aconite,* Arnica, Calendula or Hamamelis may be employed locally; at the same time administering one or another, *usually Aconite,* internally. *Atropine* should be instilled into the eye if the injury is near the centre of the cornea or if the iris is involved. If the perforation is near the periphery of the cornea *Eserine* may be substituted for the Atropine. Perfect rest should be insisted upon if the injury is extensive. If a fistulous opening should remain, a compress bandage may be necessary or even the introduction of a suture.

TUMORES.

(Tumors of the Cornea.)

(See Tumors of the Conjunctiva.)

SCLERA.

EPISCLERITIS, SCLERITIS, SCLERO-CHOROIDITIS ANT.

(Inflammation of the Sclerotic.)

The local symptoms of this disease being usually few and indefinite, we are often obliged to derive our indications for remedies from the general symptoms of the patient.

If there is great ciliary injection and pain, a solution of Atropine may be employed, but it is rarely necessary.

Aconite.—In the acute stage, if there is violent, aching, dragging, tearing, or *burning* pains in the eyeball with contracted pupil, photophobia and the characteristic reddish-blue circle around the cornea. The eye is usually quite *sensitive to touch* and feels *hot and dry.* Especially useful if caused from cold or exposure to dry cold air.

Aurum.—Low forms of scleritis in which the infiltration has extended into the parenchyma of the cornea. Moderate pain, redness and photophobia. Syphilitic dyscrasia.

Cinnabaris.—Inflammation of the sclera, with *pain over the eye*, usually aggravated at night.

Kalmia.—Sclero-choroiditis ant. Sclera inflamed, vitreous filled with opacities, glimmering of light below one eye especially on reading with the other, were indications present in one case in which Kalmia was of great service.

Mercurius.—Inflammation of the sclerotic, which is thinned so that the choroid shines through. *Steady aching pain in the eye all the time, but worse at night;* also usually some pain

around the eye, especially if the iris has become involved.
Particularly to be thought of, if of syphilitic origin. Concomitant symptoms of flabby tongue, offensive breath, night
pains, etc., are of great importance. The solubis and corrosivus have been most commonly employed, though the other
preparations may be indicated.

Nux mosch.—Nodules over external recti, very large and
painful. Patient very drowsy, with sleepy expression of eyes.

Silicea.—Sclerotic inflamed, with or without choroideal complication. The pains may be severe and extend from the eyes
to the head and are *relieved by warmth.* Aching in the occiput
corresponding to the eye affected.

Terebinth.—Inflammation of the superficial layers of the
sclera, with a considerable redness, and *intense pain in the eye
and corresponding side of the head. Urine dark* and scanty.

Thuja.—This is a very valuable remedy in all forms of inflammation of the sclera, even if no characteristic symptoms
are present. It should be the first remedy suggested to our
minds in the treatment of scleritis, sclero-choroiditis or any of
its complications as clinical experience has often verified its
usefulness in these cases. In most instances there has been
great tenderness of the globe, intolerance of light, and active
inflammation with a general cachectic condition, occurring in
persons badly nourished, either scrofulous or syphilitic, and
those long time deprived of fresh air.

The following have also been used and are recommended:
Puls., Spig. and Sulph.

STAPHYLOMA SCLERÆ ANT.

(Morbid Prominence of the Anterior Portion of the Sclera.)

We should endeavor to prevent this result by the use of
those remedies given under scleritis, but if it seems to progress
in spite of our remedies an *iridectomy* must be made.

If the staphyloma has existed for some time, it may be ab-
scised according to one of the various methods advised; if it
be extensive and sight is lost, enucleation is to be preferred.

LÆSIONES.

(Wounds and Injuries of the Sclera.)

The treatment of wounds of the sclerotic varies according to their extent and situation. If any protrusion of the contents of the globe has occurred, it should be cut off and the edges of the wound approximated as closely as possible by the aid of a bandage or the introduction of a fine suture. The patient should be kept quiet in bed and *ice compresses*, with or without applications of Arnica or Calendula solutions, employed as may be most applicable from the nature of the injury, whether contused or incised. *Aconite* should be given internally.

If the wound, however, is extensive, especially if in the ciliary region, even though the vision is not wholly lost, enucleation is far the safer method of proceeding, in order that all danger of sympathetic trouble in the other (healthy) eye may be taken away. In all cases in which a large portion of the globe has escaped and sight is irretrievably lost, enucleation is necessary.

If there is a foreign body in the sclerotic, it should be removed, but if it has penetrated the sclerotic and is within the eye, it is usually necessary to enucleate, although its extraction may be attempted if there has not been too much injury to the ciliary body. The magnet has of late been highly recommended for the removal of steel or iron from the interior of the eyeball.

IRIS.

IRITIS.

(Inflammation of the Iris.)

Under this heading will be included all varieties of iritis, idiopathic, rheumatic, syphilitic, traumatic, sympathetic, purulent, spongy and serous, also descemetitis.

The first point that demands our attention is the removal of any exciting cause, as for instance, a foreign body in the conjunctiva, cornea or interior of the eye. If it be due to swelling or dislocation of the lens forward, or to a portion of the lens substance lying against the iris, an incision should be made and the irritating object removed. When dependent upon sympathetic irritation from the other eye, which has been already destroyed, enucleation of the injured eye should be performed as early as possible. If previous synechiæ are the exciting causes, an iridectomy becomes necessary.

We are sometimes compelled to treat quite severe cases of this disease as out-patients and often with excellent results, though it is far better and safer in all cases to confine the patient to the house. If they are allowed to leave the house the eyes must be carefully guarded by bandaging the affected eye and protecting the other by a shade or colored glass. We should, however, in all cases, especially if severe, most positively insist upon the patient remaining in a darkened room and in bed, in order that perfect rest may be obtained, both from the irritation of light and from muscular movements. A low or milk diet usually proves most beneficial unless the patient is too much debilitated.

Cold applications should never be employed in iritis, except in the first stage of the traumatic form when ice compresses may be used with great advantage.

Warmth is one of our most important aids in the treatment. It may be employed in various ways, though I would especially advise *dry warmth*, covering the eye and corresponding side of the head with a large thick cotton pad, for by this the heat may be kept more uniform than by the application of moisture. Small bags, partially filled with fine table salt, applied hot to the eye will often relieve the severe iritic pain experienced at night.

The next point in the treatment of iritis is one of great importance and should always be attended to, viz., *complete dilatation of the pupil as early as possible by the use of Atropine.* As soon as the nature of the disease has been detected a solution of Atropine should be instilled strong enough to produce the desired result, and when the dilatation is complete we should endeavor to keep it so by a continued application of the mydriatic. In severe cases of iritis it may be necessary to use the Atropine every hour. Dryness of the throat or flushing of the face will indicate that it must be used at longer intervals or perhaps discontinued entirely. If the pupil is already bound down by adhesions which cannot be readily torn, it is sometimes better to discontinue the mydriatic until the inflammatory symptoms have subsided, when it may again be tried to break up the adhesions. A solution of Atropine four grains to the ounce of water is most commonly employed, though a weaker solution, even one-eighth of a grain to the ounce, may be used in mild cases if the required effect can be accomplished with it, *but the pupils must be dilated* if possible, even if we have to employ the crude substance. These remarks regarding Atropine will apply to the various forms of iritis, with the exception of the serous variety in which dilatation is not necessary. If Atropine should act as an irritant or the eye shows a great antipathy to its use, some other mydriatic, as Duboisine, Daturine, or Homatropine, may be substituted.

An *iridectomy* may be made in the later stages, or, if other treatment fails. It may also be indicated in serous iritis, if glaucomatous symptoms supervene, though *paracentesis* of the cornea is usually to be preferred.

Aconite.—In the *very first stage*, or, in a sudden reappearance, this remedy is often of the greatest value, especially, if occurring in young, full-blooded patients, and when the cause can be traced to an *exposure to a cold draught of air*. It is the most commonly indicated remedy in *traumatic iritis*. The ciliary injection is usually marked, pupils contracted, and pains often severe, beating and throbbing, especially at night. There is a sensation of *great heat, burning*, and dryness in the eyes. The eye symptoms are often accompanied by general febrile excitement.

Arnica —Rheumatic iritis has been benefited, though its special sphere of action is in the *traumatic variety*, in which it may be employed with advantage.

Arsenicum.—Iritis, with *periodic burning pains, worse at night, after midnight*, ameliorated by warm applications. Frequently indicated in serous iritis.

Asafœtida.—*Especially indicated in the syphilitic variety, and after the abuse of mercury.* (More applicable to the female sex. Liebold.) The *pains are severe* in the eye, *above it*, and in the temples, of a *throbbing, pulsating*, pressing, *burning*, or sticking character, and tend to become periodic; they extend usually from *within outwards*, and are *relieved by rest and pressure* (reverse of Aurum).

Aurum.—Chiefly serviceable in *syphilitic iritis*, and after overdosing with mercury or potash. There is much *pain, which seems to be deep in the bones* surrounding the eye, of a tearing, pressing nature, often extending down into the eyeball, with burning heat, especially on trying to open the eyes; the pressing pain is usually from *above downwards*, and from *without inwards*, aggravated on touch. The vision is clouded, as by a dark veil. The mental condition of the patient is that of great depression; this, together with the bone pains in other portions, aid us materially in our choice.

Belladonna.—Early stages of iritis, caused from a cold; or chronic plastic iritis, following cataract extraction, with much redness and severe *throbbing pain* in the eye and head, worse at night. Sensitiveness of the eyeball to touch, congestion of the face, etc.

Bryonia.—Iritis resulting from exposure to cold not unfrequently calls for this drug, especially if occurring with a rheumatic diathesis. The pains may be sharp and *shooting* in the eyes, *extending through into the head, or down into the face*, or there may be a sensation of *soreness and aching* in and around the ball, especially behind it, extending through to occiput; the patient also sometimes describes the pain "*as if the eye was being forced out of the socket.*" All the pains are generally *aggravated by moving the eyes in their sockets, or upon any exertion of them, and at night.* The seat of pain often becomes sore to touch. In the serous form it also proves serviceable.

Calendula.—Traumatic iritis.

Cedron.—This remedy is particularly of value in relieving the severe *ciliary neuralgia* observed in iritis, if *supra-orbital*, seeming to follow the course of the supra-orbital nerve, especially if there is marked periodicity. In relieving the pain it acts favorably upon the disease, by removing nervous irritation and allowing the more beneficial action of the true remedy.

China.—Iritis dependent upon the *loss of vital fluids*, or malaria. The pains are variable, but have a marked *periodicity.* The *muriate of quinine*, in appreciable doses, will often relieve the *severity of the pains*, especially when of an *intermittent type, and accompanied by chills and fever.*

Cinnabaris.—Of great value in the treatment of iritis, particularly syphilitic, and if gummata are present in the iris. The characteristic *pain commences at the inner canthus, and extends across the brow, or even passes around the eye*, though there may be shooting pains through the eye into the head, especially at inner canthus. Sharp pain over the eye, or soreness along the course of the supra-orbital nerve, and corresponding side of the head. Like mercury, the *nocturnal aggravation* is usually marked, and the symptoms intermit in severity.

Clematis.—By some, this drug is considered to be as frequently called for as mercury in iritis and kerato-iritis, though we have never used it to the same extent. Chronic syphilitic iritis, with very little pain. The pains are similar to those of Mercurius, but there is usually much heat and dryness in the eye, and great *sensitiveness to cold air*, to light and bathing. (Is said to have a marked action on the adhesions, which take place between the iris and lens.)

Conium.—Descemetitis, with *excessive photophobia*, and but little redness or apparent inflammation.

Euphrasia.—Rheumatic iritis, with constant aching, and occasional darting pain in the eye, always worse at night, ciliary injection and photophobia great, aqueous cloudy, iris discolored, and bound down by adhesions.

Gelsemium.—In *serous iritis* alone, or complicated with choroideal inflammation, Gelsem. is the most prominent remedy. There is hypersecretion, and cloudiness of the aqueous, with moderate ciliary injection and pain.

Hamamelis.—Iritis traumatica, or other forms, in which *hemorrhage has taken place into the iris or anterior chamber.*

Hepar.—Especially serviceable if the inflammation has extended to the neighboring tissues, cornea (kerato-iritis), and ciliary body (irido-cyclitis), or after gummata have ruptured, and if there is *pus in the anterior chamber* (*hypopyon*). As hypopyon is an important symptom under Hepar, we should think of this remedy in parenchymatous, or suppurative inflammation of the iris, in which this condition is present. It is also of value in *purulent irido-capsulitis* after cataract extraction. The pains are pressing, boring, or *throbbing* in the eye, *ameliorated by warmth*, and aggravated by motion. *The eye is very tender to touch.* There is usually much photophobia, and great redness of the conjunctiva, even chemosis, while the lids may be red, swollen, spasmodically closed, and sore to touch. The patient feels chilly, and wants to keep warmly covered. Payr says that it is the chief remedy for keratitis punctata.

Kali bichrom.—It is *the* remedy for true *descemetitis* characterized by fine punctate spots on the posterior surface of the cornea, especially over the pupil, with moderate redness and very little photophobia. May be required in syphilitic iritis.

Kali iod.—An important remedy in *syphilitic iritis*, especially after mercurialization and if the secondary eruption on the skin is present. The special indications are not marked, *though the inflammation is usually of high degree.* It has been given upon general principles in many instances with excellent success.

Mercurius.—Mercury in its various combinations is our

"sheet anchor" in the treatment of *all forms of iritis*, especially the syphilitic; and the cases which call for its use present a great variety of symptoms, differing widely both in character and intensity. The *pains are usually severe, of a tearing, boring, cutting, burning nature, chiefly around the eyes, in the forehead and temples,* and accompanied by throbbing, shooting, sticking pains in the eye, though in rare cases they may be almost or entirely absent; these pains as well as all the symptoms of the mercurials are *always worse at night after going to bed and in damp weather,* in this respect corresponding very closely to the disease. There is generally much heat both in and around the eye, and soreness of the corresponding side of the head to touch. *Great sensitiveness* to heat or *cold* may be found, *also to light, especially the glare of a fire.* Acrid lachrymation may be present. The *pupil is contracted* and *overspread by a thin, bluish film, while there is great tendency to the formation of adhesions* (posterior synechiæ). The iris is discolored, aqueous cloudy, and ciliary injection marked. Hypopyon may be present or not. Gummata may also be found on the iris. The lids may be red, swollen and spasmodically closed, or even normal in appearance. The concomitant symptoms of *nocturnal pains* in different portions of the body, perspiration at night, condition of tongue, mouth and throat, and eruptions on the skin, are of great importance in selecting this drug and in choosing between the different preparations.

The *Corrosivus* is most frequently employed and proves most beneficial, as the *intensity of the symptoms* is more marked under this than any other form.

The *Solubis* comes next in order of usefulness and should be given if the above symptoms are present and if the inflammation is of medium intensity or lower grade, and if certain characteristic general symptoms are observed.

The *Dulcis* is to be thought of when iritis is found in very scrofulous subjects, especially children with pale flabby skin, and when associated with corneal ulceration.

The *Protoiodide* should be chosen from concomitant symptoms, as *thick yellow coating on the base of the tongue,* enlarged glands, etc., and when *superficial ulceration of the cornea* complicates the difficulty, especially if found during the course of pannus.

Natrum salicyl.—Iritis with intense ciliary neuralgia, especially resulting from operations on the eye.

Nitric acid.—Chronic syphilitic iritis of a low degree, with very little or no nightly pain. The pains may be worse during the day and are of a pressing stinging character. Posterior synechiæ will be found.

Nux vom.—May be useful at the beginning of the disease or as an intercurrent, especially in the syphilitic form, if there is much photophobia, lachrymation, etc., *in the morning.*

Petroleum.—Syphilitic iritis accompanied by *occipital headache.* Pain in eyes pressing or stitching, and skin around the eyes dry and scurfy.

Rhus tox.—Idiopathic or rheumatic iritis, if caused by *exposure to wet,* or if found in a rheumatic patient. *Suppurative iritis, particularly if of traumatic origin, as after cataract extraction,* more often calls for Rhus than any other remedy. Also useful in kerato-iritis. *The lids are œdematously swollen, spasmodically closed, and upon opening them, a profuse gush of tears takes place. There is chemosis;* the photophobia is marked, and the pains are various, both in and around the eye, *worse at night,* especially after midnight, and in damp weather. The swelling of the lids often involves the corresponding side of the face and may be covered by a vesicular eruption. Concomitants must be taken into consideration.

Spigelia.—Rheumatic iritis, if the pains are *sharp and shooting both in and around the eye, especially if they seem to radiate from one point.*

Sulphur.—Iritis, particularly if chronic and found in strumous subjects, especially after suppression of eruptions, may find its remedy in Sulph.; also if *hypopyon* complicates the trouble. May be of service as an intercurrent, even if it does not complete the cure. The pains are usually of a *sharp, sticking character,* worse at night and toward morning. General indications will decide our choice.

Terebinth.—Rheumatic *iritis with intense pains in the eye and head,* especially if resulting from suppressed perspiration of the feet. Pain in the back and dark urine will be present.

Thuja.—*Syphilitic iritis, with gummata on the iris. Large wart-like excrescences on the iris, with severe, sharp, sticking pains in the eye, aggravated at night and ameliorated by warmth.* Usually accompanying the above we find *much heat* above and around the eye and in the corresponding side of the head; there may also be tearing, dull, aching pains in brow, or a pain above the eye (left), as if a nail were being driven in. *Ciliary injection* decided, even in some cases amounting to inflammation of the sclera. Lids may be indurated, noises in the head, etc.

The following remedies have also been employed in occasional cases with favorable results. Their meagre indications can be found by reference to Part I. Arg. nit., Crot. tig., Prunus sp., Puls., Sil., Staph. and Zinc.

IRIDO - CYCLITIS, IRIDO - CHOROIDITIS AC., CHRON. ET SYPH.; OPHTHALMIA SYMPATHICA.

(*Inflammation of the Whole or a Portion of the Uveal Tract* [*Vascular Tunic*].)

Our first object should be to prevent the disease, if possible, by properly treating every case of iritis so that no posterior synechiæ may remain to cause the inflammation. In order to do this and also to prevent or break up any adhesions which may tend to form between the iris and lens, *Atropine* should be energetically employed as early as possible and continued during the course of the disease, unless there is seclusion or occlusion of the pupil, where it will be of little service. If we have to deal with that form of irido-choroiditis, in which the iris is bulged forward in knob-like protuberances, with complete adhesion of the pupillary edge of the iris to the lens, an *iridectomy* is indicated; but if it is the parenchymatous variety, with adhesion of the whole of the posterior surface of the iris to the lens, iridectomy will do more harm than good. If a foreign body should be the cause of the inflammation, it must be removed if possible, though when the injury in the ciliary region is very great, it is better to enucleate the eye in order to prevent trouble in the other. If the inflammation of the uveal tract is caused by sympathetic irritation from an injured eye —and this is the most common form of "sympathetic ophthalmia,"—the injured eye, especially if sight is lost, should be removed upon the first symptoms of irritation or as early as possible, unless the inflammatory process is very severe, when it may be better to wait until it has subsided in some degree. If there is some sight in the injured eye, it is often difficult to decide whether enucleation is advisable or not. As a rule, an eye that has been lost from any cause and which remains painful, even if there are no symptoms of irritation in the healthy eye, should be removed. The irritation being transmitted by the ciliary nerves, division of these nerves (optico-ciliary neurotomy) has been recently proposed as a substitute for enucleation. It may be adapted to rare cases.

In old cases, in which the lens has become cataractous, various operations for its removal have been recommended.

In the treatment of all forms of inflammation of the uveal tract *complete rest* of the eye for a long period must be insisted upon. In acute cases the patient should be confined to the house and treated as for iritis. In chronic cases it is better to allow moderate exercise in the open air, with the eyes protected by a bandage or colored glasses. The diet should be nutritious and generous, especially if the patient is feeble and ill-nourished.

The chief reliance must be placed upon internal medication, but for special indications refer to the therapeutics of iritis and choroiditis. The following remedies, however, have been more commonly used with advantage, and would be among the first suggested to our minds: Apis, Ars., Asaf., Aur., *Bell.*, *Bry.*, *Gels.*, *Hepar*, *Kali iod.*, *Merc. corr. and iod.*, Prunus spin., *Rhus*, *Sil.*, Sulph. and Thuja.

SYNECHIÆ ANTERIOR. ET POSTERIOR.

(Adhesions of the Iris to Cornea or Lens.)

The common results of inflammation of the iris, after improper treatment or no treatment at all, are adhesions of this tissue to the lens or cornea (the latter more often resulting from ulceration and perforation of the cornea). This condition we are frequently called upon to treat, not only on account of its impairment of vision, but also to remove the cause of constant recurring iritis and other more serious disorders.

The first and most important measure is to endeavor to tear the adhesions by the use of strong solutions of *Atropine*, or *Eserine*, or both alternately, according to extent and situation. If we do not succeed by these means, a hook may be introduced and the adhesions torn, though this is a very delicate procedure and is rarely undertaken.

If the intra-ocular tension increases, or a chronic recurrent inflammation results, an *iridectomy* becomes necessary.

Some remedies, as Clematis, Merc. corr., Nitric ac., Sulph. and Terebinth, have seemed to have a favorable action upon recent adhesions, causing them to absorb or soften so that they can be easily torn by Atropine.

MYDRIASIS.

(*Dilatation of the Pupil.*)

This functional disturbance of the pupil is usually merely a symptom of deeper and more serious trouble, therefore requires remedies adapted to that condition. It is, however, sometimes found uncomplicated with other disorders, being dependent upon cold, trauma, etc., in which case Arnica, Bell., Caust., and a score of remedies may be indicated. The instillation of sulphate of eserine is also often of great service. As mydriasis is generally associated with paralysis of one or more of the ocular muscles, refer for treatment to paralysis of the muscles.

MYOSIS.

(*Contraction of the Pupil.*)

Contraction of the pupil, unassociated with more serious disturbance, is of rare occurrence; the cause therefore usually demands our attention. Atropine instilled into the eye may be employed, though it generally gives only temporary relief.

Jaborandi and *Physostigma ven.* are especially recommended for this condition, though various remedies which produce contraction of the pupil may be thought of.

TUMORES.

(*Tumors of the Iris.*)

Tumors of the iris are usually more successfully treated by surgical interference than by internal or external medication.

LÆSIONES.

(*Wounds of the Iris.*)

If a foreign body is lying upon or in the iris, it should be removed by making an iridectomy, excising that portion of the iris in which the foreign body is situated; after which, Atropine should be instilled, a bandage applied and the patient put to bed. If there is considerable injury to iris, or surrounding tissues. *ice compresses* will give the most favorable results.

When a portion of the iris protrudes through an opening in the cornea (prolapsus iridis) an attempt should be made to replace it by the use of Atropine or Eserine; if these measures fail, it may be excised and the patient treated as after an iridectomy. For the treatment of the inflammation produced by injuries of the iris refer to iritis.

The hemorrhage into the anterior chamber resulting from an injury to the iris will usually absorb very quickly (24 to 48 hours), without external aid. If, however, the absorption should be slow it may be hastened by a solution of *Arnica, Hamamelis* or *Ledum*, with a firm compress bandage.

CILIARY BODY.

CYCLITIS.

(Inflammation of the Ciliary Body.)

The treatment of inflammation in this portion of the uveal tract will depend almost exclusively upon internal medication. The eye must be kept warm, as in iritis, and Atropine may be necessary, as the iris is liable to become involved. Special indications for remedies are to be found under iritis.

LÆSIONES.

(Injuries of the Ciliary Body.)

Injuries implicating the ciliary region are not only dangerous on account of inflammatory complications but as a cause of sympathetic ophthalmia. Simple incised wounds may readily unite by keeping the eye at rest, or it may be necessary to use a fine suture. Extensive injuries in this region will usually necessitate enucleation, though under certain circumstances the eye may be preserved, providing the patient is intelligent and will attend to the first unfavorable symptoms which may arise. Foreign bodies must be removed, if it is possible without too much injury to the tissues, or the eye must be sacrificed.

CHOROID.

HYPERÆMIA CHOR., CHOROIDITIS.

(Hyperæmia and Inflammation of the Choroid.)

Under this section will be found both serous and plastic choroiditis, with the four varieties of the latter, choroiditis disseminata simplex, choroiditis areolaris, chorio-retinitis circumscripta seu centralis, chorio-retinitis disseminata syphilitica.

Rest in a darkened room for a long period has been recommended for inflammation of the choroid. This, together with bandaging of the eye, will answer in some cases of acute serous inflammation, but its tendency to impair the general health usually renders it unsafe, especially in chronic cases and in the disseminate form of inflammation, in which it is far wiser to allow moderate exercise in the open air, with the eyes protected from the bright light by smoke or blue glasses. *Complete rest* of the eyes from all work should always be required. Atropine may be useful in some cases, as it paralyzes the tensor choroidea, thus preventing any movement of the inflamed tissue upon change of light. In the serous variety, if the intraocular tension becomes increased, frequent paracentesis may be performed or if this does not suffice an iridectomy must be made. Abstinence from all stimulants, and proper hygienic measures are necessary.

Aurum.—Choroiditis, with or without retinal complication, especially if there is *exudation into the choroid and retina or into the vitreous,* causing haziness of the vitreous. We may have sensitiveness to light and touch, ciliary injection and some pressive pain in the eye from above downward or from without inward, aggravated on touch, or pain in the bones around the eye. A general feeling of malaise and depression of spirits is often present.

Belladonna.—An important remedy in *hyperæmia* or acute inflammatory conditions of the choroid, particularly of the disseminate variety and accompanied by congestive headaches. The optic disk is of a deep red color, and the retinal vessels enlarged, especially the veins. The pupil is slightly dilated, ciliary injection usually marked, and eyes sensitive to light, with full feeling as if pressed out of the head. Disturbances of vision are often present, as halo around the light and various flashes of light, and sparks. The headache and constitutional symptoms decide our choice.

Bryonia.—*Serous choroiditis*, or inflammation of the uveal tract, following rheumatic iritis. From *serous* infiltration into the vitreous the haziness is often so great as to seriously interfere with our view of the fundus. The vessels of the fundus are congested; the pupils may be somewhat dilated and the tension increased. *The eyeball feels sore to touch and motion, while darting pains through the eye into the head* are usually present.

Gelsemium.—It may be of service in the plastic forms of choroiditis, but its grand sphere of action is in *serous inflammation of the uveal tract*, especially if anterior to the equator, with great haziness of the humors. The impairment of vision will be great; may be slow and gradual, or subject to sudden changes. The haziness of the vitreous is usually fine; the tension may be increased, and pupil dilated. The iris may be involved, with tendency to posterior synechiæ. Transparent sensitive points or vesicles may be found on the surface of the cornea, which come and go suddenly. The pain is dull, aching, pressing, in and over the eyes; may extend to occiput and be relieved by hot applications. Eyeball sore to touch. Heaviness of the lids. Headache, general depression, loss of muscular tone, fever and thirstlessness.

Kali iod.—It is *the* remedy for *syphilitic chorio-retinitis* characterized by great haziness, and exudation into the vitreous, which may vary from day to day; also for *syphilitic disseminate choroiditis*, with little or no haziness of vitreous. Much benefit has been derived from its use in simple disseminate choroiditis even when the atrophic changes in the choroid are far advanced or when the whole uveal tract has become involved.

Kali mur.—The benefit derived from its use in the absorption of exudations has been demonstrated in exudative choroiditis.

Mercurius.—The various preparations are used, according to special indications, though the corrosivus or solubis is more often needed. Mercury is of great value in choroiditis, especially *disseminate*, and when the *iris is also involved* (iridochoroiditis). The syphilitic dyscrasia would particularly point to its use, though it is indicated in non-syphilitic cases. The tendency to the formation of adhesions of the iris to the lens is marked. *The pains are usually intense both in and around the eye*, varying to a great extent in character. The *nocturnal aggravation* of all the symptoms is of importance in the selection of this remedy, as well as the general condition of the patient.

Nux vom.—In disseminate choroiditis occurring in persons addicted to the use of stimulants, also when atrophic changes are even far advanced, Nux often seems to materially improve the degree of vision. The eyes are especially weak and *sensitive to light in the morning*. Gastric derangements and other constitutional symptoms are of great importance in selecting this drug.

Phosphorus.—Both serous and disseminate choroiditis have been benefited, especially when accompanied by *photopsies and chromopsies of various shapes and colors* (*red predominating*). We find in the proving of Phosphorus, that it has produced *hyperæmia of the choroid*, and experience shows that it is often adapted to this condition. When sexual excesses seem to be the cause of the trouble this remedy is indicated. The optic nerve and even retina may show decided hyperæmia. Black spots pass before the vision. There may be some dread of light. The eyes seem *better in the twilight*. Particularly suitable to lean slender persons, and especially if complicated with cough, etc.

Prunus spin.—Inflammation of the choroid, either with or without iritic or retinal complication. Haziness of the vitreous and other common symptoms of the disease are present, but the characteristic indication will be found in the *pain, which is usually severe, as if the eyeball were being pressed asunder, or else,* *sharp shooting and cutting through the eye and corresponding side of the head, or crushing in character.*

Pulsatilla.—Hyperæmia of the choroid or sub-acute cases of choroiditis, occurring in women of a mild, tearful, yielding disposition and when accompanied by amenorrhœa; also in tea drinkers who are subject to neuralgic headaches. Eye symptoms not characteristic.

Sulphur.—Chronic cases of choroiditis, especially if traceable to the suppression of an eruption or if occurring in a strumous subject. *Sharp darting pains* are usually present. Often assists in clearing the vitreous and completing a cure after other remedies have been used with advantage. The hemeralopia found in some cases may be relieved.

Verat. vir.—Choroiditis, especially in women with much vaso-motor disturbance. Aching pains in the eyes, becoming sharp in the evening. Photopsies. Painful menstruation and aggravation of eye symptoms at that time.

In addition to the above, the following remedies have been employed with favorable results: Acon. (first stage), Arsen. (dissem.), Duboisin, Hepar, Jaborandi (serous), Psor. (serous), Ruta (dissem.), Sil. (dissem.).

CHOROIDITIS SUPPURATIVA (PANOPHTHALMITIS).

(Suppurative Inflammation of the Whole Eyeball.)

(Syn. Parenchymatous or Metastatic Choroiditis.)

Our first endeavor should be to save the eye if possible, and with this end in view any exciting cause must be removed. If it is due to a swollen cataractous lens this must be extracted; if to an orbital abscess this must be opened; or if a foreign body is found to be the cause, as is frequently the case, we must try to remove it, unless it is too deep within the eye when it is far better to enucleate, except when the inflammatory process is very pronounced, when experience has shown that it is advisable to wait until the severity of the symptoms has subsided before we undertake the operation; but if a foreign

19

body is present within the ball, enucleation of the eye is strongly recommended after the inflammation has been subdued, for there is always danger of sympathetic irritation of the other eye.

For the disease itself, in the first stage, cold or ice compresses may be used with advantage, but if the pain becomes very severe in and around the eye, especially if suppuration has commenced, more benefit will be gained from warm applications either dry or moist. Atropine may be of advantage, early, in palliating the pain.

If the pain is very severe and the tension increased, paracentesis or an iridectomy will be found of service. If, however, suppuration has far advanced so as to destroy the eye and the pain is intense, it is best to make a deep incision at once and employ hot fomentations.

A nourishing diet, even stimulants, becomes necessary to sustain the patient's strength after suppuration has taken place.

Aconite.—*First stage*, accompanied by high fever and much thirst. *Eyelids red, swollen, hot and dry*, with much pain in the eye.

Apis.—*Lids œdematous, chemosis, stinging pains* through the eye. Drowsiness and absence of thirst usually accompany the local indications.

Arsenic.—If the patient is very *restless* and *thirsty*, with œdema of the lids and conjunctiva, and severe *burning pain.* Arsenicum cases are similar to Rhus, though the former does not compare with the latter in degree of usefulness.

Hepar.—*After suppuration has begun. Eye very sensitive to touch and the pains severe and throbbing, ameliorated by warm applications.*

Phytolacca.—Panophthalmitis, especially if traumatic. *Lids very hard, red and swollen;* chemosis, and pus in the interior of the eye. Pains quite severe.

Rhus tox.—The most commonly indicated remedy in panophthalmitis, whether it be of traumatic origin or not. It is useful in nearly every stage of the disease, though is particularly adapted to the first. The *lids are œdematously swollen,*

spasmodically closed, and upon opening them a profuse gush
of tears pours out. The *conjunctiva is œdematous*, forming a
wall around the cornea which may be slightly hazy. The
iris may be swollen, pupil contracted and aqueous cloudy,
while the pain in and around the eye is often severe, *especially
at night* and upon any change in the weather.

Asafœt., Bell., Merc., Sil., Sulph. and other remedies may in
certain cases and stages be useful.

SCLERECTASIA POSTERIOR.

(*Posterior Staphyloma.*)

(Syn. Sclerotico-Choroiditis posterior.)

As myopia always accompanies this disorder of the fundus,
the proper selection of glasses should receive our first attention, the greatest care being taken that they are. not too
strong. We should next warn the patient against over-use of
the eyes for near objects, and also to always avoid stooping or
bending forward when using the eyes at near work, as this
tends to increase the venous congestion, thus serving to accelerate the progress of the disease. It is injurious to read in
the recumbent position. These patients should, therefore, sit
upright, with head erect, when reading, and with the back to
the light, so that the page will be illuminated and the eyes
not subjected to the bright glare of the light. The work or
book should not be brought nearer as the eye becomes fatigued, but be laid aside until the eyes are thoroughly rested.
If the patient complains of dazzling from the bright light, as
is often the case, either blue or smoke glasses may be allowed.
In aggravated cases they should be required to abstain from
all near work.

The constant and continued use of *Atropine* for a long time
has been found advantageous in some instances.

Belladonna.—Sclero-choroiditis post. *with flushed face and
throbbing congestive headaches.* The eye appears hyperæmic
externally as well as internally. *The optic nerve and whole
fundus are seen congested.* Opacities may be present in the
vitreous; photopsies and chromopsies are sometimes observed.
The eyes are *quite sensitive to light.*

Phosphorus.—Fundus hyperæmic. Muscæ volitantes and flashes of light before the vision. Everything looks red.

Prunus spin.—Staphyloma posticum, accompanied by *pains in ball, as if pressed asunder, or sharp and shooting in and around the eye.* Vitreous hazy and vessels of the fundus injected.

Spigelia.—When accompanied by *sharp stabbing pains* through the eye and around it, often commencing at one point and then seeming to radiate in every direction.

Thuja—An important remedy in all *inflammatory conditions of the sclera,* especially in *strumous or syphilitic subjects.* The globe may be quite sensitive to touch and the photophobia is usually marked.

Carbo veg., Croc., Jaborandi, Lyco., Kali iod., Merc., Physostigma, Ruta and Sulph. are also remedies to be borne in mind. Compare remedies for choroiditis.

TUMORES.

(*Tumors of the Choroid.*)

Tumors of the choroid are, as a rule, malignant in character and therefore necessitate enucleation of the eye as soon as recognized. Remedies that are recommended for sarcoma and carcinoma in other portions of the body might be tried, though delay in removing the eye is unwarranted.

RUPTURA CHOR., ET HEMORRHAGIA.

(*Rupture of the Choroid, and Hemorrhage.*)

Hemorrhage is the most common symptom that demands our attention in the treatment of a rupture of the choroid, though we may have hemorrhages arising spontaneously or from inflammatory changes, etc.

The remedies chiefly called for will be *Arn.*, Bell., China, Crotalus, Hamamelis, *Lach.*, Merc. corr., or Phosph.

For special indications refer to retinitis apoplectica.

If there is hyperæmia or inflammation of the choroid present, our treatment will be guided by the rules laid down under choroiditis.

GLAUCOMA.

(*Increased Eye Tension.*)

Thanks to the genius of von Graefe, for the grandest discovery in ophthalmic science, the value of *iridectomy* in glaucoma. By the majority of the allopathic school, iridectomy is considered the only true curative treatment for this affection, and homœopathy should, by no means, cast this important aid aside, but, upon the other hand, place it at the head of our remedial agents. We do not consider it the only measure we possess to combat this terrible malady, for we have several drugs that have proved beneficial in staying the progress of the disease, especially in its incipiency, but when the premonitory stage has passed, and there is no period of remission between the attacks, no physician is justified in delaying to perform an iridectomy. This may be laid down as a rule, though there are exceptional cases in which the operation does harm, or proves of no service, as in the hemorrhagic form, though this should not deter us from operating, unless the hemorrhagic tendency is well marked, when we should first give our remedies a thorough trial.

Incision of the sclera (sclerotomy) has recently been highly recommended as a substitute for iridectomy. If properly performed, it may be advisable in certain cases, but in my experience, it does not as certainly and permanently diminish intraocular tension as iridectomy, and therefore, is not as suitable for the majority of cases, especially of acute glaucoma.

Myotomy, and other operative measures, have been recommended, though none of them can, as yet, be compared to a large iridectomy as a curative agent.

Mydriatics, especially Atropine, must be avoided, as they are liable to produce an acute attack of glaucoma. The instillation of *Eserine*, in some cases, seems to relieve the intraocular tension. It should not be substituted for iridectomy, but may be of service in the prodromal stage, when for one reason or another the operation must be temporarily postponed, or when the tension again increases after iridectomy.

In the premonitory stage, as has already been said, our endeavor should be to cure by the aid of internal medication, which may be done in many cases, if we take into consideration the constitutional disturbances, which are associated with, or cause the intra-ocular trouble. The habits of our patient should receive careful attention. The excessive use of stimulants (either alcohol or tobacco), or any exhaustive mental or physical labor must be strictly forbidden. Only moderate use of the eyes should be allowed, and, during the attacks, or when they follow each other in rapid succession, complete rest is necessary. Bright light, either natural or artificial, should be avoided, or the eyes protected by colored glasses. The diet should be good and nutritious, particularly in elderly persons, and all indigestible substances forbidden.

Asafœtida.—Glaucoma, with severe, *boring pain over the eye*, and around it.

Belladonna.—Of benefit in relieving the severe pains of glaucoma, especially if accompanied by throbbing headache, and flushed face. The eyes are injected, pupils dilated, fundus hyperæmic, and pain both in and around the eye. The pains are usually severe and throbbing; may come and go suddenly, and are *worse in the afternoon and evening*. The eyes are hot and dry, with *sensitiveness to light*. Halo around the light, red predominating. Photophobia.

Bryonia.—From its value in serous inflammations in general, this remedy has been given with benefit in glaucoma. It is more often indicated in the prodromal stage. The eyes feel full, as if pressed out, often associated with sharp, shooting pains through the eye and head. *The eyes feel sore to touch, and on moving them in any direction.* There may be a halo around the light, with heavy pain over the eye, worse at night. The usual concomitant symptoms will decide us in its selection.

Cedron.—For the relief of the pains of glaucoma, when they are severe and *shooting along the course of the supra-orbital nerve.*

Colocynth —Of service in relieving the pains of glaucoma, when they are severe, burning, aching, sticking, or *cutting* in character, in the eye and around, always *relieved by firm press-*

ure, and by walking in a warm room, aggravated by rest at night, and upon stooping.

Gelsemium.—From its usefulness in serous choroiditis it should prove of great value in glaucoma.

Nux vom.—Indicated if the *morning aggravation* is very marked, and for the resulting atrophy of the optic nerve.

Phosphorus.—Of great importance in improving vision, and removing many subjective symptoms after iridectomy. Fundus hyperæmic and hazy, halo around the light, and various lights and colors (especially red) before the eye. Sensation as if something was pulled tightly over the eyes. Vision impaired, better in the twilight.

Prunus spin.—*Pain severe, crushing, in the eye, as if eye were pressed asunder, or sharp, shooting through the eye, and corresponding side of the head* (Spig.). Aqueous and vitreous hazy, fundus hyperæmic.

Rhododendron.—Incipient glaucoma, with much pain in and around the eye, periodic in character, and *always worse just before a storm, ameliorated after the storm commences.*

Spigelia.—*Pains sharp and stabbing through the eye and head,* worse on motion, and at night.

Our range of drugs will be extensive in this affection, as we must take into consideration all the general symptoms, to make a sure prescription. The above remedies have been most often called for in the cases we have met, though the following may be found useful: Arn., Ars., Aur., Cham., Con., Crot. tig., Ham. v., Kali iod., Macrotin, Merc. and Sulph.

OPTIC NERVE AND RETINA.

HYPERÆMIA N. O. ET RET., NEURITIS, RETINITIS.

(Hyperæmia and Idiopathic Inflammation of the Optic Nerve and Retina.)

Neuro-retinitis is a more common diagnosis, as the optic nerve and retina are usually inflamed at the same time.

Hyperæmia of the retina frequently depends upon some anomaly in the accommodation or refraction of the eye, which should be corrected by suitable glasses, after which the retina returns to its normal condition.

Rest is a most important aid in all cases whether inflammatory or only hyperæmic, and the more complete it is, especially in neuritis or retinitis, the better for the patients. They should be instructed to abstain from all use of the eyes, particularly by artificial light. Some authors, as Stellwag and others, recommend the confinement of the patient in a darkened room and the employment of a bandage, thus keeping all light away from the eye for some time, when they can gradually become accustomed to bright light. Such severe measures are, however, not required except in extreme cases. It is better to allow moderate exercise in the open air, taking care that the eyes are properly protected from the irritating influence of bright light, by the use of either blue or smoke glasses.

Proper hygienic rules, according to the nature of the case, demand our most careful attention.

Belladonna.—One of the most frequently indicated remedies for both hyperæmia and inflammation of the optic nerve and retina. *The retinal vessels will be found enlarged and tortuous,* particularly the veins, while a *blue or bluish-grey film* may seem to overspread the fundus (œdema). *Extravasations of blood* may be numerous or few in number. *The optic disc is swollen* and outlines ill-defined. The vision is, of course, deteriorated. The pains are usually of an *aching,* dull character, though may be *throbbing* and severe, accompanied by *throbbing congestive head-aches* with visibly beating carotids and flushed face. Phosphenes of every shape and hue, especially red, may be observed by the patient. Decided *sensitiveness to light.* The eyes feel *worse in the afternoon* and evening, when all the symptoms are aggravated. Externally the eye may present no abnormal appearance, though generally seems weak, is injected and irritable (often with a red conjunctival line along the margins of the lids).

Bryonia.—Serous retinitis or hyperæmia, with a bluish haze before the vision and severe *sharp pain through the eye* and over it. Eyes feel full and *sore on motion* or to touch. Great heat in the head, aggravated by stooping.

Cactus.—Retinal congestions, especially if heart trouble is present.

Conium.—Fundus congested, with *much photophobia*; ciliary muscle weak.

Duboisia.—Of great value in the treatment of both hyperæmia and inflammation of the optic nerve and retina. *Retinal vessels large and tortuous,* especially the veins. *Optic papilla swollen* and outlines ill-defined (engorged papilla). Hemorrhages in the retina, aching in the eyes and *pain through the upper part of the eyeball* just beneath the brow, which may be very severe. Chronic hyperæmia of the conjunctiva.

Mercurius.—Retinitis with marked nocturnal aggravation and *sensitiveness of the eyes to the glare of a fire.* Congested conditions of the fundus found in those who work at a forge or over fires. Degeneration of the blood vessels, with hemorrhages into the retina. Concomitant symptoms will assist us in the selection.

Nux vom.—Retinitis occurring with gastric disturbances, especially in drunkards. The eye indications vary, but are usually *aggravated* in the morning.

Phosphorus. — Hyperæmia or inflammation of the optic nerve and retina, especially with *extravasations of blood.* Degeneration of the coats of the blood vessels. The eye may be sensitive to light, and vision improved in twilight. Vision impaired, muscæ volitantes, photopsies and chromopsies are present, as halo around the light. The eyeballs may be sore on motion and pain may extend from eyes to top of head.

Pulsatilla.—*Hyperæmia and inflammation of the optic nerve and retina accompanied by more or less severe pains in the head always relieved in the open air.* Sensation as if a veil were before the eyes, or the vision may be nearly lost. All the ophthalmoscopic appearances of engorged papilla or simple hyperæmia may be present. If dependent upon menstrual difficulties or associated with acne of the face or disorders of the stomach.

Veratrum viride.—*Engorged disc*, with severe pain at menses and general vaso-motor disturbances.

In addition to the above, the following remedies may be of benefit in rare cases or as intercurrents: Acon., Ars., Aurum, Chin. sulph., Gels., Kali iod., Kali mur., Lach., Spig. and Sulph.

RETINITIS SYPHILITICA.

(Inflammation of the Retina from Syphilis.)

Asafœtida.—When accompanied by *severe boring, burning pains above the brows*, especially at night; also if there is pain in the balls from within outwards ameliorated by pressure (reverse of Aurum).

Aurum.—Especially after *over-dosing with iodide of potassium or mercury* and if accompanied by detachment of the retina. Eye sensitive to touch, with pain in and around, seeming to be deep in the bones. A general syphilitic dyscrasia is perceptible in the constitutional symptoms which govern our selection of Aurum.

Kali iod.—For syphilitic retinitis this should be one of the first remedies thought of, especially if there is choroideal complication, though the chief indications for its use will be furnished by the general condition of the patient.

Mercurius.—Especially the remedy for this form of inflammation of the retina. The solubis or corrosivus have been more commonly employed, though the other preparations are also useful when special indications point to their use. The retina will be found hazy, congested and often complicated with an inflammatory condition of the choroid or neighboring tissues. The eye is particularly sensitive to artificial light. *Nocturnal aggravation of all the symptoms* is always present. More or less pain is experienced both in and around the eye, especially during the evening and after going to bed. The syphilitic taint will be perceptible in various ways that will indicate Merc.

Other anti-syphilitic remedies may be useful, given according to general indications, or we may find a remedy recommended for the other forms of retinitis, serviceable in this variety when particular indications are present.

RETINITIS ALBUMINURICA.

(*Inflammation of the Retina from Bright's Disease.*)

The principal treatment should be directed to the kidneys, the seat of the primary disease, and such hygienic and dietetic measures adopted as are recommended for Bright's disease. Benefit has sometimes been derived from keeping the patient quiet in bed, and upon a low or skim-milk diet.

Apis.—If associated with œdematous swelling of the lids and general dropsical condition. Patient very drowsy, with little thirst and scanty urine.

Arsenicum.—If the patient is restless, especially at night after midnight, with great thirst for small quantities. Urine scanty and albuminous.

Gelsemium.—Retinitis albuminurica occurring during pregnancy. White patches and extravasations of blood in the retina. Dimness of vision appears suddenly. Serous infiltration into the vitreous, making it hazy, may be observed. The patient is thirstless, and albumen is found in the urine.

Kalmia.—Nephritic retinitis accompanied by much pain in the back, as if it would break.

Merc. corr.—Has been more extensively used in *albuminuric retinitis* than any other remedy. The fatty degeneration, extravasation of blood from the weakened vessels and all the pathological changes in the eye as well as in the kidney, point to mercury as a remedy, even though no characteristic subjective symptoms are present. The results are especially favorable when pregnancy appears to be the exciting cause of the difficulty.

As hemorrhages are usually found in the retina in this form of inflammation, compare the remedies recommended for retinitis apoplectica.

Hepar, Kali acet., Plumb. and Phosph. have either been used or are highly recommended for this condition of the eye. In fact, any remedy applicable to the disease of the kidney will often prove of service in the eye complication.

RETINITIS DIABETICA.

(Inflammation of the Retina from Diabetes.)

As this form of retinitis may only be characterized by hemorrhages into the retina, compare the remedies recommended for retinitis apoplectica and albuminurica. In addition to which, *Secale* is suggested, though the chief attention must be directed to the diabetes.

RETINITIS LEUCÆMICA.

(Inflammation of the Retina from Leucocythæmia.)

This rare form of inflammation is only a symptom, therefore all the treatment must be directed to the primary disease.

RETINITIS APOPLECTICA.

(Hemorrhages into the Retina, with more or less Inflammation.)

(Syn. Retinitis hemorrhagica, Apoplexia retinæ.)

Rest for the eyes must be enforced. All undue mental or physical exertion and the use of stimulants must be strictly prohibited. If dependent upon general disturbances, these will require our attention.

Arnica.—Retinal hemorrhages of traumatic origin.

Belladonna.—Apoplexy of the retina, especially when arising from or accompanied by congestive headaches. Suppressed menstruation may be the cause of the difficulty. The retina and optic nerve will be found inflamed and congested.

Crotalus.—In the snake poisons we possess our chief agents for hastening the absorption of extravasations of blood into the retina. Crotalus has been used with great advantage, especially if the hemorrhage is unaccompanied by inflammation.

Lachesis.—From its use, hemorrhages into the retina have been seen to speedily disappear, and the accompanying inflammation rapidly diminish. It is very commonly called for when no characteristic symptoms are present with the exception of the pathological changes. The retina and perhaps optic nerve are inflamed and congested, while throughout the swollen retina may be observed extravasations of blood of various ages and sizes. General indications determine its selection.

Merc. corr.—Of great benefit in hemorrhages into the retina dependent upon pronounced degenerative changes in the coats of the bloodvessels, with or without inflammation. It not only hastens their absorption but serves to restore tone to the vessels themselves.

Phosphorus.—In a hemorrhagic diathesis, when the concomitant indications point to its selection.

Duboisia and *Pulsatilla* may also render valuable service.

RETINITIS PIGMENTOSA.

(*Pigmentary Degeneration of the Retina.*)

Over-use of the eyes and exposure to bright light must be avoided. Much attention must be given to the general health for a long period. Lyco., Nux vom. and Phos. are suggested as remedies.

ISCHÆMIA RETINÆ.

(*Anæmia of the Retina.*)

When the anæmic condition of the retina is complete (vision entirely lost), paracentesis or iridectomy, to diminish the intra-ocular tension, becomes necessary. We sometimes observe a partial anæmia of the optic nerve and retina associated with and dependent upon general anæmia. These cases should be treated by the administration of those medicines indicated by the general condition of the patient, as Calc., China, Ferrum, Phos., Puls., etc.

Agaricus has cured cases accompanied by a tendency towards chorea.

EMBOLIA ARTERIA CENTRALIS RETINÆ.

(Embolism of the Central Artery of the Retina.)

Vision may, in exceptional cases, return without any treatment though it is better to give those remedies which seem to be constitutionally required.

By reference to *Opium* a case will be found described in which a cure was effected; whether or not this was due to the Opium administered is a question.

Hemorrhage into the optic nerve often presents the same ophthalmoscopic picture as embolism; in which case remedies adapted to hemorrhagic conditions must be employed.

HYPERÆSTHESIA RETINÆ.

(Over-sensitiveness of the Retina to Light.)

(Syn. Retinal asthenopia.)

If dependent upon any anomaly of refraction, the proper glass must first be prescribed.

In rare, severe cases it may be necessary to confine the patient in complete darkness for a week or more and then gradually accustom him to the light. Though usually it is better to advise *exercise in the open air*, having the eyes protected by smoke or blue glasses or a shade. Especial attention must be paid to the general health of the patient.

Belladonna.—*Hyperæsthesia of the retina*, particularly if dependent upon some anomaly of refraction or reflex irritation. *Eyes very sensitive to light*; cannot bear it, as it produces severe aching and pain in the eye, and even *headache*. Flashes of light and sparks observed before the vision. The eye symptoms as well as the headache are usually aggravated in the afternoon and evening.

Conium.—*Over-sensitiveness of the retina to light,* especially if accompanied with asthenopic symptoms, so that one cannot read long without the letters running together; with pain deep in the eye. Excessive photopsies, but fundus normal in appearance. Photophobia. Everything looks white.

Ignatia.—Hyperæsthesia of the retina, in nervous hysterical patients. Great dread of light, and severe pain around the eye.

Lactic acid.—Hyperæsthesia of the retina, with steady aching pain in and behind the eyeball.

Macrotin.—Angell considers Macrotin more widely serviceable than any other one remedy. The ciliary neuralgia is usually marked.

Merc. sol.—Eyes more sensitive to artificial light, and in the evening.

Natrum mur.—Hyperæsthesia of the retina, especially from reflex irritation in chlorotic females; there is great photophobia, with muscular asthenopia. Some conjunctival injection. *Eyes feel stiff and ache on moving them, or on reading.* Letters run together on attempting to read. Sticking, throbbing headache in the temples.

Nux vom.—When the *photophobia is excessive in the morning,* and better as the day advances.

A large number of remedies which produce marked photophobia, may be indicated by the general symptoms and cachexia of the patient, as, Acon., Ars., China, Gels., Hep., Hyos., Puls., Rhus, Sep., Sulph., Tar. cm., etc.

AMOTIO RETINÆ.

(*Detachment of the Retina.*)

If the retina has been detached for any great length of time very little can be done to restore the vision, but if seen early the prognosis is much more favorable.

If the patient comes under treatment a short time after the detachment has occurred, or even six months afterwards, he should be confined to his bed, chiefly on his back, with the eyes bandaged. This is of great importance in aiding recovery. If it is impossible to confine the patient to his room, he must be warned to avoid all use of the eyes, and to keep as quiet as possible. If he must be out in the light, the eyes must be protected by darkly colored glasses. In many cases, the constant use of Atropine is of advantage, as it prevents accommodation, and thus keeps the eye and tissues more quiet.

Operations, to allow the escape of the fluids both into the vitreous and externally, are employed, but only temporary relief is usually obtained in this manner. They may, however, be advisable in some instances, especially if the detachment is above.

Apis.—Fluid beneath the retina. Pressive pain in the lower part of the ball, with flushed face and head. Stinging pains through the eye. Œdematous swelling of the lids.

Arnica.—*Traumatic detachment of the retina.*

Aurum.—Has been used successfully in amotio retinæ. It is especially adapted to those cases which follow over-dosing with potash or mercury. The symptom under Aurum which suggests its use is as follows: "Upper half of vision as if covered by a black body, lower half visible." The choroid, or retina, is usually inflamed, and opacities are seen in the vitreous, giving rise to the "blacks" complained of by the patient.

Digitalis.—Adapted to the general pathological condition, and has this common symptom of detachment of the retina. "As if the upper half of vision were covered by a dark cloud, evenings, on walking." Benefit has been seen from its use.

Gelsemium.—One of the most prominent remedies for *serous infiltration beneath the retina*, dependent upon injury, myopia, or ciliary neuralgia. Especially indicated if accompanied by choroiditis, with haziness of the vitreous, and some pain. A bluish haze, or wavering, is often observed.

Ars., Bry., Hep., Kali iod., Merc. and *Rhus* may also be thought of for this condition.

ATROPHIA N. OPTICI ET RETINÆ.

(Atrophy of the Optic Nerve and Retina.)

In true atrophy of the optic nerve very little can be done to restore vision, though we are often able to check its progress by the selection of appropriate remedies, as indicated by general symptoms.

The general health requires most careful attention. The diet should be nutritious and light, while tobacco and all liquors must be prohibited. Mental and physical fatigue must not be allowed.

The hypodermic injection of *Strychnia* has proved efficacious in some instances, though its internal administration is usually more satisfactory.

Nux vom.—Has been followed by more favorable results in this condition than any other remedy.

Argent. nitr., Verat vir., and others, have been used with advantage.

AMAUROSIS, AMBLYOPIA.

(Complete or Partial Loss of Vision.)

These terms should be confined to that limited class of cases in which the vision is more or less impaired without perceptible changes in the refractive media or internal tunics of the eye. Many cases are recorded in which marvelous cures of amaurosis or amblyopia have been effected under various remedies, but due allowance must be made for mistaken diagnoses, especially when the ophthalmoscope was not used.

In the treatment of these functional disturbances of vision our main reliance must be placed upon internal medication, and, as the eye indications are "nil," the prescription must be based upon the cause of the trouble and general symptoms.

The following remedies have, at present, been found most commonly indicated: Argent. nit., Aurum, *Bell.*, Ignatia, *Nux vom.*, *Phos.*, *Ruta*, Sepia, Sulph. and Tabac.

Anæsthesia of the retina which might be classed in this section has been benefited by *Hepar* and *Jaborandi*.

AMBLYOPIA POTATORUM ET NICOTIANA.

(Amblyopia from the Use of Liquor and Tobacco.)

Total abstinence from all spirituous liquors, or their reduction

20

to a minimum, must be strictly enforced, as well as the necessity of giving up tobacco. After which our attention should be turned to those remedies which will restore the whole system to its natural tone.

Arsenic seems especially adapted to loss of vision dependent upon the use of tobacco.

Nux vom. has been and probably always will be, the most important and most commonly indicated remedy in this trouble. The results following its use are often marvelous. There are no marked eye symptoms in this disease and therefore nothing to guide us to this drug with the exception of the cause.

Terebinth.—Amblyopia potatorum, with dull aching pain in the back, and dark colored urine.

HEMIOPIA.

(*Half Vision.*)

Half vision is usually only a symptom of some deep disorder of the eye, but as it is sometimes the only symptom to be found, those remedies appropriate to it will be mentioned. (It must be remembered that this is often due to intra-cranial tumors or other troubles which are irremediable.)

Upper half of visual field defective: *Aurum*, Dig. and Gels.

Right half of visual field defective: Cyclamen, *Lith. carb.* and *Lyco.*

Vertical hemiopia, either half invisible: Calc. carb., Chin. sulph., Mor., Mur ac., Nat. mur., Pb., Rhus, Sep. and Stram.

HEMERALOPIA.

(*Night Blindness.*)

As the general health is usually more or less impaired in hemeralopia, a generous diet must be ordered. Rest and protection of the eyes from bright light are first required; in severe cases it may be necessary to confine the patient to a dark room. (It must be remembered that night-blindness is frequently only a symptom of retinitis pigmentosa, which must be recognized with the ophthalmoscope.)

Lycopodium is the remedy most commonly needed in this disorder. Many cases have yielded promptly to its use.

Other remedies, as China, Hyos. and Ranunculus bulb. may be required.

NYCTALOPIA.

(*Day Blindness.*)

True nyctalopia is rarely observed in this country, though would suggest, besides careful protection of the eyes from bright light and general hygienic measures, the use of *Phos.* as the remedy most nearly adapted to this condition.

TUMORES.

(*Tumors of the Optic Nerve and Retina.*)

Tumors of the nerve layer are usually malignant in character (glioma of the retina is the most common). The only treatment which is in any degree effectual is *enucleation of the eye*, taking care to divide the optic nerve as far back toward the optic foramen as possible.

LENS.

CATARACTA.

(Opacity of the Lens.)

A large number of cases are to be found in our literature, in which the internal administration of a few doses of the properly selected remedy has worked a wonderful cure of cataract, but the great majority of these must be taken "cum grano salis," and put aside with the remark "mistaken diagnosis."

After years of experience in the treatment of cataract, I have no doubt that a careful selection of drugs, according to the homœopathic law, and their continuance for a long period, will succeed in a large proportion of cases in checking the progress of the disease, and in many cases clear up a portion of the diffuse haziness, thus improving vision to a certain extent. But after degeneration of the lens fibres has taken place, no remedy will be found of avail in restoring its lost transparency and improving the sight. We must then, providing the vision is seriously impaired, and it is senile or hard cataract, wait until it has become mature, when the lens should be extracted.

The operations for the extraction of cataract are various, nearly every surgeon having a modification of his own; they also vary according to the condition of the eye, and the character of the cataract. These operations are already well described in our standard text books on the eye.

The medical treatment will consist of the selection of remedies, according to the constitutional symptoms observed in the patient, for the objective indications are entirely or nearly absent, as we cannot yet decide from the appearance of an opaque lens, what remedy is required.

The following drugs have been found most efficacious in arresting the progress of cataract: Calc. carb. and phos., *Caust.*, Lyco., Magn. carb., *Phos.*, Puls., *Sepia*, *Sil.* and Sulph.

ECTOPIA LENTIS.

(Dislocation of the Lens.)

(Syn. Luxatio lentis.)

The treatment of a dislocated lens varies greatly, according to the condition of the eye, and the nature of the displacement. It is only by operative interference that favorable results can be obtained, except we may be able to relieve pain by the use of Atropine, or by internal medication.

VITREOUS HUMOR.

HYALITIS.

(Inflammation of the Vitreous Humor.)

Hyalitis rarely occurs idiopathically, being usually associated with severe inflammations of the fundus, especially inflammation of the whole or part of the uveal tract. The treatment must then be directed to the primary disease. Particularly study the remedies recommended for choroiditis. Traumatic inflammation of the vitreous humor is more frequently observed, especially from a foreign body, which usually necessitates the removal of the eye.

OPACITATES VITREI.

(Opacities of the Vitreous Humor.)

(Syn. Myodesopsia, Muscæ volitantes, Synchysis, Synchysis scintillans.)

Opacities of the vitreous humor usually result from some deep-seated disturbance in the internal structures of the eye, which require our special attention.

Dense membranous opacities may be torn with a fine needle, though operative measures are not usually required. If the opacity has been recent, especially if hemorrhagic, a compress bandage should be applied, and the patient kept in bed.

If there have been hemorrhages into the vitreous humor, their absorption may be hastened by Arnica, Bell., Crotal., Ham. virg., *Lach.*, Ledum or Phos. If the opacities are the result of inflammation of the choroid or retina, benefit has been derived from the following: Arg. nit., Aurum, Bell., Gelsem., Jaborandi, *Kali iod.*, Kali mur., Kalmia, Lach., Lyco., Merc., *Nat. mur.*, Phos., Prunus, Senega, Silicea and Sulph.

CORPUS ALIEN. ET CYSTICERCUS VITREI.

(Foreign Body, or Cysticercus in the Vitreous Humor.)

For years it has been the practice in cases of foreign bodies in the vitreous to enucleate the eye, as soon as possible, in order to avoid all danger of sympathetic ophthalmia. More recently, however, attempts have been made to extract foreign bodies from the vitreous, especially when they can be located with the ophthalmoscope. The success which has occasionally attended these operations, render their trial often advisable, for enucleation can be performed, if a failure to extract should result. In rare cases the foreign body becomes encapsulated, when it may be allowed to remain, providing the patient is intelligent, lives near, and will have the eye removed on the first appearance of sympathetic irritation.

The inflammation arising from injuries must be subdued by ice compresses, the instillation of Atropine, and proper internal medication. The remedies will usually be *Aconite*, Arnica, Calendula, Hamamelis, Ledum or Rhus. Cysticerci may also be removed from the vitreous, or the eye may be enucleated.

REFRACTION AND ACCOMMODATION.

MYOPIA.

(Nearsightedness.)

(Syn. Brachymetropia.)

Nearsightedness is an anomaly of refraction which requires special and careful attention, as its tendency is to constantly progress until it may terminate in complete blindness.

There are four points in the treatment of myopia which require our consideration, as follows: 1. To prevent its further development and the occurrence of secondary disturbances. 2. By means of suitable glasses to render the use of the eye easier and safer. 3. To remove any existing muscular asthenopia. 4. To combat the secondary disturbances.

Our first and most important aim should be to check the progress of the myopia, and this we are able to do, providing the patient will adhere closely to the directions given. In the beginning we must ascertain the cause of the trouble, whether due to elongation of the antero-posterior axis of the eyeball, or to spasm of the ciliary muscle. In either case, if the myopia is rapidly increasing, complete *rest* of the eyes, especially for near objects, is necessary, but if the increase is slow or nearly stationary, moderate use of the eyes may be allowed, with this condition, that they *avoid too strong convergence of the optic axes,* that is, whenever they use the eyes for near vision, either with or without glasses, to carry the object away as far as it can be seen distinctly, and not bring it nearer the eye, as is the tendency when the eyes become tired. It is also desirable that patients discontinue work, and rest the eyes from two to five minutes every half hour more or less.

A *stooping position* will also promote the increase of myopia, particularly if posterior staphyloma is present, as an increased amount of blood is sent to the eye, which accelerates the inflammatory process going on within; therefore the patient must be advised to *sit as erect as possible*, and if compelled to write, use a sloping desk. The light should be placed behind. shining over his left shoulder upon the work, and not in front, directly in the eyes, as it would irritate and increase the inflammatory symptoms. When the bright light is very dazzling and annoying, colored glasses may be allowed. If antero-posterior elongation of the eyeball be the cause of the myopia, the treatment, remedial and otherwise, recommended for sclerectasia posterior should be followed.

Within the past few years spasm of the accommodation has been placed in the foremost rank by many prominent oculists, as a cause for nearsightedness, thus rendering decided changes in the manner of treatment necessary.

The constant use of a weak solution of *Atropine* instilled into the eye for a long time, keeping the ciliary muscle at perfect rest until it has recovered its normal tone, is frequently advantageously used, though the inconvenience experienced by the abnormal dilatation of the pupil and loss of accommodation, often prevents its employment.

It is only in extremely rare cases that Atropine or any other mydriatic is necessary, as in almost every instance spasm of the accommodation can be controlled by the careful selection of a remedy according to the law of "similia," and its administration internally. *Jaborandi* and *Physostigma* are the two remedies which have proved most efficacious in this affection. For special indications refer to the treatment of "spasm of the muscles."

2. "By means of suitable glasses to render the use of the eye easier and safer." This might have been properly considered under the first point as it is of the greatest importance in preventing the development of myopia, that the proper spectacles be selected and that only these be worn, for there is nothing that causes any existing nearsightedness to increase so rapidly as the use of improper glasses, especially if too strong, as they are liable to be. In this place only a few general rules can be given regarding the selection of spectacles, when to advise their use and when to forbid.

The best general rule that can be given in prescribing spectacles for a myopic eye, though there are exceptional cases that it will not cover, is as follows: Never recommend the use of glasses for myopia if the patient can easily get along without them; but if found necessary, give the *weakest glass* that will render vision easy (though not usually perfect) and remove unpleasant symptoms. Glasses are very often prescribed in myopia for distance, that will nearly neutralize the degree, but with the advice not to wear them constantly, only employ them when wishing to see a distant object distinctly. Also glasses may be given according to the above general rule, for reading music or seeing objects two feet or more distant, with the injunction not to use them for any other distance. For reading or near vision we rarely recommend glasses unless the myopia is great or muscular asthenopia is present, and the exceptions hereafter noted are absent, in which cases they may be allowed.

The following circumstances forbid the neutralization of the myopia: 1. If the degree of myopia is slight. 2. If the range of accommodation is contracted. 3. If the acuteness of vision is materially increased. 4. If the nature of the work does not render it necessary.

3. "To relieve any existing muscular asthenopia." This may be done by *suitable concave glasses*, the use of prisms, tenotomy of the external rectus or the selection of *the indicated remedy*. (See section on asthenopia.)

4. "To combat the secondary disturbances." These, whatever they may be, must be treated according to the principles laid down in corresponding sections.

PRESBYOPIA.

(*Old Sight.*)

The recession of the near point of distinct vision in old age, often called farsightedness, is only physiological and therefore requires no treatment with the exception of the selection of the proper spectacles. As a rule those glasses should be given with which the patient can see the easiest and most distinctly at from twelve to sixteen inches without magnifying the print.

No glasses are required for distance, except occasionally in very old people when a slight degree of hypermetropia may develope.

Glasses should be prescribed for presbyopia just as soon as any difficulty or inconvenience is experienced in seeing near objects, as instead of increasing the degree of presbyopia, as many suppose, it tends to prevent its increase and relieves all asthenopic symptoms.

It must always be borne in mind that a rapid recession of the near point of vision is a prominent symptom of glaucoma, in which, of course, glasses should not be given but other measures resorted to.

HYPERMETROPIA.

(*Farsightedness.*)

(Syn. Hyperopia.)

This condition, in which the antero-posterior axis of the eyeball is too short, in opposition to myopia in which it is too long, is true farsightedness and must not be confounded with presbyopia, which is often called farsightedness.

The first and most important indication in the treatment is the selection of proper convex glasses; in fact, this is the only means of relieving this affection "per se," though the resulting symptoms of asthenopia and strabismus may require further attention. Spectacles should be prescribed for hyperopia *immediately* upon the appearance of asthenopic symptoms. In selecting these glasses we should first determine the degree of manifest hyperopia (Hm.) by finding the strongest convex glass with which the patient can see perfectly at a distance (No. 20 at 20 feet). This glass which corresponds to or neutralizes Hm. is usually the one which the patient requires for near vision, though in some cases he cannot bear as strong a glass as this to commence with, while in others it is also necessary to neutralize a portion of the latent hyperopia (Ht.). Many oculists recommend the neutralization of all of Hm. and one-fourth of Ht., but these glasses are usually found too strong for the patient.

The best general rule to follow is to give the *strongest convex glass* with which the patient can read distinctly and easily for a length of time at the usual distance for near vision.

As a rule, glasses should not be advised for distant vision, unless the hyperopia is relative or absolute, when their use becomes necessary.

Asthenopia, both accommodative and muscular, though more frequently the former, arises from hyperopia. Both are, however, relieved by the proper selection of convex glasses, and often cured by this measure alone, but if some weakness of the muscles remain, special treatment is required, as can be seen by reference to the section devoted to asthenopia.

A measure of the greatest importance for the relief of asthenopic symptoms, dependent upon hyperopia, is *systematic exercise of the eyes with convex glasses*, as first recommended by Dr. Dyer. For instance, give the proper convex glass and advise its use for reading, every morning and afternoon, at a regular time, for from three to ten minutes, according to the amount of asthenopia, and increase the time one minute each day, as long as it can be done without fatigue.

Often an irritable weakness of the ciliary muscle is produced by over-use of the eyes in hyperopia and is not relieved by suitable glasses, in which case rest of the eyes and the use of Jaborandi should be prescribed.

The treatment of strabismus convergens or any other complication can be found under appropriate heads.

ASTIGMATISMUS.

(Variation in Refraction of Different Meridians of the Eye.)

The only treatment for regular astigmatism consists in the careful selection of cylindrical glasses, either simple cylindrical, spherico-cylindrical or bi-cylindrical, according to the variety of astigmatism we have to deal with. (To prescribe glasses in astigmatism, one must thoroughly understand the theory of irregular refraction and possess the proper glasses and test types for making the examination.)

Irregular astigmatism is dependent upon irregular refraction of the lens or cornea; in the latter usually resulting from inflammatory changes. In these instances stenopaic spectacles may be necessary, or the performance of an iridectomy. Benefit may also be obtained from the use of such drugs as seem indicated by the appearance and condition of the eye.

Astigmatism, both regular and irregular, is sometimes dependent upon unequal contraction of the ciliary muscle. If such is the case much benefit may be derived from internal medication. Especially useful is *Jaborandi*, although Physostigma or Agaricus may be needed.

MUSCLES AND NERVES.

PARESIS SIVE PARALYSIS MUSCUL. OCULI.

(*Partial or Complete Paralysis of the Muscles of the Eye, including not only the Recti and Oblique Muscles, but also the Ciliary Muscle and Sphincter of the Iris.*)

The treatment varies according to the nature of the cause, which should always receive due consideration in the selection of a drug. Our chief reliance must be in internal medication.

Prismatic glasses, to which we sometimes resort, may be used for two purposes: 1. To relieve the annoying diplopia by giving that prism which neutralizes the double vision. 2. For the purpose of exercising the paralyzed muscle by using a weaker prism, which nearly fuses the double images, when by the exercise of the will they may be brought together; care must be taken, however, that these glasses are neither too weak nor too strong, or they will tend to weaken instead of strengthen the muscle.

Both *faradization and galvanization* have proved valuable aids in the cure of these disorders, either alone or in connection with the appropriate remedy.

As a last resort, careful *tenotomy* of the opposing muscle may be performed, with or without advancement of the paralyzed muscle, according to the degree of deviation.

In paralysis of the iris or ciliary muscle the local application of Eserine or Pilocarpine may be of service.

Aconite.—Paresis from exposure to a draught of cold air.

Argentum nit.—For weakness of the ciliary muscle or even paralysis of the accommodation, manifest advantage has been derived.

Arnica.—Paralysis of the muscles resulting from a blow or injury.

Causticum.—Paralysis of the muscles resulting from *exposure to cold.* It has been especially successful in paralysis of the sphincter pupillæ (mydriasis), of the ciliary muscle, levator palpebræ superioris (ptosis), orbicularis and external rectus. Its action is not found confined to any one nerve, but is useful in paralysis of any of the ocular muscles, if the particular cause and general indications are present.

Chelidonium.—Paresis of the right external rectus. Distant objects are blurred, and on looking steadily two are seen. Pain in the eye on looking up.

Cuprum acet.—Insufficiency or paralysis of the external rectus muscle.

Euphrasia.—Paralysis of the muscles, particularly of the third pair of nerves, caused from exposure to cold and wet; especially if catarrhal symptoms of the conjunctiva, blurring of the eyes relieved by winking, etc., are present.

Gelsemium.—A valuable remedy in all forms of paralysis of the ocular muscles, especially of the external rectus. Paresis from diphtheria, or associated with paralysis of the muscles of the throat.

Kali iodata.—The iodide of potassium is more commonly indicated than any other drug in *paralysis of the muscles, of syphilitic origin.* Appreciable doses are usually employed.

Merc. iod. flav.—Paralysis of the third pair, especially if syphilitic in origin.

Natrum mur.—See muscular asthenopia.

Nux vom.—Paresis or paralysis of the ocular muscles, particularly if caused or made worse by the use of stimulants or tobacco.

Opium —Paralysis of the accommodation.

Paris quad.—Paralysis of the iris and ciliary muscle, *with pain drawing from the eye to the back of the head; or pain as if the eyes were pulled into the head.* Eyes sensitive to touch.

Phosphorus.—Paralysis of the muscles caused from or accompanied by spermatorrhœa or sexual abuse.

Physostigma ven.—Has been used internally as well as locally. Paresis of the accommodation after diphtheria, and in muscular asthenopia.

Rhus tox.—A remedy often indicated in paralysis of the ocular muscles resulting from *rheumatism or exposure in cold wet weather and getting the feet wet.* Causticum is very similar in its action, though is more especially adapted to those cases resulting from exposure to cold dry weather.

Senega.—Want of power of the superior rectus or superior oblique, in which the *diplopia is relieved by bending the head backward.* The other muscles may be complicated in the trouble.

Spigelia.—When associated with *sharp stabbing pain* through the eye and head.

Alumina, Aurum, Conium, Hyoscyamus and Sulphur have also been used with advantage. Other remedies may be called for by general indications.

NYSTAGMUS, SPASMUS MUSCUL. CILIARIS.

(Oscillation of the Eyeballs, Spasm of the Ciliary Muscle.)

If strabismus coexists with nystagmus, tenotomy of the contracted muscle should be made. If there is any anomaly of refraction, it must be corrected by glasses.

In aggravated cases of spasm of the ciliary muscle the regular and prolonged use of Atropine or the constant use of convex glasses may be necessary, but usually internal medication, with rest of the eyes for near work, will suffice to diminish the spasm; after which any anomaly of refraction may be corrected.

Agaricus.—Very useful in all spasmodic affections of the muscles of the eye, especially if *associated with spasm of the lids,* or general chorea. In uncomplicated spasm of the ciliary muscle it has been of service, but is not as frequently indicated as some other drugs. *Twitchings of the lids* varying from frequent winking to spasmodic closure of them. (See blepharospasmus page 219.) *Twitchings of the eyeballs* with various sensations in and around them, chiefly pressing and aching. Eyeball sensitive to touch. *The spasmodic movements are absent during sleep but return on waking* and may be transiently relieved by washing in cold water.

Belladonna.—If accompanied by headache and hyperæsthesia of the senses.

Cicuta.—See strabismus, page 320.

Hyoscyamus.—Spasmodic action of the eyeballs.

Ignatia.—Morbid nictitation and spasmodic affections occurring in nervous hysterical women.

Jaborandi.—In *spasm of the accommodation, or irritability of the ciliary muscle,* there is no remedy so frequently useful as this. Many cases of simulated myopia have yielded to its use. *Everything at a distance is blurred without concave glasses, though near objects are seen distinctly. The vision may be constantly changing. Nausea or vertigo on using the eyes.* ·Eyes tire easily and are irritable, especially on sewing. Twitching of the lids and pain in the balls. Spasm of the internal recti muscles.

Lilium tig.—Spasm of the accommodation.

Physostigma ven.—In its proving there has been developed marked spasmodic action of the ciliary muscle and muscles of the lid. It has, therefore, been used with manifest advantage in these conditions, particularly the former; and as spasm of the ciliary muscle is frequently found in myopia, it should be thought of in this anomaly of refraction. The patient cannot read long on account of this spasm and must bring the book near the eyes. There is also generally to be seen *twitchings in the lids and around the eyes* when Physostigma is required. The pupil is contracted. (Compare Jaborandi.)

Nux, Puls. and Sulph. have also been used with benefit, as may any of that class of remedies denominated our antispasmodics.

STRABISMUS.

(Squint.)

Careful distinction must be made between concomitant and paralytic squint, as the treatment materially varies. As strabismus convergens is frequently due to hyperopia and strabismus divergens to myopia, we must always at first obtain the patient's refraction. If either be the cause, the ametropia should be neutralized, when, if the squint is recent and periodic in character, a cure may be effected by this means alone, or in connection with internal medication. In recent cases, advantage may be derived from careful and systematic exercise of the weaker muscle either with or without prisms, especially if the squint is of the paralytic variety.

In true concomitant squint, after it has become permanent, tenotomy of the contracted muscle should be performed *as early as possible*, in order that no sight be lost from non-use. Care must be taken, after the operation, to prescribe glasses, if an anomaly of refraction was the cause of the trouble, so that its return may be prevented if possible.

Cicuta vir.—Indicated in strabismus convergens occurring in children, particularly if spasmodic in nature, or caused from convulsions, to which the child is subject.

Jaborandi.—Strabismus convergens, periodic and resulting from spasm of the internal recti; also for return of squint after operation.

If helminthiasis has been the cause, Cina, Cyclamen or Spigelia may be required. If due to spasms, convulsions, or any intra-cranial disorders, Agar., Bell., Hyos., Nux or Stram. would be first suggested to our minds.

Calc. or Chin. sulph. may be indicated.

In all cases the cause of the difficulty must be determined, if possible, for this, in connection with the general condition of the patient, will govern us in the selection of the remedy.

Compare treatment given for both paralysis and spasm of the muscles of the eye.

ASTHENOPIA ACCOMMODATIVA ET MUSCULARIS.

(Weakness of the Ciliary and Internal Recti Muscles, including Kopiopia Hysterica.)

In a large proportion of cases asthenopia is due to some anomaly of refraction, which must be corrected by *suitable glasses,* before any headway can be made in the treatment; after which, properly indicated remedies are of great service. Not rarely asthenopia is dependent upon entirely different causes, as general muscular laxity, debilitating diseases, and many other constitutional disturbances; in which case our treatment should be directed to the primary seat of the trouble. Excessive use of tea may be the cause, in which case it must be stopped. After prescribing the proper spectacles in asthenopia, only a moderate, systematic use of the eyes should be encouraged, until the overworked muscles have regained their normal tone. Regular exercise of the eyes, according to the rules given on page 315, for asthenopia in hyperopia, is of great importance.

In insufficiency of the internal recti muscles, besides the spherical glasses necessary to overcome the faulty construction of the eye, prisms may be required, either to relieve any existing diplopia, and, at the same time, employ binocular vision, or used with a view of strengthening the weak muscles. Again we have observed favorable results from systematic exercise of the internal recti at regular periods, by having the patient look steadily at his finger, or a ruler, while it is slowly carried far to the right and then to the left, or by carrying it to and from the eye.

Faradism and galvanism have also proved of advantage in some cases.

As a last resort, careful tenotomy of the external recti may be performed.

Cases will be found in Part I illustrating the action of nearly all remedies.

Aconite.—Asthenopia from over-use of the eyes. Lids spasmodically closed, with a heavy feeling in them; while the eyes *feel very hot and dry* after using. Conjunctiva may be hyper

21

æmic. Cold water may relieve temporarily the heat in the eyes.

Agaricus.—Asthenopia, especially muscular, if accompanied by *sudden jerks of the ball*, twitching of the lids, etc.

Argentum nit.—Weakness of the accommodation, dependent upon errors of refraction. Letters blur, and sight vanishes on reading or writing.

Calcarea.—Pale, flabby subjects, inclined to grow fat; with coldness of the extremities, and perspiration about the head. Eyes pain after using, and are generally worse in damp weather and from warmth. Burning and cutting pains in the lids, and sticking pains in the eyes on reading. Dim vision after fine work. Objects run together.

Cinnabar.—Asthenopia, *with pain in the inner canthus, extending above or around the eye*, worse in the evening, and upon using the eyes. Soreness over exit of supra-orbital nerve.

Conium mac.—Weakness of the accommodation. Letters run together on reading. Burning pain deep in the eye. *Great dread of light.*

Duboisia.—Weakness of the ciliary muscle.

Gelsemium.—Asthenopia, with weakness of the external recti, or, if associated with blepharitis or hyperæmia of the conjunctiva.

Jaborandi.—Asthenopic symptoms, which are really dependent upon *irritability of the ciliary muscle*, especially when found in true myopia, or spasms of the accommodation. Useful when caused by reflex irritation from the uterus (kopiopia hysterica).

Kalmia.—Stiff, drawing sensation in the muscles, upon moving the eyes (Nat. mur.).

Lachesis.—Asthenopic symptoms, especially in the left eye, with a variety of pains and sensations, worse upon thinking of them, using the eyes, and on waking in the morning.

Lilium tig.—Kopiopia hysterica, and asthenopic symptoms not due to reflex irritation. Burning, smarting, and heat in the eyes after reading, relieved in the open air (Pulsat.). Photophobia.

Mercurialis peren.—Asthenopia, with a sensation of dryness of the eyes, and heaviness of the lids. Mist before the eyes in the morning. Burning pain in the eyes in evening, and upon reading.

Natrum mur.—No remedy is more often indicated in asthenopia, especially muscular, than this. Over-use of the eyes in both emmetropia and ametropia may be the cause, or it may be dependent upon reflex irritation. The vision soon becomes dim and letters run together upon using the eyes for near vision and sometimes for distant vision. The internal recti are usually weak. *The muscles feel stiff and drawn, and ache on moving the eye in any direction. Pain in the eye upon looking down.* Burning, smarting, itching and heat in the eyes upon reading or writing, with a variety of other sensations, even headache. Heaviness and drooping of the lids on use of the eyes for near vision. The eyes appear irritable, with some dread of light, so the patient desires to close them firmly.

Phosphorus.—Both accommodative and muscular asthenopia. Mistiness and vanishing of vision, with pain and stiffness in the eyeball. Light aggravates, so the patient is better in the twilight. Muscæ volitantes. Photopsies.

Physostigma ven.—Asthenopic symptoms dependent upon irritation of the ciliary muscle. Paresis of the accommodation following diphtheria, and in muscular asthenopia.

Rhododendron.—Insufficiency of the internal recti muscles, with darting pains through the eyes and head, *always worse before a storm*.

Ruta grav.—Especially indicated in *accommodative asthenopia*. *Aching in and over the eyes*, with blurring of the vision after using or straining the eyes at fine work. The *eyes feel hot* like balls of fire, appear irritable and run water, especially towards evening after working all day. Ruta is more often indicated in accommodative asthenopia and Natrum mur. in muscular.

Sepia.—Indicated if reflex irritation from the uterus is the cause of the difficulty. Smarting in the eyes and a variety of other sensations may be experienced, as can be seen by reference to the verified symptomatology. *Aggravation of the symptoms morning and evening*.

Spigelia.—If accompanied by *sharp, stabbing pains* through, the eye and around it, extending back into the head.

In addition to the above, many other remedies have been employed with success. For special indications in the selection of which, refer to the verified symptomatology and clinical application in Part I. Attention is particularly directed to the following: Ammon. carb., Apis, Arn., Asarum, Carb. veg., Caust., Crocus, Euph., Ignat., Kali carb., Ledum, Lith. carb., Macrotin, Nux vom., Paris, Phos. ac., Pulsat., Santon. and Sulphur.

NEURALGIA CILIARIS.

(Pain in the Ciliary Nerves.)

Ciliary neuralgia is usually only a symptom of some disorder of the eye, but as it is occasionally found unassociated with any ocular trouble, we shall speak briefly of those remedies adapted to this condition.

Amyl nitr.—*Severe ciliary neuralgia, with acute conjunctivitis and flushing of corresponding side of face,* dependent upon disturbance in the sympathetic system. Pupil contracted.

Asafœtida.—*Severe boring, tearing pain over the eyes,* also intense burning in brows, especially at night.

Atropine.—Used locally in the eye often proves of decided benefit in allaying the severe pain in and around the eye.

Belladonna.—*Orbital neuralgias,* especially of the infraorbital nerve, with red face, hot head and throbbing headache. Sensitive to light and noise.

Bryonia.—*Pains severe, sharp and shooting through the eye back into the head, or extending from the eye down to malar bone, and then back to occiput.* The seat of pain becomes sore to touch, *Moving the eyeball in any direction,* or the exertion of talking or walking *will aggravate the pain,* so that he wishes constantly to keep the eyes closed and at perfect rest.

Cedron. — One of the first remedies to be thought of in supraorbital neuralgia. *Pains severe, sharp and shooting, starting from one point over the eye* (generally the left) *and extending along the branches of the supraorbital nerve into the head.* May extend to temples or occiput; often worse in the evening, on lying down, and before a storm.

China.—*Intermittent ciliary neuralgia. The muriate of quinine.* in appreciable doses, will often alleviate *intense pain in and around the eye, periodic in character,* especially if malarial in origin and accompanied by chills.

Cimicifuga.—*Severe aching* pains in the eyeballs or in the temples extending to the eyes. *Sharp, shooting pains from the occiput through to the eyes or from the eyes to the top of the head.* Generally worse in the afternoon and night and relieved on lying down. *Macrotin* has been employed in similar cases with benefit.

Cinnabaris.—*Pain commencing at internal canthus and extending over or around the eye.*

Comocladia.—The *eyeballs feel too large,* painful and as if pressed out of the head. The eyeballs feel sore, especially on moving them.

Natrum salicyl. — From three to five grain doses of the salicylate of soda, frequently repeated, will often relieve severe ciliary neuralgia.

Plantago.—Ciliary neuralgia from decayed teeth.

Prunus spin.—Commonly indicated, especially if the *pain in the eyeball is severe and crushing, as if eye were pressed asunder;* or if the pain is sharp and *shooting* in character, through the eye and corresponding side of the head. These *severe sharp pains* may commence in various portions of the head and extend around and in the eye.

Rhododendron. — Pains in and around the eye usually worse at night and *always aggravated before a storm.*

Silicea.—Ciliary neuralgia; darting pains through the eye and head, often commencing at the occiput and extending forward to the eyes; caused from exposure to a draught of air, and *relieved by keeping the head warm.*

Spigelia.—Is a grand remedy in controlling the severe ciliary pain arising from various eye troubles or independent of any such disorder. The pains may intermit or not and are usually of a *sharp stabbing character* either around the eye or *extending* through the eye into the head; they often seem to commence *at one point and then radiate in different directions.* The pains are usually worse at night and on motion. Besides the above, which are most characteristic, there are a great variety of pains which have been relieved by Spigelia, as can be seen by referring to the clinical action of the drug.

Terebinth.—*Severe ciliary neuralgia with acute conjunctivitis.* The pain is intense, from a grumbling, beating, sore pain, to a severe sharp darting pain in the eye and *over* it along the course of the supraorbital nerve, *worse at night.*

Many other remedies may be indicated and useful in alleviating the severe pain in and around the eyes, chief among which may be mentioned Carbol. ac., Cham., Chel., Hypericum, Ign., Ipecac., Merc., Mez., Nat. mur., Plat., Sulph. and Thuja.

GLOSSARY.

A. Abbreviation for *accommodation*.

Abscessus corneæ. Abscess of the cornea; keratitis suppurativa.

Accommodation. Power of adjusting the eye for vision at different distances. (See *range of accommodation*.)

Acne ciliaris. Small pustules on margins of lids.

Amaurosis (Gr. αμαυρόω, to render obscure). Blindness without organic change in the eye.

Amblyopia (Gr. αμβλυς, dull; οψις, vision). Dimness of sight without apparent lesion.

Amblyopia nicotiana. Obscured vision from use of tobacco.

Amblyopia potatorum. Obscured vision from the use of alcoholic liquors.

Ametropia (Gr. α, privative; μετρον, measure; οψις, vision). Any condition of imperfect refraction in the eye.

Amotio retinæ. Separation of retina from the choroid; detachment of the retina; hydrops retinæ.

Anæsthesia retinæ. Diminished sensibility of the retina without organic change.

Anterior chamber. Space between anterior surface of iris and posterior surface of cornea.

Apoplexia retinæ. Hemorrhage into retina.

Aqueous humor. The fluid found in the anterior and posterior chambers of the eye.

Arteria centralis retinæ. The central artery of the retina, derived from the ophthalmic, and entering retina at the centre of the optic disc.

Asthenopia (Gr. ασθενης, weak; οψις, vision). Weak vision.

Asthenopia accommodativa. Weakness of ciliary muscle.

Asthenopia muscularis. Weakness of internal recti muscles.

Astigmatism (Gr. α, privative; στιγμα, a point). Condition in which degree of refraction varies in different meridians of the eye; therefore rays from a point will not be reunited in a point on the retina. In *simple a—*, the refraction is normal in one meridian and varies from normal in the other; In *compound a—*, both principal meridians are either hyperopic or myopic, but in different degrees; in *mixed a—*, one meridian is hyperopic and the other myopic. These forms are all called *regular*. *Irregular a—*, is where the refraction varies in several meridians or in different parts of the same meridian.

Atrophia nervus opticus et retinæ. Atrophy of optic nerve and retina.

Basedow's disease. See *morbus Basedowii.*

Binocular vision. Vision with both eyes.

Blepharadenitis. Glandular inflammation of the eyelids.

Blepharitis. Inflammation of the eyelids.

Blepharitis ciliaris } Inflammation of the margins of the eyelids.
Blepharitis marginalis. ∫

Blepharitis acuta. Phlegmonous inflammation of eyelids.

Blepharospasmus. Involuntary spasm of the lids.

Brachymetropia (Gr. βραχυς, short; μετρον, measure; οψις, vision). Near-sightedness; myopia.

Bulbus oculi. Eye-ball; or, globe.

Canaliculus. Canal leading from punctum to lachrymal sac.

Canthoplasty. Division of the outer canthus. More properly, *canthotomy.*

Canthus. Angle formed by junction of eyelids.

Capsule of lens. Membrane that encloses crystalline lens.

Capsulitis. Inflammation of the lens capsule.

Caries orbitæ. Caries of the bones of the orbit.

Caruncula (Lat. a little piece of flesh). A small red body lying in inner canthus of eye.

Cataracta, Catacact (Gr. καταρρασσω, to confound). Opacity of the crystalline lens; *c. dura,* hard cataract; *c.immatura,* immature cataract; *c. matura,* mature (or ripe) cataract; *c. mollis,* soft cataract; *c. traumatica,* traumatic cataract; *c. zonularis,* cataract in which only one or more layers of the lens are involved.

Cellulitis orbitæ. Orbital cellulitis; an inflammation of the cellular tissue of the orbit.

Chalazion (Gr. χαλαζα, a hail-stone). Tumor of the eyelid, caused by retained secretion of meibomian glands.

Chemosis (Gr. χημη, a gaping). Œdematous swelling of conjunctiva and sub-conjunctival tissue, causing cornea to appear sunken.

Choked disc. See *Stauungs papille.*

Choroid (Gr. χοριον, the chorion; ειδος, like). The second, or vascular tunic of the eye-ball.

Choroiditis disseminata. Disseminate inflammation of the choroid.

Choroiditis serosa. Serous inflammation of the choroid.

Choroiditis suppurativa. Suppurative inflammation of choroid.

Chorio-retinitis. Inflammation of the choroid and retina.

Chromopsies (Gr. χρωμα, color; οψις, vision). Colors before vision.

Cilia (Lat. *cilium,* an eyelash).

Ciliary injection. Congestion of ciliary vessels.

Ciliary margin. Free margin of eyelid.

Conjunctiva (Lat. *conjungen,* to join together). The mucous lining of the eye-lids, reflected upon the sclerotic, and passing slightly over the edge of the cornea.

Conjunctivitis. Inflammation of the conjunctiva; *c. catarrhalis,* catarrhal conjunctivitis; *c. crouposa,* croupous conjunctivitis; *c. diphtheritica,* diphtheritic conjunctivitis; *c. follicularis,* follicular conjunctivitis; *c. granulosa.* and *c. trachomatosa,* granular lids; *c. phlyctenularis,* phlyctenular conjunctivitis; *c. pustulosa,* pustular conjunctivitis.

Cornea (Lat. *cornu*, a horn). The transparent anterior segment of the outer tunic of the eyeball.

Corneitis. See *keratitis*.

Corpus alienum. Foreign body.

Crescentic ulcer, or **Marginal ulcer.** A form of ulceration that tends to surround cornea and cut off nutrition.

Cyclitis (Gr. *κυκλος*, a circle, and terminal *itis* denoting inflammation). Inflammation of ciliary body; also kyklitis.

Dacryocystitis (Gr. *δακρυον*, a tear; *κυστις*, a bladder, and terminal *itis*, denoting inflammation). Inflammation of the lachrymal sac; *d. catarrhalis.* Catarrhal inflammation of the lachrymal sac.

Dacryocysto-blennorhœa. Blennorrhœa of the lachrymal sac.

Descemet's membrane. Posterior limiting membrane of cornea.

Descemetitis. Inflammation of Descemet's membrane.

Dioptric. Refracting power of a lens having a focal length of one meter; designated by the letter D, written after the number.

Diplopia (Gr. *διπλοος*, double; *οψις*, vision). Double vision.

Discus opticus. The entrance of optic nerve in eyeball; the "blind spot."

Distichiasis (Gr. *διστιχια*, a double row). Double row of eyelashes.

Dyer's exercise. Systematic exercise of eyes with convex glasses (described on p. 315).

Ectopia lentis (Gr. *εκτοπος*, displaced, and Lat. *lentis*, lens). Dislocation of the crystalline lens.

Ectropion (Gr. *εκτρεπω*, to turn from). Eversion of the eyelid; also written *ectropium.*

Emmetropia (Gr. *εμμετρος*, conforming to measure; *οψις*, vision). That state of refraction in which, with the eye at rest, parallel rays are brought to a focus on the retina.

Emphysema palpebræ (Gr. *εμφυσαω*, to inflate). A collection of air in the cellular texture under the skin of the eyelids.

Enucleation. Excision of the eyeball.

Engorged disc, engorged papilla. See *Stauung's papille.*

Entropion (Gr. *εν*, in; *τρεπω*, to turn). A turning-in of free margin of eyelid; also written *entropium.*

Epiphora (Gr. *επιφερω*, to carry to). A superabundant secretion of tears.

Episcleritis. Inflammation of the superficial layers of the sclera.

Exophthalmic goitre. See *morbus Basedowii.*

Exophthalmus (Gr. *εξ*, out of; *οφθαλμος*, the eye). Protrusion of the eyeball.

Far-sightedness. Hyperopia.

Fissura palpebrarum. The opening between the eyelids.

Fistula lachrymalis. Term usually applied to fistula of the lachrymal sac.

Fundus (Lat. *fundus*, bottom). The posterior portion of the eyeball.

Glaucoma (Gr. *γλαυκος*, green). Increased tension of the eyeball (see *intraocular tension*).

Gonorrhœal ophthalmia. A form of purulent inflammation of conjunctiva, caused by inoculation with gonorrhœal pus.

Granular lids. } See *trachoma.*
Granular ophthalmia. }

H. Abbreviation denoting *hypermetropia.*

Hemeralopia (Gr. 'ημερα, a day; οψις, vision). Night-blindness.

Hemiopia (Gr. 'ημι, half; οψις, vision). Defect of vision in which only the half of an object is seen.

Herpes corneæ. Phlyctenular inflammation of the cornea.

Hordeolum (Lat. diminution of *hordeum*, barley). A small inflammatory tumor on margin of eyelid; a stye.

Humors. The more fluid contents of the eyeball.

Hyalitis (Gr. 'υαλος, glass; terminal *itis*, denoting inflammation). Inflammation of the vitreous humor.

Hydrops retinæ (Gr. 'υδωρ, water; *retinæ*, of the retina). See *amotio retinæ*.

Hypæmia. Hemorrhage into anterior chamber of the eye.

Hyperæsthesia retinæ. Oversensitiveness of the retina to light; retinal asthenopia.

Hypermetropia (Gr. 'υπερ, beyond; μετρον, measure; οψις, vision). A condition of refraction in which, with accommodation at rest, parallel rays are brought to a focus behind the retina; hyperopia; H. *Facultative h.* The least degree of h., when vision is $\frac{20}{20}$ with or without convex glasses. *Relative h.* A degree of h. when vision is $\frac{20}{20}$ only upon converging the eyes or by use of convex glasses. *Absolute h.* The highest degree of h., when vision is $\frac{20}{20}$ only with convex glasses. *Manifest h.* That amount of h. that is not neutralized by accommodative action; expressed as Hm. *Latent h.* That amount of h. that is neutralized by accommodation; expressed as Hl.

Hyperopia Contraction of *hypermetropia.*

Hypopyon, (Gr. 'υπο, under; πυον, pus). An accumulation of pus in the anterior chamber of the eye. Also written *hypopyum.*

Interstitial keratitis. See *keratitis parenchymatosa.*

Intraocular (Lat. *intra*, within; *oculus*, the eye). Pertaining to the interior of the eyeball.

Intraocular tension. Tension of the eyeball; measured by the degree of hardness of the globe; indicated by the letter T.; Tn = normal tension, T ‑ or T— = increased or diminished tension. Degree of tension represented by numbers 1, 2 and 3 placed after sign.

Iris (Gr. ιρις, a rainbow). The circular membrane suspended vertically behind the cornea; floating in the aqueous humor, and perforated to form the pupil.

Iridectomy. The operation of excision of a portion of the iris.

Irido-choroiditis. Inflammation of the iris and choroid.

Irido-cyclitis. Inflammation of the iris and ciliary body.

Iritis. Inflammation of the iris. Its varieties are: *i. idiopathica*, simple or plastic iritis; *i. purulenta*, parenchymatous or suppurative iritis; *i. rheumatica*, a form of plastic iritis dependent upon rheumatic diathesis; *i. serosa*, serous iritis (see *keratitis punctata*); *i. spongiosa*, gelatinous or spongy iritis; *i. syphilitica*; *i. traumatica.*

Ischæmia retinæ (Gr. ισχω, to suppress; αιμα, blood, and *retinæ*, of the retina). An insufficient supply of blood to the retina.

Jaeger. Name sometimes used to denote Jaeger's test type.

Keratitis (Gr. κερας, cornea and *itis*, denoting inflammation). Inflammation of the cornea; corneitis. The varieties are: *k. pannosa*, pannus, superficial keratitis; a superficial vascular opacity of the cornea; *k. parenchymatosa,* diffuse, parenchymatous, or interstitial keratitis; *k. phlyctenularis,* herpes corneæ; inflammation of the cornea with formation of vesicles; *k. punctata,* a name often given to either descemetitis or serous iritis, and characterized by punctate spots on posterior surface of cornea; *k. pustulosa,* pustular inflammation of the cornea; *k. superficialis,* same as *k. pannosa; k. suppurativa,* abscess of the cornea; *k. ulcerosa,* superficial ulceration of the cornea.

Kerato-conus. Conical cornea.

Kerato-globus. Uniform spherical bulging of the whole cornea.

Kerato-iritis. Inflammation of the cornea and iris.

Kopiopia hysterica (Gr. κοπος, weariness; οψις, and ὑστερα, the womb). Weakness of the eyes from reflex irritation, usually from the uterus.

Lachrymal duct. Name applied to portion of canal leading from lachrymal sac, including canaliculi.

Lachrymal sac. The upper dilated extremity of the nasal duct.

Lachrymation (Lat. *lachrymare,* to shed tears). Secretion of tears.

Læsiones (Lat. *lesio,* a hurting). Injuries.

L. E. Abbreviation for *left eye.*

Lens. The crystalline lens.

Lens capsule. See *capsule of lens.*

Leucoma (Gr. λευκος, white). A milky opacity of the cornea.

Leucoma adhærens. Cicatrix on cornea to which a portion of the iris is attached.

L. E. V. Abbreviation of *left eye vision.*

Levator palpebræ superioris. The levator muscle of the upper eyelid.

Luxatio lentis. Dislocation of the crystalline lens.

L. V. Left vision. See *vision.*

Macula corneæ (Heb. *machala,* blemish). A small opacity of the cornea.

Macula lutea. The "yellow spot," the most sensitive part of the retina.

Meibomian glands. Small glands located in the eyelid between the conjunctiva and tarsal cartilages.

Membrana Descemetii See *Descemet's membrane.*

Morbi glandulæ lachrymarum. Diseases of the lachrymal gland.

Morbus Basedowii. A disease characterized by palpitation of the heart, protrusion of the eyeballs and enlargement of the thyroid gland; Graves' disease; exophthalmic goitre.

Muscæ volitantes (Lat., *musca,* a fly; *volita,* to float). Floating spots in field of vision.

Musculus ciliaris. The ciliary muscle.

Mydriasis (Gr. μυδριασις; from μυδαω, to abound in moisture: so named because it was once thought to originate in redundant moisture). A morbid dilatation of the pupil.

Myodesopsia Physiological muscæ volitantes.

Myopia (Gr. μυω, to contract; οψ, the eye). A condition of refraction in which, with accommodation at rest, parallel rays are brought to a focus in front of the retina.

Myosis (Gr. μυω, to contract). Morbid contraction of the pupil.

Nasal duct. The canal leading from the lachrymal sac to the nasal cavity.

Nervus abducens. One of the cranial nerves (sixth pair).

Nervus oculo-motor. One of the cranial nerves (third pair).

Nervus opticus. The optic nerve.

Neuralgia ciliaris. Neuralgia of the ciliary nerves.

Neuralgia supra-orbitalis. Supra-orbital neuralgia.

Neuritis N. O. Inflammation of the optic nerve.

Nictitation (Lat., *nictito*, to wink often). Frequent winking.

N. O. Contraction signifying *nervus opticus*.

Nyctalopia (Gr., *νυξ*, night; *οζ'ις*, vision). Day-blindness.

Nystagmus. Oscillation of the eyeballs.   •

Ocular (Gr. *οχχαλλος*, the eye). Pertaining to the eye.

O. D. Contraction for *oculus dextra*—the right eye.

Œdema palpebræ. Œdema of the eyelid.

Old sight. Presbyopia.

Onyx (Gr. *ονυξ*, a nail). A sinking down of pus between the lamellæ of the cornea.

Opacitates vitrei. Opacities of the vitreous.

Opacitates corneæ. Opacities of the cornea.

Ophthalmia (Gr. *οφθαλμος*, the eye). Inflammation of the eye. The varieties are: *o. arthritica*, obsolete term for glaucoma; *o. blennorrhœica*, purulent conjunctivitis; *o. catarrhalis*, catarrhal conjunctivitis; *o. exanthemata*, conjunctivitis from the eruptive fevers; *o. gonorrhœica*, gonorrhœal conjunctivitis; *o. menstrualis*, inflammation of the eye dependent on menstrual disorders; *o. neonatorum*, purulent conjunctivitis in new-born infants; *o. phlyctenularis*, phlyctenular inflammation of cornea or conjunctiva ; *o. purulenta*, same as *o. blenorrhœica; o. rheumatica*, obsolete term for iritis ; *o. scrofulosa*, same as phlyctenular ophthalmia; *o. sympathetica*, any form of inflammation (usually irido-cyclitis) caused by sympathetic irritation from other eye; *o. tarsi*, inflammation of margins of lids.

Ophthalmoscope (Gr. *οφθαλμος*, the eye; *σκοπεω*, to examine). An instrument for examining the interior of the eye by reflected light.

Optic axis. An imaginary line corresponding anteriorly to the centre of the cornea and posteriorly to a point between the yellow spot and optic nerve entrance.

Optic disc. See *discus opticus*.

Optic papilla. Same as *discus opticus*.

Optico-ciliary neurotomy. Division of the optic and ciliary nerves at their point of entrance into the eyeball.

Orbit (Lat. *orbis*, a circle). The cavity in which the eyeball is located.

O. S. Contraction for *oculus sinistra*—the left eye.

O. U. Contraction for *oculi utroque*—both eyes.

Palpebræ (Lat. *palpito*, to throb). The eyelids.

Palpebral conjunctiva. The conjunctiva of the lids.

Pannus (Gr. *πηνη*, a web of cloth). A superficial vascularity of the cornea.

Pannus crassus (Gr. *πηνη*, and Lat. *crassus*, thick). An aggravated form of pannus.

Pannus herpetica. Pannus as result of phlyctenular keratitis.

Panophthalmitis (Gr. παν, all; οφθαλμος, the eye; terminal *itis*, denoting inflammation). Inflammation of the whole eye.

Paralysis of accommodation. Loss of power of adjusting the eye for vision at different distances.

Pericorneal (Gr. περι, about, and cornea). Around the cornea.

Periostitis orbitæ. Inflammation of the periosteum of the bones of the orbit.

Photophobia (Gr. φως, light; φοβεω, to dread). An intolerance of light.

Photopsia (Gr. φως, light; οψις, vision). Flashes of light before the sight.

Phthiriasis ciliaris (Gr. φθειρ, a louse). Lice on the margins of the lids.

Pinguecula (Lat. *pinguis*, fat). A conjunctival tumor near the edge of the cornea.

Posterior staphyloma. See *sclerectasia posterior*.

Posterior synechia (Gr. συνεχεια, continuity). Adhesion of iris to the capsule of the lens.

Pr. Abbreviation for *presbyopia*.

Presbyopia (Gr. πρεσβυς, an old man; οψις, vision). Physiological recession of near point of vision, from age; old sight.

Prolapsus iridis. Protrusion of iris through wound in cornea.

Pterygium (Gr. πτερυξ, a wing). Triangular hypertrophy of the conjunctiva, extending upon the cornea.

Ptosis (Gr. πτωω, to fall). Drooping of the upper eyelid.

Puncta lachrymalia. The openings of the lachrymal canaliculi.

Pupil. The opening in centre of iris.

Range of accommodation. Term used to express the distance between the nearest and farthest points of distinct vision, obtained by the formula $\frac{1}{a} = \frac{1}{p} - \frac{1}{r}$, in which p represents the near point or *punctum proximum*, and r the far point or *punctum remotissimum*.

Refraction (Lat. *refrango*, to break). The passive power possessed by the eye of bringing certain rays of light to a focus on the retina.

Retina (Lat. *rete*, a net). The expansion of the optic nerve.

Retinal asthenopia. See *hyperæsthesia retinæ*.

Retinitis. Inflammation of the retina. *R. albuminurica*, retinitis as result of Bright's disease. *R. apoplectica*, r. with extravasation of blood into retina. *R. diabetica*, r. from diabetes. *R. leucæmica*, r. from leucocythemia. *R. nephritica*, same as *r. albuminurica*. *R. nyctalopia*, same as *nyctalopia*.

Retino-choroiditis. Inflammation of retina and choroid.

R. E. V. Contraction for *right eye vision*.

Ruptura choroideæ. Rupture of the choroid.

R. V. Right vision. See *vision*.

Sclera, Sclerotic (Gr. σκληρος, hard). The outer or fibrous tunic of the eye.

Sclerectasia posterior (from sclera, and εκτασις, distension). Distension of the sclerotic, posteriorly; posterior staphyloma.

Scleritis. Inflammation of the sclera.

Sclerotico-choroiditis anterior. Inflammation of the sclera and choroid, anteriorly.

Sclerotico-choroiditis posterior. Same as *sclerectasia posterior*.

Sclerotomy (from sclera, and τεμνω, to cut). Incision of the sclerotic, near the sclero-corneal junction.

Scotomata (Gr. σκοτος, darkness). Fixed opacities in field of vision.

Serpiginous ulcer (Lat. *serpo*, to creep). Superficial spreading ulceration of the cornea.

Short sight. Myopia.

Snellen. Snellen's test type. The letters are square and their size increases in a definite ratio, so that each number is seen at an angle of five minutes; No. 1 should be seen at 1 foot, No. 2 at 2 feet, etc.

Spasm of accommodation. Spasmodic action of ciliary muscle.

Sphincter pupillæ. The circular muscular fibres of the iris.

Squint. See *strabismus*.

Staphyloma corneæ (Gr. σταφυλη, a grape). Bulging of the cornea.

Staphyloma corneæ et iridis. Bulging of cornea with displacement of iris forward.

Staphyloma scleræ anterior. Bulging of the sclera, near the cornea.

Stauungs papille. A form of optic neuritis, characterized by great swelling and engorgement of the optic disc; ascending neuritis; choked disc.

Stenopaic glasses. Spectacles which exclude more or less of the peripheral rays of light.

Stillicidium lachrymarum (Lat. *stilla*, a drop; *cado*, to fall down.) Overflow of tears from stricture of lachrymal duct.

Stilling's operation. An operation for division of strictures in the nasal duct.

Strabismus (Gr. στραβιζω, to squint). Abnormal deviation of the visual lines not dependent on paralysis nor displacement of the eyeball. *Convergent s.*, visual line deviates to inner side of object. *Divergent s.*, visual line deviates to outer side of object. *Concomitant s.*, simple strabismus.

Strictura ductus lachrymalis. Stricture of the lachrymal duct.

Sub-choroideal. Beneath the choroid.

Sub-conjunctival ecchymosis. Extravasation of blood beneath the conjunctiva.

Sub-orbital. Below the orbit.

Superciliary ridge. The bony ridge of the eyebrow.

Symblepharon (Gr. συν, together; βλεφαρον, the eyelid). Adhesion of the eyelid to the eyeball.

Synchysis scintillans (Gr. συνχεω, to confound). Sparkling bodies in the vitreous; sparkling synchysis.

Syndectomy. Excision of a circular band of conjunctiva around the cornea.

T. Abbreviation for intraocular tension.

Tarsoraphia (*tarsus*; ραφη, a suture). An operation for uniting the edges of the lids by sutures.

Tenotomy (Gr. τενον, a tendon; τεμνω, to cut). Division of the tendon of a muscle.

Tension. See *intraocular tension*.

Tinea tarsi. Blepharitis marginalis.

Tn., T+1, T+2. See *intraocular tension*.

Trachoma (Gr. τραχυς, rough). A variety of conjunctivitis characterized by granular condition of inner surface of eyelids.

Trichiasis (Gr. θριξ, animal hair). Ingrowing eyelashes.

Ulcus corneæ. Ulcer of the cornea.

Uveal tract (Lat. *uva*, a grape). The vascular tunic of the eye, iris, ciliary body and choroid; so called from its dark color.

Veruca. A wart.

Vision. The power of perceiving external objects by means of the eye. The degree of vision is expressed by a fraction in which the denominator represents the number of the test type, and the numerator the distance of the eye from the test. Thus $v.=\frac{20}{20}$ is perfect vision, $v.=\frac{10}{20}$ is one-half vision, etc.

Visual line. An imaginary line drawn from the macula lutea to the object viewed.

Vitreous humor (Lat. *vitrum*, glass). A jelly-like fluid forming about $\frac{4}{5}$ of the eyeball and filling the space between the lens and optic nerve.

Xerophthalmia. } (Gr. ξηρος, dry). Dryness of the cornea and conjunc-
Xerosis conjunctivæ. } tiva from atrophy.

INDEX.

BOERICKE & TAFEL'S
HOMŒOPATHIC PUBLICATIONS.

ALLEN, DR. T. F. The Encyclopedia of Pure Materia Medica; a Record of the Positive Effects of Drugs upon the Healthy Human Organism. With contributions from Dr. Richard Hughes, of England; Dr. C. Hering, of Philadelphia; Dr. Carroll Dunham, of New York; Dr. Adolph Lippe, of Philadelphia, and others. X volumes. Price bound in cloth, $60.00; in half morocco or sheep, . . . **$70 00**

This is the most complete and extensive work on Materia Medica ever attempted in the history of medicine—a work to which the homœopathic practitioner may turn with the certainty of finding the whole pathogenetic record of any remedy ever used in homœopathy, the record of which being published either in bookform or in journals. The volumes average about 640 pages each.

ALLEN, DR. T. F. A General Symptom Register of the Homœopathic Materia Medica. By TIMOTHY F. ALLEN, M.D., Author of the Encyclopædia of Pure Materia Medica. 1340 pages in one large volume. Price in cloth, $12.00; in sheep or half morocco, **$14 00**

This Index to the Encyclopædia of Materia Medica is at the same time the best arranged and most complete Repertory ever attempted. Its ingenious selection and arrangement of different kinds of type greatly facilitate its use.

ANGELL, DR. H. C. A Treatise on Diseases of the Eye; for the Use of Students and Practitioners. By Henry C. Angell, M.D., Professor of Ophthalmology in the Boston University School of Medicine, etc., etc. Fifth edition, enlarged and illustrated. 343 pages. 12mo. Cloth, ... **$3 00**

The fifth edition of this standard work has just been issued from the press, and shows that the whole work has been thoroughly revised and brought up to the latest dates in ophthalmology. Exquisite clear *photographic* illustrations have been added, and an exposition given of the dioptric or metric system, as applied to lenses for spectacles.

BAEHR, DR. B. The Science of Therapeutics according to the Principles of Homœopathy. Translated and enriched with numerous additions from Kafka and other sources, by C. J. HEMPEL, M.D. Two volumes. 1387 pages. **$9 00**

. . . "In short Dr. Baehr has presented us with the results of his observations at the bedside rather than of his researches in the study. It is this which renders his work valuable, and which at the same time accounts for his occasional imperfections. We know of no work of the kind in homœopathic literature where the suggestions for the choice of medicines are given in a fresher or clearer manner, or in one better calculated to interest and inform the practitioner. We have only to add that the two volumes are highly creditable to the publishers. The type is good, the paper good, and the binding excellent."—*Monthly Homœopathic Review.*

BECKER, DR. A. C. Dentition, according to some of the best and latest German authorities. 82 pages. 12mo. Cloth,. **50 cts.**

BECKER, DR. A. C. Diseases of the Eye, treated homœopathically. From the German. 77 pages. 12mo. Cloth. Out of print.

BELL, DR. JAMES B. The Homœopathic Therapeutics of Diarrhœa, Dysentery, Cholera, Cholera Morbus, Cholera Infantum, and all other loose evacuations of the bowels. 108 Second edition by Drs. Bell and Laird. 275 pages. 12mo. Cloth, **$1.50**

This little book had a very large sale, and but few physicians' offices will be found without it. The work was, without exception, very highly commended by the homœopathic press.

BERJEAU, J. PH. The Homœopathic Treatment of Syphilis, Gonorrhœa, Spermatorrhœa, and Urinary Diseases. Revised. with numerous additions, by J. H. P. FROST, M.D. 256 pages. 12mo. Cloth, ... **$1 50**

"This work is unmistakably the production of a practical man. It is short, pithy, and contains a vast deal of sound practical instruction. The diseases are briefly described; the directions for treatment are succinct and summary. It is a book which might with profit be consulted by all practitioners of homœopathy."—*North American Journal.*

BREYFOGLE, DR. W. L. Epitome of Homœopathic Medicines. 383 pages, ... **$1 25**
Interleaved with writing paper. Half morocco,. . . . **$2 25**
We quote from the author's preface :

"It has been my aim, throughout, to arrange in as concise form as possible, the leading symptoms of all well-established provings. To accomplish this, I have compared Lippe's Mat. Med.; the Symptomen-Codex ; Jahr's Epitome ; Bœnninghausen's Therapeutic Pocket-Book, and Hale's New Remedies."

BRYANT, DR. J. A Pocket Manual, or Repertory of Homœopathic Medicine, Alphabetically and Nosologically arranged, which may be used as the Physicians' *Vade-mecum*, the Travellers' Medical Companion, or the Family Physician. Containing the Principal Remedies for the most important Diseases; Symptoms. Sensations, Characteristics of Diseases, etc.; with the Principal Pathogenetic Effects of the Medicines on the most important Organs and Functions of the Body, together with Diagnosis, Explanation of Technical Terms, Directions for the selection and Exhibition of Remedies, Rules of Diet, etc. Compiled from the best Homœopathic authorities. Third edition. 352 pages. 18mo. Cloth, ... **$1 50**

BUTLER, JOHN. A Text-Book of Electro-Therapeutics and Electro-Surgery, for the Use of Students and General Practitioners. By John Butler, M.D., L.R.C.P.E., L.R.C.S.I., etc., etc. Second edition, revised and enlarged. 350 pages. 8vo. Cloth, **$3.00**

"Butler's work gives with exceptional thoroughness all details of the latest researches on

Electricity, which powerful agent has a great future, and rightly demands our most earnest consideration. But Homœopathia especially must hail with delight the advent from out the ranks of her apostles of a writer of John Butler's ability. His book will also find a large circle of non-homœopathic readers, since it does not conflict with the tenets of any therapeutic sect, and particular care has been bestowed on the technical part of electro-therapeia."—*Homœopathische Rundschau.*

DAKE, DR. WM. C. Pathology and Treatment of Diphtheria.

By Wm. C. Dake, M.D., of Nashville, Tenn. 55 pages. 8vo. Paper, **50 cts.**

This interesting monograph was enlarged from a paper read at the Third Annual Meeting of the Homœopathic Society of Tennessee, held at Memphis, September 19, 1877.

It gives a report of one hundred and seventy-six cases treated during a period of eleven months. It well repays a careful perusal.

DUNHAM, CARROLL, A.M., M.D. Homœopathy the Science of Therapeutics. A collection of papers elucidating and illustrating the principles of homœopathy. 529 pages. 8vo. Cloth, . **$3 00**

Half morocco, ... **$4 00**

"After reading this work no one will attempt to justify the practice of alternation of remedies. It is simply the lazy man's expedient to escape close thinking or to cover his ignorance. The one remedy alone can be accurate and scientific; a second or third only complicates and spoils the case, and will inevitably ruin a good reputation. But to come to more practical matters, more than one-half of this volume is devoted to a careful analysis of various drug-provings. It teaches us Materia Medica after a new fashion, so that a fool can understand, not only the full measure of usefulness, but also the limitations which surround the drug. . . . We ought to give an illustration of his method of analysis, but space forbids. We can only urge the thoughtful and studious to obtain the book, which they will esteem as second only to the *Organon* in its philosophy and learning."—*The American Homœopathist.*

DUNHAM, CARROLL, A.M., M.D. Lectures on Materia Medica.

858 pages. 8vo. Cloth, ... **$5 00**

Half morocco, ... **$6 00**

. . . "Vol. I is adorned with a most perfect likeness of Dr. Dunham, upon which stranger and friend will gaze with pleasure. To one skilled in the science of physiognomy there will be seen the unmistakable impress of the great soul that looked so long and stead-fastly out of its fair windows. But our readers will be chiefly concerned with the contents of these two books. They are even better than their embellishments. They are chiefly such lectures on Materia Medica as Dr. Dunham alone knew how to write. They are preceded quite naturally by introductory lectures, which he was accustomed to deliver to his classes on general therapeutics, on rules which should guide us in studying drugs, and on the therapeutic law. At the close of Vol. II we have several papers of great interest, but the most important fact of all is that we have here over fifty of our leading remedies presented in a method which belonged peculiarly to the author, as one of the most successful teachers our school has yet produced. . . . Blessed will be the library they adorn, and wise the man or woman into whose mind their light shall shine."—*Cincinnati Medical Advance.*

EGGERT, DR. W. The Homœopathic Therapeutics of Uterine and Vaginal Discharges. 543 pages. 8vo. Half morocco. **$3 50**

The author brought here together in an admirable and comprehensive arrangement everything published to date on the subject in the whole homœopathic literature, besides embodying his own abundant personal experience. The contents, divided into eight parts, are arranged as follows:

PART I. Treats on *Menstruation and Dysmenorrhœa;* PART II. *Menorrhagia;* PART III. *Amenorrhœa;* PART IV. *Abortion and Miscarriage;* PART V.

Metrorrhagia; Part VI. *Fluor albus;* Part VII. *Lochia;* and Part VIII. *General Concomitants.* No work as complete as this, on the subject, was ever before attempted, and we feel assured that it will meet with great favor by the profession.

"The book is a counterpart of Bell on Diarrhœa, and Dunham on Whooping-cough. Synthetics, Diagnosis and Pathology are left out as not coming within the scope of the work. The author in his preface says: Remedies and their symptoms are left out, and the symptoms and their remedies have received sole attention—that is what the busy practitioner wants. The work is one of the essentials in a library."—*American Observer.*

"A most exhaustive treatise, admirably arranged, covering all that is known of therapeutics in this important department."—*Homœopathic Times.*

GUERNSEY, DR. H. N. The Application of the Principles and Practice of Homœopathy to Obstetrics and the Disorders Peculiar to Women and Young Children. By Henry N. Guernsey, M.D., Professor of Obstetrics and Diseases of Women and Children in the Homœopathic Medical College of Pennsylvania, etc., etc. With numerous Illustrations. Third edition, revised, enlarged, and greatly improved. 1004 pages. 8vo. Half morocco, ... **$8 00**

This standard work, with the numerous improvements and additions, is the most complete and comprehensible work on the subject in the English language. Of the previous editions, almost four thousand copies are in the hands of the profession, and of this third edition a goodly number have already been taken up. There are few other professional works that can boast of a like popularity, and with all new improvements and experiences diligently collected and faithfully incorporated into each successive edition, this favorite work will retain its hold on the high esteem it is held in by the profession, for years to come. It is superfluous to add that it was and is used from its first appearance as a text-book at the homœopathic colleges.

GUERNSEY, DR. E. Homœopathic Domestic Practice. With Full Descriptions to the Dose to each single Case. Containing also Chapters on Anatomy, Physiology, Hygiene, and an abridged Materia Medica. Tenth enlarged, revised, and improved edition. 653 pages. Half leather, ... **$2 50**

GUERNSEY, DR. W. E. The Traveller's Medical Repertory and Family Adviser for the Homœopathic Treatment of Acute Diseases. 36 pages. Cloth, ... **30 cts.**

This little work has been arranged with a view to represent in as compact a manner as possible all the diseases—or rather disorders—which the non-professional would attempt to prescribe for, it being intended only for the treatment of simple or acute diseases, or to allay the suffering in maladies of a more serious nature until a homœopathic practitioner can be summoned.

HAHNEMANN, DR. S. The Lesser Writings of. Collected and Translated by R. E. Dudgeon, M.D. With a Preface and Notes by E. Marcy, M.D. With a Steel Engraving of Hahnemann from the statue of Steinhauser. 784 pages. Half bound, ... **$3 00**

This valuable work contains a large number of Essays, of great interest to laymen as well as medical men, upon Diet, the Prevention of Diseases, Ventilation of Dwellings, etc. As many of these papers were written before the discovery of the homœopathic theory of cure, the reader will be enabled to peruse in this volume the ideas of a gigantic intellect when directed to subjects of general and practical interest.

HAHNEMANN, DR. S. Organon of the Art of Healing. By
SAMUEL HAHNEMANN. Aude Sapere. Fifth American edition, translated
from the Fifth German edition, by C. WESSELHŒFT, M.D. 244 pages.
8vo. Cloth, ... $1 75

This fifth edition of "Hahnemann Organon" has a history. So many
complaints were made again and again of the incorrectness and cumber-
some style of former and existing editions to the publishers, that, yielding
to the pressure, they promised to destroy the plates of the fourth edition,
and to bring out an entire re-translation in 1876, the Centennial year. After
due consideration, and on the warm recommendation of Dr. Constantine
Hering and others, the task of making this re-translation was confided to
Dr. C. Wesselhœft, and the result of years of labor is now before the profession, who will be best able themselves to judge how well he succeeded
in acquitting himself of the difficult task.

"To insure a correct rendition of the text of the author, they (the publishers) selected as
his translator Dr. Conrad Wesselhœft, of Boston, an educated physician in every respect,
and from his youth up perfectly familiar with the English and German languages, than
whom no better selection could have been made." "That he has made, as he himself de-
clares, 'an entirely new and independent translation of the whole work,' a careful comparison of the various paragraphs, notes, etc., with those contained in previous editions, gives
abundant evidence; and while he has, so far as was possible, adhered strictly to the letter of
Hahnemann's text, he has at the same time given a pleasantly flowing rendition that avoids
the harshness of a strictly literal translation."—*Hahnemannian Monthly.*

HALE, DR. E. M. Lectures on Diseases of the Heart. In Three
Parts. Part I. Functional Disorders of the Heart. Part II. Inflamma-
tory Affections of the Heart. Part III. Organic Diseases of the Heart.
Second enlarged edition. 248 pages. Cloth, ... $1 75

**HALE, DR. E. M. Materia Medica and Special Therapeutics of
the New Remedies.** Fourth edition, revised and enlarged. In two
Volumes.

Vol. I. Special Symptomatology. With new Botanical and Pharmaco-
logical Notes. 672 pages. Cloth, ... $5 00

Vol. II. Special Therapeutics. With Illustrative Clinical Cases. 900
pages. Second enlarged edition. Cloth, . . . $5 00

N. B.—Same in half morocco, per Volume, . . . $6 00

"Dr. Hale's work on *New Remedies* is one both well known and much appreciated on this
side of the Atlantic. For many medicines of considerable value we are indebted to his researches. In the present edition, the symptoms produced by the drug investigated, and
those which they have been observed to cure, are separated from the clinical observations,
by which the former have been confirmed. That this volume contains a very large amount
of invaluable information is incontestable, and that every effort has been made to secure
both fulness of detail and accuracy of statement, is apparent throughout. For these reasons
we can confidently commend Dr. Hale's fourth edition of his well-known work on the *New
Remedies* to our homœopathic colleagues."—*Monthly Homœopathic Review.*

"We do not hesitate to say that by these publications Dr. Hale rendered an inestimable
service to homœopathy, and thereby to the art of medicine. 'The school of Hahnemann in
every country owes him hearty thanks for all this; and allopathy is beginning to share our
gain.' The author is given credit for having in this fourth edition corrected the mistake
for which the third one had been taxed rather severely, by restoring in Vol. II the 'special
therapeutics,' instead of the 'characteristics' of the third edition."—*British Journal of Homœopathy.*

HALE, DR. E. M. The Medical, Surgical, and Hygienic Treatment of Diseases of Women, especially those causing Sterility, the Disorders and Accidents of Pregnancy, and Painful and Difficult Labor. By EDWIN M. HALE, M.D., Professor of Materia Medica and Therapeutics in the Chicago Homœopathic College, etc., etc. Second enlarged edition. 378 pages. 8vo. Cloth, . . . **$2 50**

"This new work embodies the observations and experience of the author during twenty-five years of active and extensive practice, and is designed to supplement rather than supersede kindred works. The arrangement of the subjects treated is methodical and convenient; the introduction containing an article inserted by permission of Dr. Jackson, of Chicago, the author upon the ovular and ovulation theory of menstruation, which contains all the observations of practical importance known on this subject to date. The diseases causing sterility are fully described, and the medical, surgical, and hygienic treatment pointed out. The more generally employed medicines are enumerated, but their special or specific indications are unfortunately omitted. The general practitioner will find a great many valuable things for his daily rounds, and cannot afford to do without the book. The great reputation and ability of the author are sufficient to recommend the work, and to guarantee an appreciative reception and large sale."—*Hahnemannian Monthly.*

HAYWARD, DR. JOHN W. Taking Cold (the Cause of half our Diseases): Its Nature, Causes, Prevention and Cure; its frequency as a Cause of other Disease, and the Diseases of which it is the Cause, with their Diagnosis and Treatment. Fifth edition, enlarged and improved. London, 1875. 188 pages. 18mo. Cloth, ... **50 cts.**
We quote from the author's preface:

"This Essay was originally published under the conviction that, by attention to the directions it contains, persons may not only very frequently avoid taking cold, but may themselves frequently cure a cold at the onset, and thereby prevent the development of many of those serious diseases that would otherwise follow. The favorable reception it has met with is a sufficient testimony that it has been found useful."

HELMUTH, DR. W. T. A System of Surgery. Illustrated with 568 Engravings on Wood. By WM. TOD HELMUTH, M.D. Third edition. 1000 pages. Sheep, ... **$8 50**

This third edition of Dr. Helmuth's great work is already in appearance a great improvement over the old edition, it being well printed on fine paper, and well bound. By increasing the size of the page, decreasing the size of type, and setting up *solid*, fully one-half more printed matter is given than in the previous edition, albeit there are over 200 pages less. And while the old edition, bound in sheep, was sold at $11.50 by its publishers, this improved third edition is now furnished at $3 less, or for $8.50. The author brought the work fully up to date, and for an enumeration of some of the more important improvements, we cannot do better than to refer to Dr. Helmuth's own Preface.

HEMPEL, DR. C. J. The Science of Homœopathy; or, A Critical and Synthetical Index of the Doctrines of the Homœopathic School. Second edition. 180 pages. Large 8vo. Cloth, . . . **$1 75**

HEMPEL, DR. C. J., and DR. J. BEAKLEY. Homœopathic Theory and Practice. With the Homœopathic Treatment of Surgical Diseases, designed for Students and Practitioners of Medicine, and as a Guide for an intelligent public generally. Fourth edition. 1100 pages, ... **$3 00**

HERING, DR. C. Condensed Materia Medica. Second edition. More condensed, revised, enlarged, and improved, . . . **$7 00**

In February, 1877, we were able to announce the completion of Hering's *Condensed Materia Medica*. The work, as was to be expected, was bought up with avidity by the profession, and already in the Fall of 1878 the author set to work perfecting a second and improved edition. By still more condensing many of the remedies, a number of new ones could be added without much increasing the size and· the price of the work. This new edition is now ready for the profession, and will be the standard work par excellence for the practitioner's daily reference.

HEINIGKE, DR. CARL. Pathogenetic Outlines of Homœopathic Drugs. Translated from the German by EMIL TIETZE, M.D., of Philadelphia. 576 pages. 8vo. Cloth, ... **$3 50**

This work, but shortly issued, is already meeting with a large sale and an appreciative reception. It differs from most works of its class in these respects:

1. That the symptomatic outlines of the various drugs are based exclusively upon the "pathogenetic" results of provings.
2. That the anatomico-physiological arrangement of the symptoms renders easier the understanding and survey of the provings.
3. That the pathogenetic pictures drawn of most of the drugs, gives the reader a clearer idea, and a more exact impression of the action of the various remedies.

Each remedy is introduced with a brief account of its preparation, duration of action, and antidotes.

HILDEBRANDT, PROF. H. Catarrh of the Female Sexual Organs. Translated with the addition of the Homœopathic Treatment, by S. LILIENTHAL, M.D., Out of print.

HOLCOMBE, DR. W. H. Yellow Fever and its Homœopathic Treatment, ... **10 cts.**

HOLCOMBE, DR. W. H. What is Homœopathy? A new exposition of great truth. 28 pages. 8vo. Paper cover, per doz., $1.25, **15 cts.**

"Prove all things, hold fast that which is good."—*St. Paul.*

HOLCOMBE, DR. W. H. How I became a Homœopath. 28 pages. 8vo. Paper cover, per dozen, $1.25, . . . **15 cts.**

HOLCOMBE, DR. W. H. Special Report of the Homœopathic Yellow Fever Commission, ordered by the American Institute of Homœopathy for presentation to Congress. 32 pages. 8vo. Paper, per 100, $4.00, ... **5 cts.**

This Report, written in Dr. Holcombe's masterly manner, is one of the best campaign documents for homœopathy. The statistics must convince the most skeptical, and every homœopathic practitioner should feel in duty bound to aid in securing its widest possible circulation.

HOMŒOPATHIC POULTRY PHYSICIAN (Poultry Veterinarian); or, Plain Directions for the Homœopathic Treatment of the most Common Ailments of Fowls, Ducks, Geese, Turkeys. and Pigeons, based on the author's large experience. and compiled from the most reliable sources, by Dr. Fr. Schröter. Translated from the German. 84 pages. 12mo. Cloth, . . . **50 cts.**

HOMŒOPATHIC COOKERY. Second edition. With additions by a Lady of an American Homœopathic Physician. Designed chiefly for the Use of such Persons as are under Homœopathic Treatment. 176 pages, ... **50 cts.**

HUGHES, DR. R. Manual of Pharmacodynamics. 500 pages. American reprint out of print. See list of British books.

HUGHES, DR. R. Manual of Therapeutics. 540 pages. American reprint out of print. See list of British books.

HULL'S JAHR. A New Manual of Homœopathic Practice, Edited, with Annotations and Additions, by F. G. SNELLING, M.D. Sixth American edition. With an Appendix of the New Remedies, by C. J. HEMPEL, M.D. 2 vols. 2076 pages, ... **$9 00**

The *first volume*, containing the symptomatology, gives the complete pathogenesis of two hundred and eighty-seven remedies, besides a large number of new remedies are added by Dr. Hempel, in the appendix. The second volume contains an admirably arranged Repertory. Each chapter is accompanied by copious clinical remarks and the concomitant symptoms of the chief remedies for the malady treated of, thus imparting a mass of information, rendering the work indispensable to every student and practitioner of medicine.

JAHR, DR. G. H. G. Therapeutic Guide; the most Important Results of more than Forty Years' Practice. With Personal Observations regarding the truly reliable and practically verified Curative Indications in actual cases of disease. Translated, with Notes and New Remedies, by C. J. HEMPEL, M.D. 546 pages, ... **$3 00**

"With this characteristically long title, the veteran and indefatigable Jahr gives us another volume of homœopathics. . Besides the explanation of its purport contained in the title itself, the author's preface still further sets forth its distinctive aim. It is intended, he says, as a 'guide to beginners, where I only indicate the most important and decisive points for the selection of a remedy, and where I do not offer anything but what my own individual experience, during a practice of forty years, has enabled me to verify as *absolutely decisive* in choosing the proper remedy.' The reader will easily comprehend that, in carrying out this plan, I had rigidly to exclude all cases concerning which I had no experience *of my own* to offer. . . . . We are bound to say that the book itself is agreeable, chatty, and full of practical observation. It may be read straight through with interest, and referred to in the treatment of particular cases with advantage."—*British Journal of Homœopathy.*

JAHR, DR. G. H. G. Clinical Guide, or Pocket Repertory for the Treatment of Acute and Chronic Diseases.. Translated by C. J. HEMPEL, M.D. Second American revised and enlarged edition. From the third German edition, enriched by the addition of the New Remedies. By S. LILIENTHAL, M.D. 624 pages. 12mo. Half morocco. Out of print. **$2 50**

"To those of our readers who have used the old edition, nothing need be said to induce them to procure a copy of the new. To others, however, we feel free to state that as a volume of ready reference to lie on the office desk, or be used at the bedside, it is very valuable, and will save many tedious and distracting hunts through the *symptomen codex.* The typographical execution of the book is excellent."—*Hahnemannian Monthly.*

JAHR, DR. G. H. G. The Homœopathic Treatment of Diseases of Females and Infants at the Breast. Translated from the French by C. J. HEMPEL, M.D. 422 pages. Half leather. . . . **$2 00**

This work deserves the most careful attention on the part of homœopathic practitioners. The diseases to which the female organism is subject are described with the most minute correctness, and the treatment is likewise indicated with a care that would seem to defy criticism. No one can fail to study this work but with profit and pleasure.

JAHR, DR. G. H. G. Diseases of the Skin; or, Alphabetical Repertory of the Skin Symptoms, and External Alterations of Substance, together with the Morbid Phenomena observed in the Glandular, Osseous,
Mucous, and Circulatory Symptoms. Arranged with Pathological Remarks on Diseases of the Skin. Edited by C. J. HEMPEL, M.D. 515
pages. 12mo. Cloth, Out of print.

JAHR, DR. G. H. G. The Venereal Diseases, their Pathological
Nature, Correct Diagnosis, and Homœopathic Treatment.
Prepared in accordance with the author's own, as well as with the experience of other physicians, and accompanied with critical discussions.
Translated, with numerous and important additions, from the works of
other authors, and from his own experience. By C. J. HEMPEL, M.D.
428 pages. 8vo. Cloth, Out of print.

This is the most elaborate treatise on the subject in print. The work is divided into four
divisions, of which the first treats on Primary Forms of Venereal Diseases, in four chapters:
On the Venereal Phenomena in general; the Different Forms of Gonorrhœa; the Various
Forms of Chancre; and other Primary Forms of Syphilis. The second division, on Second-
ary Forms of Syphilis, treats in three chapters, of Secondary Syphilis generally; Syphilitic
Cutaneous Affections, and Intermediate Forms of Syphilis. The third division: General
Pathological Observations on Syphilis and its course generally, in three chapters; Patho-
logical Nature and Origin of Syphilis; on Venereal Contagia; General Development,
Course, and Termination of Syphilis. The fourth division: General Therapeutic Observa-
tions on the Treatment of Syphilis; General Diagnostic Remarks; General Therapeutic
Observations; Pharmaco-dynamic Observations, and Addenda.

INDEX to the first eighteen volumes of the North American Journal of
Homœopathy. Paper, ... **$2 00**

JONES, DR. SAMUEL A. The Grounds of Homœopathic Faith.
Three Lectures, delivered at the request of Matriculates of the Department of Medicine and Surgery (Old School) of the University of Michigan. By SAMUEL A. JONES, M.D., Professor of Materia Medica, Therapeutics, and Experimental Pathogenesy in the Homœopathic Medical
College of the University of Michigan, etc., etc. 92 pages. 12mo. Cloth,
per dozen, $3; per hundred, $20, ... **30 cts.**

Lecture first is on *The Law of Similars; its Claim to be a Science in that it Enables Perver-
sion.* Lecture second, *The Single Remedy a Necessity of Science.* Lecture third, *The Minimum Dose an Inevitable Sequence.* A fourth Lecture, on *The Dynomization Theory,* was to
have finished the course, but was prevented by the approach of final examinations, the preparation for which left no time for hearing evening lectures. The *Lectures* are issued in a convenient size for the coat-pocket; and as an earnest testimony to the truth, we believe they
will find their way into many a homœopathic household.

JOHNSON, DR. I. D. Therapeutic Key; or Practical Guide for the
Homœopathic Treatment of Acute Diseases. Tenth Edition. 347 pages.
Bound in linen, ... **$1 75**
Bound in flexible cover, ... **$2 25**

This has been one of the best selling works on our shelves; more copies being in circulation of this than of any two other professional works put together. It is safe to say that
there are but few homœopathic practitioners in this country but have one or more copies of
this little remembrancer in their possession.

JOHNSON, DR. I. D. A Guide to Homœopathic Practice. Designed for the use of Families and Private Individuals. 494 pages
Cloth, ... **$2 00**

This is the latest work on Domestic Practice issued, and the well and favorably known author has surpassed himself. In his book fifty-six remedies are introduced for internal application, and four for external use. The work consists of two parts. Part I is subdivided into seventeen chapters, each being devoted to a special part of the body, or to a peculiar class of disease. Part II contains a short and concise Materia Medica, i. e., gives the symptoms peculiar to each remedy. The whole is carefully written with a view of avoiding technical terms as much as possible, thus insuring its comprehension by any person of ordinary intelligence. A complete set of remedies in vials holding over fifty doses each, is furnished for $7, or in vials holding over one hundred doses each for $10, or book and case complete for $9 or $12 respectively. Address orders to Boericke & Tafel's Pharmacies at New York, Philadelphia, Baltimore, Chicago, New Orleans, or San Francisco.

JOSLIN, DR. B. F. Principles of Homœopathy. In a Series of Lectures. 185 pages. 12mo. Cloth, ... **60 cts.**

JOSLIN, DR. B. F. Homœopathic Treatment of Epidemic Cholera. Third edition, with additions. 252 pages. 12mo. Cloth, Out of print.

This work offers the advantage of a threefold arrangement of the principal medicines, viz., with reference, I—to the varieties of cholera; II—to its stages; and III—to its symptoms as arranged in repertories. These last will give the work a permanent value in treating the more frequent complaints of summer.

LAURIE AND McCLATCHEY. The Homœopathic Domestic Medicine. By Joseph Laurie, M.D. *Ninth American*, from the Twenty-first English edition. Edited and revised, with numerous and important additions, and the introduction of the new remedies. By R. J. McClatchey, M.D. 1044 pages. 8vo. Half morocco, ... **$5 00**

"We do not hesitate to indorse the claims made by the publishers, that this is the most complete, clear, and comprehensive treatise on the domestic homœopathic treatment of diseases extant. This handsome volume of nearly eleven hundred pages is divided into six parts. *Part one* is introductory, and is almost faultless. It gives the most complete and exact directions for the maintenance of health, and of the method of investigating the condition of the sick, and of discriminating between different diseases. It is written in the most lucid style, and is above all things wonderfully free from technicalities. *Part two* treats of symptoms, character, distinctions, and treatment of general diseases, together with a chapter on casualties. *Part three* takes up diseases peculiar to women. *Part four* is devoted to the disorders of infancy and childhood. *Part five* gives the characteristic symptoms of the medicines referred to in the body of the work, while *Part six* introduces the repertory."—*Hahnemannian Monthly.*

"Of the usefulness of this work in cases where no educated homœopathic physician is within reach, there can be no question. There is no doubt that domestic homœopathy has done much to make the science known; it has also saved lives in emergencies. The practice has never been so well presented to the public as in this excellent volume."—*New Eng. Med. Gazette.*

A complete set of remedies of one hundred and four vials, containing over fifty doses each, is furnished for $12, put up in an elegant mahogany case. A similar set in vials containing over one hundred doses each, is furnished for $18, or book and case complete for $17 or $23 respectively. Address orders to Boericke & Tafel's Pharmacies at New York, Philadelphia, Baltimore, Chicago, New Orleans, or San Francisco.

LILIENTHAL, DR. S. Homœopathic Therapeutics. By S. Lilienthal, M.D., Editor of North American Journal of Homœopathy, Professor of Clinical Medicine and Psychology in the New York Homœopathic Medical College, and Professor of Theory and Practice in the New York College Hospital for Women, etc. Second edition. 8vo, **$5 00**
Half morocco, ... **$6 00**

"Certainly no one in our ranks is so well qualified for this work as he who has done it, and in considering the work done, we must have a true conception of the proper sphere of such a work. For the fresh graduate, this book will be invaluable, and to all such we unhesitatingly and very earnestly commend it. To the older one, who says he has no use for this book, we have nothing to say. He is a good one to avoid when well, and to dread when ill. We also hope that he is severely an *unicum.*"—*Prof. Sam. A. Jones in American Homœopathist.*

" . . . It is an extraordinary useful book, and those who add it to their library will never feel regret, for we are not saying too much in pronouncing it the *best work on therapeutics* in homœopathic (or any other) literature. With this under one elbow, and Hering's or Allen's *Materia Medica* under the other, the careful homœopathic practitioner can refute Neimayer's too confident assertion, 'I declare it idle to hope for a time when a medical prescription should be the simple resultant of known quantities.' Doctor, by all means buy Lilienthal's *Homœopathic Therapeutics.* It contains a mine of wealth."—*Prof. Chas. Gatchel in Ibid.*

LILIENTHAL, DR. S.   A Treatise on Diseases of the Skin. A new edition in preparation for the press.

LUTZE, DR. A.   Manual of Homœopathic Theory and Practice. designed for the use of Physicians and Families. Translated from the German, with additions by C. J. HEMPEL, M.D. From the sixtieth thousand of the German edition. 750 pages. 8vo. Half leather, ... **$2 50**

This work, from the pen of the late Dr. Lutze, has the largest circulation of any homœopathic work in Germany, no less than sixty thousand copies having been sold. The introduction, occupying over fifty pages, contains the question of dose, and rules for examining the patient, and diet; the next sixty pages contain a condensed pathogenesis of the remedies treated of in the work; the description and treatment of diseases occupy four hundred and eighteen pages, and the whole concludes with one hundred and seventy-three pages of repertory and a copious index, thus forming a concise and complete work on theory and practice.

MALAN, H.   Family Guide to the Administration of Homœopathic Remedies. 112 pages. 32mo. Cloth, . . . **30 cts.**

MANUAL OF HOMŒOPATHIC VETERINARY PRACTICE. Designed for all kinds of Domestic Animals and Fowls, prescribing their proper treatment when injured or diseased, and their particular care and general management in health. Second and enlarged edition. 684 pages. 8vo. Half morocco, ... **$5 00**

"In order to rightly estimate the value and comprehensiveness of this great work, the reader should compare it, as we have done, with the best of those already before the public. In size, fulness, and practical value it is head and shoulders above the very best of them, while in many most important disorders it is far superior to them altogether, containing, as it does, recent forms of disease of which they make no mention."—*Hahnemannian Monthly.*

MARSDEN, DR. J. H.   Handbook of Practical Midwifery, with full instructions for the Homœopathic Treatment of the Diseases of Pregnancy, and the Accidents and Diseases incident to Labor and the Puerperal State. By J. H. MARSDEN, A.M., M.D. 315 pages. Cloth, ... **$2 25.**

"It is seldom we have perused a textbook with such entire satisfaction as this. The author has certainly succeeded in his design of furnishing the student and young practitioner, within as narrow limits as possible, all necessary instruction in practical midwifery. The work shows on every page extended research and thorough practical knowledge. The style is clear, the array of facts unique, and the deductions judicious and practical. We are particularly pleased with his discussion of the management of labor, and the management of mother and child immediately after the birth, but much is left open to the common-sense and practical judgment of the attendant in peculiar and individual cases."—*Homœopathic Times.*

MILLARD, DR. H. B. The Climate and Statistics of Consumption. Read before the American Geographical and Statistical Society. With extensive additions by the author. 108 pages. Cloth, . **75 cts.**

MOHR, DR. CHARLES. The Incompatible Remedies of the Homœopathic Materia Medica. By CHARLES MOHR, M.D., Lecturer of Homœopathic Pharmaceutics, Hahnemann Medical College, Philadelphia. (A paper read before the Homœopathic Medical Society of the County of Philadelphia.) Pamphlet, in paper cover, . **10 cts.**

This is an interesting paper, which will well repay perusal and study. It gives a list of fifty-seven remedies and their incompatibles, diligently collated from the best-known sources.

MORGAN, DR. W. The Homœopathic Treatment of Indigestion, Constipation, and Hæmorrhoids. Edited with Notes and Annotations by A. E. SMALL, M D. 166 pages 12mo. Cloth. **60 cts.**

Diseases resulting from irregularity or debility of the digestive organs are so frequent in their occurrence, that scarcely a family can be found in which one or more of its members are not sufferers thereby. The present work gives in a concise manner the hygienic measures as well as the medical treatment that should be observed, calculated not only to obviate the necessity of recourse to dangerous palliatives, but to promote a complete restoration of health.

MORGAN, DR. W. The Textbook for Domestic Practice; being plain and concise directions for the Administration of Homœopathic Medicines in Simple Ailments. 191 pages. 32mo. Cloth, . **50 cts.**

This is a concise and short treatise on the most common ailments, printed in convenient size for the pocket; a veritable traveller's companion.

A complete set of thirty remedies, in vials holding over fifty doses each, is furnished for $4.50, in stout mahogany case; or same set in vials holding over one hundred doses each, for $6.50; or book and case complete for $5 or $7 respectively. Address orders to Boericke & Tafel's Pharmacies, New York, Philadelphia, Baltimore, Chicago, New Orleans, or San Francisco.

MURE, DR. B. Materia Medica; or, Provings of the Principal Animal and Vegetable Poisons of the Brazilian Empire, and their Application in the Treatment of Diseases. Translated from the French, and arranged according to Hahnemann's Method, by C. J. HEMPEL, M.D. 220 pages. 12mo. Cloth, ... **$1 00**

This volume, from the pen of the celebrated Dr. Mure, of Rio Janeiro, contains the pathogenesis of thirty-two remedies, a number of which have been used in general practice ever since the appearance of the work. A faithful wood-cut of the plant or animal treated of accompanies each pathogenesis.

NEIDHARD, DR. C. On the Universality of the Homœopathic Law of Cure, ... **30 cts.**

NEW PROVINGS of Cistus Canadensis, Cobaltum, Zingiber, and Mercurius Proto-Iodatus. 96 pages. Paper, ... **75 cts.**

NORTH AMERICAN JOURNAL OF HOMŒOPATHY. Published quarterly on the first days of August, November, February, and May. Edited by S. LILIENTHAL, M.D. Vol. X, New Series, commenced in August, 1879. Subscription price per volume, in advance, . **$4 00**

Complete sets of the first twenty-seven volumes, in half morocco binding, including Index to the first eighteen volumes, . . **$90 00**

Index to the first eighteen volumes. **$2 00**

OEHME, DR. F. G. Therapeutics of Diphtheritis. A Compilation and Critical Review of the German and American Homœopathic Literature. Second enlarged edition. 84 pages. Paper, . . **60 cts.**
Same, in cloth, ... **75 cts.**

"This pamphlet contains the best compilation of reliable testimony relative to diphtheria that has appeared from the pen of any member of our school."—*Ohio Medical and Surgical Reporter.*

"Although he claims nothing more for his book than that it is a compilation, with 'critical reviews,' he has done his work so well and thoroughly as to merit all praise."—*Hahnemannian Monthly.*

"Dr. Oehme's little book will be worth many times its price to any one who has to treat this terrible disease."—*British Journal of Homœopathy.*

"It is the best monograph we have yet seen on diphtheria."—*Cincinnati Medical Advance*

PETERS, DR. J. C. A Complete Treatise on Headaches and Diseases of the Head. I. The Nature and Treatment of Headaches. II. The Nature and Treatment of Apoplexy. III. The Nature and Treatment of Mental Derangement. IV. The Nature and Treatment of Irritation, Congestion, and Inflammation of the Brain and its Membranes Based on Th. J. Rückert's Clinical Experiences in Homœopathy. 586 pages. Half leather, ... **$2 50**

PETERS, DR. J. C. A Treatise on Apoplexy. With an Appendix on Softening of the Brain and Paralysis. Based on Th. J. Rückert's Clinica Experiences in Homœopathy. 164 pages. 8vo. Cloth, **$1 00**

PETERS, DR. J. C. The Diseases of Females and Married Females. Second edition. Two parts in one volume. 356 pages Cloth, ... **$1 50**

PETERS, DR. J. C. The Diseases of Married Females. Disorders of Pregnancy, Parturition, and Lactation. 196 pages. 8vo. Cloth, **$1 00**

PETERS, DR. J. C. A Treatise on the Principal Diseases of the Eyes. Based on Th. J. Rückert's Clinical Experiences in Homœopathy. 291 pages. 8vo. Cloth, ... **$1 50**

PETERS, DR. J. C. A Treatise on the Inflammatory and Organic Diseases of the Brain. Based on Th. J. Rückert's Clinical Experiences in Homœopathy. 156 pages. 8vo. Cloth, . . **$1 00**

PETERS, DR. J. C. A Treatise on Nervous Derangement and Mental Disorders. Based on Th. J. Rückert's Clinical Experiences in Homœopathy. 104 pages. 8vo. Cloth, ... **$1 00**

PHYSICIAN'S VISITING LIST AND POCKET REPERTORY, THE HOMŒOPATHIC. By Robert Faulkner, M.D. Second edition, ... **$2 00**

"Dr. Faulkner's Visiting List is well adapted to render the details of daily work more perfectly recorded than any book prepared for the same purpose with which we have hitherto met. It commences with Almanacs for 1877 and 1878; then follow an obstetric calendar; a list of Poisons and their Antidotes; an account of Marshall Hall's ready method in Asphyxia; a Repertory of between sixty and seventy pages; pages marked for general memoranda; Vaccination Records; Record of Deaths; Nurses; Friends and others; Obstetric

Record, which is especially complete; and finally, pages ruled to keep notes of daily visits, and also spaces marked for name of the medicine ordered on each day. The plan devised is so simple, so efficient, and so clear, that we illustrate it on a scale just half the size of the original (here follows illustration). The list is not divided into special months, but its use may be as easily commenced in the middle of the year as at the beginning. We heartily recommend Faulkner's List to our colleagues who may be now making preparations for the duties of 1878."—*Monthly Homœopathic Review, London.*

RAUE, DR. C. G. Special Pathology and Diagnosis, with Thera-peutic Hints. 1072 pages. 8vo. Half morocco. Second edition, $7 00
This standard work is used as a textbook in all our colleges, and is found in almost every physician's library. An especially commendable feature is that it contains the application of nearly all the *new remedies* contained in Dr. Hale's work on Materia Medica.

RUDDOCK, DR. Principles, Practice, and Progress of Homœ-opathy, 5 cts.; per hundred, $3; per thousand, . . . $25 00

RUOFF'S REPERTORY OF HOMŒOPATHIC MEDICINE. Nosologically arranged. Translated from the German by A. H. OKIE, M.D. With additions and improvements by G. HUMPHREY, M.D. 251 pages. 12mo. Cloth, ... $1 50
As a book of reference for the practitioner, the present work far excels every other work, presenting him at a single glance what he might otherwise seek for amidst a confused mass of records and never find. The indefatigable author has drawn his matter from the infallible results of experience, leaving out all guesswork and hypothesis.

RUSH, DR. JOHN. Veterinary Surgeon. The Handbook to Vet-erinary Homœopathy; or, the Homœopathic Treatment of Horses, Cattle, Sheep, Dogs, and Swine. From the London edition. With numerous additions from the Seventh German edition of Dr. F. E. Gunther's " Ho-mœopathic Veterinary." Translated by J. F. SHEEK, M.D. 150 pages. 18mo. Cloth, ... 50 cts.

SCHAEFER, J. C. New Manual of Homœopathic Veterinary Medicine. An easy and comprehensive arrangement of Diseases, adapted to the use of every owner of Domestic Animals, and especially designed for the Farmer living out of the reach of medical advice, and showing him the way of treating his sick Horses, Cattle, Sheep, Swine, and Dogs, in the most simple, expeditious, safe, and cheap manner Translated from the German, with numerous additions from other veteri-nary manuals, by C. J. HEMPEL, M.D. 321 pages. 8vo. Cloth, $2 00

SCHWABE, DR. WILLMAR. Pharmacopœia Homœopathica Polyglottica. Second edition. Cloth, ... $3 00
Of this valuable work, the second edition has just been issued.

SHARP'S TRACTS ON HOMŒOPATHY, each, . . 5 cts.
Per hundred, ... $3 00

No. 1. What is Homœopathy?	No. 7. The Principles of Homœopathy.
No. 2. The Defence of Homœopathy.	No. 8. Controversy on "
No. 3. The Truth of "	No. 9. Remedies of "
No. 4. The Small Doses of "	No. 10. Provings of "
No. 5. The Difficulties of "	No. 11. Single Medicines of "
No. 6. Advantages of "	No. 12. Common-sense of "

SHARP'S TRACTS, complete set of 12 numbers, . . **50 cts.**
Bound, ... **75 cts.**

SMALL, DR. A. E. Manual of Homœopathic Practice, for the use of Families and Private Individuals. Fifteenth enlarged edition. 831 pages. 8vo Half leather, . . **$2 50**

SMALL, DR. A. E. Manual of Homœopathic Practice. Translated into German by C. J. HEMPEL, M.D. Eleventh edition. 643 pages. 8vo. Cloth, . . . **$2 50**

SMALL, DR. A. E. Diseases of the Nervous System, to which is added a Treatise on the Diseases of the Skin, by Dr. C. E. TOOTHACKER. 216 pages. 8vo. Cloth, ... **$1 00**

This treatise is from the pen of the distinguished author of the well-known and highly popular work entitled, "Small's Domestic Practice." It contains an elaborate description of the diseases of the nervous system, together with a full statement of the remedies which have been used with beneficial effect in the treatment of these disorders.

STAPF, DR. E. Additions to the Materia Medica Pura. Translated by C. J. HEMPEL, M.D. 292 pages. 8vo. Cloth, . . **$1 50**

This work is an indispensable appendix to Hahnemann's Materia Medica Pura. Every remedy is accompanied with extensive and most interesting clinical remarks, and a variety of cases illustrative of its therapeutic uses.

TESSIER, DR. J. P. Clinical Researches concerning the Homœopathic Treatment of Asiatic Cholera. Translated by C. J. HEMPEL, M.D. 109 pages. 8vo. Cloth, . **75 cts.**

TESSIER, DR. J. P. Clinical Remarks concerning the Homœopathic Treatment of Pneumonia, preceded by a Retrospective View of the Allopathic Materia Medica, and an Explanation of the Homœopathic Law of Cure. Translated by C. J. HEMPEL, M.D. 131 pages. 8vo. Cloth, . . . **75 cts.**

THOMAS, DR. A. R. Post-Mortem Examination and Morbid Anatomy. 337 pages. 8vo. Cloth, ... **$2 50**

VERDI, DR. T. S. Maternity; a Popular Treatise for Young Wives and Mothers. By TULLIO SUZZARA VERDI, A.M., M.D., of Washington, D. C. 450 pages. 12mo. Cloth, . . . **$2 00**

"No one needs instruction more than a young mother, and the directions given by Dr. Verdi in this work are such as I should take great pleasure in recommending to all the young mothers, and some of the old ones, in the range of my practice."—*George E. Shipman, M.D., Chicago, Ill.*

"Dr. Verdi's book is replete with useful suggestions for wives and mothers, and his medical instructions for home use accord with the maxims of my best experience in practice."—*John F. Gray, M.D., New York City.*

VERDI, DR. T. S. Mothers and Daughters: Practical Studies for the Conservation of the Health of Girls. By TULLIO SUZZARA VERDI, A.M., M.D. 287 pages. 12mo. Cloth, ... **$1 50**

"The people, and especially the women, need enlightening on many points connected with their physical life, and the time is fast approaching when it will no longer be thought singular or 'Yankeeish' that a woman should be instructed in regard to her sexuality, its organs and their functions. . . . Dr. Verdi is doing a good work in writing such books, and we trust he will continue in the course he has adopted of educating the mother and daughters. The book is handsomely presented. It is printed with good type on fine paper, and is neatly and substantially bound."—*Hahnemannian Monthly.*

WILLIAMSON, DR. W. Diseases of Females and Children, and their Homœopathic Treatment. Third enlarged edition. 256 pages. 12mo. Cloth, ...   **$1 00**

This work contains a short treatise on the homœopathic treatment of the diseases of females and children, the conduct to be observed during pregnancy, labor, and confinement, and directions for the management of new-born infants.

HOMŒOPATHIC JOURNALS.

THE NORTH AMERICAN JOURNAL OF HOMŒOPATHY.

Samuel A. Lilienthal, M.D., Editor. Boericke & Tafel, Publishers. Quarterly. Subscription price per year, payable in advance,   **$4 00**

JUST PUBLISHED.

ALLEN, DR. T. F. A General Symptom Register of the Homœopathic Materia Medica. 1330 pages. Cloth, $12.00; full sheep or half morocco, ...   **$14 00**

ALLEN, DR. H. C. The Homœopathic Therapeutics of Intermittent Fever. 232 pages. 12mo. Cloth, ...   **$1 50**

EATON, DR. M. M. A Treatise on the Medical and Surgical Diseases of Women, with their Homœopathic Treatment. Fully illustrated. 782 pages. 8vo. Sheep,   **$6 50**

EDMONDS, DR. W. A. A Treatise on Diseases peculiar to Infants and Children. 300 pages. 8vo. Cloth, ...   **$2 50**

HAGEN, DR. A. A Guide to the Clinical Examination of Patients and the Diagnosis of Disease. Translated from the second revised and enlarged edition by Dr. G. E. Gramm. 223 pages. 12mo. Cloth, ...   **$1 25**

HAHNEMANN, DR. S. Materia Medica Pura. Translated from the latest German editions by A. E. Dudgeon, M.D., with annotations by A. Hughes, M.D. Vol. I. 718 pages. 8vo. Cloth, $5.00; half morocco, $6.00. Vol. II printing.

HART, DR. C. P. Diseases of the Nervous System; being a treatise on Spasmodic, Paralytic, Neuralgic, and Mental Affections. With ample clinical illustrations. 409 pages. 8vo. Cloth, ...   **$3 00**

HEINIGKE, DR. C Pathogenetic Outlines of Homœopathic Drugs. Translated from the German by Dr. E. Tietze. 576 pages. 12mo. Cloth,   .   .   .   **$3 50**

TESTE, DR. A. A Homœopathic Treatise on the Diseases of Children. 345 pages. 12mo. Cloth, ...   **$1 50**

VON TAGEN, DR. C. H. Biliary Calculi, Perineorrhaphy, Hospital Gangrene, and its kindred Diseases, with their respective Treatments. 154 pages. 8vo. Cloth, **$1 25**

WILSON, DR. T. P. Special Indications for Twenty-five Remedies in Intermittent Fever. 53 pages. 12mo, ...   **40 cts.**

WORCESTER, DR. S. Repertory to the Modalities, in their relations to Temperature, Air, Water, Winds, Weather, and Seasons. 160 pages. 12mo. Cloth, .   **$1 25**

NOTICE TO PHYSICIANS.

Mother Tinctures. In the preparation of our Mother Tinctures, we make use of none but fresh, green plants, for the proper collection of which we have unusual facilities. Most of these are collected by ourselves within a radius of less than twenty miles from Philadelphia. Plants indigenous to the West we procure through our branch in Chicago; those of the South, through our branch in New Orleans; while plants growing on the Pacific Coast, the Sandwich Islands, etc., are furnished by our branch at San Francisco. Thus saturated tinctures made from fresh plants, gathered when in full vigor, may at all times be relied upon.

European Homœopathic Tinctures we import from the best known sources, i. e., from reputable Homœopathic Pharmacies.

The only exceptions to above rule are tinctures from plants growing in distant countries, as Nux vom., Rheum, Ignatia, etc., which of necessity are made from carefully selected dry material.

Triturations. Our Triturations are made with *Pure Sugar of Milk* in steam triturators with the latest improvements. Having ample facilities, we are enabled to accord to each trituration fully *two hours*, whereby an unusual degree of excellence is obtained. Remedies such as Sepia, Mercurius v., Graphites, are triturated four hours or longer, until the desired grade of comminution is secured.

Dilutions. Our Dilutions are all conscientiously made by hand. We commenced by running up one hundred remedies to the 30th, retaining *all intermediate attenuations* and using a separate box for each remedy. Gradually the list has increased until to-day we carry in stock over *seven hundred* remedies, and are able to supply any of them like the 12th, 15th, 24th, etc., as readily as the 3d or 6th. Each of our eight pharmacies carries such a set in stock, and our patrons thus have absolute surety of obtaining any intermediate potency called for.

Our Pharmacies are devoted exclusively to the sale of Homœopathic Medicines and Books; and as all Branch Establishments are supplied from our Laboratory in Philadelphia, Medicines of our uniform standard quality, may be obtained alike from either of our establishments.

In conclusion, we beg to assure the profession that, it has ever been our endeavor to excel in the quality of our preparations; that while furnishing our medicines at a moderate advance on cost, we do not intend to compete with establishments whose sole claims lie in cheap prices. Our endeavors have met with hearty acknowledgement by the profession, and the generous support accorded to our establishments, bears witness to our ability to give satisfaction to our many patrons.

Complete Price List and Illustrated Catalogue sent free to Physicians on application.